Religious denominations of the world : comprising a general view of the origin, history, and conditions of the various sects of Christians, the Jews, and Mahometans, as well as the pagan forms of religions existing in the different countries of the earth:

Vincent L Milner, J Newton
1803-1868 Brown, Hannah Adams

367. M. A. Carroll,
           From a friend
                      1924

John B. Dougherty
To
Orpha M. Dougherty

1874

25 ¢

Jonathan Edwards

RELIGIOUS DENOMINATIONS

OF THE

WORLD:

COMPRISING

A GENERAL VIEW OF THE ORIGIN, HISTORY, AND CONDITION OF THE
VARIOUS SECTS OF CHRISTIANS, THE JEWS, AND MAHOMETANS, AS
WELL AS THE PAGAN FORMS OF RELIGION EXISTING IN
THE DIFFERENT COUNTRIES OF THE EARTH:

WITH

Sketches of the Founders of Various Religious Sects.

FROM THE BEST AUTHORITIES.

By VINCENT L. MILNER.

A NEW AND IMPROVED EDITION,
WITH AN APPENDIX BROUGHT UP TO THE PRESENT TIME,
By J. NEWTON BROWN, D. D.,
EDITOR OF "ENCYCLOPÆDIA OF RELIGIOUS KNOWLEDGE."

SOLD ONLY BY SUBSCRIPTION.

BRADLEY, GARRETSON & CO.,
PHILADELPHIA, 66 NORTH FOURTH STREET.

WILLIAM GARRETSON & CO.,
GALESBURG, ILL.: COLUMBUS, OHIO:
NASHVILLE, TENN.: HOUSTON, TEXAS.
1872.

R. N.

PREFACE.

THE following view of the religious denominations of the world has been carefully compiled from the best authorities on the subject. In order to render it as complete as the limits of the volume would permit, the method has been followed of presenting summaries of the doctrines of each sect or religion without in general adducing the arguments by which they are sustained. The latter course would have led into too wide a field of controversy. In order to preserve the degree of impartiality which the reader is entitled to expect in a work of this kind, the compiler has confined himself to authorities in which the doctrines of the several sects are drawn from the published works of their founders or leading writers.

The subject is full of instruction. It forms a part of the history of the human intellect, as it has been exercised in different ages of the world, on topics the most interesting that can possibly claim the attention of mankind. In reviewing the various forms of faith and shades of opinion on religion which have prevailed in different ages and various parts of the world, we may learn the influence of external circumstances on internal belief; and that of speculative opinions on the actual conduct of life. We perceive also the first effect of freedom of religious inquiry, in multiplying sects and dividing extensive religious organizations into numerous branches. Above all, we may learn from this general survey of religious sects, the lesson of charity and forbearance toward those who may entertain theological opinions different from our own.

This volume will also show the gratifying truth, that while the first effect of religious freedom may be to multiply divisions, its *final* effect is to heal them. Some of the most scandalous divisions in all ages have grown out of the attempts of governments, civil and ecclesiastical, to stifle freedom of inquiry and suppress its manifestations. and while such despotism continues, no restorative process is possible. Whereas, the natural growth of Christian feeling under free institutions, tends to bring together bodies long divided and alienated, whether in the Old World or in the New. This happy effect of perfect religious freedom is most manifest in our own country at the present time. As in the beginning, Christians were "of one heart and of one soul," so it may be hoped, they will here become, through the unfettered study of the Scriptures and the influence of the same Spirit which then guided them into all truth : "for the earth shall be full of the knowledge of the Lord." Sects will disappear in the overflowing fulness of faith and love. Despotism in Church and State may produce hypocritical UNIFORMITY, but perfect religious freedom is the primary condition of CHRISTIAN UNITY.

ALPHABETICAL INDEX.

1 *

INDEX TO APPENDIX.

INTRODUCTION.

SECTION I.

STATE OF THE WORLD IN GENERAL, AT THE BIRTH OF JESUS CHRIST.

WHEN Jesus Christ made his appearance on earth, a great part of the world was subject to the Roman Empire. This empire was much the largest temporal monarchy that had ever existed, so that it was called all the world (Luke ii. 1). The time when the Romans first subjugated the land of Judea, was between sixty and seventy years before Christ was born; and soon after this the Roman Empire rose to its greatest extent and splendor. To this government the world continued subject till Christ came, and many hundred years afterwards. The remoter nations, that had submitted to the yoke of this mighty empire, were ruled either by Roman governors, invested with temporary commissions, or by their own princes and laws, in subordination to the republic, whose sovereignty was acknowledged, and to which the conquered kings, who were continued in their own dominions, owed their borrowed majesty. At the same time, the Roman people, and their venerable Senate, though they had not lost all shadow of liberty, were yet in reality reduced to a state of servile submission to Augustus Cæsar, who, by artifice, perfidy, and ᵇˡᵒᵒᵈ ... and united in his own person the pompous titles of *Emperor, Pontiff, Censor, Tribune of the People;* in a word, all the great offices of the State.

At this period, the Romans, according to Daniel's prophetic description, had trodden down the kingdoms, and by their exceeding strength devoured the whole earth. However, by enslaving the world, they civilized it; and whilst they oppressed mankind, they united them together. The same laws were everywhere established, and the same languages understood Men approached nearer to one another in sentiments and manners; and the intercourse between the most distant regions of the earth was rendered secure and agreeable. Hence, the benign influence of letters and philosophy was spread abroad in countries which had been before enveloped in the darkest ignorance.

Just before Christ was born, the Roman empire not only rose to its greatest height, but was also settled in peace. Augustus Cæsar had been for many years establishing the state of the Roman Empire, and subduing his enemies, till the very year that Christ was born: then, all his enemies being reduced to subjection, his dominion over the world appeared to be settled in its greatest glory. This remarkable peace, after so many ages of tumult and war, was a fit prelude to the ushering of the glorious Prince of Peace into the world. The tranquillity which then reigned was necessary to enable the ministers of Christ to execute with success their sublime commission to the human race. In the situation into which the providence of God had brought the world, the gospel in a few years reached those remote corners of the earth into which it could not otherwise have penetrated for many ages.

All the heathen nations, at the time of Christ's appearance on earth, worshipped a multiplicity of gods and demons, whose favor they courted by obscene and ridiculous ceremonies, and whose anger they endeavored to appease by the most abominable cruelties.

Every nation had its respective gods, over which one, more excellent than the rest, presided; yet in such a manner, that the supreme deity was himself controlled by the rigid decrees of fate, or by what the philosophers called eternal necessity. The gods of the East were different from those of the Gauls, the Germans, and other northern nations. The Grecian divinities differed from those of the Egyptians, who deified plants, and a great variety of the productions both of nature and art. Each people had also their peculiar manner of worshipping and appeasing its respective deities. In process of time, however, the Greeks and Romans grew as ambitious in their religious pretensions, as in their political claims. They maintained that their gods, though under different appellations, were the objects of religious worship in all nations; and therefore they gave the names of their deities to those of other countries.

The deities of almost all nations were either ancient heroes, renowned for noble exploits and worthy deeds, or kings and generals, who had founded empires, or women who had become illustrious by remarkable actions or useful inventions. The merit of those eminent persons, contemplated by their posterity with enthusiastic gratitude, was the cause of their exaltation to celestial honors. The natural world furnished another kind of deities; and as the sun, moon, and stars shine with a lustre superior to that of all other material beings, they received religious homage from almost all the nations of the world.

From those beings of a nobler kind, idolatry descended into an enormous multiplication of inferior powers; so that, in many countries, mountains, trees, and rivers, the earth, the sea, and wind, nay, even virtues, and vices, and diseases, had their shrines attended by devout and zealous worshippers.

These deities were honored with rites and sacrifices of various kinds, according to their respective nature and offices. Most nations offered animals, and human sacrifices were universal in ancient times. They were in use among the Egyptians till the reign of Amasis. They were never so common among the Greeks and Romans; yet they were practised by them on extraordinary occasions. Porphyry says "that the Greeks were wont to sacrifice men when they went to war." He relates, also, "that human sacrifices were offered at Rome till the reign of Adrian, who ordered them to be abolished in most places."

Pontiffs, priests, and ministers, distributed into several classes, presided over the Pagan worship, and were appointed to prevent disorder in the performance of religious rites. The sacerdotal order, which was supposed to be distinguished by an immediate intercourse and friendship with the gods, abused its authority in the basest manner, to deceive an ignorant and wretched people.

The religious worship of the Pagans was confined to certain times and places. The statues, and other representations of the gods, were placed in the temples, and supposed to be animated in an incomprehensible manner — for they carefully avoided the imputation of worshipping inanimate beings — and therefore pretended that the divinity, represented by the statue, was really present in it, if the dedication was truly and properly made.

Besides the public worship of the gods, to which all, without exception, were admitted, there were certain religious rites celebrated in secret by the Greeks, and several eastern countries, to which a small number was allowed access. These were called mysteries; and persons who desired an initiation, were obliged previously to exhibit satisfactory proofs of their fidelity and patience, by passing through various trials and ceremonies of the most disagreeable kind. The secret of these mysteries was kept in the strictest manner, as the initiated could not reveal anything that passed in them, without exposing their lives to the most imminent danger.

These secret doctrines were taught in the mysteries of Eleusis, and in those of Bacchus and other divinities. But the reigning religion was totally external. It held out no body of doctrines, no public instruction to participate on stated days in the established worship. The only faith required, was to believe that the gods exist, and reward virtue, either in this life or in that to come; the only practice, to perform at intervals some religious acts, such as appearing in the solemn festivals, and sacrificing at the public altars

The spirit and genius of the Pagan religion was not calculated to promote moral virtue. Stately temples, expensive sacrifices, pompous ceremonies, and magnificent festivals, were the objects presented to its votaries. But just notions of God, obedience to His moral laws, purity of heart, and sanctity of life, were not once mentioned as ingredients in religious service. No repentance of past crimes, and no future amendment of conduct, were ever prescribed by the Pagans, as proper means of appeasing their offended deities. Sacrifice a chosen victim, bow down before an hallowed image, be initiated in the sacred mysteries,— and the wrath of the gods shall be averted, and the thunder shall drop from their hands.

The gods and goddesses, to whom public worship was paid, exhibited to their adorers examples of egregious crimes, rather than of useful and illustrious virtues It was permitted to consider Jupiter, the father of the gods, as an usurper, who expelled his father from the throne of the universe, and is, in his turn, to be one day driven from it by his son The priests were little solicitous to animate the people to virtuous conduct, either by precept or example. They plainly enough declared, that all which was essential to the true worship of the gods, was contained in the rites and institutions which the people had received by tradition from their ancestors. Hence the wiser part of mankind, about the time of Christ's birth, looked upon the whole system of religion as a just object of ridicule and contempt.

The consequence of this state of theology was an universal corruption of manners, which discovered itself in the impunity of the most flagitious crimes.

When the Romans had subdued the world, they lost their own liberty. Many vices, engendered or nourished by prosperity, delivered them over to the vilest of tyrants that ever afflicted or disgraced human nature. Despotic power was accompanied with all the odious vices which are usually found in its train, and they rapidly grew to an incredible pitch. The colors are not too strong which the apostle employs in drawing the character of that age, in Rom. i. 21, 22, etc., and in Eph. iv. 17–19.

At the time of Christ's appearance on earth, the religion of the Romans, as well as their arms, had extended itself throughout a great part of the world. Besides the religious rites, which

Numa and others had instituted for political views, the Romans added several Italian and Etrurian fictions to the Grecian fables, and gave also to the Egyptian deities a place among their own.

In the provinces subjected to the Roman government, there arose a new kind of religion, formed by a mixture of the ancient rites of the conquered nations with those of the Romans. Those nations, who, before their subjection, had their own gods, and their own particular religious institutions, were persuaded by degrees to admit into their worship a great variety of the sacred rites and customs of the conquerors.

When, from the sacred rites of the ancient Romans, we pass to review the other religions which prevailed in the world, it will appear obvious, that the most remarkable may be properly divided into two classes — one of which will comprehend the religious systems which owe their existence to political views; and the other, of those which seem to have been formed for military purposes The religion of most of the eastern nations may be ranked in the former class, especially that of the Persians, Egyptians, and Indians, which appears to have been solely calculated for the preservation of the State, the support of the royal authority and grandeur, the maintenance of public peace, and the advancement of civil virtues. The religious system of the northern nations may be comprehended under the military class; since all the traditions among the Germans, the Bretons, the Celts, and the Goths, concerning their divinities, have a manifest tendency to excite and nourish fortitude, ferocity, an insensibility of danger, and contempt of life.

At this time Christianity broke forth from the east like a rising sun, and dispelled the universal religious darkness which obscured every part of the globe. "The noblest people," says Dr. Robertson, "that ever entered upon the stage of the world, appear to have been only instruments in the Divine Hand, for the execution of wise purposes concealed from themselves The Roman ambition and bravery paved the way, and prepared the world, for the reception of the Christian doctrine. They fought and conquered, that it might triumph with the greater ease (see (saiah x. 7). By means of their victories, the overruling providence of God established an empire, which really possesses that perpetuity and eternal duration which they vainly arrogated to their own. He erected a throne which shall continue forever, and of the "*increase of that government there shall be no end.*"

It has been mentioned to the honor of Christianity, that it rose and flourished in a learned, inquiring, and discerning age; and made the most rapid and amazing progress through the immense empire of Rome, to its remotest limits, when the world was in its most civilized state, and in an age that was universally distinguished for science and erudition.

SECTION II.

STATE OF THE JEWISH NATION AT THE BIRTH OF JESUS CHRIST

THE state of the Jews was not much better than that of other nations, at the time of Christ's appearance on earth. They were governed by Herod, who was himself tributary to the Roman people. His government was of the most vexatious and oppressive kind. By a cruel, suspicious, and overbearing temper, he drew upon himself the aversion of all, not excepting those who lived upon his bounty

Under his administration, and through his influence, the luxury of the Romans was introduced into Palestine, accompanied with the vices of that licentious people. In a word, Judea, governed by Herod, groaned under all the corruption which might be expected from the authority and example of a prince who, though a Jew in outward profession, was, in point of morals and practice, a contemner of all laws, human and divine.

After the death of this tyrant, the Romans divided the government of Judea between his sons. In this division, one-half the kingdom was given to Archelaus, under the title of Exarch. Archelaus was so corrupt and wicked a prince, that at last both Jews and Samaritans joined in a petition against him to Augustus, who banished him from his dominions, about ten years after the death of Herod the Great. Judea was by this sentence reduced to a Roman province, and ordered to be taxed.

The governors whom the Romans appointed over Judea, were frequently changed, but seldom for the better. About the sixteenth year of Christ, Pontius Pilate was appointed governor, the whole of whose administration, according to Josephus, was one continual scene of venality, rapine, and of every kind of savage cruelty. Such a governor was ill calculated to appease the ferments occasioned by the late tax. Indeed, Pilate was so far from attempting to appease, that he greatly inflamed them, by taking every occasion of introducing his standards, with images, pictures, and consecrated shields, into their city; and at last by attempting to drain the treasury of the temple, under pretence of bringing an aqueduct into Jerusalem. The most remarkable transaction of his government, however, was his condemnation of Jesus Christ; seven years after which he was removed from Judea.

However severe was the authority which the Romans exercised over the Jews, yet it did not extend to the entire suppression of their civil and religious privileges. The Jews were, in some measure, governed by their own laws, and permitted the enjoyment of their religion. The administration of religious ceremonies was committed, as before, to the high priest, and to the Sanhedrim; to the former of whom the order of priests and Levites was in the usual subordination; and the form of outward worship, except in a very few points, had suffered no visible change. But, on the other hand, it is impossible to express the disquietude and disgust, the calamities and vexations, which this unhappy nation suffered from the presence of the Romans, whom their religion obliged them to regard as a polluted and idolatrous people; in a particular manner, from the avarice and cruelty of the prætors, and the frauds and extortions of the publicans. So that, all things considered, their condition, who lived under the government of the other sons of Herod, was much more supportable than the state of those who were immediately subject to the Roman jurisdiction.

It was not, however, from the Romans only, that the calamitie: of this miserable people proceeded. Their own rulers multiplied their vexations, and debarred them from enjoying any little comforts, which were left them by the Roman magistrates The leaders of the people, and the chief priests, were, according to the account of Josephus, profligate wretches, who had purchased their places by bribes, or by other acts of iniquity, and who maintained their ill-acquired authority by the most abominable crimes   The inferior priests, and those who possessed any shadow of authority, were become dissolute and abandoned to the highest degree.   The multitude, excited by these corrupt examples, ran headlong into every kind of iniquity; and by their endless seditions, robberies, and extortions, armed against themselves both the justice of God and vengeance of man

About the time of Christ's appearance, the Jews of that age concluded the period pre-determined by God to be then completed, and that the promised Messiah would suddenly appear. Devout persons waited day and night for the consolation of Israel; and the whole nation, groaning under the Roman yoke, and stimulated by the desire of liberty or of vengeance, expected their deliverer with the most anxious impatience.

Nor were these expectations peculiar to the Jews.   By their dispersion among so many nations; by their conversation with the learned men among the heathens; and by the translations of their inspired writings into a language almost universal, the principles of their religion were spread all over the East.   It became the common belief, that a Prince would arise at that time in Judea, who would change the face of the world, and extend his empire from one end of the earth to the other.

Two religions flourished at this time in Palestine; the Jewish and Samaritan.   The Samaritans blended the errors of Paganism with the doctrines of the Jews.   The whole body of the people looked for a powerful and warlike deliverer, who, they supposed, would free them from the Roman authority.   All considered the whole of religion as consisting in the rites appointed by Moses, and in the performance of some external acts of duty.   All were unanimous in excluding the other nations of the world from the hopes of eternal life.

The learned among the Jews were divided into a great variety of sects. The Pharisees, the Sadducees, and Essenes, eclipsed the other denominations.

The most celebrated of the Jewish sects was that of the Pharisees. It is supposed by some, that this denomination subsisted about a century and a half before the appearance of our Saviour. They separated themselves not only from Pagans, but from all such Jews as complied not with their peculiarities. Their separation consisted chiefly in certain distinctions respecting food and religious ceremonies. It does not appear to have interrupted the uniformity of religious worship, in which the Jews of every sect seem to have always united.

This denomination, by their apparent sanctity of manners, had rendered themselves extremely popular. The multitude, for the most part, espoused their interests; and the great, who feared their artifice, were frequently obliged to court their favor. Hence they obtained the highest offices both in the State and priesthood, and had great weight both in public and private affairs. It appears from the frequent mention which is made by the evangelists of the Scribes and Pharisees in conjunction, that the greatest number of Jewish teachers or doctors of the law, (for those were expressions equivalent to scribe) were, at that time, of the Pharisaical sect.

The principal doctrines of the Pharisees are as follows: That the oral law, which they suppose God delivered to Moses by an archangel on Mount Sinai, and which is preserved by tradition, is of equal authority, with the written law: That, by observing both these laws, a man may not only obtain justification with God, but perform meritorious works of supererogation: That fasting, alms-giving, ablutions, and confessions, are sufficient atonements for sin: That thoughts and desires are not sinful, unless they are carried into action. This denomination acknowledged the immortality of the soul, future rewards and punishments, the existence of good and evil angels, and the resurrection of the body. They maintained both the freedom of the will and absolute predestination, and adopted the Pythagorean doctrine of the transmigration of souls, excepting the notoriously wicked, whom they supposed consigned to eternal punishment.

The peculiar manners of this sect are strongly marked in the writings of the evangelists, and confirmed by the testimony of the Jewish authors. They fasted the second and fifth day of the week, and put thorns at the bottom of their robes, that they might prick their legs as they walked. They lay upon boards covered with flint stones, and tied thick cords about their waists. They paid tithes as the law prescribed, and gave the thirtieth and fiftieth part of their fruits, adding voluntary sacrifices to those which were commanded. They were very exact in performing their vows. The Talmudic books mention several distinct classes of Pharisees; among whom were the Truncated Pharisee, who, that he might appear in profound meditation, as if destitute of feet, scarcely lifted them from the ground; and the Mortar Pharisee, who, that his contemplations might not be disturbed, wore a deep cap in the shape of a mortar, which would only permit him to look upon the ground at his feet Such expedients were used by this denomination to captivate the admiration of the vulgar; and under the appearance of singular piety, they disguised the most licentious manners.

The sect of the Sadducees derived its origin and name from one Sadoc, who flourished in the reign of Ptolemy Philadelphus, about two hundred and sixty-three years before Christ. The chief heads of the Sadducean doctrine are as follows: All laws and traditions, not comprehended in the written law, are to be rejected as merely human inventions. Neither angels nor spirits have a distinct existence, separate from their corporeal vestment. The soul of man, therefore, expires with the body. There will be no resurrection of the dead, nor rewards and punishments after this life. Man is not subject to irresistible fate, but has the framing of his condition chiefly in his power. Polygamy ought to be practised.

The practices of the Pharisees and Sadducees were both perfectly suitable to their sentiments. The former were notorious hypocrites; the latter, scandalous libertines.

The Essenes were a Jewish sect. Some suppose they took their rise from that dispersion of their nation, which took place after the Babylonian captivity. They maintained that rewards and punishments extended to the soul alone, and considered the body as a mass of malignant matter, and the prison of the immortal spirit. The greatest part of this sect considered the laws of Moses as an allegorical system of spiritual and mysterious truth, and renounced all regard to the outward letter in its explanation. The leading traits in the character of this sect were, that they were sober, abstemious, peaceable lovers of retirement, and had a perfect community of goods. They paid the highest regard to the moral precepts of the law, but neglected the ceremonial, excepting what regarded personal cleanliness, the observation of the Sabbath, and making an annual present to the temple at Jerusalem. They commonly lived in a state of celibacy, and adopted the children of others, to educate them in their own principles and customs. Though they were, in general, averse to swearing, or to requiring an oath, they bound all whom they initiated by the most sacred vows, to observe the duties of piety, justice, fidelity, and modesty; to conceal the secrets of the fraternity; to preserve the books of their instructors; and with great care to commemorate the names of the angels.

Philo mentions two classes of Essenes; one of which followed a practical institution. The other professed a theoretical institution. The latter, who were called Theraputæ, placed their whole felicity in the contemplation of the Divine nature. Detaching themselves entirely from secular affairs, they transferred their property to their relations and friends, and retired to solitary places, where they devoted themselves to an holy life The principal society of this kind was formed near Alexandria, where they lived, not far from each other, in separate cottages, each of which had its own sacred apartments, to which the inhabitants retired for the purposes of devotion.

Besides these eminent Jewish sects, there were several of inferior note, at the time of Christ's appearance: the Herodians, mentioned by the sacred writers; and the Gaulonites, by Josephus.

The Herodians derived their name from Herod the Great. Their distinguishing tenet appears to be, that it is lawful, when constrained by superiors, to comply with idolatry and with a false religion Herod seems to have formed this sect on purpose to justify himself in this practice, who, being an Idumean by nation, was indeed half a Jew and half a Pagan. He, during his long reign, studied every artifice to ingratiate himself with the emperor, and to secure the favor of the principal personages in the court of Rome. Josephus informs us, that his ambition, and his entire devotion to Cæsar and his court, induced him to depart from the usages of his country, and, in many instances, to violate its institutions. He built temples in the Greek taste, and erected statues for idolatrous worship, apologizing to the Jews that he was absolutely necessitated to this conduct by the superior powers We find the Sadducees, who denied a future state, readily embraced the tenets of this party: for the same persons, who, in one of the gospels, are called Herodians, are, in another called Sadducees.

The Gaulonites were Galileans, who derived their name from one Judas Theudas, a native of Gaulon in Upper Galilee, who, in the tenth year of Jesus Christ, excited his countrymen, the Galileans, and many other Jews, to take arms, and venture upon all extremities, rather than pay tribute to the Romans. The principles he instilled into his party were, not only that they were a free nation, and ought not to be in subjection to any other; but that they were the elect of God; that he alone was their governor; and that, therefore, they ought not to submit to any ordinance of man. Though Theudas was unsuccessful, and his party, in their very first attempt, entirely routed and dispersed, yet, so deeply had he infused his own enthusiasm into their hearts, that they never rested, till in their own destruction, they involved the city and temple.

Many of the Jews were attached to the oriental philosophy concerning the origin of the world. From this source the doctrine of the Cabala is supposed to be derived. That considerable numbers of the Jews had imbibed this system, appears evident both from the books of the New Testament, and from the ancient history of the Christian church.   It is also certain that many of the Gnostic sects were founded by Jews.

Whilst the learned and sensible part of the Jewish nation was divided into a variety of sects, the multitude was sunk into the most deplorable ignorance of religion, and had no conception of any other method of rendering themselves acceptable to God than by sacrifices, washings, and other external rites and ceremonies of the Mosaic law.   Hence proceeded that dissoluteness of manners which prevailed among the Jews during Christ's ministry on earth.   Hence also the divine Saviour compares the people to sheep without a shepherd, and their doctors to men who, though deprived of sight, yet pretended to show the way to others.

In taking a view of the corruptions both in doctrine and practice, which prevailed among the Jews at the time of Christ's appearance, we find that the external worship of God was disfigured by human inventions.   Many learned men have observed that a great variety of rites was introduced into the service of the temple, of which no traces are to be found in the sacred writings This was owing to those revolutions, which rendered the Jew more conversant than they had formerly been, with the neighboring nations.   They were pleased with several of the ceremonies which the Greeks and Romans used in the worship of the Pagan deities, and did not hesitate to adopt them in the service of the true God, and add them as an ornament to the rites, which they had received by divine appointment.

The Jews multiplied so prodigiously, that the narrow bounds of Palestine were no longer sufficient to contain them.   They poured, therefore, their increasing numbers into the neighboring countries with such rapidity, that, at the time of Christ's birth, there was scarcely a province in the empire where they were not found carrying on commerce and exercising other lucrative arts. They were defended in foreign countries against injurious treatment by the special edicts of the magistrates.   This was absolutely necessary; since, in most places, the remarkable difference of their religion and manners from those of other nations, exposed them to the hatred and indignation of the ignorant and bigoted multitude. "All this," says Dr. Mosheim, "appears to have been most singularly and wisely directed by the adorable hand of an interposing Providence, to the end, that this people, which was the sole depository of the true religion, and of the knowledge of one supreme God, being spread abroad through the whole earth, might be everywhere, by their example, a reproach to superstition, contribute in some measure to check it, and thus prepare the way for that yet fuller discovery of divine truth, which was to shine upon the world from the ministry and gospel of the Son of God."

SECTION III.

AN ACCOUNT OF THE PHILOSOPHICAL SYSTEMS WHICH WERE IN VOGUE AT THE TIME OF CHRIST'S APPEARANCE.

At the important era of Christ's appearance in the world, two kinds of philosophy prevailed among the civilized nations. One was the philosophy of the Greeks, adopted also by the Romans; and the other, that of the Orientals, which had a great number of votaries in Persia, Syria, Chaldea, Egypt, and even among the Jews. The former was distinguished by the simple title of *philosophy*. The latter was honored by the more pompous appellation of *science* or *knowledge;* since those who adhered to the latter sect pretended to be the restorers of the knowledge of God, which was lost in the world. The followers of both these systems, in consequence of vehement disputes and dissensions about several points, subdivided themselves into a variety of sects. It is, however, to be observed, that all the sects of the Oriental philosophy deduced their various tenets from one fundamental principle, which they held in common; but the Greeks were much divided about the first principles of science.

Amongst the Grecian sects there were some who declaimed openly against religion, and denied the immortality of the soul; and others, who acknowledged a Deity, and a state of future rewards and punishments. Of the former kind were the Epicureans and Academics; of the latter, the Platonists and Stoics

The Epicureans derived their name from Epicurus, who was born in the hundred and ninth olympiad, 242 years before Christ. He accounted for the formation of the world in the following manner: A finite number of that infinite multitude of atoms, which, with infinite space, constitutes the universe, falling fortuitously into the region of the world, were, in consequence of their innate motion, collected into one rude and indigested mass. All the various parts of nature were formed by those atoms, which were best fitted to produce them. The fiery particles formed themselves into air; and from those which subsided, the earth was produced. The mind or intellect was formed of particles most subtle in their nature, and capable of the most rapid motion. The world is preserved by the same mechanical causes by which it was framed; and from the same causes it will at last be dissolved.

Epicurus admitted that there were in the universe divine natures. But he asserted that these happy and divine beings did not encumber themselves with the government of the world: yet, on account of their excellent nature, they are proper objects of reverence and worship.

The science of physics was, in the judgment of Epicurus, subordinate to that of ethics; and his whole doctrine concerning nature was professedly adapted to rescue men from the dominion of troublesome passions, and lay the foundation of a tranquil and happy life. He taught, that man is to do everything for his own sake; that he is to make his own happiness his chief end, and do all in his power to secure and preserve it. He considered pleasure as the ultimate good of mankind; but asserts that he does not mean the pleasures of the luxurious, but principally the freedom of the body from pain, and of the mind from anguish and perturbation. The virtue he prescribes is resolved ultimately into our private advantage without regard to the excellence of its own nature, or of its being commanded by the Supreme Being.

The followers of Aristotle were another famous Grecian sect. That philosopher was born in the first year of the ninety-ninth olympiad, about 384 years before the birth of Christ.

Aristotle supposed the universe to have existed from eternity.

He admitted, however, the existence of a deity, whom he styled the *first mover*, and whose nature, as explained by him, is something like the principle which gives motion to a machine. It is a nature wholly separated from matter, immutable, and far superior to all other intelligent natures. The celestial sphere, which is the region of his residence, is also immutable; and residing in his first sphere, he possesses neither immensity nor omnipresence. Happy in the contemplation of himself, he is entirely regardless of human affairs. In producing motion, the deity acts not voluntarily, but necessarily; not for the sake of other beings, but for his own pleasure.

Nothing occurs in the writings of Aristotle which decisively determines whether he supposed the soul of man mortal or immortal.

Respecting ethics, he taught that happiness consisted in the virtuous exercise of the mind, and that virtue consists in preserving that mean in all things which reason and prudence describe. It is the middle path between two extremes, one of which is vicious through excess, the other through defect.

The Stoics were a sect of heathen philosophers, of which Zeno, who flourished about 350 years before Christ, was the original founder. They received their denomination from a place in which Zeno delivered his lectures, which was a portico at Athens. Their distinguishing tenets were as follows: That God is underived, incorruptible, and eternal; possessed of intelligence and goodness; the efficient cause of all the qualities and forms of things; and the constant preserver and governor of the world. That matter is also underived and eternal, and by the powerful energy of the Deity impressed with motion and form: That though God and matter subsisted from eternity, the present regular frame of nature had a beginning, and will have an end. That the element of fire will at last, by an universal conflagration, reduce the world to its pristine state. That at this period all material forms are lost in one chaotic mass, all animated nature is reunited to the Deity, and matter returns to its original form. That from this chaotic state, however, it again emerges, by the energy of the efficient principle; and gods and men, and all forms of regulated nature, are renewed, to be dissolved and renewed in endless· succession. That at the restoration of all things, the race of men will return to·life. Some imagined that each individual would return to its former body; while others supposed that after the revolution of the great year, similar souls would be placed in similar bodies.

Those among the Stoics who maintained the existence of the soul after death, supposed it to be removed into the celestial regions of the gods, where it remains, till, at the general conflagration, all souls, both human and divine, shall be absorbed in the Deity. But many imagined, that before they were admitted among the divinities, they must purge away their inherent vices and imperfections by a temporary residence in the aerial regions between the earth and the moon, or in the moon itself. It was supposed that depraved and ignoble souls are agitated after death in the lower region of the air till the fiery parts are separated from the grosser, and rise, by their natural levity, to the orbit of the moon, where they are still further purified and refined.

According to the doctrine of the Stoics, all things are subject to an irresistible and irreversible fatality : and there is a necessary chain of causes and effects, arising from the action of a power, which is itself a part of the machine it regulates, and which, equally with the machine, is subject to the immutable laws of necessity.

The moral doctrine of the Stoics depends upon the preceding principles. They make virtue to consist in an acquiescence in the immutable laws of necessity, by which the world is governed. The resignation they prescribe appears to be part of their scheme to raise mankind to that liberty and self-sufficiency which it is the great end of their philosophy to procure. They assert that virtue is its own proper reward, and vice its own punishment; that all external things are indifferent; and that a wise man may be happy in the midst of tortures. The ultimate design of their philosophy was to divest human nature of all passions and affections; and they make the highest attainments and perfection of virtue to consist in a total apathy and insensibility of human evils.

The Platonic philosophy is denominated from Plato. who was born in the eighty-seventh olympiad, 426 years before the nativity of Jesus Christ. ·He founded the old academy on the opinions of Heraclitus, Pythagoras, and Socrates; and by adding the information he had acquired to their discoveries, he established a sect of philosophers, who were esteemed more perfect than those who had before appeared in the world.

The outlines of Plato's philosophical system were as follows: That there is one God, an eternal, immutable, and immaterial being, perfect in wisdom and goodness, omniscient and omnipresent. That this all-wise and perfect Being formed the universe out of a mass of pre-existing matter, to which he gave form and arrangement. That there is in matter a necessary, but blind and refractory force, which resits the will of the Supreme Artificer, so that he cannot perfectly execute his designs; and this is the cause of the mixture of good and evil which is found in the material world. That the soul of man was derived by emanation from God; but that this emanation was not immediate, but through the intervention of the soul of the world, which was itself debased by some material admixture. That the relation which the human soul, in its original constitution, bears to matter, is the source of moral evil. That when God formed the universe, he separated from the soul of the world inferior souls, equal in number to the stars, and assigned to each its proper celestial abode. · That these souls were sent down to earth to be imprisoned in mortal bodies; hence proceed the depravity and misery to which human nature is liable. That the soul is immortal; and by disengaging itself from all animal passions, and rising above sensible objects to the contemplation of the world of intelligence, it may be prepared to return to its original habitation. That matter never suffered annihilation, but that the world will remain forever; but that by the action of its animating principle, accomplishes certain periods, within which everything returns to its ancient place and state. This periodical revolution of nature is called the Platonic or great year.

- The Platonic system makes the perfection of morality to consist in living in conformity to the will of God, the only author of true felicity; and teaches that our highest good consists in the contemplation and knowledge of the Supreme Being, whom he emphatically styles ταυγαθον, the *good*. The end of this knowledge is to make men resemble the Deity as much as is compatible with human nature. This likeness consists in the possession and practice of all the moral virtues.

After the death of Plato, many of his disciples deviated from his doctrines. His school was then divided into the old. the middle, and the new academy. The old academy strictly adhered to his tenets. The middle academy receded from his system without entirely deserting it. The new academy, founded by Carneades, an African by birth, almost entirely relinquished the original doctrines of Plato, and verged towards the sentiments which were taught by the Skeptic philosophy.

The Skeptic or Pyrrhonic sect of philosophers derive their name from Pyrrho, a Grecian philosopher, who flourished at Peloponnesus, in the hundred and ninth olympiad. This denomination was in little esteem till the time of the Roman emperors; then it began to increase, and made a considerable figure.

Every advance which Pyrrho made in the study of philosophy involved him in fresh uncertainty. Hence he left the school of the dogmatists, and established a school of his own on the principles of universal skepticism.

On account of the similarity of the opinions of this sect and those of the Platonic school in the middle and new academy, many of the real followers of Pyrrho chose to screen themselves from the reproach of universal skepticism by calling themselves Academics.

Pyrrho and his followers rather endeavored to demolish every other philosophical structure than to erect one of their own They asserted nothing, but proposed positions merely by way of enunciation, without deciding on which side, in any disputed question, the truth lay, or even presuming to assert that one proposition was more probable than another. On the subject of morals the Skeptics suspended their judgment concerning the ground of the distinction admitted by the Stoics and others, between things in their nature good, evil, or indifferent.

The chief points of difference between the Pyrrhonists and Academics are these. The Academics laid it down as an axiom, that nothing can be known with certainty; the Pyrrhonists maintained that even this ought not to be positively asserted. The Academics admitted the real existence of good and evil; the Pyrrhonists suspended their judgment on this point. The Academics, especially the followers of Carneades, allowed different degrees of probability in opinion; but the Skeptics rejected all speculative conclusions, drawn either from the testimony of the senses, or from reasoning; and concluded that we can have no good ground for affirming or denying any proposition, or embracing any one opinion rather than another.

The Eclectic philosophy was in a flourishing state at Alexandria when our Saviour was upon earth. Its founders formed the design of selecting from the doctrines of all former philosophers such opinions as seemed to approach nearest the truth, and of combining them into one system. They held Plato in the highest esteem; but they did not scruple to join with his doctrines whatever they thought conformable to reason in the tenets of other philosophers. Potamo, a Platonist, appears to have been the first projector of this plan. The Eclectic system was brought to perfection by Ammonias Saccas, who blended Christianity with the tenets of philosophy.

. The moral doctrine of the Alexandrian school was as follows· The mind of man, originally a portion of the Divine Being, having fallen into a state of darkness and defilement by its union with the body, is to be gradually emancipated from the chain of matter, and rise by contemplation to the knowledge and vision of God. The end of philosophy, therefore, is the liberation of the soul from its corporeal imprisonment. For this purpose the Eclectic philosophy recommends abstinence, with other voluntary mortifications and religious exercises.

In the infancy of the Alexandrian school, not a few of the professors of Christianity were led, by the pretensions of the Eclectic sect, to imagine that a coalition might, with great advantage, be formed between its system and that of Christianity. This union appeared the more desirable, as several philosophers of this sect became converts to the Christian faith The consequence was, that Pagan ideas and opinions were by degrees mixed with the pure and simple doctrines of the gospel.

The Oriental philosophy was popular in several nations at the time of Christ's appearance. Before the commencement of the Christian era it was taught in the East, whence it gradually spread through the Alexandrian, Jewish, and Christian schools.

The Oriental philosophers endeavored to explain the nature and origin of all things by the principle of emanation from an eternal fountain of being. The forming of the leading doctrines of this philosophy into a regular system has been attributed to Zoroaster, an ancient Persian philosopher. He adopted the principle generally held by the ancients, that from nothing, nothing can be produced. He supposed spirit and matter, light and darkness, to be emanations from one eternal source. The active and passive principles he conceived to be perpetually at variance; the former tending to produce good; the latter, evil; but that, through the intervention of the Supreme Being, the contest would at last terminate in favor of the good principle. According to Zoroaster, various orders of spiritual beings, gods, or demons, have proceeded from the Deity, which are more or less perfect, as they are at a greater or less distance in the course of emanation from the eternal fountain of intelligence, among which the human soul is a particle of divine light, which will return to its source and partake of its immortality; and matter is the last or most distant emanation from the first source of being, which, on account of its distance from the fountain of light, becomes opaque and inert, and whilst it remains in that state, is the cause of evil; but, being gradually refined, it will at length return to the fountain from whence it flowed.

Those who professed to believe the Oriental philosophy were divided into three leading sects, which were subdivided into various factions. Some imagined two eternal principles, from whence all things proceeded; the one presiding over light, the other over matter, and, by their perpetual conflict, explaining the mixture of good and evil that appears in the universe. Others maintained that the being which presided over matter was not an eternal principle, but a subordinate intelligence, one of those whom the supreme God produced from himself. They supposed that this being was moved by a sudden impulse to reduce to order the rude mass of matter which lay excluded from the mansions of the Deity, and also to create the human race. A third sect entertained the idea of a triumvirate of beings, in which the *supreme deity* was distinguished both from the *material* evil principle, and from the Creator of this sublunary world. That these divisions did really subsist, is evident from the history of the Christian sects which embraced this philosophy.

From blending the doctrines of the Oriental philosophy with Christianity, the Gnostic sects, which were so numerous in the first centuries, derive their origin Other denominations arose, which aimed to unite Judaism with Christianity. Many of the Pagan philosophers, who were converted to the Christian religion, exerted all their art and ingenuity to accommodate the doctrines of the gospel to their own schemes of philosophy. In each age of the church new systems were introduced, till, in process of time, we find the Christian world divided into that prodigious variety of sentiment which is exhibited in the following pages.*

* For the above introduction, we are indebted to Miss Hannah Adams " View of Religions."—ED.

C

HISTORY OF RELIGIONS.

BAPTISTS.

THE members of this denomination are distinguished from all other professing Christians, by their opinions respecting the ordinance of Christian Baptism. Conceiving that positive institutions cannot be established by *analogical* reasoning, but depend on the will of the Saviour, revealed in *express precepts*, and that apostolical example illustrative of this is the rule of duty, they differ from their Christian brethren with regard both to the *subjects* and the *mode* of baptism.

With respect to the *subjects*, from the command which Christ gave after his resurrection, and in which baptism is mentioned as *consequent* to *faith* in the *gospel*, they conceive them to be those, and *those only*, who *believe* what the apostles were then *enjoined to preach*.

With respect to the *mode*, they affirm that, instead of sprinkling or pouring, the person ought to be *immersed* in the water, referring to the primitive practice, and observing that the baptizer as well as the baptized having *gone down into* the water, the latter is baptized *in it*, and both *come up out of it*. They say that John baptized *in the Jordan*, and that Jesus, after being baptized, *came up out*

(35)

of it. Believers are also said to be *buried with Christ by baptism into death, wherein also they are raised with him* · a doctrinal allusion, incompatible with any other mode. Rom. vi. 4, Col. ii, 12. For baptism here appears as an appointed and expressive emblem of the death of Christ, through which our sins are remitted or washed away, and of the resurrection of Christ, through which the Holy Spirit confers upon us a new spiritual life, in which every true believer enters into fellowship with him. In other words, Christian baptism is a figurative representation of *that*, which the Gospel of Christ is in testimony. To this, therefore, the mind of the baptized believer is naturally led, and every spectator in like manner is impressed with the gospel, not only as truth, but life, derived by faith from the crucified and glorified Redeemer. The Baptists, therefore, think that none ought to be baptized, but such as with all their heart believe the gospel, and that immersion is not properly a *mode* of baptism, but baptism itself.

Holding convictions at once so clear and sacred, drawn from the very fountain of truth, the Baptists, while differing from other Christians, disclaim the spirit of schism. Feeling the authority of the Great Commission, which remains unchanged to the end of the world, they aim to carry out all its parts in the prescribed order, with the fidelity of a good conscience, as under law to Christ, and responsible alone to Him, on whose promised presence and aid they humbly rely. Matt. xxviii : 19, 20. They profess to love all Christians as brethren ; but they own no other Master than Christ ; no other law in religion than his word ; no baptism but that which is hallowed by faith ; no church, but that which is the living body of Christ, pervaded and animated by his Spirit. Neither birth, nor age, nor sex, nor nation, nor condition, in their view, can qualify for Christian ordinances, but the *faith that worketh by love,* and which naturally unfolds in obedience to *all things whatsoever* Christ has commanded.

As to Church organization and government, Baptists believe in the spiritual Unity of the Church, the collective body of believers, of which Christ is the head. This unity it is a duty to preserve and cherish, by subjection to Him in all things. Local churches, composed of believers in a particular place, who, being duly baptized, are embodied by mutual consent, under the law of Christ, for extending his kingdom, are the first scriptural means of *manifesting* this spiritual unity. The government of these churches is congregational; that is to say, being immediately dependent on Christ, they are severally independent of all other authority as churches; though as citizens, individually subject to the civil power, and loyal in its support. Each church is completely competent to manage its internal affairs, such as the choice of officers reception, dismission, or discipline of members. Here is the only tribunal in which Christ presides, ratifying in heaven what is done according to his will on earth. But this principle of local church independence is not held by Baptists as a law of isolation, for it is balanced by the principle of intercommunion between the churches, which binds them into one. This intercommunion is the highest form of *visible* unity, and is never without necessity to be interrupted. On this principle, Baptist churches associate for the accomplishment of all common ends, and especially for diffusing the gospel throughout the world. Councils also are called to advise and assist in the formation of churches, the ordination of ministers, and the settlement of any serious difficulties; but these councils are strictly such, having no judicial or appellate powers. They are composed of both ministers and laymen; between whom there is no distinction, but that of office. Ministers are

4

ordained, both as evangelists and pastors, and deacons also, after due examination, by prayer and the laying on of hands in solemn benediction. There are no higher officers recognized than these—no prelacy, no hierarchy— all pastors are equally bishops, in their sacred charge of the flock of Christ.

The Baptists are zealous friends of ministerial educa- tion, as their numerous Colleges and Theological Semina- ries show ; but they do not regard such education as in- dispensable to the Christian ministry, where all the scrip- tural qualifications are found; as in John Bunyan and Andrew Fuller, who are among their brightest ornaments. Dr. Sprague's volume on the "Baptist Pulpit," is a monument of their eminent men, from the foundation of this country. Dr. Baird, also, in his great work on "Religion in America," has said: "The ministry of the Baptists comprehends a body of men, who in point of talent, learning, and eloquence, as well as in devoted piety, have no superiors in the country." Through their labors, accompanied by the Divine blessing, the Baptists are now, with a single exception, the largest denomination of Christians in the United States, being spread through every State and Territory, and growing at a rate which outstrips the rapid growth of population. This fact is the more remarkable, as they are less indebted to emigration from Europe than most other denominations ; discard on principle infant baptism and birth-right membership, as incompatible with the genius of Christianity, and depend on the power of truth and the Holy Spirit alone for the vital increase of their churches. It is the more remarkable still, because on all sides they are reproached for their strictness of practice on Church communion ; as they think, reproached wrongfully. A few words there- fore may be necessary on this point.

Baptists believe that, according to the scriptures, the Holy Supper is a church ordinance, intended to express their common fellowship with Christ, as the source and support of spiritual life; and that each church must therefore judge for itself on its responsibility to Christ, of the scriptural qualifications of all who apply for admission In requiring baptism and church fellowship among these qualifications, they agree with almost all Christians in every age and country; they differ only in their views of baptism. If their views of baptism are correct, they are bound to apply them impartially to all who apply for admission to communion. The very fact that it is the Lord's table, and not their own, forbids them, even if they would, from changing at their pleasure the divine laws of approaching it. All who agree with them are welcome to come; those who do not, and cannot with a good conscience, are at perfect liberty to join elsewhere. Hard cases may arise with individuals, but the churches are not responsible. The right of private judgment is sacred, but it is equally so on both sides; and the conscience of the individual cannot over-ride the conscience of the church; for the fellowship of the Spirit cannot be forced. These views, so far from being narrow and bigoted, as some suppose, the Baptists believe to present the only true solution of this question of conscience, when viewed in its broadest aspect, and in the spirit of brotherly love. The strictest Baptists therefore claim, that their communion, in any proper use of the term, is *free*. A laxer and less consistent view obtains to some extent among Baptists in England; but as it rests on no scriptural precept or practice, it is regarded by Baptists in the United States as a perilous anomaly, to be avoided rather than imitated. Not one of their twelve thousand churches indorses it not because they do not love and esteem other Christians but because love to their brethren must be regulated in its manifestations by the word of God. *By this we know that we love the children of God, when we love God and keep his commandments.* 1 John v. 2.

It is this clear conviction of the truth and equity of their principles, that has made the Baptists the pioneers of religious liberty in its full extent, both in the Old World and in the New. Before William Penn, before Lord Baltimore, before Jeremy Taylor, Milton, or Locke, even before William I. of Orange, in the sixteenth century, their clear testimony is on record. And theirs is the high honor of establishing in the little colony of Rhode Island, in 1636, the first civil government in modern times which declared that conscience should be free; in which noble declaration, fifty years later, they were followed by the Friends, of Pennsylvania; and since, the Revolution of 1776, by all the United States. This honor history now awards them. But how few know what toils and sacrifices, what vigilance, patience, prayers, tears and blood, it cost the Baptists to win this boon of freedom for all mankind.

As will be evident from the above exposition of their principles, the Baptists claim their origin from the ministry of Christ and his Apostles. They further claim, that all the Christian churches of the first two centuries after Christ, were founded and built up upon these principles; in proof of which they appeal to the highest authorities in church history, such as Mosheim and Neander. Amid the growing defection of later times, they claim to be able to trace their history in a succession of pure churches, under various names, down to the Reformation of the sixteenth century. From the fifth and sixth centuries, these churches became the objects of relentless persecution · but though persecuted, they were not forsaken; though scattered, not destroyed; a bush forever.   c   , but unconsumed. The seeds of their principles had long been sown throughout Europe; the Waldenses had held them fast; the Paterines suffered for them; the Lollards diffused them; Wickliffe embraced them. At the first dawn of the Reformation, they emerged on all sides, and after fifty years of unparalleled suffering, from Romanists and Protestants alike, at last found protection under the Prince of Orange, the founder of the Dutch Republic. They were called indiscriminately Anabaptists, (or Rebaptizers,) but they of course disowned the name, as incompatible with their principles, and still more, as disgraced by a small party of fanatics in Munster, with whom they had not the slightest identity or connection, What the main body really were, and how they bore their terrible sufferings, let Cardinal Hosius, President of the Council of Trent, testify : "If you behold their cheerfulness in suffering persecution, the Anabaptists run before all the heretics, (i. e. Protestants.) If you have regard to the number, it is likely that they would swarm above all others, if they were not grievously plagued and cut off by the knife of persecution. If you have an eye to the outward appearance of godliness, both the Lutherans and the Zuinglians must needs grant that they far pass them. If you will be moved by the boasting of the word of God, these be no less bold than Calvin to preach; and their doctrine must stand aloft above all the glory of the world, must stand invincible above all power, because it is not their word, but the word of the living God."

If there be a tinge of irony in the last sentence, there is certainly none in the honorable testimony to the antiquity of the Baptists, in the following passage from the "History of the Reformed Church of the Netherlands," by Drs. Ypeig and Dermout, clergymen of the highest standing in that church, and published in Breda,

4 *

in 1819. " We have now seen that the Baptists, who were formerly called Anabaptists, and in later times Mennonites, were the original Waldenses, and have long, in the history of the church received the honor of that origin. On this account the Baptists may be considered as the only Christian community which has stood since the days of the Apostles; and as a Christian society which has preserved pure the doctrines of the Gospel through all ages."

In regard to the value of religious forms, this body of Cnristians seem to hold a middle place between the Roman Catholics, who multiply them at will, and magnify their efficacy to salvation, and the Friends, or Quakers, who discard them altogether as inconsistent with a spiritual religion. In opposition to the first view, the Baptists hold that no forms but those of scriptural institution are valid, thus repudiating all *traditions of men;* and in reference to those of Divine institution, the sacraments of Baptism and the Lord's Supper, that they have no inherent virtue, or saving efficacy of the Holy Spirit, independent of the receiver's faith. In opposition to the Quaker view, the Baptists hold that the reception of the Holy Spirit, though essential to spiritual religion, does not make void the authority of Baptism and the Lord's Supper, or supersede their value as the appointed expressions and auxiliaries of faith; and they particularly point to the conversion of the Gentiles in the house of Cornelius, at Cesarea, in proof; where Peter, full of the Holy Ghost himself, said, *Can any man forbid water, that these should not be baptized, who have received the Holy Ghost as well as we? And he commanded them to be baptized in the name of the Lord.* (Acts x. 47, 48.)

Instead of magnifying the efficacy of Baptism and making it a saving ordinance, the Baptists affirm that they make less of it than most religious denominations;

for they believe that infants are saved without it; in proof of which, they adduce the fact that Christ *blessed* little children, without baptizing them. Baptism (meaning immersion) is in their view but the symbol of faith, and it *saves* us, as Peter says, only in a figure, or so far only as it is *the answer of a good conscience toward God.*

In their doctrine, the Baptists are in a high degree evangelical, holding the views commonly called Calvinistic, as set forth in the writings of Bunyan, Gill, and Fuller. The Confessions of 1643, 1689, 1742, and 1833, are all in harmony, differing only in the choice of language and fulness of exposition. These Confessions are never regarded as binding creeds.

There is a close affinity between the Baptists and the Congregationalists, and they are divided only on the point of baptism. The late Dr. Woods, of Andover, Mass., in 1854, thus expresses his views of this affinity : " For myself, I entertain feelings of the most cordial esteem, love and confidence, toward the Baptists as a denomination. I have had the freest intercourse and the sincerest friendship with Baptist ministers, theological students, and private Christians. And I have wished that our denomination was as free from erratic speculations, and as well grounded in the doctrines and experimental principles of the Puritans as the Baptists. It seems to me that they are the Christians who are likely to maintain pure Christianity, and to hold fast the form of sound words; while many of our denomination are rather loose in their opinions, and are trying to introduce innovations into the system of evangelical doctrines. And I think that Congregationalists in general regard the Baptists much as I do, though it may be that my better acquaintance with them has led me to esteem them more highly than some of my breth en do." See CONGREGATIONALISTS.

The Baptist "Missionary Union," from its origin in Dr. Judson's change of views on baptism, as well as from the common aim of its endeavors, is in cordial sympathy with the "American Board of Commissioners for Foreign Missions" established by the Congregationalists in 1810. The following comparative table of their successful operations, drawn up from the reports of the two societies in 1866, will be found of great value and interest. It should be observed that the figures of the American Board, except in the item of schools and scholars, include the returns from the Sandwich Islands, and the figures of the Missionary Union include all their European missions, from which no schools are reported.

	American Board		Missionary Union
Date of organization	June, 1810		May, 1814.
Income the past year	$446,942 44	....	$175,354 32
Expenditures	440,275 47	....	173,484 57
Missions now maintained	20	....	19
Stations and out-stations	526	....	1700
Missionaries, male and female	312	....	84
Native helpers	815	....	700
Churches	194	....	487
Members added last year	1119	....	2672
Total present members	23,240	....	36.000
Schools of all kinds	428	....	157
Total number of scholars	10,901	....	3295
Printing establishments	2	....	1
Pages printed last year	13,659,826	....	4,375,950

The strength of the American Board in its resources, its missionary force, its vigorous schools, of which sixteen are theological and training schools, and its multiplication of books, is very manifest from this table. The Missionary Union's more exclusive attention to simple evangelization, with much less income and fewer missionaries, is also evident in its appropriate fruits. God's blessing has rested richly upon both. A like blessing has at-

tended their labors in Home Missions, as might be shown
if the figures were at hand. The Baptists have indeed
spread far more widely, and gathered converts more rapidly; from a much smaller beginning, now outnumbering
the Congregationalists in this country fourfold. But, on
the other hand, the Congregationalists, with a narrower
field, have cultivated it more richly. At present there
is a sort of interchange in the character of their home
labors, the Baptists devoting themselves to a higher culture, and their Congregational brethren to a more energetic effort of expansion. Their history, too, both in
England and in this country, has flowed on in parallel
streams, and the waters have often intermingled. The
great names that adorn them are alike dear to both, and
it may be hoped time will cement and perfect the union.

The unity of the Baptist denomination, which is almost
equally spread over all the United States, does not consist
in any external bond of authority distinct from the Bible,
but in the internal fellowship of the churches and members in "one Lord, one faith, and one baptism." (Eph.
iv. 6.) It was formerly expressed also by free co-opera
tion in the same general missionary and benevolent societies. This was gradually interrupted, as in other denominations, by the different position of the North and
the South on the questions of slavery and of secession,
which culminated in the civil war of 1861. As early as
1845, the Southern Baptists, partly from the wish to avoid
agitation, and partly from the desire to engage their
members more fully in the missionary enterprise by con-
centrated action, withdrew, and organized separate general societies for the South, which still continue in operation, though greatly crippled by the war. The general
societies for benevolent effort at the North were never so
energetic so well sustained, or so successful, as at the

present. Since secession and slavery have now passed away, it is to be hoped that time will restore a more perfect internal fellowship than before, on the New Testament principles of equity, loyalty, and love.

The changes created by the war in the Southern States make it impossible to obtain complete returns of Baptist communicants. The Baptist Year Book gives the total North and South for 1870 as 799 Associations, 17,745 Churches, 10,818 ordained ministers; 77,795 baptized within the year, and 1,419,493 communicants. Grand total for North America, including the British colonies, 1,464,638. If the minor sects of Baptists, of all sorts, are added, the whole amounts to 2,075,000. Population about 10,500,000. Baptist Colleges, 29; Theological Seminaries, 9; Academies and high schools for both sexes about 100; periodical organs, 48.

EPISCOPALIANS;

OR,

PROTESTANT EPISCOPAL CHURCH.

THE denomination of Christians called the Protestant Episcopal Church had its origin in England, where it is called the Church of England.

The king is the supreme head; by this authority he convenes and prorogues the convocations of the clergy. The church is governed by two archbishops and twenty-five bishops.

The Archbishop of Canterbury is styled the *Primate of all England*, and to him belongs the privilege of crowning the kings and queens of England. The province of

William White

Canterbury comprehends twenty-one bishoprics. In the province of the Archbishop of York, who is called the *Primate of England*, there are four bishoprics.

Archbishops and bishops are appointed by the king, by what is called a *congé d'élire*, or leave to elect, which is sent to the dean and chapter, naming the person to be chosen.

The bishop of London, as presiding over the capital, has the precedence of all the others. The Bishop of Durham has certain prerogatives, as presiding over a see that constitutes a county palatine; the Bishop of Winchester is third in dignity; the others take rank according to seniority of consecration. The archbishops and bishops (except the Bishop of Sodor and Man) have seats in the House of Lords, and are styled the *spiritual lords*.

The archbishops have the title of *grace*, and *most reverend father in God, by divine providence;* bishops are addressed by the title of *lord*, and *right reverend father in God, by divine permission.* The former are said to be *enthroned*, the latter *installed.*

To every cathedral belong several prebendaries and a dean, who form the dean and chapter, or council of the bishop. The next order of the clergy is that of archdeacons; their number is sixty; their office is to reform abuses, and to induct into benefices.

The most numerous and laborious order of the clergy are the deacons, curates, vicars, and rectors. The office of the deacon is confined to baptism, reading in the church, and assisting the priest at the communion.

A parson is one who has full possession of all the rights of a parish church; if the great tithes are *impropriated*, the priest is called a *vicar;* if not, a *rector :* a *curate* is one who is not instituted to the cure of souls, but exercises the spiritual office in a parish under a rector or vicar.

The convocation of the clergy, which is the highest ecclesiastical court, has not been permitted by government to do·any business since 1717, and is merely convened as a matter of form. The doctrines of the Church of England are contained in the thirty-nine articles ; the form of worship is directed by a liturgy.

The first steps to the establishment of the English Church were slow. It retained at first many of the features of the Roman Church, both in regard to doctrine and rites.

After the parliament had declared Henry VIII. the only supreme head of the Church, and the convocation of the clergy had voted that the Bishop of Rome had no more jurisdiction in England than any other foreign bishop, the articles of faith of the new Church were declared to consist in the Scriptures and the three creeds, the Apostolic, the Nicene, and the Athanasian ; the real presence, the use of images, the invocation of saints, &c were still maintained.

Under Edward the new liturgy was composed in English, and took the place of the old mass ; the doctrines were also stated in forty-two articles. With the reign of Mary, the old religion was re-established ; and it was not till that of Elizabeth that the Church of England was finally instituted. As no change was made in the episcopal form of government, and some rites and ceremonies were retained which many of the Reformed considered as superstitious, this circumstance gave rise to many future dissensions.

The controversy concerning the ceremonial part of divine worship commenced with those exiles who, in 1554, fled from the persecutions of Queen Mary, and took refuge in Germany. On the accession of Elizabeth they returned, and renewed the contest at home which had begun abroad.

These were called *Puritans*, and at one time comprised many distinguished members of the English clergy.

On the accession of James, the Puritans hoped for some relief; but an Episcopal hierarchy was more favorable to his views than the Presbyterian form of government, and he publicly adopted the maxim, "No bishop, no king."

When the English divines returned from the Synod of Dort, the king and the majority of the Episcopal clergy discovered an inclination to the sentiments of Arminius, which have since prevailed over Calvinism among the English clergy.

Under Charles I., the attempts made, through the instrumentality of Laud, to reduce all the churches of Great Britain under the jurisdiction of bishops, and the suppression of the opinions and institutions that were peculiar to Calvinism, cost the Archbishop of Canterbury his head, and had no little effect in imbittering the civil contest between the throne and the parliament. After the death of Laud, the parliament abolished the Episcopal government, and condemned everything in the ecclesiastical establishment that was contrary to the doctrine, worship, and discipline of the Church of Geneva.

As soon as Charles II. was restored to the throne, the ancient forms of ecclesiastical government and public worship were restored; and, in 1662, a public law, entitled *the act of uniformity*, was enacted, by which all who refused to observe the rites and subscribe the doctrines of the Church of England, were entirely excluded from its dominion.

In the reign of William III., and particularly in 1689, the divisions among the friends of Episcopacy gave rise to the two parties called the *high-churchmen*, or *nonjurors*, and *low-churchmen*. The former maintained the doctrine of passive obedience, or non-resistance to the

5　　　　　　D

sovereign under any circumstance whatever; that the hereditary succession to the throne is of divine institution, and cannot be interrupted: that the Church is subject to the jurisdiction of God alone; and, consequently, that certain bishops deposed by King William remained, notwithstanding, true bishops; and that those who had been appointed in their places were rebels and schismatics, and all who held communion with them were guilty of rebellion and schism.

The gradual progress of civil and religious liberty during the last one hundred and fifty years, has settled practically many such controversies. The great increase of the dissenters in recent times (they are estimated to be more numerous than the members of the established Church) has led to new concessions in their favor; the repeal of the corporation and test acts, and the *Catholic emancipation*, as it is called, are among the important events of the late reign.

We have said that the doctrines of the Church of England are contained in the thirty-nine articles; we are not ignorant that the most eminent English divines have doubted whether they are Calvinistic or Lutheran, that some have denominated them *articles of peace*, and that not a few have written in direct opposition to them. But they are the established confession of the English Church, and, as such, deserve a short analysis. The five first articles contain a profession of faith in the Trinity; the incarnation of Jesus Christ, his descent to hell, and his resurrection; the divinity of the Holy Ghost. The three following relate to the canon of the Scripture. The eighth article declares a belief in the Apostles', Nicene, and Athanasian creeds. The ninth and following articles contain the doctrines of original sin, of justification by faith alone, of predestination, &c. The nineteenth, twentieth, and twenty-first declare the Church to be the assembly of the faithful; that it can decide nothing except by the Scriptures. The twenty-second rejects the doctrine of purgatory, indulgences, the adoration of images, and the invocation of saints. The twenty-third decides that only those lawfully called shall preach or administer the sacraments. The twenty-fourth requires the liturgy to be in English. The twenty-fifth and twenty-sixth declare the sacraments effectual signs of grace (though administered by evil men), by which God excites and confirms our faith. They are two ; baptism and the Lord's Supper. Baptism, according to the twenty-seventh article, is a sign of regeneration, the seal of our adoption, by which faith is confirmed and grace increased. In the Lord's Supper, according to article twenty-eighth, the bread is the communion of the body of Christ, the wine the communion of his blood, but only through faith (art. twenty-ninth) ; and the communion must be administered in both kinds (art. thirty). The twenty-eighth article condemns the doctrine of transubstantiation, and the elevation and adoration of the host; the thirty-first rejects the sacrifice of the mass as blasphemous ; the thirty-second permits the marriage of the clergy ; the thirty-third maintains the efficacy of excommunication. The remaining articles relate to the supremacy of the king, the condemnation of Anabaptists, &c.

In the United States, the members of the Church of England, or Episcopalians, form a large and respectable denomination. When the Revolutionary War began, there were only about eighty parochial clergymen of this Church to the northward and eastward of Maryland; and they derived the greater part of their subsistence from the English Society for the Propagation of the Gospel in Foreign Parts. In Maryland and Virginia, the Episcopal

Church was much more numerous, and had legal establishments for its support.   The inconvenience of depending
on the mother Church for ordination, and the want of an
internal Episcopacy, was long severely felt by the American Episcopalians.   But their petitions for an Episcopate
of their own were long resisted by their superiors in Eng
land; and their opponents in the United States objected
to the measure from an apprehension that bishops from
England would bring with them an authority which would
interfere with the civil institutions of this country, and be
prejudicial to the members of other communions.   After
the United States had become independent of Great
Britain, a new difficulty arose on the part of the English
bishops: they could not consistently depart from their
own stated forms of ordination, and these contained political tests improper for American citizens to subscribe.
Dr. L' wth, then Bishop of London, obtained an act of
Parliament allowing him to dispense with these political
requisitions.   Before this act was passed, Dr. Seabury
was consecrated at Aberdeen by the *non-juring* bishops of
Scotland; and, not long after, Dr. W. White, of Philadelphia. Dr. Provoost, of New York, and Dr. James Madison,
of Virginia, were consecrated by the English archbishops.

In 1792 there were four bishops and about 200 clergy.
In 1832 there were fifteen bishops and 583 clergy.   In
1855 the number of bishops had increased to thirty-eight,
and the clergy to 1714, while the communicants were reported to be 105,350.   In 1859 there were 1422 churches,
with accommodations for 625,213 persons.   The total
value of church property was $11,261,970.

Some changes in the liturgy of the American branch
of the Episcopal Church were early made, in accommodation to the American clergy, and the difference in the
political condition of the two countries.

The three orders of bishops, priests, and deacons, are retained. The churches choose their pastors, but their installation or induction requires the consent of the bishop of the diocese. The churchwardens are chosen by the communicants, the vestry by the parish.

Each diocese holds an Annual Convention, composed of clergy and lay delegates elected by the people, in which the bishop presides.

Every three years a General Convention is held, composed of the bishops, who form the House of Bishops; and clerical and lay delegates from each diocese, who form the House of Delegates: and the Episcopal Church throughout the United States is governed by the canons of the General Convention.

DUTCH REFORMED CHURCH.

THE colony of New Amsterdam, now New York, was settled in 1612 by the Dutch. Missionaries and pious immigrants arrived here in the very beginning of the colony, but it is not known at what time a church was first organized. The Collegiate Church is supposed to have been formed in 1619. The Dutch Reformed Church is by many years earlier than any other Presbyterian church in this country. It differs but slightly from the other American Presbyterian churches. Unfortunately, the names used for its officers and ecclesiastical bodies, and the name of the church itself, do not impart to the English reader a clear view of the things represented. It should be remembered, then, that the Dutch Reformed Church is no longer a Dutch church. Its services are all performed in

English, and all its modes of action are naturalized to our country; so that no church among us is more perfectly American, or better adapted to make an effectual movement in the propagation of religion among our varied population.

If its name were changed, and its dominie were called a minister, its consistory a session, its classis a presbytery, and its general synod a general assembly, there would be little remaining to distinguish it from the American Presbyterian Church.

From the commencement of the Dutch Reformed Church in this country, it was subordinate to the classis of Amsterdam till 1737. In this year a movement was made to throw off dependence on the parent classis. This occasioned a violent contest, which was not terminated till 1771: when the Rev. Dr. Livingston, having previously convinced the classis of Amsterdam of the desirableness of the measure, and having prepared the way by conciliating wise men of both parties, induced the consistory of his church to call a convention. The convention met in New York in October, and resulted in a harmonious arrangement for a complete organization of the Dutch Reformed Church in this country as an independent body. It receives the confession of faith, as adopted by the national synod of the Council of Dort in the years 1618 and 1619, with the Heidelberg Catechism, the Compend of the Christian religion, and the canons of the Council of Dort on the famous five points. It is strictly Calvinistic.

The Dutch Reformed Church has a limited liturgy, which is allowed to be used by those who, through a defective education or inexperience, need such helps. The only part which is enjoined is the reading of the Ten Commandments in the opening of the morning service, the form of baptism, the short prayer before the vows taken by parents in the baptism of infants, and the formula of the holy communion of the Lord's Supper. This last is read by the minister, while all the members carefully and devoutly follow him, with the book open before them. There is a single point in which their government differs from other branches of the Presbyterian Church. The ruling elders, instead of being elected for life, are appointed for two years. If acceptable to the church, they may be appointed again after having been out of office for one year.

The government of the Dutch Reformed Church is Presbyterian. It is fully described in the article on Presbyterians. They only use a different nomenclature, in some respects, in speaking of ecclesiastical affairs. The consistory, or session, is composed of the minister, or bishop, ruling elders, and deacons. The pastor and elders meet as a spiritual court to transact the spiritual concerns, such as the admission of members, and the exercise of discipline. The deacons are charged with the care of the poor. The consistory, *including the deacons*, meet as a board of trustees, for the transaction of the secular business of the church. On great occasions, such as the calling of a minister, what is termed the grand consistory is called together. · This is composed of the acting session, and all who have previously belonged to that body. The next court is the classis, or presbytery; the next, *the particular synod*, which, like the classis, is a representative body. It consists of two ministers and two elders from each classis within its bounds. The highest court, from which there is no appeal, is *the general synod*. This is composed of three ministers and three elders from each classis of the whole church. It holds its sessions annually, and conducts its affairs much in the same method with the General Assembly of the Presbyterian Church.

The college and theological seminary at New Brunswick, N. J., are an honor to the Dutch Church. Amply endowed, and furnished with able professors, they exert their full share of influence, in raising up a learned and able ministry. This church reports in the Minutes of the General Synod for 1847 — particular synods, 2; classes, 24; ministers, 289; churches, 276; communicants, 32,840; members of congregations, 110.977.

In the American Almanac for 1859, the Dutch Reformed Church is stated to have 324 churches, accommodations for 181,986 worshippers, and church property to the amount of $4,096,730.

The sessions of the General Synod held during the war were marked by weighty and earnest declarations of sympathy with the government in its struggle to maintain the integrity of the nation, and by more guarded yet sufficiently clear utterances in favor of the removal of slavery as the source of our troubles.

No Church has a more honorable record in the work of Foreign Missions than this, and no names in this department are more favorably known to the Christian world than her Abeel, Pohlman, and above all her Scudders, father and sons. In 1817 the General Synod united with the Presbyterian and the Associate Reformed churches in forming the United Foreign Missionary Society. In 1826 this was merged in the American Board of Commissioners for Foreign Missions. In 1857 an amicable separation from the Board took place, when the Reformed Dutch Church undertook the foreign missionary work through the ordinary denominational channels. In the separation, the Amoy mission in China and the Arcot mission in India, which had been founded and carried on by ministers of the Dutch Church exclusively, were set over to that denomination, and they have been among the most prosperous missions in that part of the world.

At the time of the separation, the General Synod requested the ministers and churches in China, after the example of those in India, to form themselves into a classis, according to the order of the Dutch Church. This they declined doing, preferring to form, with the flourishing congregations of the English Presbyterian Mission, a separate organization, called "The Great Presbyterial or Classical Council of Amoy."

In 1863 missionaries were sent to Japan. In 1866 Rev. S. R. Bowen, missionary at Yokohama, sent a circular of great interest to Christians in all parts of the world, showing the marvellous preparation for the entrance of the Gospel in that country. He asked the coöperation of Christendom in the work of evangelizing Japan. Four of the foremost princes have requested a missionary to superintend their educational interests. Two governors consulted with the missionary on the same subject, and large numbers of Christian books in Chinese have been purchased or distributed among the natives.

In 1866, a committee of the General Classis was appointed to inquire into the expediency and propriety of dropping the word "Dutch" from the name of the denomination. Next year the General Synod, by 102 to 7, voted in favor of the change, and on submitting the question to the classes, 25 voted in favor and 6 against it. The adjourned meeting of the General Synod in November ratified the action of the classes by a vote of 112 to 7. By this action, the name and style of the Church became "The Reformed Church in America." The charter of the Church was amended to conform to this change by the Legislature of New York.

Statistics for 1870: 33 classes, 464 churches, 493 ministers, 61,444 communicants. Contributions to general benevolence $281,647.36; to congregational purposes $906,034.27.

GERMAN REFORMED CHURCH.

THE German Reformed Church in the United States dates its origin in about 1740, and was formed by immigrants from Germany and Switzerland. It commenced its existence in this country in the eastern portion of Pennsylvania, and is almost entirely confined to the German population. At an early period, however, congregations were formed in Virginia, the Carolinas, Maryland, New Jersey, and New York.

The German Reformed Church consists, at this time, of two independent synods. They are bound together by a triennial convention. But this convention at first was not a court of appeal, and possessed none of the power of a general synod. In 1810 or 1812, the Rev. Jacob William Dechaut was sent out as a missionary to the State of Ohio. He was stationed at Miamisburg, Montgomery County. The Rev. Messrs. Winters and Weis joined him; and their labors were attended with so much success that a classis was organized in 1819; and in 1823 or 1824 the majority of the classes separated from the parent body, and became an independent judicatory, calling themselves the Synod of Ohio. In 1836 the classis of Western Pennsylvania obtained permission to unite with the Synod of Ohio, which now bore the title of "The Synod of Ohio and the adjoining States;" and by a late act, this synod, which nad previously, been subdivided into three district synods, received a new organization agreeably to the plan of the constitution of the eastern church. The western church is now divided into classes, and its synod is a delegated body composed of the representatives of the classes.

The government of the German Reformed Church is strictly Presbyterian. While there was no general synod, appeals could not be carried so far by one court as in the Dutch Reformed and American Presbyterian churches. For an explanation of the terms consistory, classes, etc., see the preceding article.

An appeal could be taken from the consistory to the classes, and from the classes to the synod, whose decision was final.

The German Reformed Church in this country is now spread over the whole of Pennsylvania and Ohio, and over portions of Maryland, Virginia. North Carolina, Missouri, Illinois, Indiana, Michigan, and New York. There is a church in the city of New Orleans; others formerly subsisted in New Jersey, South Carolina, Tennessee, and Kentucky; and some members are still scattered over the several States of the Union.

The eastern portion of the church is the original and parent body; and its synod, existing before the other, bears the title of "The Synod of the German Reformed Church in the United States." Its territory extends in Pennsylvania westward to the Alleghany Mountains; northward it includes portions of New York; and on the south, Maryland, Virginia, and Carolina. It has under its jurisdiction ten classes, viz.: Philadelphia, Goshenhoppen, East Pennsylvania, Lebanon, Susquehanna, Zion, Mercersburg, Maryland, Virginia, and North Carolina.

The doctrines of this church are Calvinistic; that is to

say, the Heidelberg Catechism is their symbol, though a large portion of the laity lean to Arminian doctrines touching the subject of predestination. They practise the rite of confirmation; which is, however, little else than a ceremony admitting candidates, who give evidence of regeneration, to full communion. They have a theological seminary founded in 1827, and a college established in 1836; both are located in Pennsylvania, and are in a flourishing state. They have a Board of Foreign Missions, and sustain one missionary station at Broosa, in Asia Minor. Their foreign missionary transactions are all made through the American Board of Commissioners for Foreign Missions, with which body a connection has been formed for that purpose. According to the published Minutes of 1845, the Eastern Synod then comprised 10 classes, 155 ministers, 471 congregations, and 31,170 communicants. The Western Synod contained 6 classes, 72 ministers, 236 congregations, and 7,885 communicants. A summary of the whole force of the German Reformed Church in this country, then, was — 2 synods, containing 16 classes, 227 ministers, 707 churches. and 39,055 communicants. It is remarkable that such a disproportion should exist between the number of ministers and churches. This arises from a peculiar usage of intrusting several congregations to the charge of a single minister.

In the American Almanac for 1859, the German Reformed Church is stated to have 327 churches, accommodations for 156.932 worshippers, and church property to the amount of $965,880.

Much agitation upon the expediency of a more elaborate and authoritative ritual, and upon "High Church" views, taught in the seminary at Mercersburg, chiefly by Dr. Nevin, has been experienced in the past quarter century of this church's history. The Western Synod has adhered to more strictly Protestant ground, but in the Eastern Synod the powerful influence of Dr. Nevin and his able associates has, until lately, quite overborne that of Dr. Bomberger and his associates upon the other side, such men as Dr. Berg and Dr. Helfenstein having meanwhile withdrawn from the body, to seek more congenial relations in the Reformed Dutch and Presbyterian Churches. In 1863 the Triennial General Convention was clothed with judicial power. A resolution admonishing the subordinate bodies of the duty of loyalty to the government was adopted. The tercentenary of the Heidelberg Catechism was celebrated this year, by a series of meetings lasting from the 17th to the 23d of January. The addresses and essays were subsequently published in a large memorial volume. A superb edition of the Catechism, in Latin, German and English, was also published as a memorial of the occasion. The tercentenary contributions to be applied to theological institutions and benevolent objects reached $103,000.

In 1866, the two classes in the South, which had been hindered but not estranged by the war, were again fully represented in the Triennial Convention. Proposals to co-operate with the Reformed Dutch Church in the work of Foreign Missions were received and considered, without final action. The classes were requested, a second time, to take action upon the proposal to drop the word "German" from the title of the Church, the majority having previously voted in the negative. The discussions on the liturgy were very animated. The Western Synod, which is "Low Church," reported that they were still engaged on the work of revising a liturgy, but were not prepared to report finally. The Eastern Synod had for some time been using a liturgy considered "High Church," and which they desired the Convention to endorse and authorize for the whole body. By a close vote (64 to 57) it was decided to recommit the liturgy of the Eastern and the unfinished work of the Western Synod to new hands, and to require a new revised liturgy to be presented at the next triennial session. A convention of those opposed to the "High Church" liturgy was held at Meyerstown, Pennsylvania, in September, 1867, which was very emphatically condemned at a subsequent meeting of the Eastern Synod as irregular and schismatic. At the last general synod, in 1869, it appeared that twenty-four out of the thirty-one classes had voted in favor of dropping the word "German" from the name, and the change was declared carried. The body is therefore known as the "Reformed Church in the United States." Overtures looking to organic union from the Reformed (Dutch) Church in America were favorably entertained, but the time for definite action was not considered to have arrived. In regard to a liturgy, it was left optional with classes which to employ.

The statistics for 1870 give 31 classes, 526 ministers, 1179 congregations, 217,910 "members," 96,728 being "communicants." The benevolent contributions were $76.453.15. In 1868 there were connected with the church six colleges, two seminaries, and one mission house.

The Foreign Missionary work of this church is done through the American Board of Foreign Missions. One of the most successful missionaries of that Board is Rev. B. Schneider, of the Reformed Church, whose services in connection with the great church of Aintab in the Armenian mission are well known to the Christian public. Congregations of from twelve to fifteen hundred assembled regularly in the church under his care, and the remarkable movements among the Armenian Churches towards self-support and independent evangelistic effort appeared here at a very early date.

The Ursinus College, recently founded by Dr. J. H. A. Bomberger and others, mainly of Philadelphia, is designed to serve as a counteractive to the educational and theological tendencies of Mercersburg.

THE EVANGELICAL LUTHERAN CHURCH.

THE Lutheran Church is that body of Christian confessors, or aggregate of particular Churches, who adhere to the Augsburg Confession, as a correct exhibit of the great doctrines taught in the sacred Scriptures of the Old and New Testaments. These Churches are found in the Germanic States, Prussia, Austria, France, Denmark, Norway, Sweden, Russia, Poland, Finland, Hungary, Bohemia, the Netherlands, European Turkey, England, the United States, Canadas, Nova Scotia, East and West Indies, South America, Africa, and other parts of the world. Some of them adhere to the Augsburg Confession with more rigidness than others; but, in some form, that great Confession is their acknowledged Symbol, by which they testify to each other, and to the world, their mutual affiliation, and their distinctness from all others.

It has been said that the birthday of the Lutheran Church was the 31st of October, 1517, when Luther nailed upon the Church-door of Wittenberg his ninety-five Theses against the infamous traffic in indulgences, setting forth the only way of forgiveness in Christ Jesus; that the day of her baptism was the 17th of April, 1521, when Luther appeared before the Diet of Worms, and, in the face of all the powers on earth, avowed his unflinching adherence to conscience and the plain word of God;

that the day of her confirmation was the 25th of June, 1530, when the Lutheran princes stood up before the imperial throne of Charles V., at the Diet of Augsburg, and gave out that noble Confession of the true Christian faith, which will ever remain "the heroic monument of the most admirable acts with which Christian history makes us acquainted;" and that the day when she reached her maturity, and became of age, was the 26th of September, 1555, when the religious wars of Germany terminated in the Peace of Augsburg, and gave to Protestant Christians their political recognition and the free enjoyment of their faith.

But Lutherans say it was not there, nor thence, that their principles were derived, nor those great events that originated what is known as the Lutheran Church. They say that its root runs back into the ages of Prophets and Apostles, that its true birth was in the birth of Jesus, and that its true baptism, that which occurred at Jerusalem on the day of Pentecost. "Whilst Luther amended the gravest errors and vices of the Church of Rome, and restored the Church to a happier condition, he did not frame a new Church," says Buddeus. "The Reformers desired not, and are not to be considered founders of a new Church, but simply renewers of the old upon its ancient foundation," says Sartorius. "The doctrine of the Lutherans," says Walch, "is no new doctrine; it is the same which has been steadfastly preserved in the Church from old, and from the times of the Apostles: for we teach nothing in our Churches, except what the pure, ancient, apostolic Christian Church teaches."

Lutherans are very particular to distinguish between the Romish Church, in the specific sense of the papal system, and the true Catholic Church of Christ, of which the papacy had taken possession. The one is human; the other is divine. The one originated with the Apostles,

and with Christ, whose earthly body it is; the other arose during the sixth and seventh centuries after Christ. The one existed before there was a pope, or a papal system, and hence, of course, does not cease with the expulsion and abandonment of the pope and his system. Departure from the corruptions and false authorities which had risen up in the true Church, does not, by any means, involve departure from the Church itself. "No one, therefore," says Heerbrand, "can justly charge us with apostasy; for we have in no way departed from the true Church of God, but only from that of malignants and Antichrist, which has hated us, and from which the Holy Ghost also directs and commands us to depart." When the Lutherans renounced the papacy and its abominations, they took with them the same Bible, the same Ecumenical Confessions, the same holy Faith, and the same apostolic ministry and sacraments, which distinguished the true Church from the beginning, and hence the same historic Church-life, which took its rise in the incarnation of the Son of God, trickled feebly through the rubbish and darkness of the middle ages, and never was, or could be, entirely lost.

The Church before the Reformation had three general Creeds, the Apostles', the Nicene, and the Athanasian.

The Apostles' Creed took its being and shape from the Formula of Baptism given by the Lord Himself, and was the natural and necessary fruit of it, by which all the earliest Churches, almost simultaneously, and without formal agreement, united in the expression of their one common faith.

Out of this primary Creed as naturally grew the Nicene, necessitated as it was by the great controversies of the third and fourth centuries, concerning the Trinity, and especially by the heretical tenets of the Arians and Macedonians. Then came the Nestorian and Eutychian agitations, which called for still closer definitions and stricter guards of the great substance of the faith. These were realized in the Athanasian Creed.

All these Creeds thus having a necessary and unrelinquishable connection with the Church's utterance and preservation of what she received direct from Christ and His inspired Apostles and Evangelists, the Lutherans hold, cannot be abandoned without unmaking the Spirit-moved history of the universal body of the truest and best disciples Christ had upon earth in the course of more than a thousand years, as they show us the true Catholic faith as wrought out in the consciousness of the members of the true body of Christ, and rest directly and only on the Holy Scriptures.

To these essential and Catholic expressions of the faith, the Lutheran Church adheres, next to the Scriptures, as right utterances of the contents of God's word with regard to the questions and circumstances which gave them being. So far, then, she is soundly Catholic, and vitally conjoined with the only proper Church, for the first fifteen centuries of its existence.

At the time of the Reformation, there were still other relations of the contents of the Gospel, which it had become as necessary to define as those with which the Ecumenical symbols dealt.

The Augsburg Confession, therefore, it is claimed, is as deeply inlaid with the historic conservation of the Gospel in the convictions and belief of men, as any of the older Creeds; that it grew out of similar necessities, was fashioned by a like law, proceeded from a corresponding Spirit-moved source, and to the same end; and that it can no more be abandoned now, and yet the pure Catholic faith be retained, than the Ecumenical symbols which went before it.

And upon the Augsburg Confession, as necessarily, in

their degree, followed the Apology, and the Smalcald Articles, polemically dealing with Romish perversions and contradictions; and then the Form of Concord, to dispose of the internal disputes which troubled the Reformation itself. Many of the sublimest reminiscences of Protestantism pertain to the history of the Lutheran Church.

The first successful attempt to reform the corrupt Church of the Middle Ages was made by the Lutherans. There were reformers before Luther, but there was no effective reformation, except that which he led. Those ninety-five Theses, nailed to the door of the Church of All Saints at Wittenberg, on the morning of the 31st of October, 1517; the seventeen Articles of Torgau, prepared by his hand in obedience to the command of one of the most praiseworthy of rulers; the magnificent protest of the Lutheran princes at the Diet of Spires; and the triumphant Confession of Augsburg, along with the hymns and sermons, translations, and other writings of Luther and his associates, must ever be acknowledged as the first effective disclosure to modern nations of those ancient and undying truths which make up the real essence of Christianity. Luther found the Bible chained in the cloister, and he was the first, in modern times, to break its fetters, and to set it free. He himself translated it into the common language of the people, in a version which stands to this day as the best extant, which has largely formed the basis and led the way for all subsequent translations, and which laid at once the foundations of Protestantism and German literature—the ruling religion and literature of the earth.

It is also claimed that the Lutheran Church, by her Confessions and masters in theology, has, either directly or indirectly, given to all orthodox Christendom its Creed. As remarked by one of her doctors: "The Augsburg Confession has been substantially inwrought into all the subsequent evangelical symbols, both in and out of Germany; and, in the opposition which it provoked, even determined the decisions of the Council of Trent."

As to that branch of the Reformation which took the name of *Reformed*, Bossuet says: "The Calvinists, particularly, cannot deny that they have always looked upon Luther and the Lutherans as the authors of their Reformation; and, not to speak of Calvin, who often mentioned Luther with great regard, as the head of the Reformation, all the Calvinists, Germans, English, Hungarians, Poles, Dutch, and all others, in general, who assembled at Frankfort through the influence of Queen Elizabeth, all these having acknowledged those of the Confession of Augsburg, namely, the Lutherans, as the first who gave a new birth to the Church."

As to the Church of England, with her daughter, the Protestant Episcopal Church of the United States, Tytler, the historian, has very properly observed, that she has chiefly conformed her tenets to the Lutheran system of Reformation. "The principles upon which our Reformation was conducted," says Archbishop Laurence, "were manifestly Lutheran." In the construction of the Thirty-nine articles, Bishop Burnet affirms his conviction, that "great regard was had to the Lutheran Churches, with whom a conjunction was much endeavored." Laurence says of them, that they "were neither the production of Parker nor the convocation," but "*were borrowed from a Lutheran Creed.*" He notes "a manifest resemblance between them and that boast of Germany and pride of the Reformation, the Confession of Augsburg, which in some instances amounts to a direct transcript of whole passages" and "entire extracts, without the slightest omission or important variation." Bishop Whittingham, of Maryland, speaking of the Thirty-nine Articles, in his

charge for 1849, says, that "with the Augsburg Confession
their connection is of a nature 'the most intimate and direct, substantiable by superabundant evidence, both internal and circumstantial. In more than one respect,"
he continues, "the Confession of Augsburg is the source
of the Thirty-nine Articles of the Church of England
and America—their prototype in form, their model in
doctrine, and the very fountain of many of their expressions; while others are drawn from its derivative expositions and repetitions." Palmer, Hare, Short, Chapin,
Proctor, Humphrey, Hardwick, and other prominent
Episcopalians, have made the same acknowledgment.
And even the English Book of Common Prayer is largely
indebted to the Lutheran Reformers. It was, to a large
extent, based upon a book of "directions for the public
services and administration of the sacraments, with forms
of prayer and a litany," given out by authority of Herr-
man, Prince Archbishop of Cologne, as a form of doctrine
and worship for his subjects, and *prepared by Melancthon
and Bucer.* Humphrey says of this book, that "it was
not so much a new composition as a revision of the ancient formularies, and was taken in great measure from a
Liturgy prepared by Luther and used at Nuremberg."
And Proctor, in his History, says, that "the litany, the
exhortations in the communion service, and portions of
the baptismal services, are mainly due to this book,
through which the influence of Luther may be traced in
our (English) Prayer Book, where additions or considerable changes were made in translating the old Latin
Services."

It is, therefore, with justice that the Lutheran Church
takes to herself the high appellation of *The Mother of
Protestants.* Evangelical Christendom owes more to the
Lutherans, for everything pure, blessed, and great in its

religion, than to any other class of men since the Apostles fell asleep.

To Luther, and the Reformation he conducted, under God, are modern freemen also indebted for the privilege of thinking, believing, preaching and worshiping, as conscience and Scripture may direct, without danger of being burned for blasphemy, or having their bones broken for heresy. When Luther stood before the august Diet of Worms on trial for his faith, the liberties of the world trembled in his lone heart. And when he lifted up his hand before God, in the face of all Europe's potentates, and declared in solemn oath, that, unless convinced by clear testimonies of holy Scripture and solid reasons, he could not and would not retract, modern freedom drew its first breath, and independence once more began to pulsate in the arteries of man.

A Romish writer bears witness, that "Luther has been the restorer of liberty in modern times;" that "if he did not create, he at least courageously affixed his signature to that great revolution, which rendered the right of examination lawful in Europe;" and that "if we at this day exercise, in all its plenitude, this first and highest privilege of human intelligence, it is to him we are mostly indebted for it."

Nor is the Lutheran Church any less distinguished for her patronage of learning, and her contributions to theology and science, than in the particulars just cited. Her literature is the richest in the world. "The Romish Church," says Lange, "is the Church of priests; the Lutheran Church is the Church of Theologians." Her universities have been the glory of Germany for the last three hundred years; and her critics and religious teachers have been the leading instructors of Christendom from the days of Luther until now.

These Churches of the Augsburg Confession generally have connected with them the name of Luther, and are often called *Lutherans*, or Lutheran Churches. This title was first applied by Romanists, as an expression of disrespect and derision. It is no part of the proper designation of these Churches. As a party name, over against the proper historical Church, they protest against it, and reject it. They claim to be simply the Evangelical Church, as distinguished from a church which rests upon tradition, popes, or human idiosyncrasies. Luther was wholly unwilling to have his name used as a sectarian watchword. "I beg," says he, "that my name may be passed in silence, and that people call themselves not *Lutherans*, but Christians. Who is Luther? The doctrine is not mine; I have not been crucified for any one. Why, then, should the children of Christ take the unhallowed name of a frail, vile mortal like me? Do it not; let us put away party names, and bear the name of Christ, whose doctrine we hold."

And yet, there is a sense in which the name of Luther is significant and dear. Being historically associated with the restoration of the pure Gospel, and the exode of the Church of Christ from its bondage under popery and superstition, Lutherans feel that they cannot entirely discard it. With the pious George, the Margrave of Brandenburg, they say, "We were not baptized in the name of Luther. He is not our God and Saviour. We do not rest our faith in him. And, therefore, in this sense, we are no *Lutherans*. But if it be asked whether, with heart and lips, we profess the doctrines which God restored to light through the instrumentality of his blessed servant, Dr. Martin Luther, we neither hesitate, nor are we ashamed to call ourselves *Lutherans*. In this sense we are, and while we live, will remain *Lutherans*."

The great cardinal principles of the Lutheran Church are thus summed up by one of its writers:

1. *An open Bible, man's only guide to heaven;* as eloquently affirmed in the Formula of Concord, where it is said: "We receive and adopt, with all the heart, the prophetic and apostolic writings of the Old and New Testaments, as the clear and pure fountains of Israel; and hold, that these sacred Scriptures alone are the true and infallible rule by which all teachers and doctrines are to be tried and judged."

2. *Private judgment, man's inalienable birthright;* as so thrillingly asserted by Luther before the Diet of Worms, and so vigorously re-echoed in the Protest of the Princes at the Diet of Spires.

3. *Christ and Him crucified, man's only Saviour;* as unequivocally affirmed and taught in all the Symbols and accepted theologians of the Church, which never cease to refer to Christ as true God and true man in one Person, who is "the only Propitiator and Mediator ordained between God and man, the only Saviour, the only High Priest and Advocate before God."

4. *Faith in Christ, man's only availing righteousness;* as everywhere declared by the Lutheran Symbols, "that we cannot obtain forgiveness of sins and righteousness before God through our strength, merits and works; but that we are pardoned and justified gratuitously for Christ's sake through faith;" "that faith is the sole medium and instrument by which we apprehend Christ;" and that "this faith is not a bare historic knowledge of Christ, but a divine gift, by which we truly apprehend Christ our Redeemer, as presented in the Gospel message, and trust in him, for the sake of whose righteousness alone our sins are graciously forgiven, we are justified before God the Father, and entitled to expect eternal salvation."

The Lutheran Church has but few special peculiarities. It is presented as her chief characteristic that she aims at exhibiting a full, rotund, and complete Christianity, in a form in all directions true to the word and appointments of its Divine Author, and conformed to the common necessities of man, in all ages, in all places, and in all circumstances.

One of her authors says of her: "Taking the deepest and broadest foundations of the Christian religion, and working ever from its inner essence and spirit, there is nothing good or praiseworthy in faith or practice which does not harmonize with her, or which may not be realized as her own proper fruit. She held and taught a sovereign salvation, by grace only, before Calvin was freed from the shackles of papal superstition. She confessed and believed that Jesus Christ tasted death for every man, before Arminius was born. She approved and practiced the holding of meetings for prayer and mutual edification, before there was a Wesley, or any followers of his method. She had her Liturgies and forms of devotion,—the models and sources of the best that have followed,—when England was yet in the arms of the papacy, and the English Book of Common Prayer had not been thought of. She had her bishops before there were any Episcopalians, so-called, though ever denying that diocesan Episcopacy is at all necessary to the integrity of the Church. In government, she prescribes for the pure preaching of the Word, and the administration of the Sacraments according to that Word, but leaves all questions of outward forms to be regulated as the circumstances may render most convenient or desirable. And in all things she is as many-sided as the graces of the Holy Spirit, or the glorious character of her Lord.

"Her name is *Evangelical*, and her office in the world

7

is EVANGELIZATION, according to Christ's own word and commandments. In fulfillment of this office, she approaches men, while yet in the helplessness of infancy, and marks them with God's token and seal of mercy in the Holy Sacrament of Baptism, teaching that 'children are thereby consecrated to God, and received into His favor;'—gathers them into classes and schools for instruction in the things of faith and piety as their minds unfold,—and, as soon as the evidences of fitness appear, introduces them into full fellowship and communion by the solemn rite of Confirmation. She builds sanctuaries, and delights in ornamenting and embellishing them with every pure art, for the honor and glory of God, and educates her young men of suitable gifts and spiritual graces, to serve in them as pastors and teachers, whom she solemnly and officially sets apart for their office by laying on of hands and prayer. She sets forward her pulpits, and the preaching of the Word, as the great central and divinely-instituted power of the Gospel. She puts 'psalms and hymns and spiritual songs' into the lips of her people, to strengthen their faith, exercise their devotional feelings, and refresh their souls. She calls upon all her members, at convenient intervals, to renew their profession at the sacred altar of that one sacrifice of our Lord, of which it is the privilege of men to participate in the Holy Supper. She watches over them with a godly and merciful discipline and maternal solicitude while they live. And, finally, when their race is run, she lays their bodies down with solemn care in the house of the dead,—'earth to earth, ashes to ashes, dust to dust'—looking for the resurrection of the last day, and the life of the world to come, through our Lord Jesus Christ. And whatever on earth can contribute to the furtherance or establishment of the doctrine and truth of God, among the civilized or savage, at home or abroad, and whatever may add to the true comfort and peace of man, she always lays hold of as an instrument for her service, and sanctifies it unto the Lord.

"She claims, that the Gospel can live and flourish in connection with the State, with all the embarrassments which such an unnatural relation entails, and that it can live and flourish in entire separation from it. She consents to all established government, whether despotic and monarchical, or free and republican, as lawful, and, for the end of government, an ordinance of God, to be obeyed in all matters not touching the direct obligations of conscience to the great Judge of all, as a part of every Christian's duty. She proclaims in her principal Confession, 'that Christians may hold either legislative, judicial or executive offices without sin; may decide causes, pronounce judgments, and punish transgressors, agreeably to imperial or other established laws; may wage just wars, and serve in them, make lawful contracts, take oaths when required, hold property, marry, and be married.' She stringently denies that a higher holiness is to be obtained by an abandonment of the ordinary stations, relations and duties of life, or that God cannot be as well and purely served in them as in separation from them. Nor does she suppose that the true Church of Jesus Christ has ceased to be, where imperfect or spurious members may be found among the confessors of his name."

In agreement with this, it was the remark of an Episcopal clergyman, respecting the Lutheran Church, that it "breathes the free spirit of Luther, and the mild spirit of Melancthon;" occupying the ground of a great mediator for the truth between many conflicting parties. It is claimed that she has successfully laid a doctrinal, liturgical, and government basis, which leaves no possible excuse for sectarianism; that the Episcopalian can come into her communion, and yet feel that he has in no way departed from the Church, and find much more solid and unequivocal instruction than his own standards contain; that the Dissenter may worship at her altars, without being oppressed and outraged with rigid, weakening, corrupt, or invariable forms, and yet come into much closer and wholesome contact with the proper Church; that the Presbyterian may hear of her preachers his favorite theme of sovereign grace, freed from the repulsive and questionable forms and inferences with which his Confession accompanies it, and learn lessons concerning the Sacraments about which he is too much in the dark; that the Methodist may find food in her pastures to give consistency to his fervor, and in her treasures the original sources of what he most admires in Wesley, without the unchurchliness and one-sided subjectivism with which he is sometimes reproached; that for all men, there is not on earth a more reliable, well-tried and satisfactory guide to the full truth, a sanctified life, and everlasting salvation, than that which is presented in the Evangelical Lutheran Church, wherever she is properly herself; that what she demands, is what no one may neglect or despise without danger to his soul; and that in nothing does she so heartily rejoice, as in the triumph of the simple truth as it is in Jesus, unwilted by sectarian bigotries, and unmutilated by the proud presumptuous hand of rationalizing philosophy, or by the enervations of a mistaken liberalism.

The Lutheran Church accordingly claims to be Catholic and not sectarian. The only notes and marks which she finds for the Church properly so called, are "the pure and sound doctrine of the Gospel, and the right use of the Sacraments." It is part of her Confession, that, "for the true unity of the Christian Church, it is not necessary that uniform ceremonies, instituted by men, should be

everywhere observed." All that she requires on this
point is, that the saying of Paul, Eph. iv. 4, 5, be realized: "One body and one Spirit, even as ye are called
in one hope of your calling; one Lord, one Faith, one
Baptism." As expressed by the Wurtemburg Confessors,
"We think that men are to judge by the authority, both
of the Holy Scripture and of the ancient fathers, that the
true Catholic and Apostolic Church is not tied to one certain place or nation. Where the Gospel of Christ is sincerely preached, and His sacraments rightly administered
according to his institution, where the Word of God is
preached, and where the Gospel is acknowledged by faith,
there God hath his Church, wherein he is effectual unto
eternal life."

The Lutherans do not claim that theirs is the only true
Church. In the Apology of their chief Confession, it is
said: "We affirm, and know in truth, that there are children of God scattered throughout all the world, in various kingdoms, islands, countries and cities, from the rising
to the setting of the sun, who truly know Christ and the
Gospel. . . And although among those built upon the
right foundation, that is, on Christ and the faith, there
are many weak ones, who build upon this foundation
wood, hay and stubble, that is, certain human conceits
and opinions, nevertheless, as they do not thereby overthrow or thrust aside the foundation, Christ, they are still
Christians, and may be forgiven such defects. . . Thus
even the Fathers sometimes build hay and stubble upon
the foundation, not intending, however, thereby to overthrow it. . . Hence, we conclude, according to the Scriptures, that the true Christian Church is the company of
those, *throughout all the world*, who really believe the
Gospel of Christ, and have the gift of the Holy Ghost. . .
We may so appears, holy and just, the children of God and

Christians, without observing the same ceremonies that are in use in *other Churches*. . . People can be in the Church of Christ even though they do not wear German or French garments."

The Lutheran Church has her Church-year, in harmony with the Ancient Churches, in which she seeks to reflect, in her computation of times and seasons, the course and progress of salvation both in the acts of Jesus and in the renewal of the soul and life. She has her appointed festivals of her Saviour's birth, and of the showing forth of his grace and power. She has her fixed period for coming into special sympathy with his great humiliation and passion, in taking her guilt upon him, and making himself an offering for her sins. She has her allotted days for the glad commemoration of his triumphant resurrection and ascension, and of the outpouring of the Holy Ghost in fulfillment of his gracious promises. She has her time for the special celebration of the adorable Trinity and the attributes of a life fully consecrated to Him. She does not canonize or worship saints, but remembers those whose faith she is to follow, and such as have by their lives and labors illustrated the way of holiness, and left the impress of their good deeds upon the world. She has her regular *Pericopes*, or Lessons of Holy Scripture, designated for every week, and for the special celebration of each great fact by which salvation was achieved, and on which the faith of the Church reposes. Leaving the Jewish Sabbath as no longer binding in its ancient form, she follows the example of the Apostles and the early Church, in setting apart the first day of the week as holy unto the Lord, in which secular employments and cares are to be laid aside, and God, His word, and His worship made to occupy and fill the attention. And in all these things she seeks to exemplify and perpetuate a living and true Christianity, first of all fulfilling what Christ has commanded and enjoined, and then conforming to the truest, best, and most wholesome convictions and developments of the Church itself in the purest periods of its history and worthiest portions from the beginning onward.

It is the habit of some to speak and think disparagingly of the Lutheran Church, and to assign it the position of an obscure sect, differing but little from Romanists, and scarcely any longer existing. This is altogether unwarranted by the facts. So far from being a mere obscure sect, the Lutheran Church is the oldest and largest of all Protestant denominations. She cannot be rightly reckoned as a mere branch of the Protestant Church; for, as remarked by one of her theologians, she is the great body and trunk of it. Christianity, in its Protestant form, started with her; and from her have all the Protestant Churches derived their being as Protestant Churches. Neither has she become lost in branches which have absorbed her strength and diverted her proper historic continuation. Up to this present moment, she is the massive and living trunk still. She possesses more territory now than any other two of the great Protestant families, and embraces a larger population than all other orthodox communions combined. From fifty to sixty millions of souls are at this hour under her spiritual care and training, and about thirty millions are enrolled as communicants at her altars. Nor has there ever been a people who more earnestly or more effectively protested against the errors of Rome.

In the United States, the Lutheran Church stands fourth in the list of denominations; the Baptists, Methodists and Presbyterians alone exceeding the Lutherans in numbers. It embraces fifty-four synods, four general organizations, and more than 600,000 communicants. It has (1872) seven theological seminaries, sixteen colleges, six seminaries for young ladies, six publication establishments, and twenty-nine regular periodicals. Among its living theologians are, Drs. C. F. and C. W. Schaeffer, W. J. Mann, C. P. Krauth and J. A. Seiss, of Philadelphia; Drs. S. S. Schmucker, J. A. Brown and M. Valentine, of Gettysburg; Drs. G. F. Krotel and H. I. Schmidt, of New York; Dr. J. G. Morris, of Baltimore; Dr. F. A. Muhlenberg, of Allentown, Dr. W. A. Passavant, of Pittsburg, and Dr. E. G. Greenwald, of Lancaster, Pa.; Dr. C. F. Walther, of St. Louis, Mo.; Dr. Bittle, of Salem, Va., and Dr. A. R. Rude, of Columbia, S. C.

METHODISTS.

It is not generally known that the name of Methodist had been given long before to a religious sect in England, or, at least, to a party in religion which was distinguished by some of the same marks as are now supposed to apply to the Methodists. John Spence, who was librarian of Sion College in 1657, in a book which he published, says, "Where are now our Anabaptists and plain pikestaff Methodists, who esteem all flowers of rhetoric in sermons no better than stinking weeds?" But the denomination to which we here refer was founded in the year 1729, by one Mr. Morgan and Mr. John Wesley. In the month of November that year, the latter, being then fellow of Lincoln College, began to spend some evenings in reading the Greek Testament with Charles Wesley, student, Mr. Morgan, commoner of Christ Church, and Mr. Kirkham, of Merton College. Not long afterwards, two or three of the

Engraved by A.B. Walter.

pupils of Mr. John Wesley obtained leave to attend these meetings. They then began to visit the sick in different parts of the town, and the prisoners also, who were confined in the castle. Two years after they were joined by Mr. Ingham, of Queen's College, Mr. Broughton, and Mr. Hervey; and in 1735 by the celebrated Mr. Whitfield, then in his eighteenth year. At this time their number in Oxford amounted to about fourteen. They obtained their name from the exact regularity of their lives, which gave occasion to a young gentleman of Christ Church to say, "Here is a new sect of Methodists sprung up!" alluding to a sect of ancient physicians who were called Methodists, because they reduced the whole healing art to a few common principles, and brought it into some method and order.

At the time that this society was formed, it is said that the whole kingdom of England was tending fast to infidelity. "It is come," says Bishop Butler, "I know not how, to be taken for granted by many persons that Christianity is not so much as a subject of inquiry; but that it is now at length discovered to be fictitious; and accordingly they treat it as if, in the present age, this were an agreement among all people of discernment, and nothing remained but to set it up as a principal subject of mirth and ridicule, as it were, by way of reprisals for its having so long interrupted the pleasures of the world." There is every reason to believe that the Methodists were the instruments of stemming this torrent. The sick and the poor also tasted the fruits of their labors and benevolence. Mr. Wesley abridged himself of all his superfluities, and proposed a fund for the relief of the indigent; and so prosperous was the scheme, that they quickly increased their fund to eighty pounds per annum. This, which one should have thought would have been attended with praise instead of censure, quickly drew upon them a kind of persecution; some of the seniors of the university began to interfere, and it was reported "that the college censors were going to blow up the *godly club*." They found them selves, however, patronized and encouraged by some men eminent for their learning and virtue; so that the society still continued, though they had suffered a severe loss, in 1730, by the death of Mr. Morgan, who, it is said, was the founder of it. In October, 1735, John and Charles Wesley, Mr. Ingham, and Mr. Delamotte, son of a merchant in London, embarked for Georgia, in order to preach the gospel to the Indians. After their arrival they were at first favorably received, but in a short time lost the affection of the people; and, on account of some differences with the storekeeper, Mr. Wesley was obliged to return to England. Mr. Wesley, however, was soon succeeded by Mr. Whitfield, whose repeated labors in that part of the world are well known.

After Mr. Whitfield returned from America in 1741, he declared his full assent to the doctrines of Calvin. Mr. Wesley, on the contrary, professed the Arminian doctrine, and had printed in favor of perfection and universal redemption, and very strongly against election — a doctrine which Mr. Whitfield believed to be scriptural. The difference, therefore, of sentiments between these two great men, caused a separation. Mr. Wesley preached in a place called the Foundry, where Mr. Whitfield preached but once, and no more. Mr. Whitfield then preached to very large congregations out of doors, and soon after, in connection with Mr. Cennick, and one or two more, began a new house in Kingswood, Gloucestershire, and established a school that favored Calvinistic preachers. The Method ists, therefore, were now divided; one part following Mr. Wesley, and the other Mr. Whitfield.

The doctrines of the Wesleyan Methodists, according to

their own account, are the same as the Church of England, as set forth in her liturgy, articles, and homilies. This, however, has been disputed. Mr. Wesley, in his appeal to men of reason and religion, thus declares his sentiments: "All I teach," he observes, "respects either the nature and condition of justification, the nature and condition of salvation, the nature of justifying and saving faith, or the Author of faith and salvation. That justification whereof our articles and homilies speak signifies present forgiveness, and consequently acceptance with God: I believe the condition of this is faith: I mean not only that without faith we cannot be justified, but also that, as soon as any one has true faith, in that moment he is justified. Good works follow this faith, but cannot go before it; much less can sanctification, which implies a continued course of good works, springing from holiness of heart. But it is allowed that sanctification goes before our justification at the last day, Heb. xii. 14. Repentance, and fruits meet for repentance, go before faith. Repentance absolutely must go before faith; fruits meet for it, if there be opportunity. By repentance I mean conviction of sin, producing real desires and sincere resolutions of amendment; by salvation, I mean not barely deliverance from hell, but a present deliverance from sin. Faith, in general, is a divine supernatural evidence, or conviction of things not seen, not discoverable by our bodily senses: justifying faith implies not only a divine evidence or conviction that God was in Christ reconciling the world unto himself, but a sure trust and confidence that Christ died for my sins, that he loved me, and gave himself for me. And the moment a penitent sinner believes this, God pardons and absolves him; and as soon as his pardon or justification is witnessed to him by the Holy Ghost, he is saved.

From that time (unless he make shipwreck of the faith)
salvation gradually increases in his soul.

"The Author of faith and salvation is God alone.
There is no more of power than of merit in man; but as
all merit is in the Son of God, in what he has done and
suffered for us, so all power is in the Spirit of God. And,
therefore, every man, in order to believe unto salvation,
must receive the Holy Ghost." So far Mr. Wesley. Re
specting original sin, free will, the justification of men,
good works, and works done before justification, he refers
us to what is said on these subjects in the former part of
the ninth, the tenth, the eleventh, the twelfth, and thirteenth articles of the Church of England. One of Mr.
Wesley's preachers bears this testimony of him and his
sentiments: "The gospel, considered as a general plan of
salvation, he viewed as a display of the divine perfections,
in a way agreeable to the nature of God; in which all the
divine attributes harmonize, and shine forth with peculiar
lustre. The gospel, considered as a means to attain an
end, appeared to him to discover as great fitness in the
means to the end as can possibly be discovered in the
structure of natural bodies, or in the various operations of
nature, from a view of which we draw our arguments for
the existence of God. Man he viewed as blind, ignorant,
wandering out of the way, with his mind estranged from
God. He considered the gospel as a dispensation of
mercy to men, holding forth pardon, a free pardon of sin
to all who repent and believe in Christ Jesus. The gospel, he believed, inculcates universal holiness both in heart
and in the conduct of life. He showed a mind well instructed in the oracles of God, and well acquainted with
human nature. He contended that the first step to be a
Christian is to repent; and that, till a man is convinced
of the evil of sin, and is determined to depart from it;

till he is convinced that there is a beauty in holiness, and something truly desirable in being reconciled to God, he is not prepared to receive Christ. The second important and necessary step, he believed to be faith, agreeable to the order of the apostle, 'Repentance toward God, and faith toward our Lord Jesus Christ,' Acts xx. 20. 21. In explaining sanctification, he accurately distinguished it from justification, or the pardon of sin. Justification admits us into a state of grace and favor with God, and lays the foundation of sanctification, or Christian holiness, in all its extent. There has been a great clamor raised against him because he called his view of sanctification by the word *perfection;* but he often explained what he meant by this term. He meant by the word *perfection,* such a degree of the love of God, and the love of man; such a degree of the love of justice, truth, holiness, and purity, as will remove from the heart every contrary disposition towards God or man; and that this should be our state of mind in every situation, and in every circumstance of life. He maintained that God is a God of love, not to a part of his creatures only, but to all; that He who is the Father of all, who made all, who stands in the same relation to all his creatures, loves them all; that He loved the world, and gave his Son a ransom for all without distinction of persons. It appeared to him, that to represent God as partial, as confining his love to a few, was unworthy our notions of the Deity. He maintained that Christ died for all men; that he is to be offered to all; that all are to be invited to come to him; and that whosoever comes in the way which God has appointed, may partake of his blessings. He supposed that sufficient grace is given to all, in that way and manner which is best adapted to influence the mind. He did not believe salvation was by works. So far was he from putting works in the place of the blood of

8

Christ, that he only gave them their just value: he considered them as the fruits of a living, operative faith, and as the measure of our future reward; for every man will be rewarded not for his works, but according to the measure of them. He gave the whole glory of salvation to God from first to last. He believed that man would never turn to God, if God did not begin the work: he often said that the first approaches of grace to the mind are irresistible; that is, that a man cannot avoid being convinced that he is a sinner; that God, by various means, awakens his conscience; and, whether the man will or no, these convictions approach him." In order that we may form still clearer ideas respecting Mr. Wesley's opinions, we shall here quote a few questions and answers as laid down in the *Minutes of Conference.* Q. "In what sense is Adam's sin imputed to all mankind?" A. "In Adam all die, *i. e.*, 1. Our bodies then became mortal. 2. Our souls died, *i. e.*, were disunited from God. And hence, 3. We are all born with a sinful, devilish nature; by reason whereof, 4. We are children of wrath, liable to death eternal," Rom. v. 18; Eph. ii. 3. Q. "In what sense is the righteousness of Christ imputed to all mankind, or to believers?" A. "We do not find it expressly affirmed in Scripture that God imparts the righteousness of Christ to any, although we do find that faith is imputed for righteousness. That text, 'As by one man's disobedience all men were made sinners, so by the obedience of one all were made righteous,' we conceive, means by the merits of Christ all men are cleared from the guilt of Adam's actual sin." Q. "Can faith be lost but through disobedience?' A. "It cannot. A believer first inwardly disobeys; inclines to sin with his heart; then his intercourse with God is cut off, *i. e.* his faith is lost; and after this he may fall into outward sin, being now weak, and like another man."

Q. "What is implied in being a *perfect Christian?*" A. "The loving the Lord our God with all our heart, and with all our mind, and soul, and strength." Q. "Does this imply that all inward sin is taken away?" A. "Without doubt; or how could we be said to be saved *from all our uncleanness?*" Ezek. xxxvi. 29. Q. "How much is allowed by our brethren who differ from us with regard to *entire sanctification?*" A. "They grant, 1. That every one must be entirely sanctified in the article of death. 2. That till then a believer daily grows in grace, comes nearer and nearer to perfection. 3. That we ought to be continually pressing after this, and to exhort all others to do so." Q. "What do we allow them?" A. "We grant, 1. That many of those who have died in the faith, yea, the greater part of those we have known, were not sanctified throughout, not made perfect in love, till a little before death. 2. That the term *sanctified* is continually applied by St. Paul to all that were justified, that were true believers. 3. That by this term alone he rarely (if ever) means saved from all sin. 4. That consequently it is not proper to use it in this sense, without adding the word 'wholly, entirely,' or the like. 5. That the inspired writers almost continually speak of or to those who were justified, but very rarely either of or to those who were sanctified. 6. That it consequently behoves us to speak in public almost continually of the state of justification; but more rarely in full and explicit terms concerning entire sanctification." Q. "What, then, is the point wherein we divide?" A. "It is this: Whether we should expect to be saved from all sin before the article of death." Q. "Is there any clear Scripture promise of this, that God will save us from *all* sin?" A. "There is. Ps. cxxx. 8: 'He shall redeem Israel from *all* his iniquities.' This is more largely expressed in Ezek. xxxvi. 25, 29; 2 Cor. vii. 1;

Deut. xxx. 6; 1 John iii. 8; Eph. v. 25, 27; John xvii. 20, 23; 1 John iv. 17."

These are the tenets of the Wesleyan Methodists, given in their own words, in order to prevent misrepresentation.

The doctrine of the Calvinistic Methodists are those of Calvin.

A considerable number both of the Calvinist and Arminian Methodists approve of the discipline of the Church of England, while many, it is said, are dissenters in principle. Mr. Wesley and Mr. Whitfield were both brought up in, and paid peculiar respect to that Church. They did not, however, as it is well known, confine themselves to her laws in all respects as it related to discipline.

Mr. Wesley having formed numerous societies in different parts, he, with his brother Charles, drew up certain rules, by which they were, and it seems in many respects still are, governed. They state the nature and design of a Methodist society in the following words:

"Such a society is no other than a company of men having the form and seeking the power of godliness; united in order to pray together, to receive the word of exhortation, and to watch over one another in love, that they may help each other to work out their own salvation.

"That it may the more easily be discerned whether they are indeed working out their own salvation, each society is divided into smaller companies, called *classes*, according to their respective places of abode. There are about twelve persons (sometimes fifteen, twenty, or even more) in each class; one of whom is styled their leader. It is his business, 1. To see each person in his class once a week, at least, in order to inquire how their souls prosper; to advise, reprove, comfort, or exhort, as occasion may require; to receive what they are willing to give to the poor or toward the gospel — 2. To meet the minister and the stewards of the society once a week, in order to inform the minister of any that are sick, or of any that walk disorderly and will not be reproved; to pay to the stewards what they have received of their several classes in the week preceding; and to show their account of what each person has contributed.

" There is only one condition previously required of those who desire admission into these societies: namely, *a desire to flee from the wrath to come; to be saved from their sins :* but wherever this is really fixed in the soul, it will be shown by its fruits.   It is, therefore, expected of all who continue therein, that they should continue to evidence their desire of salvation.

" First, By doing no harm; by avoiding evil in every kind; especially that which is most generally practised, such as the taking the name of God in vain; the profaning the day of the Lord, either by doing ordinary work thereon, or by buying or selling; drunkenness; *buying or selling spirituous liquors,* or *drinking them,* unless in cases of extreme necessity; fighting, quarrelling, brawling; brother *going to law* with brother; returning evil for evil. or railing for railing; the *using many words* in buying or selling; the *buying or selling uncustomed goods;* the *giving or taking things on usury,* i. e. unlawful interest.

"*Uncharitable* or *unprofitable conversation;* particularly, speaking evil of magistrates or of ministers.

" Doing to others as we would not they should do unto us.

" Doing what we know is not for the glory of God; as the *putting on gold or costly apparel;* the *taking such diversions* as cannot be used in the name of the Lord Jesus.

" The *singing* those *songs,* or *reading* those *books,* which do not tend to the knowledge or love of God; softness and

8 *

needless self-indulgence; laying up treasure upon earth; borrowing without a probability of paying; or taking up goods without a probability of paying for them.

"It is expected of all who continue in these societies that they should continue to evidence their desire of salvation,

Secondly, By doing good; by being in every kind merciful after their power, as they have opportunity; doing good of every possible sort, and as far as possible to all men: to their *bodies*, of the ability which God giveth; by giving food to the hungry, by clothing the naked, by visiting or helping them that are sick, or in prison; to their *souls*, by instructing, reproving, or exhorting all we have any intercourse with; trampling under foot that enthusiastic doctrine of devils, that 'We are not to do good, unless *our hearts be free to it.*'

"By doing good, especially to them that are of the household of faith, or groaning so to be; employing them preferably to others; buying one of another; helping each other in business; and so much the more, because the world will love its own, and them only; by all possible *diligence and frugality*, that the gospel be not blamed; by running with patience the race set before them, *denying themselves and taking up their cross daily;* submitting to bear the reproach of Christ; to be as the filth and offscouring of the world, and looking that men should *say all manner of evil of them falsely for the Lord's sake.*

"It is expected of all who desire to continue in these societies, that they should continue to evidence their desire of salvation.

"Thirdly, By attending on all the ordinances of God: such are — The public worship of God; the ministry of the word, either read or expounded; the supper of the

Lord; family and private prayer; searching the Scriptures: and fasting and abstinence.

"These are the general rules of our societies, all which we are taught of God to observe, even in his written word: the only true rule, and the sufficient rule, both of our faith and practice; and all these we know his Spirit writes on every truly awakened heart. If there be any among us who observe them not, who habitually break any of them, let it be made known unto them who watch over that soul, as they who must give an account. We will admonish him of the error of his ways; we will bear with him for a season; but then, if he repent not, he hath no more place among us: we have delivered our own souls.

"*May* 1, 1743.   John Wesley.
                         Charles Wesley."

In Mr. Wesley's connection, they have circuits and conferences, which we find were thus formed:—When the preachers at first went out to exhort and preach, it was by Mr. Wesley's permission and direction; some from one part of the kingdom, and some from another; and, though frequently strangers to each other, and those to whom they were sent, yet on his credit and sanction alone they were received and provided for as friends by the societies wherever they came. But having little or no communication or intercourse with one another, nor any subordination among themselves, they must have been under the necessity of recurring to Mr. Wesley for directions how and where they were to labor. To remedy this inconvenience, he conceived the design of calling them together to an annual conference; by this means he brought them into closer union with each other, and made them sensible of the utility of acting in concert and harmony. He soon found it necessary, also, to bring their itinerancy under

certain regulations, and reduce it to some fixed order, both
to prevent confusion, and for his own ease; he therefore
took fifteen or twenty societies, more or less, which lay
round some principal society in those parts, and which
were so situated that the greatest distance from one to
another was not much more than twenty miles, and united
them into what was called a circuit. At the yearly conference, he appointed two, three, or four preachers to one
of these circuits, according to its extent, which at first was
very often considerable, sometimes taking in a part of
three or four counties. Here, and here only, were they to
labor for one year, that is, until the next conference. One
of the preachers on every circuit was called the assistant,
because he assisted Mr. Wesley in superintending the
societies and other preachers; he took charge of the societies within the limits assigned him; he enforced the rules
everywhere, and directed the labors of the preachers associated with him. Having received a list of the societies
forming his circuit, he took his own station in it, gave to
the other preachers a plan of it, and pointed out the day
when each should be at the place fixed for him, to begin a
progressive motion round it, in such order as the plan
directed. They now followed one another through all the
societies belonging to that circuit, at stated distances of
time, all being governed by the same rules, and under-
going the same labor. By this plan every preacher's daily
work was appointed beforehand; each knew, every day,
where the others were, and each society when to expect
the preacher, and how long he would stay with them.—It
may be observed, however, that Mr. Wesley's design in
calling the preachers together annually, was not merely
for the regulation of the circuits, but also for the review
of their doctrines and discipline, and for the examination
of their moral conduct; that those who were to administer

with him in holy things might be *thoroughly furnished for every good work.*

The first conference was held in June, 1744, at which Mr. Wesley met his brother, two or three other clergymen, and a few of the preachers whom he had appointed to come from various parts to confer with them on the affairs of the societies.

"Monday, June 25," observes Mr. Wesley, "and the five following days, we spent in conference with our preachers, seriously considering by what means we might the most effectually save our own souls, and them that heard us; and the result of our consultations we set down to be the rule of our future practice."

Since that time a conference has been held annually, Mr. Wesley himself having presided at forty-seven. The subjects of their deliberations were proposed in the form of questions, which were amply discussed, and the questions with the answers, agreed upon, were afterwards printed under the title of "Minutes of several Conversations between the Rev. Mr. Wesley and others," commonly called *Minutes of Conference.*

As to their preachers, the following extract from the above-mentioned Minutes of Conference will show us in what manner they are chosen and designated: *Q.* "How shall we try those who think they are moved by the Holy Ghost to preach?" *A.* "Inquire, 1. Do they know God as a pardoning God? Have they the love of God abiding in them? Do they desire and seek nothing but God? And are they holy in all manner of conversation? 2. Have they *gifts* as well as *grace* for the work? Have they, in some tolerable degree, a clear, sound understanding? Have they a right judgment in the things of God? Have they a just conception of salvation by faith? And has God given them any degree of utterance? Do they speak justly, readily, clearly ?—3. Have they *fruit?* Are any truly convinced of sin and converted to God by their preaching?

"As long as these three marks concur in any one, we believe he is called of God to preach. These we receive as sufficient proof that he is *moved thereto by the Holy Ghost.*

Q. "What method may we use in receiving a new helper?" *A.* "A proper time for doing this is at a conference, after solemn fasting and prayer; every person proposed is then to be present, and each of them may be asked,—

" Have *you* faith in Christ? Are *you going on to perfection?* Do you expect to be perfected in love in this life? Are you groaning after it? Are you resolved to devote yourself wholly to God and to his work? Have you considered the rules of a *helper?* Will you keep them for conscience' sake? Are you determined to employ *all* your time in the work of God? Will you preach every morning and evening? Will you diligently instruct the children in every place? Will you visit from house to house? Will you recommend fasting both by precept and example?

" We then may receive him as a probationer, by giving him the Minutes of the Conference, inscribed thus : — ' To A. B. You think it your duty to call sinners to repentance. Make full proof hereof, and we shall rejoice to receive you as a fellow-laborer.' Let him then read and carefully weigh what is contained therein, that if he has any doubt it may be removed."

" To the above it may be useful to add," says Mr. Benson, "a few remarks on the method pursued in the choice of the *itinerant preachers,* as many have formed the most erroneous ideas on the subject, imagining they are employed with hardly any prior preparation. 1. They are received as private members of the society on trial. 2. After a quarter of a year, if they are found deserving, they are admitted as proper members. 3. When their grace and abilities are sufficiently manifest they are appointed leaders of classes. 4. If they then discover talents for more important services, they are employed to exhort occasionally in the smaller congregation, when the preachers cannot attend. 5. If approved in this line of duty, they are allowed to preach. 6. Out of these men who are called *local preachers,* are selected the *itinerant preachers,* who are first proposed at a quarterly meeting of the stewards and local preachers of the circuit; then at a meeting of the travelling preachers of the district; and lastly, in the conference; and, if accepted, are nominated for a circuit. 7. Their characters and conduct are examined annually in the conference; and, if they continue faithful for four years of trial, they are received into full connection. At these conferences, also, strict inquiry is made into the conduct and success of every preacher, and those who are found deficient in abilities are no longer employed as itinerants; while those whose conduct has·not been agreeable to the Gospel, are expelled, and thereby deprived of all the privileges even of private members of the society.''

Since Mr. Wesley's death, his people have been divided; but this division, it seems, respects discipline more than sentiment. Mr. Wesley professed a strong attachment to the established church of England, and exhorted the societies under his care to attend her service, and receive the Lord's supper from the regular clergy. But in the latter part of his time he thought proper to ordain some bishops and priests for America and Scotland; but as one or two of the bishops have never been out of England since their appointment to the office, it is probable that he intended a regular ordination should take place when the state of the connection might render it necessary. During his life, some of the societies petitioned to have preaching in their own chapels in church hours, and the Lord's Supper administered by the travelling preachers. This request he generally refused, and where it could be conveniently done, sent some of the clergymen who officiated at the New Chapel in London, to perform these solemn services. At the first conference after his death, which was held at Manchester, the preachers published a declaration, in which they said that they would "take up the *Plan* as Mr. Wesley had left it." This was by no means satisfactory to many of the preachers and people, who thought that religious liberty ought to be extended to all the societies which desired it. In order to favor this cause, so agreeable to the spirit of Christianity and the rights of Englishmen, several respectable preachers came forward; and by the writings which they circulated through the connection, paved the way for a plan of pacification, by which it was stipulated, that in every society where a three-fold majority of class-leaders, stewards, and trustees desired it, the people should have preaching in church hours, and the sacraments of baptism and the Lord's Supper administered to them. The spirit of inquiry being roused did not stop here; for it appeared agreeable both to reason and the customs of the primitive church, that the people should have a voice in the temporal concerns of the societies, vote in the election of church-officers, and give their suffrages in spiritual concerns. This subject produced a variety of arguments on both sides of the question: many of the preachers and people thought that an annual delegation of the general stewards of the circuits, to sit either in the conference or the district meetings, in order to assist in the disbursement of the yearly collection, the Kingswood School collection, and the preachers' fund, and in making new or revising old laws, would be a bond of union between the conference and connection at large, and do away the very idea of arbitrary power among the travelling preachers. In order to facilitate this good work, many societies in various parts of the kingdom sent delegates to the conference held at Leeds in 1797; they were instructed to request that the people might have a voice in *the formation of their own laws, the choice of their own officers, and the distribution of their own property.* The preachers proceeded to discuss two motions: Shall delegates from the societies be admitted into the conference? Shall circuit stewards be admitted into the district meetings? Both motions were negatived, and consequently all hopes of accommodation between the parties were given up. Several friends of religious liberty proposed a plan for a new itinerancy. In order that it might be carried into immediate effect, they formed themselves into a regular meeting in Ebenezer Chapel, Mr. William Thom being chosen president, and Mr. Alexander Kilham, secretary. The meeting proceeded to arrange the plan for supplying the circuits of the new connection with preachers, and desired the president and secretary to draw up the rules of the church government, in order that they might be circulated through the societies for their approbation. Accordingly, a form of church government, suited to an itinerant ministry, was printed by these two brethren, under the title of "Outlines of a Constitution proposed for the Examination, Amendment, and Acceptance of the Members of the Methodist New Itinerancy." The plan was examined by select committees in the different circuits of the connection, and, with a few alterations, was accepted by the conference of preachers and delegates. The preachers and people are incorporated in all meetings for business, not by temporary concession, but by the essential principles of their constitution; for the private members choose the class-leaders; the leaders meeting nominates the stewards; and the society confirms or rejects the nomination. The quarterly meetings are composed of the general stewards and representatives chosen by the different societies of the circuits, and the fourth quarterly meeting of the year appoints the preacher and delegate of every circuit that shall attend the general conference. For a further account of their principles and discipline, we must refer the reader to a pamphlet, entitled *General Rules of the United Societies of Methodists in the New Connection.*

The Calvinistic Methodists are not incorporated into a body as the Armenians are, but are chiefly under the direction or influence of their ministers or patrons.

It is necessary to observe here that there are many congregations in London, and elsewhere, who, although they are called Methodists, yet are neither in Mr. Wesley's, Mr. Whitfield's, nor the new connection. Some of these are supplied by a variety of ministers; and others, bordering more upon the congregational plan, have a resident minister. The clergy of the church of England who strenuously preach up her doctrines and articles, are called Methodists. A distinct connection upon Mr. Whitfield's plan was formed and patronized by the late Lady Huntingdon, and which still subsists. The term Methodist, also, is applied by way of reproach to almost every one who manifests more than common concern for the interests of religion, and the spiritual good of mankind.

Methodism in this country, as in Great Britain, was at first an arm of the Church of England, without an ordained ministry, and without ordinances. It aimed chiefly at the revival of true religion, and the conversion of sinners to God. Commencing with a congregation of five persons in the house of an Irish emigrant named Philip Embury, a lay or local preacher in New York, in 1766, the missionary spirit of the movement soon extended to other parts of the country. Societies were formed and the cause greatly advanced by Captain Webb, a British officer, who zealously preached the doctrines held by Wesley, and met with wonderful success. The classes grew and multiplied on every hand until 1773, when, at a Conference held that year in Philadelphia, there were reported ten itinerant preachers and over one thousand communicants.

The political revolution of 1776 occasioned some derangement in the work, and resulted in an entire change in the relations of American Methodism. The breaking up of the Church of England, and the return to that country of many English clergymen, left the societies destitute of the needed services of an ordained ministry. Mr. Wesley was importuned on the subject, and about the close of the war inaugurated measures for the independency of the societies in the United States. This led to the formal organization and establishment of

THE METHODIST EPISCOPAL CHURCH.

In its Book of Discipline the origin and structure of the Church are thus set forth: "The preachers and members of our society in general, being convinced that there was a great deficiency of vital religion in the Church of England in America, and being in many places destitute of the Christian Sacraments, as several of the clergy had forsaken their churches, requested the late Rev. John Wesley to take such measures, in his wisdom and prudence, as would afford them suitable relief in their distress.

"In consequence of this, our venerable friend, who, under God, has been the father of the great revival of religion now extending over the earth by the means of the Methodists, determined to ordain ministers for America, and for this purpose, in the year 1784, sent over three regularly ordained clergy; but preferring the Episcopal mode of Church government to any other, he solemnly set apart, by the imposition of his hands and prayer, one of them, namely, Thomas Coke, doctor of civil law, late of Jesus College, in the University of Oxford, and a presbyter of the Church of England, for the episcopal office; and having delivered to him letters of episcopal orders, commissioned and directed him to set apart Francis Asbury, then general assistant of the Methodist society in America, for the same episcopal office, he, the said Francis Asbury, being first ordained deacon and elder. In consequence of which, the said Francis Asbury was solemnly set apart for the said episcopal office by prayer and the imposition of the hands of the said Thomas Coke, other regularly ordained ministers assisting in the sacred ceremony. At which time the General Conference held at Baltimore did unanimously receive the said Thomas Coke and Francis Asbury as their bishops, being fully satisfied of the validity of their episcopal ordination."

The "General Conference" above referred to, was convened December 25, 1784. The polity which has since mainly governed the Church was approved. But two orders in the ministry were recognized, that of deacon and elder or presbyter, the bishop being different from the latter only in office. Mr. Wesley was led to this opinion, as he declared, by reading Lord King's account of the Primitive Christian Church. The two American bishops thus providentially constituted immediately prepared and presented a patriotic address to General Washington, in the name of the people they represented, receiving from him as the first President of the United States a cordial recognition and the assurance of personal regard.

In less than one hundred years from the date of its organization, Methodism has covered the whole continent, showing by the latest census returns, a membership in all its branches of 2,723,252, and a ministry, travelling and local, of over 37,000 men.

The officers of the Methodist Episcopal Church are class leaders, stewards, trustees, exhorters, local preachers, pastors in charge, presiding elders of districts, and general superintendents or bishops, the duties of each being defined in the Book of Discipline.

The itinerant ministers, although springing directly from the people, held the legislative, executive, and judicial departments in their own hands until very recently. The right of lay representation, long a subject of controversy and the occasion of schism, is now conceded, and incorporated in the government of the Church. A General Conference, which meets quadrennially, possesses full powers to revise any part of the discipline, except certain restrictive rules relating to doctrine and the maintenance of the system of itinerancy, the concurrence of three-fourths of all the Annual Conferences being necessary to the alteration of any important measure needing revision.

The bishops are required to travel extensively, taking the oversight of the entire work. They are elected to office by the General Conference, to which body they are amenable. They preside at all the Annual Conferences, of which there are over seventy, ordain the deacons and elders by the imposition of hands, and appoint the pastors to their several circuits and stations.

An immense book-concern in New York and Cincinnati, with branches in all the leading cities, from Boston

9 *

to the Pacific coast, supplies the literary wants of the denomination. It is under the control of the General Conference, and publishes about 2000 bound volumes and over 1000 tracts in the English, German, Welsh, Swedish, Danish, and French languages. The periodical literature of the Church consists of an able Quarterly Review, several monthly magazines, ten official, and as many semi-official and independent weekly papers, with a great variety of publications for Sunday-schools, all of which have an extensive circulation.

The Missionary department embraces a working force of six hundred, and a membership in foreign lands of between forty and fifty thousand souls.

Under the auspices of the Church Extension Society, new edifices for religious worship are being constantly and rapidly built, the total number of churches owned by the denomination being 13,500, with capacity to accommodate five millions of people, and estimated, with parsonage property, to be worth $30,000,000.

The literary institutions of this Church include 6 theological seminaries; 27 universities and colleges; and 69 academies and seminaries. The number of teachers, including presidents and professors, is given as about 750, students, 20,000, and aggregate value of property, $8,000,000.

The latest statistics (1870) show 8 bishops, 9193 travelling and 11,404 local preachers, and 1,367,134 communicants, 16,912 Sunday-schools, 189,412 officers and teachers, and 1,221,393 scholars. The benevolent contributions of the Church are reported at an average of $1,000,000 per year.

THE METHODIST EPISCOPAL CHURCH, SOUTH,

was formed in 1844. At the General Conference of that year, differences of opinion on the subject of slavery became so antagonistic that a separation was effected, and 1155 ministers, with 639,164 members belonging in the Southern States, became a distinct ecclesiastical body. Its enterprise and ratio of increase corresponded with that of the parent Church, until the breaking out of the civil war, which brought serious disaster upon all Southern institutions. Since the return of peace the Southern Methodists have displayed uncommon energy in "building up the waste places," reviving their literature, and enlarging the borders of their territory. They now number some 35 Annual Conferences, 9 bishops, 8000 travelling and local preachers, and a membership of over 600,000.

A book-publishing house at Nashville, Tennessee, and official papers in various sections, with an adequate supply of periodical literature, schools, colleges, and all the machinery of an active organization, give vigor and vitality to this branch of Methodism.

OTHER BRANCHES.

From time to time there have been divisions and secessions among the "people called Methodists," mostly on account of Church government, the leading doctrines remaining intact, and held fast by all in common.

In 1792 a secession took place in Virginia headed by a presiding elder named James O'Kelly, who objected to the absolute power of the bishops in appointing the preachers, and contended for an appeal to the Conference. This Mr. O'Kelly was a man of very considerable popularity, and had great influence over the minds of those with whom he associated. The spirit of dissension was fomented by the publication of appeals to the preachers and people, and a number in southern Virginia and North Carolina joined themselves to his standard. They took the name of "REPUBLICAN METHODISTS," though better known as O'Kelleyites. Their system of church polity was liberal, and for a time succeeded well; but in a few years they began to decline, and finally amalgamated with a branch of Baptists known as Christians.

Another small secession took place in Vermont, A. D. 1804, which resulted in the formation of

THE REFORMED METHODIST CHURCH.

The government established by this branch is essentially Congregational, all power being in the churches. To the annual and general conferences are delegated power to transact business of a general character, for which they are held strictly accountable to the churches. The churches select their own ministers, and stipulate with them in respect to time and salary. In the beginning the churches ordained their own ministers, but subsequently lay ordination was discontinued. In the fall of 1841 an association was formed between the Reformed Methodists, Society Methodists, and several churches of Wesleyan Methodists, for mutual aid. And after the organization of the Wesleyan Methodist Church in 1843, preliminary steps were taken with a view to the union of the two bodies. At that time they had 5 conferences, about 50 ordained preachers, and 3000 members. At present, 1870, they have 20,000 members.

In 1820, a third secession from the old connection in New York took the name of

THE METHODIST SOCIETY.

They adopted the representative form of government. It required a majority of laymen in their conferences to form any rules for the government of the churches. The preachers remain in the same charge as long as they can agree with the churches. Prosperity attended them for a few years; but most of their ministers and members united with the Methodist Protestant Church. The most prominent minister of the society is William M. Stilwell, pastor of the church in New York. No statistics have been furnished, from which to ascertain the number of their membership. They probably do not exceed 5000.

In 1821, an animated discussion of the principles of church polity was introduced into a periodical entitled the Wesleyan Repository, edited and published by William S. Stockton, a layman of the Methodist Episcopal Church in Trenton, N. J. It attracted general attention, and continued to spread as a little leaven through the whole lump. Memorials praying for lay representation were addressed to the General Conference of 1824. Union societies were formed for the purpose of concentrating strength. These measures alarmed the powers that be, and the work of expulsion commenced; secession followed. A convention of reformers was held. The General Conference of 1828 denied the right of lay representation, and refused redress. All hope of reform fled. The expelled and their friends organized churches, known as ASSOCIATED METHODISTS; and in 1830 a General Convention was held in Baltimore, which formed a Constitution and Discipline, adopting as the name of the association,

THE METHODIST PROTESTANT CHURCH.

Thirteen annual conferences were represented in the convention. Episcopacy was rejected as a spurious order, and ministerial parity asserted. The elementary principles of the government acknowledge the individuality of the local assemblies as churches of Christ — the Lord Jesus as the only Head of the Church — the Word of God the only rule of faith and practice — and private judgment as the right of man. They secure the freedom of speech and press — protect church membership, and define the origin of power.

The constitution recognises the mutual rights of ministers and laymen, and grants an equal representation to both. The doctrines taught — the means of grace — mode of worship and usages common to Methodists, are retained. The Church has been steadily progressing ever since: and, at present, is extended over the whole of the United States There are 30 annual conferences, about 1500 ministers, and about 230,000 members.

In 1843, a convention of seceders from the Methodist Episcopal Church, and other Methodist societies opposed to slavery, was held in Utica, N. Y., and founded

THE WESLEYAN METHODIST CHURCH.

They adopted the same principles of church government held by the Methodist Protestants, but abjure all connection with slavery and slaveholders. The distinguishing feature of the association is its anti-slavery character. They have been strengthened by secessions from all the other Methodist churches, and now number 10 annual conferences, 1000 ministers (of whom 600 are travelling preachers), and 5),000 members, confined to the free States.

THE EVANGELICAL ASSOCIATION,

or Albrights, are in fact German Methodists, as they are familiarly called. The first society was organized in 1800, under their leader, Jacob Albright. In 1803 he was elected presiding elder, and ordained by the other preachers, and ecclesiastical regulations adopted. Their bishops, so called, are elected quadrennially. They have hitherto confined their labors to the German population chiefly. They have 16 annual conferences, about 500 ministers, and 72,979 members.

THE PRIMITIVE METHODISTS

have a number of societies in this country, planted by emigrants from England. They have (1870) 2000 members, and 20 preachers.

CONGREGATIONAL, OR INDEPENDENT METHODISTS.

Churches having no connection with any ecclesiastical body exist in many places. A very respectable association of such might be formed, but at present they are not generally known beyond the localities in which they are found. It is believed there are several thousand members of this class.

Besides the above, there are several distinct associations of colored Methodists. In 1816, a number of colored persons finding their connection with the Methodist Episcopal Church subjected them to serious inconveniences, assembled in Philadelphia, and organized

THE AFRICAN METHODIST EPISCOPAL CHURCH.

They copied after the Methodist Episcopal Church, Rev. Richard Allen being their first bishop. They have now 5 bishops, 4000 preachers, travelling and local, and a membership of 375,000 in the United States and Canada.

THE AFRICAN M. EPISCOPAL ZION CHURCH

was organized by a body of seceders from the Methodist Episcopal Church in New York, October 25, 1820. This church is not strictly episcopal. Their bishops are styled superintendents, and elected quadrennially, and hold the office four years. They have 1500 travelling preachers, and 172,000 members.

Another small body called UNION METHODISTS, and several congregational churches of colored persons, amounting in all to several thousand members, exist; but of their peculiar views little is known.

KIRK OF SCOTLAND.*

THE conversion of the Scots to the Christian faith began through the ministry of Paladius, about the year 430, and from the first establishment of Christianity in that country till the Reformation in the reign of Mary, mother of James I. and of Mary I. of England, their church government was episcopacy; but the Presbyterian discipline was not finally established in Scotland, until the reign of King William and Mary, A. D. 1689, when episcopacy was totally abolished. The Westminster Confession of Faith was then received as the standard of the national creed; which all ministers, and principals and professors in universities, are obliged to subscribe as the confession of their faith, before receiving induction into office.

The Church of Scotland is remarkable for its uncommon simplicity of worship; it possesses no liturgy, no altar, no instrumental music, no surplice, no fixed canonical vestment of any kind. It condemns the worship paid to saints, and observes no festival days. Its ministers enjoy a parity of rank and of authority; it enforces that all ministers, being ambassadors of Christ, are equal in commission; that there is no order in the church, as established by the Saviour, superior to presbyters; and that bishop and presbyter, though different words, are of the same import. It acknowledges no earthly head: its judicatories are quite distinct from, and independent of, any civil judicatory; insomuch, indeed, that the decisions of the one are often contrary to those of the other, yet both remain unaffected and unal-

---

* The word *Kirk* is of Saxon origin, and signifies *Church*; or, according to others, it is a contraction of the Greek word meaning the *House of God*.

tered. When, for example, a clergyman has been presented to a parish by a patron, and induction and ordination have followed on that presentation, if afterwards it be found that the patron, who had given the presentation, has not that right, and that it belongs to another, the clergyman may be ejected as to all the temporalities of the office; but *quoad sacra*, he may continue minister of the parish, and exercise all the sacred functions: and though a new presentee may obtain a right to the civil endowments of the benefice, he can perform none of the sacred duties, while the other chooses to avail himself of his privilege.

There are four ecclesiastical judicatories. —namely, the Kirk Session, the Presbytery, the Synod, and the General Assembly, from each of which there is a power of appeal to the other; but the decision of the General Assembly is supreme.

The lowest court is the Kirk Session, which is composed of the minister of the parish, who is the moderator or president of it, and a number of the most grave and respectable laymen, members of the congregation. Their number varies in different parishes, five or six being about the average number; and their services are entirely gratuitous. They are something like churchwardens in England, only they have a spiritual jurisdiction, as it is a part of their duty to visit the sick, &c. The Kirk Session takes cognisance of cases of scandal, such as fornication, Sabbath-breaking, profane swearing. It also manages the funds of the poor, a duty in which it formerly was assisted by deacons, a class of men inferior to elders, as they had no spiritual jurisdiction; but not being found necessary, they are consequently disused.

The Presbytery, which is the court next in dignity, is composed of the ministers of a certain district, with an elder from each parish. The number of presbyteries is seventy-eight. Their chief duty consists in the management of such matters as concern the church within their respective bounds. But they may originate any matter, and bring it under the view of the Synod or General Assembly. They have also the superintendence of education within their bounds, such as the induction of teachers, and the examination of schools.

The Synod is the next intermediate court. There are fifteen synods, each consisting of the clergymen of a certain number of presbyteries, with elders, as in presbyteries. Presbyteries meet generally once a month; synods twice a year, though some remote synods, such as that of Argyle, only once.

The General Assembly is the last and supreme court, and meets yearly in the month of May, in Edinburgh, and continues its sittings for twelve days. The king presides by his representative, who is always a nobleman, and is denominated *the Lord High Commissioner*. The General Assembly is a representative court, consisting of 200 members representing presbyteries, and 156 elders representing burghs or presbyteries, and five ministers or elders representing universities, — making altogether 361 members. They choose a moderator or president, out of their own number, distinct from the Royal Commissioner, the duty of the latter consisting merely in convening and dissolving the court, and in forming the medium of communication between it and the throne. The moderator is now always a clergyman, though previously to 1688, laymen sometimes held that office.

The duties of the Scotch clergy are numerous and laborious. They officiate regularly in the public *worship of God;* and in general, they must go through this duty twice every Sunday (exclusively of other occasional appearances), delivering every Sunday a *lecture* and a *sermon,* with *prayers.* It is also expected, throughout Scotland, that the prayers and discourses shall be of the minister's own composition; and the prayers, in all cases, and the discourses, in most instances, are delivered without the use of papers. They are expected to perform the alternate duties of *examining* their people from the Scriptures and catechisms of the church, and of visiting them from house to house, with prayers and exhortations. This is done commonly once in the year, being omitted only in those cases in which the ministers deem it impracticable, or not acceptable, or at least not necessary. The charge of the poor devolves, in a very particular manner, on the clergy, and in them also is vested the superintendence of all schools within their bounds.

Baptism in this church is practised by none but ministers, who do it by sprinkling; and whether performed in private or in public, it is almost always preceded by a sermon.

The Lord's Supper is not administered so frequently in Scotland as in some other places. Some time before this sacrament is dispensed, it is announced from the pulpit. The week before, the Kirk Session meets, and draws up a list of all the communicants in the parish, according to the minister's examination-book, and the testimony of the elders and deacons. According to this list, tickets are delivered to each communicant, if desired, and the ministers and elders also give tickets to strangers who bring sufficient testimonials. None are allowed to communicate without such tickets, which are produced at the table. Those who never received are instructed by the minister, and by themselves in the nature of the sacraments, and taught what is the proper preparation thereunto. The Wednesday or Thursday before, there is a solemn fast, and on the Saturday there are two preparatory sermons. On Sunday morning, after singing and prayer as usual, the minister of the parish preaches a suitable sermon; and when the ordinary worship is ended, he in the name of Jesus Christ forbids the unworthy to approach, and invites the penitent to come and receive the sacrament. Then he goes into the body of the church, where one or two tables, according to its width, are placed, reaching from one end to the other, covered with a white linen cloth, and seats on both sides for the communicants. The minister places himself at the end or middle of the table. After a short discourse, he reads the institution, and blesses the elements; then he breaks the bread, and distributes it and the wine to those that are next him, who transmit them to their neighbors; the elders and deacon attending to serve, and see that the whole is performed with decency and order. While these communicate, the minister discourses on the nature of the sacrament; and the whole is concluded with singing and prayer. The minister then returns to the pulpit, and preaches a sermon. The morning-service ended, the congregation are dismissed for an hour; after which the usual afternoon worship is performed. On the Monday morning, there is public worship, with two sermons; and these, properly speaking, close the communion-service. No private communions are allowed in Scotland.

Marriage is solemnized nearly after the manner of the Church of England, with the exception of the ring, which is deemed a great relic of " popery." By the laws of Scotland, the marriage-knot may be tied without any ceremony of a religious nature: a simple promise in the presence of witnesses, or a known previous cohabitation, being sufficient to bind the obligation. The most ridiculous, often immoral, and almost always injurious practice, of marrying at *Gretna-Green* was, till lately, in use; a person said to have been a blacksmith performed the ceremony at Gretna according to the rites of the church.

The Funeral ceremony is performed in total silence. The corpse is carried to the grave, and there interred without a word being spoken on the occasion.

Dr. Evans, in his usual liberal strain, gives the following account of the *Seceders:* —

"Dissenters from the kirk, or church of Scotland, call themselves *Seceders;* for, as the term Dissenter comes from the Latin word *dissentio,* to differ, so the appellation Seceder is derived from another Latin word, *secedo,* to separate or to withdraw from any body of men with which we may have been united. The secession arose from various circumstances, which were conceived to be great defections from the established church of Scotland. The Seceders are rigid Calvinists, rather austere in their manners, and severe in their discipline. Through a difference as to civil matters, they are broken down into *Burghers* and *Anti-burghers.* Of these two classes the latter are the most confined in their sentiments, and associate therefore the least with any other body of Christians. The Seceders originated under two brothers, Ralph and Ebenezer Erskine, of Stirling, about the year 1730. It is worthy of observation, that the Rev. George Whitfield, in one of his visits to Scotland, was solemnly reprobated by the Seceders, because he refused to confine his itinerant labors wholly to them. The reason assigned for this monopolization was, that they were exclusively God's people. Mr. Whitfield smartly replied, that they had, therefore, the less need of his services; for his aim was to turn sinners from the error and wickedness of their ways, by preaching among them glad tidings of great joy.

"The Burgess' oath, concerning which the Seceders differed, is administered in several of the royal boroughs of Scotland, and runs thus: 'I protest before God and your lordships, that I profess and allow with my heart the

H

true religion presently professed within this realm, and
authorized by the laws thereof; I shall abide thereat, and
defend the same to my life's end, renouncing the Roman
religion called papistry.' The Messrs. Erskine and others
maintained there was no inconsistency in Seceders taking
this oath, because the established religion was still the
true religion, in spite of the faults attaching to it, and
hence were called Burghers. Messrs. Moncrieff and others
thought the swearing to the religion, as professed and
authorized, was approving the corruptions, therefore the
oath was inconsistent and not to be taken; hence Anti-
burghers. The Kirk of Scotland, both parties say, still
perseveres in a course of defection from her professed
principles, and therefore the secession continues, and is
increasing to the present day. (See an Historical Account
of the Rise and Progess of the Secession, by the late Rev.
John Brown, of Haddington.) The Seceders are strict
Presbyterians, having their respective associate synods,
and are to be found not only in Scotland, but also in Ireland and in the United States of America. Both classes
have had among them ministers of considerable learning
and piety.

"There is also a species of Dissenters from the Church
of Scotland called *Relief*, whose only difference from the
Kirk is, the choosing of their own pastors. They arose in
1752, and are respectable as to numbers and ability.
(See a Compendious View of the Religious System maintained by the Synod of Relief, by P. Hutchinson; and
also Historical Sketches of the Relief Church, &c., by J.
Smith.) The Relief are Calvinists as well as Presbyterians,
but liberal in their views, admitting to their communion
pious Christians of every denomination. They revere the
union of faith and charity."

In 1835, an attempt was made by the Church of Scotlard to place itself on a more popular basis, by giving to the heads of families, communicants, a veto upon the nomination of the patron; but the ecclesiastical action by which this was sought to be effected having been declared, by the Supreme Court, to be a civil act beyond the jurisdiction of the church, and no disposition being manifested by the Parliament to aid in removing the difficulty, a number of its most distinguished members, in 1843, withdrew in a body, and formed the "Free Church of Scotland." It is probable they anticipated that a step so decided would move the legislature to action on their behalf. One of their most dearly-cherished and prominent principles was the obligation of the state to provide for the religious instruction of the people, and the insufficiency of the voluntary principle for this purpose; but the state's declining to act, left them to make a beautiful exemplification of the mistake of their own theory. They seemed to have proved, by logic, that a church could not sustain itself on the voluntary principle; they are demonstrating, by experiment, that it can do it, not only, but also that it can do it with signal advantage to its spiritual interests. The late eminent Doctor Chalmers, Doctors Candlish, Cunningham, and many others distinguished for their learning and piety, took part in securing the division. Since the separation, the Free Church has erected 676 churches, 487 of which are free from debt. They number now about 600 minis ters, and have raised in less than five years 7,500,000 dol lars for sustaining their interests.

ENGLISH PRESBYTERIANS.

THE appellation *Presbyterian* is in England appropriated to a large denomination of dissenters, who have no
attachment to the Scotch mode of church government any
more than to episcopacy amongst us, and therefore to this
body of Christians the term *Presbyterian*, in its original
sense, is improperly applied.   This misapplication has occasioned many wrong notions, and should be rectified.
English Presbyterians, as they are called, adopt nearly
the same mode of church government with the Independents.   Their chief difference from the Independents is,
that they are less attached to Calvinism, and consequently
admit a greater latitude of religious sentiment.   It may
be added, that their mode of admitting members into communion differs from that commonly practised among the
Presbyterians.

Recently a remarkable change has taken place in the
ecclesiastical arrangements of the English Presbyterians.
The Free Church of Scotland has erected its banner in England, and is now rallying its forces.   The character of this
new Presbyterian church in England, is the same with that
of the Free Church.   The general principles of its doctrines, order of worship and government, may be found in
the article on American Presbyterians.

Under the care of the Presbyterian Synod of England,
besides a Theological College, there are seven Presbyteries, viz.: Berwick-on-Tweed, Birmingham, Cumberland,
Lancashire, London, Newcastle-on-Tyne, and Northumber-
land.   In these Presbyteries there are 79 clergymen, 78
churches, and 2 foreign missionaries.   The Synod also

attends to various schemes of benevolence, among which are prominent, foreign and home missions, and ministerial education. Considering the comparatively short time in which this progress has been made, it appears to be highly encouraging.

AMERICAN PRESBYTERIANS.

THE word Presbyterian is often used in a wide sense as characterizing a large portion of the Protestant church. It embraces all those denominations which are opposed to prelacy. In prelatical church government and usages, a large number of sects are included. Thus, the Greek Church alone is made up of "The Greek Church proper," "The Russian Greek Church," "The Georgian and Mingrelian Churches," "The Nestorian Churches," "The Christians of St. Thomas," "The Jacobites," "The Copts," "The Abyssinians," "The Armenians," and many other minor denominations. "The Roman Church," "The English Episcopal Church," and "The American Episcopal Church," are also each of them a portion of that great family of churches included under the term Prelacy. These all agree in one great fundamental principle. They believe that ecclesiastical government is a gift from Christ to priests, and that they possess the power of transmitting this authority to their successors. They differ in respect to their acknowledged head; some of the Greek Christians acknowledging one Patriarch, and some another, and some the Roman Pontiff. Some Romanists also acknowledge the Pope, and some deny his supremacy. The English Episcopal Church acknowledge the king, or, during the present reign, the queen, as their head; while American Episcopalians account diocesan bishops as the highest ecclesiastical officers.

Presbyterians differ from Prelatists in respect to the source of ecclesiastical authority; and are divided, perhaps, into an equal number of minor denominations. They hold that all ecclesiastical authority is derived from the church itself; that the teaching office is transmitted by a plurality of presbyters or bishops; and that the whole body of believers, either as associated, or by their representatives, participate in the government. A bishop, according to the views of Presbyterians, is the pastor of a single congregation. Sometimes, as in the church of Ephesus, mentioned Acts xx. 28, several bishops or pastors unitedly presided over the spiritual instruction of a single worshipping assembly. This general system is sometimes termed "parity," because a leading feature of it is the equal official dignity of Christian ministers. Prelacy and Parity divide the Christian world.

The Presbyterian church, in this general denomination, includes Lutherans, Dutch Reformed, Congregationalists, Baptists, Scotch, English, and American Presbyterians. Among these, the English Presbyterians, Congregationalists, and Baptists. allow the popular will in ecclesiastical matters to be expressed by the members of the church as occasion may demand; while the Dutch Reformed, Scotch, and American Presbyterians call for the exercise of popular liberty in the election of lay elders, as making a part of the ecclesiastical courts, and in the election and dismission of pastors, and in the entire control of the church edifices and congregational funds.

Presbyterianism acknowledges no authority, in respect to the doctrines and duties of the Christian church, but the will of God as found in the sacred Scriptures. It maintains that God alone is Lord of the conscience, and hath left it free from the doctrines and commandments of men; and that the rights of private judgment, in all matters that respect religion, are universal and inalienable. It holds, that all ecclesiastical power is only ministerial and declarative; that is to say, that the Holy Scriptures are the only rule of faith and manners; that no church judicatory ought to pretend to make laws to bind the conscience in virtue of their own authority, and that all their decisions ought to be founded upon the word of God. Ecclesiastical discipline is purely moral and spiritual in its object, and ought not to be attended with any civil effects; hence it can derive no force whatever but from its own justice, the approbation of an impartial public, and the favor and blessing of the great Head of the church.

The officers of the Presbyterian church are bishops or pastors, ruling elders, and deacons. The pastor is the spiritual teacher of the congregation. He is expected to preach the gospel in the church on the Lord's day, to instruct the people by occasional lectures, to superintend the catechismal teaching of the young, and to visit the sick and bereaved, and console them by spiritual counsel adapted to their necessities. Ruling elders are elected by the people as their representatives in the ecclesiastical courts, and to co-operate with the pastor in watching over the spiritual interests of the congregation. They are designated by the Apostle Paul under the title of "governments," and as "those who rule well," in distinction from such as labor in word and doctrine. Deacons are secular officers whose duty is the care of the poor, and the reception and disbursement of the charities of the congregation.

The Session is the primary court of the church, and consists of the pastor and the ruling elders. The pastor is the president, and has the title of "Moderator of the session." In this primary court originates all the legislative action of the church. If the superior courts would take any step involving new constitutional princi ples, they are obliged to send the question down to the church sessions, that they may thus know the will of the church itself, before any revolutionary measures can be adopted. The session is also charged with the duty of watching over the spiritual interests of the congregation. It can summon offenders to an account for their irregular- ities, or their neglect of Christian duty. It can investi- gate charges presented by others, and admonish, rebuke, or suspend or exclude from the Lord's table, those who are found to deserve censure, according to the degree of their criminality. It is the business of the session also to ap- point a delegate of its own body to attend, with the pas- tor, the higher judicatories of the church. It is required of the session to keep a fair record of all its proceedings, as also a register of marriages, baptisms, persons admitted to the Lord's Supper, deaths, and other removals of church members, and to transmit these records, at stated periods, to the presbytery for their inspection.

A Presbytery consists of all the ministers, and one ruling elder from each church within a certain district. Three ministers and as many elders as may be present are necessary to constitute a quorum. The presbytery has power to receive and issue appeals from church sessions, and references brought before them in an orderly manner; to examine and license and ordain candidates for the holy ministry; to install, remove, and judge ministers; to exa- mine and approve or censure the records of church ses- sions; to resolve questions of doctrine or discipline, seriously and reasonably proposed; to condemn erroneous opinions which injure the purity or peace of the Church; to visit particular churches for the purpose of inquiring into their state, and redressing the evils that may have arisen in them; to unite or divide congregations, at the request of the people, or to form or receive new congregations; and, in general, to perform whatever may be deemed necessary to the spiritual welfare of the churches under their care.

A Synod consists of several presbyteries united. Not less than three presbyteries are necessary to compose a synod. It is not made up of representatives from the presbyteries, as presbyteries are of representatives from the sessions. On the contrary, each member of all the presbyteries included in its bounds is a member of the synod, so that a synod is nothing different from a larger presbytery, constituted by a combination of several presbyteries into one. The synod reviews the records of presbyteries, approving or censuring their proceedings, erecting new presbyteries, uniting or dividing those which were before erected, taking a general care of the churches within its bounds, and proposing such measures to the General Assembly as may be for advantage to the whole church. The synod is a court of appeal for the presbyteries within its bounds, having the same relation to the presbyterial courts which the presbyteries have to the sessions.

The General Assembly is the highest judicatory in the Presbyterian Church. It is constituted of an equal delegation of pastors and elders from the presbyteries. In one branch of the Presbyterian Church in America, the General Assembly is an appellate court; in the other it is only an advisory council, except that it possesses power to review the proceedings of the inferior bodies, and to decide, as a supreme court, the meaning of the constitution.

The General Assembly is not necessary to the most perfect development of Presbyterian Church government, nor, indeed, is any court higher than the Presbytery; but it has this obvious advantage, of representing all the congregations of this denomination under the same civil government in a single body. Thus, the General Assembly of the Kirk of Scotland and the General Assembly of the United States, before either was divided, presented an imposing influence in the visible unity of each.

The Church Sessions meet at stated periods, as often as may be deemed necessary. In some churches they convene once in each week; in others less frequently. Presbyteries hold two stated meetings in a year, while the synods in the United States meet annually. In the two great branches of the Presbyterian Church in the United States, one General Assembly meets annually, and the other triennially. It is a rule in all the judicatories of the Presbyterian Church, that the meetings shall be constituted with prayer. In the stated meetings of presbyteries, synods, and the General Assembly, the session is opened by a sermon from the Moderator, or presiding officer of the preceding meeting.

The Doctrines of the Presbyterian Church are Calvinistic — the doctrines of all the leading Reformers; of the Waldenses, for five or six hundred years before the Reformation; of Augustin and the primitive Church. They are substantially the same with the doctrinal symbols of the Synod of Dort, the Heidelberg Confession and Catechism, and of the Thirty-nine Articles of the Church of England, and of the Episcopal Church of the United States. No other branch of the Reformed Churches has maintained Calvinistic doctrines with so much tenaciousness as Presbyterians. While the Earl of Chatham could say of his own Church of England, " We have a Popish liturgy, a Calvinistic creed, and an Arminian clergy;" and while that denomination seem to be engaged in an interminable controversy to decide whether their branch of the Church ought to be considered Arminian or Calvinistic, the Presbyterian Church is unitedly Calvinistic, so that any man who should avow himself Arminian could not obtain ordination in the Presbyterian Church of either Scotland or America.

The system of doctrine is clearly set forth in the Westminster Confession of Faith, and the Larger and Shorter Catechisms.

The Presbyterian Church in the United States originated in a union of immigrants from Ireland and England — a blending of Irish Presbyterianism and English Congregationalism. The first presbytery formed in this country was the presbytery of Philadelphia, organized in 1704. The synod of Philadelphia was erected in 1716, and was composed of the presbyteries of Philadelphia, Snow Hill, Newcastle, and Long Island.

In 1741 the Church was divided in consequence of the inharmonious elements of which it was composed, and the synod of New York was formed. Fifteen years after the separation, in 1758, the synods of New York and Philadelphia were united again. In 1789, the year of the first meeting of the General Assembly, there were in the Church 188 Presbyterian ministers and 419 churches. In 1832 there were 21 synods, 110 presbyteries, 935 ministers, 2281 churches, and 17,348 communicants. In 1837, the Presbyterian Church was again thrown into a state of disunion, and divided into two nearly equal portions. Among so able and pious a body of men, the principles of the gospel are justly expected to exert their legitimate influence; it can subserve no benefit to record the grounds of a dissension which, it is hoped, will be only temporary.

These two branches of the Church are distinguished from each other by the circumstance that one holds the meeting of its General Assembly annually; while the other meets only triennially.

According to the Minutes of the General Assembly (Old School) of the Presbyterian Church in the United States for 1859, that branch of the Church has in connection with the Assembly 33 synods, 168 presbyteries, 297 licentiates, 493 candidates for the ministry, 2577 ministers, 3487 churches, and 279,630 communicants; and the whole amount contributed for congregational and other purposes in the year ending May, 1859, was $2,835,147.

By the Minutes of the General Assembly (New School) of the Presbyterian Church in the United States for 1859, that branch of the Church has 108 presbyteries, 1545 ministers, 134 licentiates, 370 candidates, 1542 churches, 137,990 communicants; and it expends annually on Domestic Missions, $91,402; on Foreign Missions, $67,796; on Education, $65,707; and on Publications, $44,667.

REFORMED PRESBYTERIAN CHURCH.

In 1588 the Scotch Protestants entered into an association which they denominated " *The Covenant*." The object of this arrangement was to protect themselves against an expected invasion from Spain by the famous "invincible armada." The union of the crowns of Scotland and England in 1603 resulted in a hierarchy, which was deemed dangerous, in the last degree, to the Presbyterian interests. This united in still closer bonds the friends of parity, and of ecclesiastical liberty. In 1637 the new liturgy, modelled after the English, was ordered to be introduced into the churches of Scotland. The most determined resistance ensued, which terminated in a new covenant the year fol lowing. While Charles I. and the Parliament were contending, the Protestants in Scotland entered into "a solemn league and covenant" with the English Parliament, by which the independence of the Presbyterian churches was confirmed. On the restoration of the Stuarts in 1661, this covenant was abolished. These successive struggles seemed to have engendered a habit of making firm compacts for maintaining what they considered important principles; a habit which continues till this day.

At the accession of William and Mary in 1689, Episcopacy was established in England and Ireland, and Presbyterianism in Scotland.

A portion of the Scottish Kirk declined to avail themselves of an establishment of this kind, and covenanted to resist it, and protested that it was at variance with the "solemn league and covenant" which they considered a part of the constitution of the empire. They maintained that the civil rulers had usurped an authority over the church which conflicted with the proper headship of the Redeemer.

For fifteen or sixteen years these staunch and determined men remained without pastors, preserving their distinct social existence by uniting in praying societies, and meeting statedly for religious worship.

In 1706 the Rev. John MacMillan joined them from the Established Church. In 1743, the Rev. Mr. Nairne, from the Secession Church, then recently organized, acceded to them; and these two clergymen, with ruling elders, constituted the "Reformed Presbytery." Several families had, in the meantime, emigrated to the American colonies.

About the same time in which the "Reformed Presbytery" was organized in Scotland, the Rev. Mr. Craighead collected the Covenanters of Pennsylvania, and induced them to bind themselves together by a solemn public en

11 *

gagement to maintain their peculiar principles. Their body was slowly augmented, mostly by immigration, till they were joined by the Rev. Mr. Cuthbertson, from the Reformed Presbytery of Scotland, in 1752; and Rev. Messrs. Lin and Dobbin, from the Reformed Presbytery in Ireland, in 1774. This year the Reformed Presbytery was organized in the colony of Pennsylvania.

Their growth was slow till 1782, when a union was effected between the Reformed Presbytery and the Associate Presbyterian Church. Hence arose a new organization, denominated, from the name of its two constituent elements, the "Associate Reformed Church."

This union, instead of combining two bodies in one, left a small minority in each of the elementary portions, which perpetuated the original organizations; so that, in fact, two churches were divided into three, — an instructive instance of the influence of hasty and forced combinations of bodies of men.

The doctrinal principles of the Reformed Church are thoroughly Calvinistic. The Reformed Presbyterians objected to the Constitution of the United States, when it was formed, on account of its having no exclusive religious character, and its tolerating Jews, Mohammedans, Deists, and Atheists. They also objected to its recognition of slavery. They declared that they would not take the oath of allegiance.

In 1830, a portion of their ministers began to entertain different views, and were in favor of acknowledging the government of this country, and avowing allegiance to it This led to what was called the New Light Controversy, and the formation of two organizations, which still remain separated.

The entire body of the Reformed Presbyterians in the United States, including both these organizations, embraces

108 ministers, 15 licentiates, 25 students of Theology, 160 congregations, and 14,000 communicants. Among the well-known and distinguished ministers of this connection are the late Alexander McLeod, D. D., and Rev. Samuel B. Wylie.

The two bodies are known as "The General Synod" (which acknowledges the Constitution of the U. S.) and "the Synod of the Reformed Presbyterian Church" (which denounces the Constitution as sinful). The General Synod had one congregation in the South at the outbreak of the rebellion, at Fayetteville, Tennessee. Strenuous efforts were in vain made to induce the people to swear allegiance to the rebel government. Every one refused, and as a consequence most of the members had to flee to the free States.

In 1867, the General Synod numbered 8 Presbyteries, 66 ministers, 91 congregations and 8324 members. Given for all purposes, $123,097.34, or more than $15 per member. The theological seminary had an endowment of $23,000 and 16 students. The next year showed a farther increase. There were 77 pastors and 8487 members. This was the culmination of its prosperity. Wide and irreconcilable differences were arising in the body, which, though not created, were developed, by the movement for reunion going on among Presbyterians.

Those broad sentiments of Christian sympathy and liberality which had been developed among evangelical Christians of the North by the war, and especially by the labors of the Christian Commission, had their embodiment in a leading member of this denomination, who had been the president of the Christian Commission. Mr. George H. Stuart earnestly desired to see his church take the honored place of a pioneer in the reunion of the various Presbyterian Churches. It was due to his zeal and activity, that the Reformed Presbyterian Church, at the meeting of the general Synod, May, 1867, invited a National Convention of Presbyterians of all branches to meet in Philadelphia, to consider the subject of a general union.   This Convention met in November, and embraced delegates from six different organizations.   The first Reformed Presbyterian Church, Dr. Wylie pastor, was the place of meeting, and Mr. Stuart was elected chairman. Offence was given to the more rigid portion of the Reformed body by the enthusiastic proceedings of this Convention.   The adherents of an inspired psalmody were shocked at the singing of hymns.   They were in no hurry to surrender their distinctive principles.   So, when the General Synod met the next year, a very decided opposition to the movement was shown by the majority of the members.   Union only with those whose doctrines, order, and worship corresponded with their own, was now advocated, and all direct overtures were confined to psalm-singing and close-communion bodies.

Mr. George H. Stuart and his friends being thus outvoted, and yet boldly maintaining the rightfulness of their liberal position, it was decided by a majority vote to censure and suspend Mr. Stuart for singing hymns and communing with persons not members of the Reformed Church.   Thirteen delegates to the Synod issued a formal protest against this action.

Mr. Stuart was sustained by his pastor, Dr. Wylie, by the First Church and by his Presbytery.   Consequently, at the meeting of the next General Synod, the delegates from the Presbytery were refused admission.   The Presbytery has since suspended relations with the Synod, and remains in that condition.

The Allegheny Presbytery, also sympathizing with Mr. Stuart, sent a protest against Synod's action, and was pronounced out of communion, in reply. In 1870 it was received by the General Assembly of the reunited Presbyterian Church.

The missionary Presbytery of Saharanpur having, on similar grounds, suspended relations to the Synod, it was declared in secession. Steps were taken, however, to retain it in communion if possible, and to secure to the Synod control of its property.

A basis of union was agreed upon in 1869 for an organic union with the United Presbyterians, but it has not yet (1871) been carried into effect.

The total number of ministers and licentiates reported in 1870 was 41; the attendance at the synod of 1871 was 24.

"The Synod of the Reformed Presbyterian Church," at its meeting in 1869, formally reiterated its position of hostility toward the Constitution of the United States, as an irreligious document, which could not be accepted and approved by a Christian people without sin, and declared it the duty of citizens to refuse to co-operate with a government thus founded.

There is a college at Northwood, Ohio, and a theological seminary connected with this Church; it has a mission among the freedmen at Washington. In 1870 it had 8 Presbyteries, 87 congregations, 86 ministers, 8577 communicants. The total of contributions reported exceeded $150,000.

THE ASSOCIATE PRESBYTERIAN CHURCH, OR SECEDERS.

THIS, like the church just described, is an offshoot from the Church of Scotland. The cause of the secession was almost identical in its nature with that of the great secession of 1843, by means of which the Free Church was created. In 1649, the patronage of kirks had been formally abolished by parliament, as " an evil and bondage," as " a custom popish," and as " prejudicial to the liberties of the people."

The act of parliament above referred to remained in force until the year 1712, when the doctrine of patronage was again revived. Many protested against it loudly at the time. The right of patronage was, for a while, exercised with great moderation. A case arose, however, in which a minister was forced upon a congregation against the wishes of the great body of the people. The proceeding came before the General Assembly at its next session in May, 1732, and this, together with other similar cases, led to the adoption of an act "*Anent planting vacant churches*," wherein the general doctrine of patronage was strongly asserted. In the October following, the Rev. Ebenezer Erskine, a minister of distinguished ability and influence, in a sermon preached at the opening of the Synod of Perth and Sterling, denounced, with great freedom, the Act of Assembly above referred to. Mr. Erskine was censured by the synod, and hence arose the secession and the organization of the "Associate Presbytery of Scotland." This organization occurred November 17th, 1733. Its growth, as might have been expected, was rapid, and in 1744 a synod was formed. The year following, a controversy commenced, which resulted in the division of the synod into two parties, each claiming to be the "Associate Synod." The occasion of the disruption was the taking or not taking the burghers' oath. In order to be admitted burghers, or freemen of towns, an oath was required containing the following clause: "I protest before God and your lordship, that I profess and allow, with all my heart, the true religion, presently professed within this realm, and authorized by the laws thereof; that I shall abide thereat, and defend the same to my life's end, renouncing the Roman religion called Papistry." The controversy turned on the question whether it was right to take an oath which implied an approval of the established church. The division was completed in 1746. Those who opposed the lawfulness of the oath were termed Anti-burghers, and its advocates Burghers. The act requiring the oath objected to, being repealed, the parties again coalesced, taking the title of The United Secession Church, with the exception of a small minority of the Anti-burghers, who only are represented in the United States by a regular organization.

At an early day some of the secession emigrated to this country. The Rev. Messrs. Gellatly and Arnot were sent over by the Synod to organize congregations and to constitute them into a presbytery. They reached the province of Pennsylvania in 1754, and organized the Associate Presbytery in the November of that year.

In 1776, the number of ministers having increased to

thirteen, the presbytery was divided, and the eastern portion was denominated the "Presbytery of New York."

In 1782, the division occurred by which the Associate Reformed Church came into existence, a more full history of which may be found in the preceding account of the Reformed Church.

By this division, the Associate Church in this country was almost extinguished.

The Synod of Scotland, however, despatched assistance, and the church was gradually strengthened until the formation of the Synod in 1800. This was denominated "The Associate Synod of North America." It held its first meeting in Philadelphia, May, 1801. This body was subordinate to the Associate Synod in the mother country, till it was declared a co-ordinate Synod by the General Associate Synod of Scotland, in 1818.

In 1841, a controversy arose in respect to principles involved in some cases of discipline, and the minority declared themselves the Synod. Since that time, until recently, there have been two bodies claiming the same name. Within a short time the two bodies have coalesced.

From the larger of these bodies another secession took place in 1845, denominating itself "The Associate Presbytery of Philadelphia."

The Associate Presbyterian Church in this country is, in all its branches, decidedly Calvinistic in doctrine. It insists upon the use of the literal translation of the Psalms in its singing. It maintains a high standard of duty in respect to the education of its children in the fear of God, making it an offence worthy of discipline if parents neglect to teach their children the Shorter Catechism. It possesses a learned and pious ministry. It has a Theological Seminary at Xenia, Ohio. with two Professorships, one of didactic theology and Hebrew, and one of pastoral theology and biblical literature.   Students 45.

The strength of the whole Associate Church in this country is 20 presbyteries, 164 ministers, 267 congregations, 21,588 communicants.

THE ASSOCIATE REFORMED CHURCH.

THIS branch of the Presbyterian family of churches was called into existence, and took its name from a union that was formed between large portions of the Associate and the Reformed Presbyterian churches at Pequa, Pennsylvania, in June, 1782.   Modifying the doctrine of the Westminster Confession of Faith concerning the power of the civil magistrate in matters of religion, and adapting the form of church government and the directory of worship to the Word of God, and the circumstances of the church in this country, the synod formally issued its constitution and standards at Greencastle, Pa,, May 31, 1799.

Soon afterwards, there being, from various quarters, an urgent demand for sound and faithful ministers, the erection of a theological seminary was taken into serious consideration ; and, in 1801, the Rev. John M. Mason was sent to Great Britain and Ireland with authority to procure a suitable number of evangelical ministers and probationers, and to solicit donations, in money and books, for establishing an institution to train young men for the gospel ministry.   He met with considerable success ; and, immediately on his return, the synod (which, in the autumn of 1802, had divided itself, for the convenience of its members, into four synods, and formed these into a general synod, to meet by delegation, and to hold its first meeting at Greencastle, May, 1804) took steps for establishing its theological

school   Their arrangements were completed in **May,**
1805.   The Rev. J. M. Mason, D. D., was appointed professor; and on the 1st of November following, the institu-
tution went into successful operation.   It was the **first**
theological seminary in the United States

Thus established, the synod pursued its course, and **was**
largely prospered until about the year 1816, when, from **a**
gradual relinquishment of some of its distinctive features,
and the withdrawal, on that account, of the synods of Scioto
into the West, and of the Carolinas, in the South, its interests
materially declined.

In May, 1822, a partial union was formed with the General Assembly of the Presbyterian Church, and the General
Synod was dissolved.   The subordinate synods, however,
continued their existence, and were active and useful in
their work.   Again the demand for ministers trained in
the church, and sympathizing with it, in everything in which
it was peculiar, was strong and urgent.   Shortly afterwards,
therefore, the synod of the West established a seminary at
Alleghany, Pa.   The Rev. Joseph Kerr was its first professor; and under his care, and that of his successors, Rev.
Mungo Dick and Rev. John T. Pressly, D. D., it has been
instrumental in furnishing the churches with a large number of able ministers of the New Testament.   In 1829 the
Synod of New York revived the seminary at Newburgh,
and placed it under the care of the Rev. Joseph MacCarroll,
D. D.   Already it has sent many laborers into the field;
and with an excellent building, a most valuable library, **a**
good location, and an able professor, it presents most important facilities for a theological education.   A younger,
but flourishing and valuable theological institution was also
formed in 1839 by the second synod of the West, at Oxford,
Ohio, under the presidency of the Rev. Joseph Claybaugh,
D. D.   At Due-west-corner, Abbeville district, S. C., an

institution with literary and theological departments has also been opened, under the most auspicious circumstances. It is under the charge of four professors appointed by the synod of the South, and already numbers over one hundred students.

In each of these synods there is a periodical devoted to the interests of the Associate Reformed Church, namely, in the order of their history: The Evangelical Guardian, edited by the Rev. D. Macdill, D. D., at Hamilton, Ohio; The Christian Magazine of the South, by Rev. J. Boyce, in Fairfield district, S. C.; The Preacher, by Rev. D. R. Kerr, at Pittsburg, Pa.; and The Christian Instructor, by Rev. J. B. Dales, at Philadelphia. Besides projecting and sustaining these institutions and publications, the Associate Reformed Church has commenced a most interesting mission to Palestine; taken incipient steps for one in Western Africa; appointed two ministers to explore Texas during the coming season, and resolves upon a special effort to seek the lost sheep of the house of Israel in our large cities, and point them to the true Messiah, as soon as the proper men can be employed.

The Associate Reformed Church is the most liberal and efficient of all the branches of the early Scotch Secession churches. It has numbered among its ministry some of the most brilliant lights of learning and religion in this country. It is thoroughly Calvinistic in doctrine, maintains the literal psalmody, and is very strict in its discipline.

The Rev. John Mason, and his son, John M. Mason, D. D.; Rev. James Proudfit, and Alexander Proudfit, D. D., the late eminent and beloved advocate of African colonization, were men to adorn any church, and any age. At the present time the Associate Reformed Church comprises 5 synods, 84 presbyteries, upwards of 315 ministers, more than 375 churches, and about 40,000 members.

UNITED PRESBYTERIANS.

In 1858, the "Associate Reformed" and the "Associate" Presbyterian Churches (the two last-named bodies) were united into one organization, called the United Presbyterian Church in North America, and forming a body more than fifty thousand strong. They hold to the obligation of using only an inspired psalmody in worship, and they are exclusive in their terms of communion. Otherwise they cannot be distinguished from the great body of Presbyterians in America in polity or in doctrine. Their membership is almost exclusively Scotch or Scotch-Irish, or the immediate descendants of such. Their position on national questions is strongly anti-slavery, and though owning allegiance to the Constitution, they have always shown great desire to secure an amendment distinctly recognizing at least the being of God in that instrument. Strong loyal and anti-slavery resolutions were adopted during the war.

Rev. W. C. McCune, one of the ministers of the body, was arraigned before his Synod in 1866, for holding loose or liberal views on the terms of communion and admission to church membership. The Synod cleared him, but the case coming up on appeal to the General Assembly of the following year, the course of the Synod was condemned by an overwhelming vote, and the case was referred back to Mr. McC.'s Presbytery. Mr. McCune withdrew to another branch of the Presbyterian Church where the terms are less stringent.

In 1868, by a unanimous vote, the General Assembly declared that the terms of union between all the Presbyterian branches in America, proposed by the Philadelphia convention of 1867, as a whole, would not answer the purpose. There must be no relinquishment of principle for union, and especially is unqualified assent to the Confession and Catechisms indispensable.

Statistics of 1870: 8 synods, 56 presbyteries, 553 ministers, 729 congregations, 69,807 members. Contributions to general benevolence, $178,155. Total contributions, $827,126. Average per member, $11.64. Salaries of pastors averaged by Synods, $787.

The Associate Reformed Synod of the South reported 63 ministers in 1870. Negotiations for union with the Southern Presbyterian Church were carried on about the close of the war, but without result. One of the Presbyteries, however, was received by the Synod of Alabama in 1866.

The Associate Reformed Synod of New York had, in 1867, 16 ministers and 1631 communicants.

The Associate Synod of North America also had 22 ministers and 778 communicants.

The last two bodies are fragments of the Associate and Associate Reformed Presbyterian Churches, who refused to go with the mass of their fellow-members into the union by which the United Presbyterian Church was formed.

CUMBERLAND PRESBYTERIANS.

ABOUT the beginning of the present century there arose a remarkable revival of religion among a portion of the Presbyterian church in Kentucky. Meetings were held in the open air; and multitudes flocked together from the distance of fifty, and even in some instances, a hundred miles. This was the origin of camp-meetings. As the number of converts was great, and religion was extended into destitute and neglected regions, a strong necessity was felt for a more rapid multiplication of Christian ministers. This led the Cumberland Presbytery, in 1801, to encourage four laymen, without a classical education, to prepare written discourses with a view to the receiving of license to preach the gospel. In 1803 Mr. Alexander Anderson, and Mr. Finis Ewing, were ordained to the work of the ministry. Others were licensed as probationers, and several candidates were received under the care of the presbytery.

In 1805, the Synod of Kentucky, in reviewing the book of records of the Cumberland Presbytery, took notice of their having introduced men into the sacred office who had not acquired a regular education, and who were understood to have taken exceptions to the doctrinal standards of the Church. This led to the appointment of a commission, with full powers to act in the place of the synod, both in holding a friendly conference with the presbytery, and in judicially terminating the case.

The commission demanded that all those persons who had been ordained or licensed without an examination on all the branches of learning and doctrine required in the Confession of Faith, should appear before themselves, and submit to a full and regular examination. To this demand the presbytery declined to submit.

The commission then passed a resolution that those who had been thus licensed or ordained without a full examination, should be prohibited from the exercise of official functions, until such times as they should submit themselves to their jurisdiction.

The members of presbytery continued to exercise their ministry, but not without making various efforts, during a period of five years, to obtain through the General Assembly a "redress of grievances." Having failed in all these endeavors, the Rev. Messrs. Ewing, King, and McAdow, in 1810, declared themselves independent, and constituted the Cumberland Presbytery, which was the germ of the present Cumberland Presbyterian Church. In constituting the church, the following statement is made as defining their position:

"We, Samuel McAdow, Finis Ewing, and Samuel King, regularly ordained ministers of the Presbyterian Church, against whom no charge either of immorality or heresy has ever been exhibited before any judicature of the church, having waited in vain more than four years, in the mean time petitioning the General Assembly for a redress of grievances, and a restoration of our violated rights, have and do hereby agree and determine to constitute ourselves into a presbytery, known by the name of the Cumberland Presbytery, on the following conditions:

"All candidates for the ministry, who may hereafter be licensed by this presbytery, and all the licentiates or probationers who may hereafter be ordained by this presbytery, shall be required, before such licensure and ordination, to receive and accept the Confession of Faith and Discipline of the Presbyterian Church, except the idea of fatality that seems to be taught under the mysterious doctrine of predestination. It is to be understood, however, that such as can clearly receive the Confession of Faith without an exception, will not be required to make any. Moreover, all licentiates, before they are set apart to the whole work of the ministry, or ordained, shall be required to undergo an examination in English Grammar, Geography, Astronomy, Natural and Moral Philosophy, and Church History. It will not be understood that examinations in Experimental Religion and Theology will be omitted. The presbytery may also require an examination on any part, or all, of the above branches of knowledge before licensure, if they deem it expedient."

So rapid was their growth, that three years after, in 1813, they became three presbyteries, and constituted a synod. At the sessions of the synod in 1828, three new synods were erected, and measures were taken for the organization of a general assembly. The first meeting of the General Assembly occurred at Princeton, Ky., in 1829.

The doctrines of this church are a modification of the Westminster Confession. The chief point of difference is their rejecting the doctrine of election, as in their view tending to fatality. They are strictly Presbyterian in government and order.

No church, perhaps, has increased more rapidly than has this young and vigorous denomination. Its doctrines seem to have been popular not only with the masses, but with those of high culture and refinement. Although a classical course of instruction is not made a *sine qua non* to entering the sacred profession, yet no ecclesiastical organization, it is believed, more strongly favors a highly educated ministry. As confirmation of this, the church, though in its infancy, not only stands abreast with the older and more powerful denominations in the institutions of learning established for the education of both sexes, but it now embraces in its ministry many of the fine scholars and vigorous thinkers of the age. Nor is this denomination behind others in its periodical literature, as its highly respectable weeklies, monthlies, and quarterlies will testify.

A prominent trait in this body of Christians is its *conservatism*. The great civil war between the North and the South—a conflict which deluged the United States with blood, and which rent in twain the leading denominations not before severed—was not sufficient, it seems, to divide the Cumberland Presbyterian Church! This denomination has never prostituted to political ends either the pulpit or the religious press. With it the church has ever been considered an asylum for the heart, and not an arena for fierce, bitter controversies in reference to the kingdom of Cæsar.

The General Assembly has under its superintendence 24 synods, 100 presbyteries, 1400 congregations, 1250 ministers, 250 licentiates, 300 candidates for the ministry, and over 125,000 communicants. The number of communicants in some estimates has been placed considerably higher than this. The lowest has here been stated. Reckoning four children, and other adherents, to each communicant, which it will be acknowledged is a very low estimate, there will be found 500,000 persons connected with this branch of the Redeemer's kingdom.

MORAVIANS.

THE *Unitas Fratrum*, or *Church of the Bohemian and Moravian Brethren*, was founded by followers of John Huss in the year 1457, sixty years before the Reformation. It rapidly grew and spread. In 1621, Ferdinand of Tyrol issued an edict for the suppression of the Church. The Bibles were burned and the Brethren exiled, and for a while the Unitas Fratrum seemed to be extinct. But a " hidden seed " remained. Among the mountains of Bohemia there dwelt a few devoted men who kept alive the faith of the fathers, and in Poland there survived a couple of the bishops of the Church. In 1722 some of the Moravians from Bohemia found an asylum upon the estates of Nicholas Lewis, Count de Zinzendorf. Here they founded a town and called it Herrnhut. Through the Polish bishops the episcopal succession of the ancient Brethren was transmitted to the church at Herrnhut and the ancient discipline revived. Moved by a great spiritual awakening, the exiles, whose numbers were swelled by devout men from all parts of Europe, approached the work of Foreign Missions. In 1732 the first missionaries went to the West Indies and the year following to Greenland. As the pioneers in the work of Protestant missions the Brethren are chiefly known in later times. The Church has missions in Greenland, Labrador, the West Indies, Central America, Surinam, Africa, Australia, Thibet, Palestine and among the North American Indians.

The Church is divided into four provinces (two American, and a British and a Continental). The government of the province is administered by Synods, which meet triennially, and the affairs of the Church at large are administered by a General Synod, which convenes in

Europe every ten years. The will of the Synods is executed by the Boards elected for that purpose.

The orders in the ministry are bishops (of the so-called Apostolical Succession), presbyters and deacons.

The doctrinal position of the Church is strictly evangelical. The ritual of the Church is simple. Litanies are used in connection with the various services, though their use is not binding upon the officiating clergyman. Music holds a prominent place in connection with worship. The festivals, as Epiphany, Christmas and Easter, are observed. "Lovefeasts," consisting of a meal of light cakes with tea and coffee, are partaken of in imitation of the apostolical "Agapæ." The Moravians do not hold to a community of goods.

In the year 1736 the first colony of Moravians came to Georgia in company with John Wesley. The first permanent settlement was made in 1742 at Bethlehem, Pennsylvania. In 1749 an Act was passed by Parliament recognizing the Moravian Church as "An ancient, evangelical, episcopal Church," and encouraging the emigration of its members to America. A large colony proceeded to Salem, N. C. The membership in the United States is at present about 14,000. There are 63 congregations and about 100 clergymen in service, including 3 bishops. The home membership throughout the world is about 25,000; the membership in the mission-field is 70,000. The Church has large schools for the education of females at Bethlehem and Lititz, Pa., at Salem, N. C., and at Hope, Ind. The seminary at Bethlehem has educated over 5000 young ladies. The publications of the American Province are the "Moravian," the "Brueder Botschafter" (German), "The Little Missionary" and the "Text-Book."

FREE-WILL BAPTISTS.

THE founder of this denomination was the Rev. Benjamin Randall. He was originally a preacher connected with the Calvinistic Baptists. Having embraced Arminian views, and being disowned by his brethren as unsound in the faith, he organized a church in New Durham, N. H., on the 30th day of June, 1780. Soon after this, other churches were formed on the same plan; and these churches united together, and constituted the New Durham Quarterly Meeting.

They were first called Free Willers, by way of reproach. Subsequently they assumed the name as one by which they are willing to be designated. They are nearly allied to the English *General Baptists*.

They have three missionaries in India; also a home mission society, a Sunday-school union, and an education society for training men for the sacred office.

Their ecclesiastical government is a mixture of Congregationalism and Presbyterianism. The discipline of private members belongs to the churches with which they are connected. They have quarterly meetings, consisting of ministers and lay delegates. To these bodies ministers are amenable. The quarterly meeting possesses very much the character of a presbytery. Several quarterly meetings, united in an annual council, make what they term a yearly meeting. All the annual meetings are convened together triennially as a general conference.

The denomination has been divided by the question of slavery, the greater portion of the church having withdrawn from about four thousand communicants in South Carolina, on account of their being slaveholders. For the same reason they declined receiving into their connection some twelve thousand from Kentucky, who sent a delegation to

Engraved by A.B. Walter

Roger William

the general conference to solicit a union. They hold what is commonly understood by Armenian doctrines, denying the doctrine of personal election and the inadmissibleness of grace. They have a book concern and printing establishment at Dover, N. H. Its trustees are appointed by the general conference.

If we reckon in the statistics of the denomination those who have been disowned on account of their connection with slavery, we shall find that they had, according to the Baptist Register of 1846, 115 quarterly meetings, comprised in 25 yearly meetings, 1249 churches, 1076 ministers, and 55,323 communicants. They have now 133 associations, 1720 churches, 965 ordained ministers, 158 licentiates, and 56,026 communicants.

DISCIPLES OF CHRIST.

THE Church established by Christ and his Apostles was a unit, and was designed to remain so through all time. It had the one sure "foundation," and the one Divine rule for building thereon. The gospel was preached to the people; they heard it, believed it, and obeyed it. These obedient ones were instructed to "keep the unity of the Spirit in the bond of peace," to "continue steadfastly in the Apostles' doctrine and fellowship, and in breaking of bread and of prayers."

Now, it is evident that there have been many innovations upon and departures from the teaching and practice of the primitive Church as laid down in the New Testament Scriptures. Divisions, strifes, and speculations exist; and while these exist, the world cannot be converted to Christianity. The aim of the Disciples of Christ is to restore the faith and practice of the Apostolic Church, to unite all of God's people on the "one foundation," and to have the gospel preached among all nations.

As individuals, this people wear the name of "Disciples of Christ," or "Christians." In their organized capacity they are known as "The Church of Christ," "Church of God," or simply "The Christian Church," believing that these names are authorized by the Word of God, and were, by the Holy Spirit, applied to the Church in the days of the Apostles.

Scarcely fifty years have transpired since the reformatory movement began, yet it has attained large proportions already, and is rapidly extending its influence. Churches of this faith are found in all parts of the United States, in the Dominion of Canada, in England, Ireland, Scotland, Australia, and Jamaica. They number fully 600,000 communicants. They have 3000 preachers in the field, many of whom are distinguished for their talent and scholarship. They publish 30 periodicals: 9 of these are weeklies, 1 quarterly, and the rest monthlies. 1 is published in Canada, 2 in England, 1 in Australia, and the rest in the United States.

The Disciples are distinguished for their interest in education. Their oldest literary institution is Bethany College, founded by Alexander Campbell, who for many years presided over it. Kentucky University, at Lexington, Kentucky, has 800 students in attendance. The university at Indianapolis, Indiana, is in a flourishing condition. Besides these, they have 12 or 15 colleges and a large number of academies and seminaries under their control. They have taken steps to found a college in Australia to meet the wants of the Church in that locality.

They are a missionary people. They have a general missionary society, directed by a "Board of Managers," through which the offerings of the brotherhood are applied for the extension and upbuilding of the Church. They have also State and local organizations of a missionary character, which co-operate with the General Society.

The following statement, taken from the writings of Mr. Campbell and others, is a very explicit declaration of the object and principles of the Disciples of Christ:

"The constitutional principle of this Christian association and its object are clearly expressed in the following resolution: — 'That this society, formed for the sole purpose of promoting simple evangelical Christianity, shall, to the utmost of its power, countenance and support such ministers, and such only, as exhibit a manifest conformity to the original standard, in conversation and doctrine, in zeal and diligence; only such as reduce to practice the simple original form of Christianity, expressly exhibited upon the sacred page, without attempting to inculcate anything of human authority, of private opinion, or inventions of men, as having any place in the constitution, faith, or worship of the Christian church.'

"But to contradistinguish this effort from some others almost contemporaneous with it, we would emphatically remark, that, whilst the remonstrants warred against human creeds, evidently because those creeds warred against their own private opinions and favorite dogmas, which they wished to substitute for those creeds, — this enterprise, so far as it was hostile to those creeds, warred against them, not because of their hostility to any private or favorite opinions which were desired to be substituted for them; but because those human institutions supplanted the Bible, made the Word of God of non-effect, were fatal to the intelligence, union, purity, holiness, and happiness of the disciples of Christ, and hostile to the salvation of the world. We had not at first, and we have not now, a favorite opinion or speculation, which we would offer as a substitute for any human creed or constitution in Christendom.

"With various success, and with many of the opinions of the various sects imperceptibly carried with them from the denominations to which they once belonged, did the advocates of the Bible cause plead for the union of Christians of every name on the broad basis of the apostles' teaching. But it was not until the year 1823, that a restoration of the original gospel and order of things began to be advocated in a periodical, edited by Alexander Campbell, of Bethany, Virginia, entitled 'The Christian Baptist.'

"He and his father, Thomas Campbell, renounced the Presbyterian system, and were immersed in the year 1812. They and the congregation which they had formed, united with the Redstone Baptist Association; protesting against all human creeds as bonds of union, and professing subjection to the Bible alone. But in pressing upon the attention of that society and the public the all-sufficiency of the Sacred Scriptures for everything necessary to the perfection of the Christian character, whether in the private or social relations of life, in the church or in the world, they began to be opposed by a strong creed-party in that association. After some ten years' debating and contending for the Bible alone, and the apostles' doctrine, Alexander Campbell, and the church to which he belonged, united with the Mahoning Association of Ohio—that association being more favorable to his views of reform.

"In his debates on the subject and action of baptism with Mr. Walker, a seceding minister, in the year 1820, and with Mr. M'Calla, a Presbyterian minister, in 1823, his views of reformation began to be developed, and were very generally received by the Baptist society, as far as these works were read.

"But in his 'Christian Baptist,' which began July 4, 1823, his views of the need of reformation were more fully exposed; and as these gained ground by the pleading of various ministers of the Baptist denomination, a party in opposition began to exert itself, and to oppose the spread of what they were pleased to call heterodoxy. But not till after great numbers began to act upon these principles, was there any attempt towards separation. After the Mahoning Association appointed Walter Scott an evangelist, in 1827, and when great numbers began to be immersed into Christ under his labors, and new churches began to be erected by him and other laborers in the field, did the Baptist associations begin to declare non-fellowship with the brethren of the Reformation. Thus by constraint, not of choice, they were obliged to form societies out of those communities that split upon the ground of adherence to the Apostles' doctrine. The distinguishing character·istics of their views and practices are the following : —

"They regard all the sects and parties of the Christian world as having, in greater or less degree, departed from the simplicity of faith and manners of the first Christians. This defection they attribute to the great varieties of speculation and metaphysical dogmatism of the countless creeds, formularies, liturgies, and books of discipline adopted and inculcated as bonds of union and platforms of communion in all the parties which have sprung from the Lutheran Reformation. The effects of these synodical covenants, conventional articles of belief, and rules of ecclesiastical polity, has been the introduction of a new nomenclature, a human vocabulary of religious words,

13 *

phrases, and technicalities, which has displaced the style of the living oracles, and affixed to the sacred diction ideas wholly unknown to the apostles of Christ.

"To remedy and obviate these aberrations, they propose to ascertain from the Holy Scriptures, according to the commonly received and well established rules of interpretation, the ideas attached to the leading terms and sentences found in the Holy Scriptures, and then to use the words of the Holy Spirit in the apostolic acceptation of them.

"By thus expressing the ideas communicated by the Holy Spirit, in the terms and phrases learned from the apostles, and by avoiding the artificial and technical language of scholastic theology, they propose to restore a pure speech to the household of faith; and by accustoming the family of God to use the language and dialect of their heavenly Father, they expect to promote the sanctification of one another through the truth, and to terminate those discords and debates which have always originated from the words which man's wisdom teaches, and from a reverential regard and esteem for the style of the great masters of polemic divinity; believing that speaking the same things in the same style is the only certain way to thinking the same things.

"They make a very marked distinction between faith and opinion; between the testimony of God and the reasonings of men: the words of the Spirit and human inferences. Faith in the testimony of God and obedience to the commandments of Jesus are their bond of union; and not an agreement in any abstract views or opinions upon what is written or spoken by divine authority. Regarding all the opposing theories of religious sectaries as extremes begotten by each other, they cautiously avoid them, as equidistant from the simplicity and practical tendency of the promises and precepts, of the doctrine and facts, of the exhortations and precedents of the Christian institution. They look for unity of spirit and the bonds of peace in the practical acknowledgement of 'one faith, one Lord, one immersion, one hope, one body, one Spirit, one God and Father of all;' not in unity of opinions, nor in unity of forms, ceremonies, or modes of worship.

"The Holy Scriptures of both Testaments they regard as containing revelations from God, and as all necessary to make the man of God perfect, and accomplished for every good word and work: the New Testament, or the living oracles of Jesus Christ, they understand as containing the Christian religion; testimonies of the four evangelists they view as illustrating and proving the great proposition on which our religion rests, namely, — that Jesus of Nazareth is the Messiah, the only begotten and well-beloved Son of God, and the only Saviour of the world; the Acts of the Apostles as a divinely authorized narrative of the beginning and progress of the reign or kingdom of Jesus Christ, recording the full development of 'the gospel' by the Holy Spirit sent down from heaven, and the procedure of the apostles in setting up the Church of Christ on earth; the Epistles as carrying out and applying the doctrine of the apostles to the practice of individuals and churches, and as developing the tendencies of the gospel in the behavior of its professors, and all as forming a complete standard of faith and morals, adapted to the interval between the ascension of Christ, and his return with the kingdom which he has received from God.

"Every one who sincerely believes the testimony which God gave of Jesus of Nazareth, saying, 'This is my Son, the beloved, in whom I delight,' or, in other words, believes what the evangelists and apostles have testified concerning him, from his conception to his coronation in heaven, as

Lord of all, and who is willing to obey him in everything, they regard as a proper subject of immersion into the name of the Father, and of the Son, and of the Holy Spirit, and no one else. They consider Christian baptism, after a public, sincere, and intelligent confession of the faith in Jesus, as necessary to admission to the privileges of the kingdom of the Messiah, and as a solemn pledge on the part of heaven, of the actual remission of all past sins, and of adoption into the family of God.

"The Holy Spirit is promised only to those who believe and obey the Saviour. No one is taught to expect the reception of that heavenly monitor and Comforter as a resident in his heart, till he obeys the gospel. Thus, while they proclaim faith and repentance, or faith and a change of heart, as preparatory to immersion, remission of sins, and the gift of the Holy Spirit, they say to all penitents, or all those who believe and repent of their sins, as Peter said to the first audience addressed after the Holy Spirit was bestowed after the glorification of Jesus, 'Be immersed, every one of you, in the name of the Lord Jesus, for the remission of sins, and you shall receive the gift of the Holy Spirit.' They teach sinners that God commands all men everywhere to repent or to turn to God; that the Holy Spirit strives with them so to do by the apostles and prophets; that God beseeches them to be reconciled through Jesus Christ, and that it is the duty of all men to believe the gospel and turn to God.

"The immersed believers are congregated into societies according to their nearness to each other, and taught to meet every first day of the week in honor and commemoration of the resurrection of Jesus, and to attend to the Lord's Supper, which commemorates the death of the Son of God, to read and hear the living oracles, to teach and admonish one another, to unite in all prayer and praise, to contribute to the necessities of saints, and to perfect holiness in the fear of the Lord.

"Every congregation chooses its own overseers and deacons, who preside over and administer the affairs of the congregations; and every church, either from itself, or in co-operation with others, sends out, as opportunity offers, one or more evangelists, or proclaimers of the word, to preach the word and to immerse those who believe, to gather congregations, and to extend the knowledge of salvation as far as their means extend. But every church regards these evangelists as its servants, and therefore they have no control over any congregation, each church being subject to its own choice of presidents or elders, whom they have appointed. Perseverance in all the work of faith, labor of love, and patience of hope, is inculcated by all the Disciples, as essential to admission into the heavenly kingdom.

"Such are the prominent outlines of the faith and prac tice of those who wish to be known as the disciples of Christ; but no society among them would agree to make the preceding items either a confession of faith or a standard of practice; but, for the information of those who wish an acquaintance with them, are willing to give at any time a reason for their faith, hope, and practice.

"On the design of baptism, and the benefits resulting from this ordinance to the penitent believer through the blood of Christ, the Disciples have been greatly minunderstood. That the blood of Jesus is the only procuring cause of the remission of sins, is believed by every Disciple. Baptism, they teach, is designed to introduce the subjects of it into the participation of the blessings of the death and resurrection of Christ, who died for our sins, and rose again for our justification. But it has no abstract efficacy. Without previous faith in the blood of Christ, and deep and unfeigned repentance before God, neither immersion in water nor any other action can secure to us the blessings of peace and pardon. It can merit nothing. Still to the believing penitent it is the *means* of receiving a formal, distinct, and specific absolution, or release from guilt. Therefore none but those who have first believed in Christ and repented of their sins, and that have been intelligently immersed into his death, have the full and explicit testimony of God, assuring them of pardon. In reference to generation the Disciples teach that an individual who is first begotten of God, whose heart is imbued with the word of God, is enabled to enjoy the life thus bestowed when immersed into Christ, as it gives him an introduction to the happiness and society of the pardoned and the spiritual. Baptism, succeeding faith and repentance, consummates regeneration. The new birth as a change of state, is a formal ingress of a penitent believer, a prior spiritual creation, into the family and kingdom of our Lord Jesus Christ. Formed for a new state by faith and repentance, he enjoys its heavenly adaptations the moment he enters the kingdom by being baptized in the name of Christ. The waters of baptism in connection with the death of Jesus, afford him as great an assurance of safety, as did their type, the waters of the Red Sea, to the redeemed Israelites, when they engulphed Pharaoh and his hosts. Thus are we taught that penitent believers are born the children of God by baptism — that salvation is connected with baptism when accompanied by faith — that remission of sins is to be enjoyed by baptism through the blood of Christ — that persons, having previously believed and repented, wash away their sins in baptism, calling on the name of the Lord — that they profess to be dead to sin and alive to God in the action of baptism—that believers put on Christ when baptized into Christ — that the church is cleansed by baptism and belief of the Word of God — that men are saved by baptism in connection with the renewing of the Holy Spirit—and that the answer of a good conscience is obtained in baptism through the resurrection of Christ.

"As the Disciples endeavor to call Bible things by Bible names, they have repudiated all words and phrases in respect to Father, Son, and Holy Spirit, not sanctioned by divine usage. Never employing such terms as 'trinity,' 'eternal generation,' 'eternal filiation,' 'eternally begotten,' 'eternal procession,' 'co-essential and consubstantial,' and all others of the same category, they have sometimes been denominated, but most unjustly so, Unitarians. They believe that Christ is absolutely divine, infinitely above any super-human or even super-angelic being. They believe Christ to be 'God' *in nature*, and not *in office* only, or because he is invested with divine prerogatives, as Moses is said to have been made 'a god unto Pharaoh,'' and as the magistrates of Israel are called 'gods,' as being engaged in administering divine laws."

BAPTISTS—MINOR DENOMINATIONS.

UNDER this head it is proposed to place in a group several denominations of Baptists that are less important than those before mentioned, because fewer in their numbers.

SEVENTH-DAY BAPTISTS.

" The terms Sabbatarian and Seventh-day Baptists are used to designate those Christians who observe the seventh or last day of the week as the Sabbath. The former term was adopted in England soon after the Reformation, when the word Sabbath was applied exclusively to the seventh day, and when those who observed that day were regarded as the only true Sabbath-keepers, or Sabbatarians. In the year 1818, this term was rejected by the General Conference in America, on account of its supposed indefiniteness; and the term Seventh-day Baptist was adopted in its stead, as more descriptive of the opinions and practices of the people.

"The Seventh-day Baptists are distinguished from Baptists generally by the views which they entertain of the Sabbath. In respect to this, they believe that the seventh day of the week was sanctified and blessed for the Sabbath in Paradise, and was designed for all mankind; that it forms a necessary part of the Ten Commandments, which are immutable in their nature, and universally binding; that no change as to the day of the Sabbath was made by divine authority at the introduction of Christianity; that those passages in the New Testament which speak of the first day of the week, do not imply either the substitution of that day for the seventh as the Sabbath, or its appointment as a day of religious worship; that whatever respect the early Christians paid to the first day of the week, on the supposition of its being the day of Christ's resurrection, yet they never regarded it as the Sabbath, but continued to observe the seventh day in that character until, by edicts of emperors and the decrees of councils, the first day was made gradually to supersede it.

"At what precise time the observers of the seventh day took a denominational form, it is not easy to say. According to Ross's 'Picture of all Religions,' they appeared in Germany late in the fifteenth or early in the sixteenth century. According to Dr. Chambers, they arose in England in the sixteenth century. Assuming the beginning of the sixteenth century as the true period of their origin, would carry them back as far as any of the modern denominations of Christians date. But whatever difficulty there may be in fixing the precise time of their origin as a denomination, the Seventh-day Baptists think there is no difficulty in proving the antiquity of their sentiments. Indeed, they believe that there has been no period since the commencement of the Christian era, when there were not upon the earth more or less Christians observing the seventh day.

"They hold, in common with other Christians, the distinguishing doctrines of Christianity. There were lately two congregations of the Sabbatarians in London; one among the General Baptists, meeting in Mill Yard, the trust-deeds of which date as far back as 1678, but which is now greatly reduced in number; the other among the Particular Baptists, in Cripplegate. There are also a few to be found in different parts of the kingdom.

"The Seventh-day Baptists in America date from about the same period that their brethren in England began to organize regular churches. Mr. Stephen Mumford was one of the earliest among them. He came from England to Newport, R. I., in 1665, and 'brought with him the opinion, that the Ten Commandments, as they were delivered from Mount Sinai, were moral and immutable, and that it was an anti-Christian power which changed the Sabbath from the seventh to the first day of the week.' He joined the First-day Baptist church in Newport, and soon won several members of that church to his views. They continued to walk with the church, however, for a time, until a difficulty arose in consequence of the hard things which were said of them by their brethren, such as, that the Ten Commandments, being given to the Jews, were not binding upon the Gentiles, and that those who observed the seventh day were gone from Christ to Moses. In November, 1671, they came to an open separation, when Stephen Mumford, William Hiscox, Samuel Hubbard, Roger Baster, and three sisters, entered into church covenant together, thus forming the first Seventh-day Baptist church in America. William Hiscox was chosen and ordained their pastor, which office he filled until his death, in 1704, in the 66th year of his age. He was succeeded by William Gibson, a minister from London, who continued to labor among them until he died, in 1717, at the age of 79 years. Joseph Crandall had been his colleague for two years, and was selected to succeed him. When he died, in 1737, Joseph Maxson was chosen pastor, and discharged the duties of the office until 1743. He was followed by William Bliss, who served the church as pastor until his death, in 1808, at the age of 81 years. Henry Burdick succeeded him in the pastoral office, and occupied that post until a few years ago, when he died. Besides the regular pastors, this church has ordained several ministers, from time to time, who have labored with great usefulness, both at home and abroad. It has also included among its members several distinguished characters, two of whom, Richard and Samuel Ward, governors of the State of Rhode Island, are well known to history.

"For more than thirty years after its organization, the Newport church included nearly all persons observing the seventh day in the States of Rhode Island and Connecticut; and its pastors were accustomed to hold stated meetings at several distant places, for the better accommodation of the widely-scattered members. But in 1708, the brethren living in what was then called Westerly R. I., (comprehending all the south-western corner of the State,) thought best to form another society. Accordingly they proceeded to organize the Hopkinton church, which had a succession of worthy pastors, became very numerous, and built three meeting-houses for the accommodation of the members in the different neighborhoods. At present, there are seve[r] churches in Rhode Island, and one in Connecticut."

There are four Seventh-day Baptist churches in New Jersey, more than twenty in the State of New York, and many more of later origin scattered over the South and West.

It is now nearly a century and a half since a yearly meeting was established by this denomination in our country. A general conference was formed in 1800. The conference comprises four associations.

According to the Baptist Almanac for 1860, they have 70 ordained ministers, 10 licentiates, 56 churches, and 6577 communicants, and 4 associations.

EPHRATA SOCIETY OF SEVENTH-DAY BAPTISTS

The Ephrata Society arose out of a division of the Dunkers, in about 1730. They observe the seventh day as the Sabbath. They form a settlement near Lancaster, Pa., much on the plan of the old Moravian communities.

The Society was originated by Conrad Beissel, a native of Germany, and a Dunker. In 1725, he published a tract in defence of observing the seventh day as a holy time. This discussion attracted to his views several other Dunkers from the society at Mill Creek, Lancaster County. In 1728, they formally adopted the seventh day as the day for public worship. In 1732, they established a monastic society at Ephrata. They adopted the habit of the Capuchin friars. The men wear a shirt, trowsers, and vest, with a long white gown, and cowl. The dress of the sisters is the same, except that they wear petticoats in the place of trowsers, and a cowl of different shape. In 1740, there were in the cloister thirty-six single brethren and thirty-five sisters. No monastic vows were taken, and a community of goods was maintained. They consider celibacy a virtue, and favorable to eminent holiness, but do not prohibit marriage. They receive the Sacred Scriptures as the only rule of faith. They hold to the divinity of Christ, the doctrine of the Trinity, salvation by grace alone, the baptism of believers only, which they administer by trine immersion, with the laying on of hands, while the recipient remains kneeling in the water. Their numbers are greatly diminished, and are now inconsiderable.

MENNONITES.

Edwards, the Baptist historian, informs us that "some Mennonite families were in the province of Pennsylvania as early as the year 1692, who came hither from New York government, which at first belonged to the Dutch, and was called New Netherlands, extending from the river Delaware to the river of Connecticut. They settled in the neighborhood now called Germantown and Frankfort, &c. Other families soon followed; and after them many came directly from Europe, insomuch that May 23, 1708, there was a church settled at Germantown, consisting of 52 members, which exists to this day, (1770,) and is not only the first in the province, but, in some sort, the mother of all the rest. In about sixteen years after, this church had branched out to Skippeck, Conestoga, Great Swamp, and Monatony, and become five churches, to which appertained sixteen ministers, viz.: Rev. Messrs. Jacob Gottschalk, Henry Kolb, Martin Kolb, Cleas Johnson, Michael Zeigler, John Gorgas, John Concrads, Cleas Rittinghausen, Hans Burghaltzer, Christian Heer, Benedict Hirchy, Martin Beer, Johannes Bowman, Velter Clemer, Daniel Langaneckor, and Jacob Beghtly. The present (1770) state of the Mennonites in this province is as follows: 1st, their churches, which contain many branches, are 13; 2d, the meeting-houses belonging to them are 42; 3d, their or-

dained ministers or bishops are 15; 4th, their probationary
or licensed preachers are 53; 5th, the families are about
810, which, allowing five to a family, contain 4050 souls;
whereof 1448 persons are baptized and members of their
churches.   This account, I believe, is pretty exact, except
the county of Lancaster hath introduced any error into it;
for in that county I have not met with as much readiness
to give me the information I sought as in the other counties, owing, I believe, to a suspicion that a knowledge of
their state would, some way or other, be to their prejudice.

"The Mennonites, in common with other communities,
spread abroad in different directions.   They formed settlements, and now have congregations and churches in Virginia, Ohio, and Western New York, and the Canadas;
but they are the most numerous in the State where they
first planted their standard on the American soil.   This
remark holds true of both the old and new connection.

"The new connection of Mennonites was formed by a
seceding party from the old body, in 1811.   Connected
with it are about 700 members in Pennsylvania, from 150
to 200 in New York, about 200 in Upper Canada, and
small detachments of them are found in Maryland, Ohio,
Indiana, &c.   The cause of the separation was purely on
the principles of experimental religion, which the new
interest sought to inculcate and maintain, in the spirit as
well as the letter, according to the pattern set them by
Menno Simon and his associates.   They complain that the
old body 'have deviated from time to time and fallen
away, particularly in the spiritual part of religion — have
become lukewarm and carnally-minded, seeking transitory
things more than spiritual, holding more to the letter and
outward form, than to the spirit and real substance of
religion.'

"The Mennonites in the old world, for ages past, have

14   L

as a general thing, administered Laptism by pouring and laying on of hands; and the same is true of them in this country, both of the old and new connection; they are, however, the decided opponents of infant baptism in all its forms." The Mennonites have now 300 churches, 250 ministers, and 36,280 communicants, as reported in the Baptist Almanac for 1860.

TUNKERS OR DUNKERS.

" The first appearing of these people in America was in the fall of the year 1719, when about twenty families landed in Philadelphia, and dispersed themselves, some to Germantown, some to Skippeck, some to Oley, some to Conestoga, and elsewhere. This dispersion incapacitated them to meet for public worship, and therefore they began to grow lukewarm in religion. But in the year 1722, Messrs. Baker, Gomery, Gantz, and the Trautes, visited their scattered brethren, which was attended with a great revival, insomuch that societies were formed wherever a number of families were within reach one of another. But this lasted not above three years. They settled on their lees again, till about thirty families more of their perse-cuted brethren arrived in the fall of the year 1729, which both quickened them again and increased their number everywhere. These two companies had been members of one and the same church, which originated at Schwardze-nau, in the year 1708. The first constituents were Alex ander Mack and wife, John Kipin and wife, George Grevy, Andreas Bloney, Lucas Fetter, and Joanna Nethigeim. These had been bred Presbyterians, except Kipin, who was a Lutheran; and being neighbors, they consorted together to read the Bible, and edify one another in the way they had been brought up, for as yet they did not know there were any Baptists in the world. However, believers' bap-

tism and a congregational church soon gained upon them,
insomuch that they had determined to obey the gospel in
these matters.   They desired Alexander Mack to baptize
them; but he, deeming himself in reality unbaptized, refused; upon which they cast lots to find who should be
administrator.   On whom the lot fell hath been carefully
concealed.   However, baptized they were in the river
Eder, by Schwardzenau. and then formed themselves into
a church, choosing Alexander Mack to be their minister.
They increased fast, and began to spread their branches to
Merienborn and Epstein, having John Naass and Christian
Levy to their ministers in those places.   But persecution
quickly drove them thence, some to Holland and some to
Creyfelt.   Soon after, the mother church voluntarily removed from Schwardzenau to Serustervin, in Friezland,
and from thence migrated towards America, in 1719; and
in 1729, those of Creyfelt and Holland followed their
brethren.

"Thus we see that all the Tunker churches in America
sprang from the church at Schwardzenau, in Germany;
that that church began in 1708, with only seven souls, and
that in a place where no Baptist had been in the memory
of man, nor any now are.   In sixty-two years that *little
one became a thousand, and that small one a great nation.*"

One of their body, in a letter to Benedict, says of their
doctrinal views, that "they have been charged with holding the sentiments of the *Universalists*, which they all
deny, and often testify against them."

"This statement, I suppose, refers to the no-future-pun-
ishment system, as he admits that by some of this community 'the writings and reasonings of Elhanan Winchester
have been well received.'   He also mentions a schism in
this body in 1790, when a party of decided Universalists
drew off under the ministry of one John Ham, a man of

great talents and popular address.   Some of his followers afterward moved into the Green River country, Ky., and caused great confusion among the brotherhood there as well as in North Carolina, where Ham himself lived at the time of the division.   'Those who have imbibed his opinions are thought to be in union and fellowship with the German Baptist Brethren, which has not been the case since the Yearly Meeting which was held in Franklin County, Virginia, fifty years ago, or upwards.'

"This class of Tunkers, at present, reside in Kentucky, in the southern part of Illinois, in Missouri, and Iowa.

"Summary statement of the Tunkers: Congregations and churches, 500; ministers of all grades, about 2000; communicants, 100,000.

CHRISTIANS.

This denomination call themselves Christians; but as the name does not distinguish them from other Christians, and as the public must have a distinguishing appellation, the first part of the name is commonly pronounced as we pronounce the word Christ, when written by itself.   Hence they are commonly called Christ-ians.   One of their own writers gives the following account of their origin:

"About fifty years ago, several Methodist preachers in the State of Virginia and in the Carolinas, became dissatisfied with the discipline of that church, and withdrew. They then agreed to search the Scriptures for a rule of life, and to believe, preach, and walk as they should direct. The result was, they soon became agreed that Christian was the appropriate name for all the followers of Christ, as all true believers hold; and that while others go farther, and take some sectarian name of human origin, they ought not, and would not, receive or use among themselves any other   By thus searching the Scriptures for a rule, they became satisfied that as that book contained the whole of the rule of duty and faith, so no other was necessary ; and all others, if authoritative, served to divide and lead astray. Here they settled down upon the broad plan of the name all believers take—Christian ; and the rule they all acknowledge—*the Bible*.

"A few years after this, several ministers of the Presbyterian order, in the State of Kentucky, broke off from that body because of the government under which it acted ; and several of their usages appeared to them both unscriptural and oppressive. This act threw them upon the Bible, as the like act had thrown the seceders from the Methodists in Virginia ; and with the same result—for they soon agreed to be nothing but Christians, and to have no discipline or rule but the Bible.

"About the same time, a few ministers in New England, who had been connected with the Baptists, were led to see that human creeds were both useless and hurtful, and, in relinquishing these, they too were thrown upon the Bible alone. As they found there none of their names but Christian, and none of the modern denominational titles, they also soon agreed on that name, and on the Bible as their only rule of faith and practice.

"Here, then, were three companies in the United States, all agreeing in these two points. But they were strangers to each other, and even to the fact that such companies existed. But in a few years each learned that others existed, and by means of letters, and a periodical which was soon commenced among the New England Christians, a correspondence was opened, and a union created, so that the three became one, and have to this day been known as the 'Christian Connection in the United States of America.'

"They are Unitarians in doctrine, and Baptists both in respect to the mode and the subjects of baptism.

"The education of many of the ministers of the connection, who universally preach extempore, is defective. Their maxim has been, 'Let him who understands the gospel teach it;' yet the sentiment is fast gaining ground among them, that literature and science are very useful auxiliaries in the illustration and enforcement of divine truth; and a charter was obtained, in 1832, from the legislature of Indiana, for a Christian College, to be located in New Albany.

"They are Independents in Church polity, yet represented in associations composed of ministers and laymen, after the manner of presbyteries and synods, but without judicial authority. For the purpose of promoting the general interest and prosperity of the connection by mutual efforts and joint counsels, associations were formed, denominated conferences. Ministers and churches, represented by delegates, formed themselves, in each State, into one or more conferences, called State Conferences, and delegates from these conferences formed the United States General Christian Conference. This general conference has been given up. The local or State conferences are still continued, possessing, however, no authority or control over the independence of the churches.

"They number 40 associations, or conferences, 1100 ministers, 1200 churches, and 80,000 communicants."

SIX PRINCIPLE BAPTISTS.

"The appellation of Six Principle Baptists is applied at the present time to a few churches in Rhode Island and a few other States, who, grounding their belief on Heb. vi. 1–3, make the imposition of hands on all newly baptized members an indispensable pre-requisite to church fellow-

ship and communion.   As the people of this sentiment
were among the first settlers in the State, where most of
them now reside, the *Old Baptists* is a term very commonly
applied to them, to distinguish them from their brethren
of less rigid views on the rite in question.   For a long
time after the settlement of Rhode Island, the Baptist
brotherhood who carry out to the letter the *six principles*
laid down by the apostle Paul to the converted Hebrews,
had a controlling influence in Baptist affairs in the State;
but some of their churches have become extinct, and others
have ceased to maintain on this point the sentiments of
their progenitors; and the *Orthodox, Free Will*, and other
classes of Baptists occupy a large portion of the ground
where the *old order* formerly almost exclusively prevailed.

"They have twenty churches, twenty-two ministers,
and 3500 communicants."

WINEBRENNARIANS.

This is a small denomination of Baptists, which received
its origin from the Rev. John Winebrenner, of Harrisburg,
Pa., in 1830.   They assumed to themselves the name of
THE CHURCH OF GOD.   It is certainly allowed to every
religious body to assume whatever name they choose in our
free and happy country.   If such name should not distinguish them from others, no great evil can arise from that
circumstance, inasmuch as the right of others is equally
perfect to bestow a name upon them by which they shall
be really distinguished.

The Winebrennarian Baptist Church was organized in
1830; and, through a fervent zeal in preaching the gospel,
has secured a very considerable degree of success.   They
reject creeds and are Arminians in doctrine.   They reject
infant baptism, and practise immersion, and the literal
washing of the saints' feet as an appointed ordinance.

They hold that domestic slavery and civil war are sinful, and believe in the personal reign of Christ. In ecclesiastical government they are Presbyterian. They number at the present time 132 ministers, 275 churches, and 13,800 communicants, existing in three presbyteries, which they term elderships.

UNITARIANS.

UNITARIANS take their name from that point of belief whereon they first diverged from the generally held views of Christians. Their fundamental principle may be stated to be the trustworthiness of the human faculties, and their competency, when duly trained and freed from prejudice, to receive moral and religious, no less than scientific, truths. In pursuance of this principle, they have carried to the farthest point yet reached by any denomination the Protestant belief in the right of private judgment and reverence for the individual conscience. They do not hesitate to bring all theological systems and the sacred writings of both Jews and Christians to this test. What does the best instructed reason, the clearest ascertained science, and the most enlightened conscience decide upon them? Believing truth to be infinite, they have always declined to lay down any set of dogmas which should pretend to include it all, or to make a belief in special dogmas a test of fellowship. A very wide range of individual opinion is hence included in this body, it having always been its cardinal doctrine that unity of spirit and aim should take precedence of unity of thought. There is, however, a general similarity of conclusion arrived at by this free action of mind upon religious thought, of which the following is an outline: (1.) A belief in a supreme God of unchanging goodness and wisdom, whose will and attributes are made known to us in the universal order of things so far as we can understand it, in human experience so far as it has been transmitted to us, and in our own reason and conscience so far as we will examine them. (2.) A grateful recognition of Jesus as the Founder of the Christian religion, and the great Leader and Inspirer of all who seek to lead a holy life, with a growing tendency to see in him this entire and perfect humanity. (3.) A persuasion that man's highest duty is to live in love toward his fellow-man, and in perfect fidelity to those convictions of truth which he has attained. (4.) A belief that the moral order which reigns here reigns throughout the universe, eternally rewarding all right action and purpose, and eternally overthrowing and punishing all wrong action and purpose.

In this country, the divergence of many of the Congregational churches of New England from the older standards toward this type came into notice about a century ago. Among a people so interested in theology as New Englanders then were, earnest discussion was at once provoked, and it was finally found that about a third of the churches held these views. New England, especially Massachusetts, still remains the centre of this form of faith, though single churches are found in almost all the large cities of the North and West. Statistics give a total of 330 churches and about 400 ministers. There are also two Divinity schools, one at Cambridge, Massachusetts, the other at Meadville, Pennsylvania. The two principal organizations connected with this body are the American Unitarian Association and the National Conference of Unitarian and other Christian Churches. There are published in the denomination Old and New, a monthly magazine; The Religious Magazine, also monthly; The Christian Register and Liberal Christian, weekly, and The S. School Gazette, bi-monthly.

UNIVERSALISTS.

THERE are two classes of Christians that have passed under this general name — Universalists, so called, and Restorationists. They were formerly reckoned one.

The Restorationists held the doctrine of punishment in the future state, but maintained that all mankind would be ultimately restored.

The other class, which embraces but few of either clergy or laity, maintain that every human being, on dying, passes immediately into a state of eternal happiness. They are Unitarians in doctrine; and allege that sin brings its own punishment, and consequently that to punish men in a future state would be unjust. The early Universalists in this country were Restorationists. Of this class was Dr. Benneville, of Germantown, Pa., and Rev'd John Murray, who came hither from England in 1770.

In 1780, Rev. Elhanan Winchester, a Baptist preacher, embraced the doctrine of Universalism. About ten years subsequent to this, the Rev. Hosea Ballou embraced the same doctrine, but on the principles first described in this article. He may be properly regarded as the founder of the Church in the United States.

The Universalist Expositor gives the following statistics of the denomination:

" The ministry of the Universalist denomination in the United States hitherto has been provided for, not so much by the means of schools, as by the unaided but irresistible influence of the gospel of Christ. This has furnished the denomination with its most successful preachers. It has turned them from other sects and doctrines, and brought them out from forests and fields, and from secular pursuits of almost every kind, and driven them, with inadequate literary preparation, to the work of disseminating the truth. This state of things has been unavoidable, and the effect of it is visible. It has made the ministry of the Universalist denomination very different from that of any other sect in the country; studious of the Scriptures, confident in the truth of their distinguishing doctrine, zealous, firm, industrious : depending more on the truths communicated for their success, than on the manner in which they were stated. It has had the effect, too, to give the ministry a polemic character,—the natural result of unwavering faith in the doctrine believed, and of an introduction into the desk without scholastic training. But the attention of the denomination in various parts of the country has of late been turned to the education of the ministry; and conventions and associations have adopted resolves, requiring candidates to pass examinations in certain branches of literature. The same motives have governed many in their effort to establish literary and theological institutions."

They have recently engaged quite earnestly in this work, and have now several flourishing literary institutions under their superintendence. Among these are Tuft's College, Medford, Mass., Dean Academy, Franklin, Mass., Westbrook Seminary, Westbrook, Maine, Green Mountain Institute, Barre, Vt., St. Lawrence University, Canton, N. Y., Clinton Liberal Institute, Clinton, N. Y., Lombard University, Galesburg, Ill., and six or seven others.

In 1779, the first Universalist Society was organized at Gloucester, Mass. There are now 917 societies professing this faith.

In 1799, the General Convention (organized in 1785) was the only association of the clergy. There are now

the General Convention of the United States, 13 state
conventions, and more than 70 associations.

The first Universalist newspaper in the United States
(the "Universalist Magazine") was commenced in Boston,
July 3, 1819, with less than one thousand subscribers.
There are now 17 periodicals of this description, with an
aggregate list of about 30,000 subscribers.

We have not been able to find any reliable account of the
number of communicants. They have accommodations for
205,462 worshippers, and about $2,000,000 worth of church
property.

In 1864 the Convention passed resolutions sustaining
the government in the war for the Union, condemning
oppression, and remonstrating against any concession to
traitors, and any movement or adjustment which might
put our colored soldiers at the mercy of their old masters.
During the two years, 1864 and 1865, it was stated that
the denomination had raised over half a million dollars
for educational purposes. At the Convention of 1865 a
Board of Missions was elected, and it was resolved to
raise one hundred thousand dollars for their use. In
1866 the Convention met at Galesburg, Illinois, when it
was reported that but seventeen thousand dollars of this
amount had been raised. Stringent resolutions against
the policy of the President, and in favor of impartial
suffrage, were adopted. Resolutions of sympathy with
Unitarians, and offering to unite with them in any way
practicable in the Christianizing of the world, were
adopted by a large majority. In the Convention of the
following year, this action was qualified, if not virtually
rescinded, by a resolution affirming the divine authority
of Scripture and the Lordship of Christ, as tests of
church membership. Only one person voted in the negative. A Universalist preacher in Boston, who had had

trouble with his congregation on account of the extreme Unitarian views which he preached, was refused admission to the Convention by a vote of 95 to 16. At this Convention, it was again resolved to raise one hundred thousand dollars for denominational purposes. The Convention received an act of incorporation, March 9, 1866. In 1868 resolutions were adopted recognizing a call for a general spiritual awakening and recommending conference and prayer meetings, wherever practicable. In 1869 two new State Conventions, those of Missouri and Kansas, were recognized and admitted by their delegates into the General Convention, and arrangements were perfected for a very earnest demonstration in behalf of all the interests of the body during the following year, which was the centenary of the establishment of Universalism as an organized church in America.

The Register for 1871 says that the preceding or centenary year was one of unprecedented activity throughout the denomination. The proposed Murray Centenary, Fund of two hundred thousand dollars was nearly all raised. The income only is to be used and applied to aid theological students, in the distribution of denominational literature, and in church extension.

Statistics of 1870: 74 associations, 917 parishes, 692 meeting-houses, 625 ministers, 36 new churches built, 18 installations, including one woman, 28 ordinations, contributed or pledged for benevolent enterprises, beside the Murray Fund and ordinary parish expenses, nine hundred thousand dollars. Three colleges are in operation, and three more are projected. There are two divinity schools and one law school, with seven academies. These institutions own property and funds to the amount of $1,832,000.

The denomination has 5 weekly papers, and 8 monthly,

15 *

quarterly, and semi-monthly periodicals. The number of the membership is not given. The Register claims it as "ground for just pride and congratulation that we are dealing with living forces, not with fossils and petrifactions capable of exact enumeration and classification." It also specifies "the better education of our ministers, the improving tone of spiritual culture among our people, the multiplying and strengthening of our religious, educational and benevolent institutions" as exhibited by the record of the preceding year. These evidences of prosperity will strike the public more forcibly, when the rolls of a large and permanent membership can be made out and the results spread before the eye.

SWEDENBORGIANS.

THE Swedenborgians are so called from the late Hon. Emanuel Swedenborg, son of Jasper Swedenborg, bishop of West-Gothia. He was born at Stockholm, in the year 1689; and died in London, 1772.

He early enjoyed all the advantages of a liberal education, having studied with great attention in the academy of Upsal, and in the universities of England, Holland, France, and Germany. Endued with uncommon talents for the acquirement of learning, his progress in the sciences was rapid and extensive; and, at an early period in life, he distinguished himself by various publications on philosophical subjects.

His philosophic studies led him to refer natural phenomena to spiritual agency, and to suppose that there is a close connection between the two worlds of matter and spirit. Hence his system teaches us to consider all the visible universe, with everything that it contains, as a theatre and representation of the invisible world, from which it first derived its existence, and by connection with which it continually subsists.

Swedenborg's extraordinary genius and learning, accompanied with the purity of his life and uprightness of his character, attracted the public notice. Hence he received various literary and political honors. These, however, he considered of small importance, compared with the distinguished privilege of having, as he supposed, his spiritual sight opened, and conversing with spirits and angels in the spiritual world.

He first began to have his revelation in London. He asserted that, on a certain night, a man appeared to him in the midst of a strong shining light, and said, "I am God, the Lord, the Creator, and Redeemer; I have chosen thee to explain to men the interior and spiritual sense of the sacred writings. I will dictate to thee what thou oughtest to write." He affirmed that, after this period, his spiritual sight was opened so far that he could see, in the most clear and distinct manner, what passed in the spiritual world, and converse with angels and spirits in the same manner as with men. Accordingly, in his "Treatise concerning Heaven and Hell," he relates the wonders which he saw in the invisible worlds, and gives an account of various and heretofore unknown particulars, relating to the peace, the happiness, the light, the order of heaven, together with the forms, the functions, the habitations, and even the garments of the heavenly inhabitants. He relates his conversations with angels, and describes the condition of Jews, Mahometans, Christians, clergymen of every denomination, laity, &c., in the other world.

Swedenborg called the doctrines which he delivered, "The Heavenly Doctrines of the New Jerusalem." It is thus styled, for, according to his system, the New Jerusalem signifies the new church upon earth, which is now about to be established by the Lord, and which is particularly described, as to its glory and excellency, in Rev. xxi., and many other parts of the sacred word.

The holy city, or New Jerusalem, he interpreted as descriptive of a new dispensation of heavenly truth, breaking through and dissipating the darkness which at this day prevails on earth. The laws of divine order, and the economy of God's kingdom, providence, and operation, will be more clearly and fully understood, and the hearts of men will thus be opened to a nearer intercourse with heaven, and rendered admissive of the purer influences of gospel love and charity in their lives and conversation.

The following extract contains the general outlines of Swedenborg's theological system:

First. That the Sacred Scripture contains three distinct senses, called *celestial*, *spiritual*, and *natural;* and that, in each sense, it is divine truth, accommodated respectively to the angels of the three heavens, and also to men on earth.

2dly. That there is a correspondence between all things in heaven and all things in man; and that this science of correspondences is a key to the spiritual or internal sense of the Sacred Scriptures, every page of which is written by correspondences, that is, by such things in the natural world as correspond unto and signify things in the spiritual world.

3dly. That there is a divine trinity of Father, Son, and Holy Ghost, or, in other words, of the all-begetting Divinity, (*Divinum a quo*) the divine human, and the divine proceeding or operation; and that this trinity consisteth not of three distinct persons, but is united, as body, soul, and operation in man, in the one person of the Lord Jesus Christ, who, therefore, is the God of heaven, and alone to be worshipped, being Creator from eternity, Redeemer in time, and Regenerator to eternity.

4thly. That redemption consisteth not in the vicarious sacrifice of the Redeemer, and an atonement to appease the Divine wrath, but in a real subjugation of the powers of darkness; in a restoration of order and good government in the spiritual world: in checking the overgrown influences of wicked spirits on the souls of men, and opening a nearer and clearer communication with the heavenly and angelic powers; in making salvation, which is regeneration, possible for all, who believe on the incarnate God, and keep his commandments.

5thly. That there is an universal *influx* from God into the souls of men. The soul, upon receiving this influx from God, transmits it, through the perceptive faculties of the mind, to the body. The Lord, with all his divine wisdom, consequently with all the essence of faith and charity, entereth by influx into every man, but is received by every man according to his state and form. Hence it is that good *influxes* from God are changed, by the evil nature of their recipients, into their opposites, good into evil, and truth into falsehood.

6thly. That we are placed in this world, subject to the influences of two most opposite principles; of good from the Lord and his holy angels; of evil from hell or evil spirits. While we live in this world, our spirits have their abode in the spiritual world, where we are kept in a kind of spiritual equilibrium by the continual action of those contrary powers, in consequence of which, we are at perfect liberty to turn to which we please. That, without this *free will* in spiritual things, regeneration cannot be effected. If we submit to God we receive real life from him; if not, we receive that life from hell, which is called in Scripture, *spiritual death.*

7thly. That heaven and hell are not arbitrary appointments of God. Heaven is a state arising from the good affections of the heart, and a correspondence of the words and actions, grounded on sincere love to God and man, and hell is the necessary consequence of an evil and thoughtless life, enslaved by the vile affections of self-love and love of the world without being brought under the regulations of heavenly love by a right submission of the will, the understanding, and actions, to the truth and spirit of heaven.

8thly. That there is an intermediate state for departed souls which is called *the world of spirits*, and that very few pass directly to heaven or hell. This is a state of purification to the good; but to bad spirits it is a state of separation of all the extraneous good from the radical evil which constitutes the essence of their natures.

9thly. That, throughout heaven, such as are of like dispositions and qualities are consociated into particular fellowships; and such as differ in these respects are separated, so that every society in heaven consists of similar members.

10thly. That man, immediately on his decease, rises again in a spiritual body, which was inclosed in his material body; and that, in this spiritual body, he lives as a man to eternity, either in heaven, or in hell, according to the quality of his past life.

11thly. That those passages in the Sacred Scripture generally supposed to signify the destruction of the world by fire, &c., commonly called the *last judgment*, must be understood according to the above-mentioned science of correspondences, which teaches, that by the end of the world or consummation of the age, is not signified the destruction of the world, but the end or consummation of the present Christian church, both among Roman Catholics and Protestants of every description and denomination.

That this consummation, which consists in the total falsification of the Divine truth, and adulteration of the Divine good of the word, has actually taken place; and, together with the establishment of a new church, in place of the former, is described in the Revelations, in the internal sense of that book; in which the new church is meant, as to its internals, by the new heaven, and as to its externals, by the new earth; also, by the *New Jerusalem descending by God out of heaven.*

It is one of the leading doctrines of Swedenborg, in his explanation of the other books of Scripture, that one of the principal uses for which the Word is given, is that it might be a medium of communication between the Lord and man; also, that earth might be thereby conjoined with heaven, or human minds with angelic minds; which is effected by correspondences, and natural things with spiritual, according to which the Word is written; and that, in order to its being divine (*divinum verum in ultimo*), it could not be written otherwise. That hence, in many parts of the letter, the Word is clothed with appearances of truths accommodated to the apprehension of the simple and unlearned; as, when evil passions are attributed to the Lord, and where it is said, that he withholdeth his mercy from man, forsakes him, casts him into hell, doeth evil, &c.; whereas such things do not at all belong to the Lord, but are so said, in the same manner as we speak of the sun's rising and setting, and other natural phenomena, according to the appearance of things, or as they appear to the outward senses. To the taking up such appearances of truth from the letter of Scripture, and making this or that point of faith, derived from them, the essential of the church, instead of explaining them by doctrine drawn from the genuine truths, which, in other parts of the Word, are left naked, Swedenborg ascribes

the various dissensions and heresies which have arisen
in the church, and which, he says, could not be prevented, consistently with the preservation of man's free
agency, both with respect to the exertion of his will, and
of his understanding. But yet, he says, every one, in
whatever heresy he may be with respect to the understanding, may still be reformed and saved, provided *he
shuns evils as sins,* and does not confirm heretical tastes
in himself; for, by *shunning evils as sins,* the will is reformed, and by the will, the understanding, which then
first emerges out of darkness into light. That the word,
in its lowest sense, is thus made the medium of salvation
to those who are obedient to its precepts; while this sense
serves to guard its internal sanctities from being violated
by the wicked and profane, and is represented by the
cherubim placed at the gates of Eden, and the flaming
sword turning every way to guard the tree of life.

His doctrine respecting differences of opinion in the
church is summed up in these words: "There are three
essentials of the church: an acknowledgment of the Lord's
divinity; an acknowledgment of the holiness of the Word;
and the life, which is charity. Conformable to his life,
i. e. to his charity, is every man's *real faith.* From the
Word he hath the knowledge of what his life ought to be;
and from the Lord he hath reformation and salvation. If
these three had been held as essentials of the church, intellectual dissensions would not have divided it, but would
only have varied it, as the light varieth colors in beautiful
objects, and as various jewels constitute the beauty of a
kingly crown."

The moral doctrines of the New Jerusalem Church are
comprised under general heads, collected from Swedenborg's writings, and prefixed to some proposals, published

SWEDENBORGIANS. 181

in England, for the organization and establishment of a society.

Under those general heads, it is proposed to promote marriages upon the principles of the new church, which are, that true conjugal love consists in the most perfect and intimate union of minds, which constitutes one life, as the will and understanding are united in one. That this love exists only with those who are in states of regeneration. That, after the decease of conjugal partners of this description, they meet, and all the mere natural loves being separated, the mental union is perfected, and they are exalted into the wisdom and happiness of the angelic life.

Swedenborg founded his doctrines on the spiritual sense of the Word of God, which he declared was revealed to him immediately from the Lord out of heaven. As his language is peculiar, his reasoning cannot be abridged so as to be rendered intelligible to the generality of readers. Those who are desirous of farther information are referred to his numerous and singular productions.

Those who embrace the tenets of Swedenborg are numerous in England, Germany, Sweden, &c. Societies are also formed in different parts of Europe, for spreading his doctrines; and, where societies have not been formed, there are individuals who admire his writings and embrace his sentiments, particularly in England, France, Germany, Holland, Sweden, Russia, Poland, Turkey, and even in the East and West Indies, and America.

Their ecclesiastical order is a mixture of Presbyterianism and Congregationalism.

They practise baptism and the Lord's Supper, and use confirmation, the solemnization of matrimony, after the ordinary ceremony at church, and a burial service. They approximate to an independent form of church govern

16

ment, but their discipline is not yet definitely settled. No candidate for ordination can be admitted till after he has been baptized into the faith of the new church, the formula of which is—"I baptize thee into the name of the Lord Jesus Christ, who is Father, Son, and Holy Spirit."

The first person who introduced Swedenborgianism into this country was a Mr. Glen, who delivered lectures on the subject in Philadelphia, in 1784. The first American minister was ordained in 1798. Their increase has been slow.

There is a General Convention of the New Jerusalem Church in the United States, in which are represented associations in the States of Illinois, Maine, Maryland, Massachusetts, Pennsylvania, and Ohio, besides 4 isolated societies; and there are receivers of Swedenborg's doctrines scattered through all the other States. The number of ordaining ministers connected with the General Convention, is 6; pastors and missionaries, 29; licentiates and ministers, 14.

There are many societies not connected with the General Convention. There are probably not more than 15 or 20 church edifices belonging to this denomination in the United States, and the number of communicants probably does not exceed 10,000. The Journal of Proceedings of the General Convention furnishes no information as to the aggregate number of believers.

CONGREGATIONALISTS.

SCRIPTURAL Congregationalism denotes a system of self-governed local churches, each free and yet all in fellowship with each other. Each church is composed of regenerated men statedly meeting in one place, united by a covenant for the worship of God and for holy living in all things. The Bible is regarded by them as the only and sufficient rule of ecclesiastical order, as well as of faith. There is no legislative or judicial power above the local church. Each church has full power to choose its officers, to receive members, to exercise discipline, and to do all things required for the common welfare. Congregational churches, though thus free and self-governed, are not so disjoined as to be insulated elements, but are united to Christ in one common cause, are in sympathy and fellowship with each other, which is to be manifested in all appropriate ways—by exchange of members by letter, by regarding and sustaining the discipline of each other, by meeting in council as occasion may require, and, if necessary, by admonition and reproof. If any church becomes unsound in doctrine or scandalous or immoral in practice, and will not be reformed by admonition and council, the sound churches are to withdraw fellowship from the offending church.

On these principles were the apostolic churches organized, as is confessed by Mosheim, Gibbon, Barrow, and other eminent scholars of all denominations. These principles were in process of time suppressed by centralized and despotic organizations, though in every age some have held to them to some extent. But after the Reformation restored the study of the Bible they were once more fully developed and reduced to practice by the modern Congregational churches.

The freedom and self-government of the local churches were developed and reduced to practice by Robert Brown in 1586. But he did not as fully develop the fellowship of the churches as the scriptural ideal requires. Those who adopted his views were at first called Brownists. Others who more fully but not completely developed the fellowship of the churches, throwing off his name, were called Independents. In New England the name Independents was also rejected, and the fellowship of the churches was fully developed, and the name Congregationalist assumed in the Cambridge platform. For a time, in England, the name Independents was used to denote Congregationalists, but there also the name Congregationalist has superseded it, as may be seen in the Savoy declaration, and in the declaration of the Congregational Union of England and Wales.

Having given this general view of the use of names and the relations of Brownists, Independents, and Congregationalists, let us follow the course of historical development. Robert Brown became prominent among those who, in 1567, resisted the attempts of Queen Elizabeth of England to suppress, by forcible measures, the doctrines and assemblies of the Puritans. Brown contended that each church or society of Christians meeting in a single place was a body corporate, possessing full power within itself to admit or exclude members, to choose and ordain officers, and also to depose them, without being in any respect responsible to synods, councils, or any other ecclesiastical authority. He denied the supremacy of the queen in religious and ecclesiastical matters, he refused to admit that the established Church of England was a scriptural church, and asserted that the Scriptures were the only authoritative guide in matters of faith and discipline. He also held that the labors of a pastor should be confined to a single church, and that five orders or offices should be recognized in the Christian Church—namely, pastor, teacher, elder, deacon, and widow. He also asserted that the priesthood should not be regarded as a distinct order from the laity. Brown arrived at the conviction of all these doctrines, and publicly proclaimed them as a separate system of belief, in 1586.

As might have been naturally expected in such an age, and among such a community as England then was, the announcement of such opinions soon led to persecution. Brown was hooted in the streets, pelted with stones, and became the victim of general obloquy. Nevertheless, he persisted in his course, and succeeded in assembling and organizing the first church on independent principles known to exist in modern times. This fact only led to more violent persecution, and the members of his society were visited with fines, arrests, imprisonments, and in some instances with death, until at last the condition of the persecuted Puritans became intolerable. They accordingly resolved to escape, and fled in a body to Holland. Brown subsequently ventured to return to England, but he was unable to accomplish anything there, in consequence of the general outburst of persecution which overwhelmed him, not only from the fanatical mobs in the streets and in the community, but even from the pulpits and from the judicial bench.

In 1602 a second society called Independents or Congregationalists was formed in the north of England, of whom John Robinson was the pastor. By them the fellowship of the churches was more fully developed, especially in New England. Robinson was a man of strong mind and superior intelligence. Although he and his associates lived blamelessly in the world, merely worshipping God according to the dictates of their own consciences, yet they were soon surrounded and afflicted with the severest persecution. The whole power of the government and of the prelatical establishment was brought to bear upon them, and they soon found it necessary to seek repose and safety in flight. Mr. Robinson and his associates projected a plan of escape to Holland, but their purpose was frustrated by the treachery of the captain of the vessel which they had engaged. He happened to be a prelatist, and betrayed them to the authorities. They were imprisoned for a time, as a punishment for offences the nature of which was undefined and unknown.

Undaunted by these reverses, a portion of Robinson's followers made a second attempt to flee from the heavy hand of tyranny, which proved more successful. In the spring of 1608, Robinson, in company with Brewster, Bradford, Carver, Wilson, and other leading men, accompanied by their families, met at night on a lonely heath in Lincolnshire, intending to escape during the night. They had secretly hired a vessel for that purpose, and at the appointed time it appeared in the offing. The work of embarkation commenced, although the wind was high and the sea rough. Only a portion of the fugitives succeeded in getting on board before the remainder were surprised by a troop of horse, were arrested, and again conveyed to prison. But these, after the lapse of some time, were released, and eventually joined their friends, who had arrived in Holland and obtained a home and protection in Amsterdam.

In that city a society still existed which traced its origin to Robert Brown. The associates of Robinson united with it, and at first all went on harmoniously. But dissensions soon afterward broke out among them, and Robinson's friends removed to Leyden. Here they remained ten years. Some of these had been men of wealth, but they were at that time so impoverished, by not receiving their means from England, that they were reduced to the utmost indigence, and were compelled to learn mechanical trades. Brewster became a printer, and Bradford a silk dyer. During the period of their residence at Leyden these Congregationalists were exempted from persecution, and Robinson published several works, in which he set forth and defended the following points as constituting his belief:

1. That no church ought to consist of more numbers than can conveniently meet together for worship and discipline. 2. That the churches of Christ are to consist of those who believe in and obey Him. 3. That any competent number of such have the right, when conscience obliges them, to form themselves into a distinct and separate church. 4. That this incorporation must be effected by means of some contract or covenant, either expressed or implied. 5. That when thus incorporated they have full power and authority to choose their own officers. 6. That these officers should consist of pastors, or teaching elders, ruling elders, and deacons. 7. That the elders, though chosen and ordained, have no power to rule over the church, except by the consent of the brethren. 8. That all elders and churches are perfectly equal in their powers and privileges. 9. That baptism is to be administered to believers and their infant children. That the Lord's Supper is to be received sitting at the table, and is to be taken every Lord's Day. That ecclesiastical censures and penalties should be wholly spiritual, and not attended with temporal punishments.

10. That no holy days were to be observed, except the Sabbath, though occasional days of fasting and thanksgiving were to be recommended.

It was in 1617 that Robinson conceived the idea of removing to America. The tone of morals then prevalent in Holland was very corrupt, and the Puritans were fearful that their children might be contaminated by the surrounding influences. The New World was then an almost unknown wild, but perfect freedom and purity were the boons which tempted the adventurers to undertake the perilous voyage. They first selected Virginia as the spot to which their course should be directed. A committee was appointed to confer with the then existing Virginia Company, for the purpose of securing liberty and religious toleration within the limits of their jurisdiction. Although the company were sensible that the Puritans would be valuable colonists, and desired them to reside on their territory, they could not promise them absolute security, nor would the prelates of the Anglican Church promise them immunity from ecclesiastical interference, or perfect religious toleration. At length, however, the archbishop of London promised *"to connive"* at their presence and religious views in Virginia, and they resolved to set sail. In 1620 the preparations for their departure were completed. As their vessels could not convey all the members of the community, they were divided, and a portion of them embarked on board the *Mayflower*, while the remainder waited for the return of the vessel, to convey them on the second voyage. The emigrants were placed under the direction of Elder Brewster, while Robinson remained with the other party.

It was at Delft Haven that Robinson bestowed his blessing upon about a hundred persons previous to their embarkation, who constituted this extraordinary expedition. He died in 1625, before he and his associates could accomplish their intended voyage to America. Subsequently a few of them sailed for America, though the majority remained in Holland. The Mayflower reached Plymouth in safety, and the intrepid exiles disembarked upon a country which they were destined to render illustrious by their own virtues and those of their descendants. The second Congregational church established in the New World was that founded at Salem, on August 6, 1629. In 1630 another church was organized at Charlestown. On the 30th of July, in that year, the governor, deputy governor, and the minister, Mr. Wilson, entered into a "church covenant." Several days afterward, five others joined them. At a later period other accessions were made to the society, and they then elected Mr. Wilson as their pastor, and ordained him to that office. Emigrants continued to arrive from England who sympathized with the Congregationalists in their opinions, and thus churches continued to be gradually organized around the original settlers of Plymouth. In 1633, Mr. Cotton arrived from England, by whose means the scriptural plan of church government was developed, and generally adopted, which then received the name, and embodied the principles, of Congregationalism. In this the fellowship of the churches was first fully developed. In 1638 the Congregationalists resolved to become independent of the mother country in regard to the supply of ministers for their growing churches, and accordingly, in that year, they established Harvard College at Cambridge, which is the oldest literary institution in the United States.

The Congregationalist churches gradually extended over the New England colonies. In 1648 a synod was held, at which a system of church order was adopted which has since become widely known as the Cambridge Platform. It was in 1680 that a confession or creed which had been previously adopted by the English Congregational Churches was examined and approved by a synod assembled at Boston, and thus became the authoritative doctrinal declaration of the New England Congregationalists. It is held by these Congregationalists that there is no "Congregational Church" in this or in any country, in the sense in which the word "church" is applied to other sects, such as the Presbyterian Church, or Methodist Church. But there is a collection of Congregational churches in fellowship with each other who constitute the denomination. The Congregationalists define a church to be an organization of professed believers statedly meeting in one place, and united together by a covenant or agreement mutually to watch over and edify each other, and for the maintenance of the ordinances of the Gospel. A church, as thus understood, differs from a congregation, which includes all those who assemble in a place of worship, non-communicants as well as communicants. A church also differs from a "society," which is a legal phrase intended to represent those persons who are incorporated by the law of the land for the purpose of holding and transferring property, and providing for the expenses of the church. The church also differs from the "parish," which last is a term properly employed only to designate territorial limits.

Congregationalists insist upon the competence of each church to elect its own officers, to regulate its own affairs, to receive or reject candidates for membership, to pronounce censure upon any member who is guilty of impropriety, and that its allegiance in all these matters is due to Christ alone. In the administration of church affairs all the members have equal rights. Each male member of full age is entitled to vote on all questions appertaining to the interests of the society. The internal structure of Congregational societies is of the simplest nature. Their only officers are pastors and deacons, for the office of ruling elder was disused about the year 1745, first at Plymouth, and afterward in all the churches. The deacons are elected from and by the church members. The pastors are chosen by the members of the church from among those persons who are either already in the ministry, and settled over other churches, or are recommended by well-known clergymen as fit to assume the functions of the pastoral office. In electing a pastor, it is usual for the "church" to nominate a person to the "society," and, upon the concurrence of the latter, to give an invitation to the candidate to settle. Provision for the support of the pastor is made, either by a voluntary subscription, or a tax, or from the pew rents. When a pastor who is selected accepts the congregation tendered him, he is inducted into office by a council of ministers, being ordained by them if he has never before been set apart to the ministry; if otherwise, simply installed. Each church selects a clerk, who keeps their records, (and in some churches a committee appointed by the members examines candidates for admission, in connection with the pastors and deacons, and has a general superintendence over the interests of the church.) The pastor is the moderator of the church, the spiritual counsellor of its members, their authorized teacher, and has full control over the pulpit, administers the ordinances of baptism and the Lord's Supper, and performs the marriage ceremony. The deacons distribute the alms of the church, visit the sick and needy, and are the counsellors of the minister whenever he desires the benefit of their advice.

Congregationalists believe in the parity of the ministry,

and hold that there is but one order of ministers. The deacons they regard as belonging to the laity. Licentiates are not ministers, but merely candidates for the sacred office. Those ministers who are employed to preach to churches from one year to another, without being installed, are termed stated supplies. The terms bishop and elder are not often used by Congregationalists, but when they are employed, they are intended merely to represent the pastors. Excommunication is enforced as the penalty upon those who make themselves amenable to church discipline by irregularities of conduct.

The liturgy and form of worship of Congregationalists are simple. The ordinary service of the Sabbath consists of extemporaneous prayers, the singing of psalms and hymns, the reading of the Scriptures, and the delivery of a sermon either written or unwritten. Although they are careful to preserve their congregational independence, yet they endeavor to promote sympathy and unity of aims between their churches. Hence the pastors of neighboring churches frequently exchange pulpits, and meet in deliberative consociations, in which, though they have no legislative or judicial power or authority, they consult together, and suggest ways and means of mutual usefulness. The fellowship of the churches is also expressed in councils for the ordination or dismission of pastors, or for advice on questions of doctrine or practice. Such councils are commonly composed of the nearest churches, but if occasion calls for it, distant churches can be invited. Councils vary in size, being generally local, but on special occasions national. If a member of the church supposes himself aggrieved by church action, he has the right to request the church to summon a council of the pastors and deacons of neighboring churches, to examine into the facts of his case and recommend such action as may seem to them just. If they refuse, he has a right to call an *ex parte* council to give information and advice. In the Congregational system, the individual church is the source of all ecclesiastical authority; hence the action of councils is advisory, and cannot interfere with the free and absolute determination of the aggregate members of any church in reference to the control or decision of their own affairs.

The doctrines held by the Orthodox Congregationalists are the same in substance as those taught in the Confession of the Westminster Assembly of Divines which convened in 1643. They are Calvinistic, believing in absolute decrees in reference to man's salvation. They are Pædobaptists, holding to the right of infants to be baptized. They believe in man's total depravity by nature; in the trinity, atonement, regeneration, justification by faith, and in the eternity of future punishment for the finally impenitent. In 1750, Unitarian sentiments began to be diffused among the Congregationalists of New England. A public separation of such churches as espoused this system took place about the year 1815, but Unitarian churches everywhere still retain the Congregational form of church government. Harvard College is under their control, from the divinity school of which their candidates for the ministry are sent forth. But these churches are entirely distinct from the Orthodox Congregational churches, from which they originally sprung, and resemble them only in the form of their ecclesiastical government. Among the most eminent men whose names adorn the annals of Orthodox Congregationalism are those of Jonathan Edwards, Timothy Dwight, S. Hopkins and Joseph Bellamy. The denomination co-operates efficiently with all the benevolent enterprises of the American Church, such as the American Bible Society, American Board of Foreign Missions, Home Missions, etc. The denomination occupies a very prominent and eminent place for numbers, usefulness, and influence, among the various branches of the American Church. The Baptist churches are organized on Congregational principles, (see p. 37.) Adding to them all other churches Congregationally organized, we find in this country and England 25,000, and in this country more than one-half of all the churches of all names in the United States are Congregationally organized, so great has been the spread of Scripture principles of church order.

THE MORMONS.

THE Mormons, or Latter Day Saints, are a denomination of recent origin, having been founded by Joseph Smith within the present century. This remarkable man was born at Sharon, Windham County, Vermont, on the 23d of December, 1805. His father was a small farmer; and the first ten years of the life of the future prophet were spent at the place of his birth. In 1815 his parents removed to Palmyra, in the State of New York; and after a period of four years they again changed their abode to Manchester, in the same State. During this interval Joseph was employed in the various labors of agriculture; and his opportunities for literary culture were very limited. It was with difficulty that he could read, or write, or perform the simplest processes of arithmetic.

It was when he was about fifteen years of age that Smith seems to have received his first religious impressions. He professes to have then examined into the claims of the various existing denominations, and to have discovered such confusion and contradiction among them, that he turned from all of them in disgust. Then it was that he determined to put in practice the advice of St. James: "If any man lack wisdom, let him ask of God, who giveth to all men liberally and upbraideth not, and it shall be given him." Accordingly he retired to a secret place in a grove, and began to call upon the Lord. He declares that he was then favored with a heavenly vision; that

he saw two glorious personages, who resembled each
other in form and feature, and were surrounded by a
light brighter than that of the sun; that they informed
him that all the existing sects were in error, and had
wandered from the truth; and that they promised to
reveal to him, at some future day, the Gospel of Truth
in all its fulness, which he should afterward proclaim
with great success throughout the world. He was also
assured that he was the chosen instrument in introducing this new dispensation; and he was furnished
with mysterious information in reference to the Abori-
ginal inhabitants of this country.

Smith alleged that the promise of a second vision
was fulfilled in September, 1823; and that while praying, a personage appeared to him who proclaimed himself the angel and messenger of God, and informed
Smith where there were deposited a number of golden
plates, upon which were written the records of the
early inhabitants of this country, and which narrated
how our Saviour, after his resurrection, made his appearance on this continent, and established here his
true religion, with the various orders of priests, prophets, and teachers; how the people were all cut off in
consequence of their sins, and the last of their prophets
had been commanded to write on those plates a narrative of those events, and bury them, that they might
afterward be found, and used in the latter days for the
establishment and universal diffusion of the true religion in the chosen time.

These plates Smith alleged that he afterward obtained, and that they contain the volume known as the
"Book of Mormon." A very different account of the
origin of this remarkable production is given by another
person, whose testimony is regarded by many as un-

biased and true. It is asserted that the Book of Mormon is a religious romance, which was written by a person named Solomon Spaulding. He was a graduate of Dartmouth College, and became a clergyman, but afterward relinquished his profession, and entered into mercantile pursuits. He subsequently removed to Ohio; there he wrote this book, and in 1812 brought the manuscript to Pittsburg, and offered it to a publisher named Patterson. Before any arrangement was made in reference to the matter, Spaulding died. The manuscript remained with Patterson till his death in 1826, when it passed into the possession of Sidney Rigdon, by whose means it came into the hands of Joseph Smith. Then it was that Smith conceived the idea of founding a new religion based upon the romantic and curious details contained in this volume, in reference to the early history of the Lost Tribes of Israel, who are represented as being the ancestors of the American Aborigines, and other details. The identity of Spaulding's book with the Book of Mormon was supported by the affidavits of several persons of undoubted veracity, who had seen the manuscript of Spaulding, and afterward examined the Book of Mormon.

In whatever way Smith obtained possession of the Book of Mormon, it answered his purpose admirably as a means to aid in founding a new sect, upon the accomplishment of which purpose he had resolved. He proceeded to announce his divine mission as the chosen apostle of a new dispensation, to his immediate family and relations. His pretensions were at first received with derision and contempt; and some time elapsed before any of his own family even pretended to believe in his claims. But his earnestness and zeal prevailed, after a time; and first one and then another of his partizans announced themselves as converts. The first church of the Latter Day Saints was organized in the town of Manchester, in New York, on the 6th of April, 1830; and from that time there commenced one of the most extraordinary histories ever presented in the annals of religion. The new sect were immediately visited by persecution, and the indignation of the public, at what they regarded as an unparalleled instance of mingled impudence and fraud, broke forth. Notwithstanding these obstacles, Smith continued to preach zealously, and to gather around him a number of adherents.

At length the Mormon leaders became convinced that it was for the benefit of their cause for them to remove to a distant locality; and accordingly Smith and his adherents, of whom Sidney Rigdon was the chief, proceeded westward, and established themselves, after various wanderings, in Jackson County, Missouri. Here they remained during four years, when the persecutions of their incensed neighbors compelled them to remove. Smith now selected a spot in Illinois which he called Nauvoo, or the New Jerusalem— the future home of the saints. Here his followers, who now numbered several thousand, commenced in April, 1841, to erect dwellings, public edifices, and a temple of large and imposing dimensions. In two years' time a numerous community assembled there, a city gradually arose; many missionaries were sent forth to proclaim the new faith; journals were established; and the Mormon community attained a degree of prosperity which justly excited the astonishment, while it provoked the hostility and resentment, of the general public.

At that period Nauvoo contained fifteen thousand inhabitants. But success rendered them quarrelsome, and hostile factions arose among themselves. A party opposed to Smith commenced a suit against him for the alleged destruction of a printing press; but the warrant could not be served upon the prophet in Nauvoo. He accordingly proceeded to the neighboring town of Carthage to surrender himself on the warrant; but the popular excitement had become so intense, that on the 27th of June, 1844, the jail was surrounded by a furious mob, who overpowered the guard, and eventually shot Smith, and several of his associates.

Some time afterward the whole Mormon community, harrassed by the persecution to which they were continually subjected, resolved to remove to a new and more remote location. Brigham Young, who had succeeded Smith in the supreme authority among them, was the leader in this new exodus; and in the year 1847 four thousand persons of all ages and both sexes reached Salt Lake Valley, in Utah, under his guidance. There a numerous community has since congregated, amounting perhaps to thirty thousand, who now constitute the chief bulk of this extraordinary people. The doctrines which the Mormons entertain may be briefly stated as follows:

They believe the Bible to be the word of God, as far as it is correctly translated; but at the same time they hold that the Book of Mormon is also inspired, and possessed of equal authority. They believe in the Father, Son, and Holy Ghost; that all men may be saved through the atonement of Christ. They hold that the Gospel ordinances are four: Faith in Christ, Repentance, Baptism by immersion, and laying on of hands, for the gift of the Holy Ghost. They believe in the power of miracles, of healing, prophecy, revelation, gift of tongues and visions among the saints at the present time. They believe in the literal gathering of Israel, the restoration of the Lost Ten Tribes, and the personal reign of Christ on the earth during a thousand years of millenial glory, when the saints will reign with him, and judge the Gentiles and unbelievers. They practice polygamy, and the spiritual wife system; that is, every wife, except the first, is *sealed* to her husband, in order thereby to obtain salvation, inasmuch as none but the saints and their families will become partakers of heaven and the millenial glory.

PURITANS.

THE name *Puritans* was given in the primitive Church to the Novatians, because they would never admit to communion any one who, from dread of death, had apostatized from the faith; but the word has been chiefly applied to those who were professed favorers of a further degree of reformation and purity in the Church before the Act of Uniformity, in 1662. After this period, the term Nonconformists became common, to which succeeds the appellation Dissenter.

"During the reign of Queen Elizabeth, in which the royal prerogative was carried to its utmost limits, there were found many daring spirits who questioned the right of the sovereign to prescribe and dictate to her subjects what principles of religion they should profess, and what forms they ought to adhere to. The ornaments and habits

worn by the clergy in the preceding reign, when the
Romish religion and rites were triumphant, Elizabeth was
desirous of preserving in the Protestant service. This
was the cause of great discontent among a large body of
her subjects; multitudes refused to attend at those churches
where the habits and ceremonies were used; the conforming clergy they treated with contumely; and, from the
superior purity and simplicity of the modes of worship to
which they adhered, they obtained the name of *Puritans*.
The Queen made many attempts to repress everything that
appeared to her as an innovation in the religion established
by her authority, but without success; by her almost unlimited authority she readily checked open and avowed
opposition, but she could not extinguish the principles of
the Puritans, 'by whom alone,' according to Mr. Hume,
'the precious spark of liberty had been kindled and was
preserved, and to whom the English owe the whole freedom
of their constitution.' Some secret attempts that had
been made by them to establish a separate congregation
and discipline, had been carefully repressed by the strict
hand which Elizabeth held over all her subjects. The
most, therefore, that they could effect was to assemble in
private houses for the purpose of worshipping God according to the dictates of their own consciences. These practices were at first connived at, but afterwards every means
was taken to suppress them, and the most cruel methods
were made use of to discover persons who were disobedient
to the royal pleasure.

The severe persecutions carried on against the Puritans
during the reigns of Elizabeth and the Stuarts, served to
lay the foundation of a new empire in the western world.
Thither, as into a wilderness, they fled from the face of
their persecutors, and, being protected in the free exercise
of their religion, continued to increase, till in about a cen-

tury and a half they became an independent nation. The different principles, however, on which they originally divided from the Church establishment at home, operated in a way that might have been expected when they came to the possession of the civil power abroad. Those who formed the colony of Massachusetts Bay, having never relinquished the principles of a national Church, and of the power of the civil magistrate in matters of faith and worship, were less tolerant than those who settled at New Plymouth, at Rhode Island, and at Providence Plantations. The very men (and they were good men too) who had just escaped the persecutions of the English prelates, now in their turn persecuted others who dissented from them, till at length the liberal system of toleration established in the parent country at the Revolution, extending to the colonies, in a good measure put an end to these proceedings.

Neither the Puritans, before the passing of the Bartholomew act, in 1662, nor the Nonconformists, after it, appear to have disapproved of the articles of the established Church in matters of *doctrine*. The number of those who did so, however, was very small. While the great body of the bishops and clergy had, from the days of Archbishop Laud, abandoned their own articles in favor of Arminianism, they were attached to the principles of the first Reformers; and by their labors and sufferings the spirit of the Reformation was kept alive in the land. But after the Revolution, one part of the Protestant Dissenters, chiefly Presbyterians, first veered towards Arminianism, then revived the Arian controversy, and by degrees many of them settled in Socinianism. At the same time another part of them, chiefly Independents and Baptists, earnestly contending for the doctrines of grace, and conceiving, as it would seem, that the danger of erring lay entirely on one side, first veered towards high Calvinism; then forbore inviting the unregenerate to repent, believe, or do anything practically good, and by degrees many of them, it is said, settled in Antinomianism.

Such are the principles which have found place amongst the descendants of the Puritans. At the same time, however, it must be acknowledged that a goodly number of each of the three denominations have adhered to the doctrine and spirit of their forefathers; and have proved the efficacy of their principles by their concern to be holy in all manner of conversation. See articles BROWNISTS, INDEPENDENTS, and NONCONFORMISTS, in this work.

BROWNISTS,

A sect that arose among the Puritans towards the close of the sixteenth century; so named from their leader, Robert Brown. He was educated at Cambridge, and was a man of good parts and some learning. He began to inveigh openly against the ceremonies of the church, at Norwich, in 1580: but being much opposed by the bishops, he, with his congregation, left England, and settled at Middleburgh, in Zealand, where they obtained leave to worship God in their own way, and form a church according to their own model. They soon, however, began to differ among themselves; so that Brown, growing weary of his office, returned to England, in 1589, renounced his principles of separation, and was preferred to the rectory of a church in Northamptonshire. He died in prison in 1630. The revolt of Brown was attended with the dissolution of the church at Middleburgh; but the seeds of Brownism which he had

sown in England were so far from being destroyed, that
Sir Walter Raleigh, in a speech in 1592, computes no less
than 20,000 of this sect.

The articles of their faith seem to be nearly the same as
those of the church of England. The occasion of their
separation was not, therefore, any fault they found with the
faith, but only with the discipline and form of government
of the churches in England. They equally charged corruption on the Episcopal and Presbyterian forms; nor
would they join with any other reformed church, because
they were not assured of the sanctity and regeneration of
the members that composed it. They condemned the solemn
celebration of marriages in the church, maintaining that
matrimony being a political contract, the confirmation
thereof ought to come from the civil magistrate; an opinion in which they are not singular. They would not allow
the children of such as were not members of the church to
be baptized. They rejected all forms of prayer, and held
that the Lord's prayer was not to be recited as a prayer,
being only given for a rule or model whereon all our prayers are to be formed. Their form of church government
was nearly as follows: When a church was to be gathered,
such as desired to be members of it made a confession of
their faith in the presence of each other, and signed a covenant, by which they obliged themselves to walk together in
the order of the Gospel. The whole power of admitting
and excluding members, with the decision of all controversies, was lodged in the brotherhood. Their church officers
were chosen from among themselves, and separated to their
several offices by fasting, prayer, and imposition of hands.
But they did not allow the priesthood to be any distinct
order. As the vote of the brethren made a man a minister,
so the same power could discharge him from his office, and
reduce him to a mere layman again; and as they main

tained the bounds of a church to be no greater than what could meet together in one place, and join in one commu- nion, so the power of these officers was prescribed within the same limits. The minister of one church could not administer the Lord's Supper to another, nor baptize the children of any but those of his own society. Any lay brother was allowed the liberty of giving a word of exhor- tation to the people ; and it was usual for some of them after sermon to ask questions, and reason upon the doc- trines that had been preached. In a word, every church on their model is a body corporate, having full power to do everything in themselves, without being accountable to any class, synod, convocation, or other jurisdiction what- ever. The reader will judge how near the Independent churches are allied to this form of government. See INDE- PENDENTS. The laws were executed with great severity on the Brownists ; their books were prohibited by queen Eli- zabeth, their persons imprisoned, and some hanged. Brown himself declared on his death-bed that he had been in thirty- two different prisons, in some of which he could not see his hand at noon-day. They were so much persecuted, that they resolved at last to quit the country. Accordingly, many retired and settled at Amsterdam, where they formed a church, and chose Mr. Johnson their pastor, and after him, Mr. Ainsworth, author of the learned Commentary on the Pentateuch. Their church flourished near 100 years. Among the Brownists, too, were the famous John Robin- son, a part of whose congregation from Leyden, in Holland, made the first permanent settlement in North America ; and the laborious Canne, the author of the marginal refer- ences to the Bible.

18

THE INDEPENDENTS

ARE a sect of Protestants, so called from their maintaining that each congregation of Christians which meet in one house for public worship is a complete church; has sufficient power to act and perform everything relating to religious government within itself; and is in no respect subject or accountable to other churches.

Though the Episcopalians contend that there is not a shadow of the independent discipline to be found either in the Bible or the primitive church, the Independents, on the contrary, believe that it is most clearly to be deduced from the practice of the apostles in planting the first churches The Independents, however, were not distinguished as a body till the time of queen Elizabeth. The hierarchy established by that princess in the churches of her dominions, the vestments worn by the clergy in the celebration of divine worship, the book of Common Prayer, and, above all, the sign of the cross used in the administration of baptism, were very offensive to many of her subjects, who, during the persecutions of the former reign, had taken refuge among the Protestants of Germany and Geneva. These men thought that the church of England resembled in too many particulars the anti-christian church of Rome; they therefore called perpetually for a more thorough reformation, and a *purer* worship. From this circumstance they were stigmatized with the general name of *Puritans,* as the followers of Novatian had been in the ancient church Elizabeth was not disposed to comply with their demands and it is difficult to say what might have been the issue of the contest, had the Puritans been united among them selves in sentiments, views, and measures. But the case was quite otherwise: that large body, composed of persons of different ranks, character, opinions, and intentions, and unanimous in nothing but their antipathy to the Established Church, was all of a sudden divided into a variety of sects. Of these the most famous was that which was formed about the year 1581, by Robert Brown, a man insinuating in his manners, but unsteady and inconsistent in his views and actions of men and things. Brown was for dividing the whole body of the faithful into separate societies or congregations; and maintained that such a number of persons as could be contained in an ordinary place of worship ought to be considered as a *church*, and enjoy all the rights and privileges that are competent to an ecclesiastical community. These small societies he pronounced *independent, jure divino*, and entirely exempt from the jurisdiction of the bishop, in whose hands the court had placed the reins of a spiritual government: and also from that of presbyteries and synods, which the Puritans regarded as the supreme visible sources of ecclesiastical authority. But as we have given an account of the general opinions and discipline of the Brownists, we need not enumerate them here, but must beg the reader to refer to that article. The zeal with which Brown and his associates maintained and propagated his notions, was, in a high degree, intemperate and extravagant. He affirmed that all communion was to be broken off with those religious societies that were founded upon a different plan from his; and treated more especially the church of England as a spurious church, whose ministers were unlawfully ordained; whose discipline was popish and anti-christian; and whose sacraments and institutions were destitute of all efficacy and virtue. His followers not being able to endure the severe treatment which they met with from an administration that was not distinguished for its mildness and indulgence, retired into the Netherlands, and founded churches at Middlebourg, Amsterdam, and Leyden. Their founder, however, returned into England, renounced his principles of separation, and took orders in the Established Church. The Puritan exiles, whom he thus abandoned, disagreed among themselves, were split into parties. and their affairs declined from day to day. This engaged the wiser part of them to mitigate the severity of their founder's plan, and to soften the rigor of his uncharitable decisions.

The person who had the chief merit of bringing about this reformation was one of their pastors, of the name of Robinson, a man who had much of the solemn piety of the times, and no inconsiderable portion of learning. This distinguished reformer, perceiving the defects that reigned in the discipline of Brown, and in the spirit and temper of his followers, employed his zeal and diligence in correcting them, and in new-modelling the society in such a manner, as to render it less odious to his adversaries, and less liable to the just censure of those true Christians who look upon charity as the end of the commandments. Hitherto the sect had been called Brownists ; but Robinson having in his apology affirmed that all Christian congregations were so many *independent* religious societies, that had a right to be governed by their own laws, *independent* of any further or foreign jurisdiction, the sect was first called *Independents,* afterward Congregationalists, of which the apologist was considered as the founder.

The first independent or congregational church in England was established by a Mr. Jacob, in the year 1616. Mr. Jacob, who had fled from the persecution of Bishop Bancroft, going to Holland, and having imparted his design of setting up a separate congregation, like those in Holland, to the most learned Puritans of those times, it was not condemned as unlawful, considering there was no prospect of a national reformation. Mr. Jacob, therefore, having summoned several of his friends together, and having obtained their consent to unite in church fellowship for enjoying the ordinances of Christ in the purest manner, they laid the foundation of the first independent church in England in the following way : Having observed a day of solemn fasting and prayer for a blessing upon their undertaking, towards the close of the solemnity, each of them made an open confession of their faith in Christ ; and then, standing together, they joined hands, and solemnly covenanted with each other, in the presence of Almighty God, to walk together in all God's way and ordinances, according as he had already revealed, or should further make known to them. Mr. Jacob was then chosen pastor by the suffrage of the brotherhood ; and others were appointed to the office of deacons, with fasting and prayer, and imposition of hands.

The Independents were much more commendable than the Brownists ; they surpassed them, both in the moderation of their sentiments, and in the order of their discipline. They did not, like Brown, pour forth bitter and uncharitable invectives against the churches which were governed by rules entirely different from theirs, nor pronounce them, on that account, unworthy of the Christian name. On the contrary, though they considered their own form of ecclesiastical government as of Divine institution, and as originally introduced by the authority of the apostles, nay, by the apostles themselves, they had yet candor and charity enough to acknowledge that true religion and solid piety might flourish in those communities which were under the jurisdiction of bishops, or the government of synods and presbyteries. They were also much more attentive than the Brownists in keeping on foot a regular ministry

in their communities; for, while the latter allowed promis
cuously all ranks and orders of men to teach in public,
the Independents had, and still have, a certain number of
ministers, chosen respectively by the congregations where
they are fixed: nor is it common for any person among
them to speak in public before he has submitted to a
proper examination of his capacity and talents, and been
approved of by the heads of the congregation.

From 1642, the Independents are very frequently mentioned in the English annals. The charge alleged against
them by Rapin, (in his History of England, vol ii p. 114,
folio edition,) that they could not so much as endure
ordinary ministers in the church, &c., is groundless. He
was led into this mistake by confounding the Independents
with the Brownists. Other charges, no less unjustifiable,
have been urged against the Independents by this celebrated historian and others. Rapin says, that they ab-
horred monarchy and approved of a republican government: this might have been true with regard to many
persons among them, in common with other sects; but it
does not appear, from any of their public writings, that
republican principles formed their distinguishing characteristic; on the contrary, in a public memorial drawn up
by them in 1647, they declare that they do not disapprove
of any form of civil government, but do freely acknowledge
that a kingly government, bounded by just and wholesome
laws, is allowed by God, and also a good accommodation
unto men. The Independents, however, have been generally ranked among the regicides, and charged with the
death of Charles I. Whether this fact be admitted or
denied, no conclusion can be fairly drawn from the greater
prevalence of republican principles, or from violent proceedings at that period, that can affect the distinguishing
tenets and conduct of the Independents in our times. It

is certain that the present Independents are steady friends to a limited monarchy. Rapin is further mistaken when he represents the religious principles of the English Independents as contrary to those of all the rest of the world. It appears from two confessions of faith, one composed by Robinson, in behalf of the English Independents in Holland, and published at Leyden, in 1619, entitled, *Apologia pro Exulibus Anglis, qui Brownistæ vulgo appellantur;* and another drawn up in London, in 1658, by the principal members of their community in England, entitled, "A Declaration of the Faith and Order owned and practised by the Congregational Churches in England, agreed upon and consented unto by their Elders and Messengers, in their meeting at the Savoy, October 12th, 1658," as well as from other writings of the Independents, that they differed from the rest of the reformed in no single point of any consequence, except that of ecclesiastical government; and their religious doctrines were almost entirely the same with those adopted by the church of Geneva. During the administration of Cromwell, the Independents acquired very considerable reputation and influence; and he made use of them as a check to the ambition of the Presbyterians, who aimed at a very high degree of ecclesiastical power, and who had succeeded, soon after the elevation of Cromwell, in obtaining a parliamentary establishment of their own church government. But after the restoration, their cause declined; and in 1691 they entered into an association with the Presbyterians residing in and about London, comprised in nine articles, that tended to the maintenance of their respective institutions. These may be found in the second volume of Whiston's Memoirs, and the substance of them in Mosheim. At this time the Independents and Presbyterians, called from this association the *United Brethren,* were agreed with regard to

doctrines, being generally Calvinists, and differed only
with respect to ecclesiastical discipline. Independentism
is peculiar to Great Britain, the United States, and the
Netherlands. It was carried first to the American colonies in 1620, and by successive Puritan emigrants, in
1629 and 1633, from England, and there developed more
fully the fellowship of the churches, and was called Congregationalism. One Morel, in the sixteenth century,
endeavored to introduce it into France; but it was condemned at the synod of Rochelle, where Beza presided;
and again at the synod of Rochelle, in 1644.

Many of the Independents reject the use of all creeds
and confessions drawn up by fallible men, though they
require of their teachers a declaration of their belief in
the Gospel and its various doctrines, and their adherence
to the Scriptures as the sole standard of faith and practice. They attribute no virtue whatever to the right of
ordination, upon which some other churches lay so much
stress. According to them, the qualifications which constitute a regular minister of the New Testament, are, a
firm belief in the Gospel, a principle of sincere and unaffected piety, a competent stock of knowledge, a capacity
for leading devotion and communicating instruction, a
serious inclination to engage in the important employment
of promoting the everlasting salvation of mankind, and
ordinarily an invitation to the pastoral office from some
particular society of Christians. Where these things concur, they consider a person as fitted and authorized for
the discharge of every duty which belongs to the ministerial function; and they believe that the imposition of
hands of bishops or presbyters would convey to him no
powers or prerogatives of which he was not before possessed. But though they attribute no virtue to ordination,
as conveying any new powers, yet they hold with and

practise it. Many of them, indeed, suppose that the essence of ordination does not lie in the act of the ministers who assist, but in the choice and call of the people, and the candidate's acceptance of that call; so that their ordination may be considered only as a public declaration of that agreement. They consider it as their right to choose their own ministers and deacons. They own no man as head of the church. They disallow of parochial and provincial subordination; but though they do not think it necessary to assemble synods, yet, if any be held, they look upon their resolutions as prudential counsels, but not as decisions to which they are obliged to conform. They consider the Scriptures as the only criterion of truth. Their worship is conducted in a decent, plain, and simple manner, without the ostentation of form, and the vain pomp of ceremony.

The congregations of the Independents are very numerous, both in England and America, and generally very respectable. This denomination has produced many characters as eminent for learning and piety as any church in Christendom; whose works, no doubt, will reflect lasting honor on their characters and abilities.

NEONOMIANS.

NEONOMIANS, so called from the Greek νεος, *new*, and νμος, *law*, signifying *new law*, the condition whereof is imperfect, though sincere and persevering obedience.

Neonomianism seems to be an essential part of the Arminian system. " The new covenant of grace which, through the medium of Christ's death, the Father made with men, consists, according to this system, not in our being justified by faith, as it apprehends the righteousness of Christ; but in this, that God, abrogating the exaction of perfect legal obedience, reputes or accepts of faith itself, and the imperfect obedience of faith, instead of the perfect obedience of the law, and graciously accounts them worthy of the reward of eternal life." This opinion was examined at the synod of Dort, and has been canvassed between the Calvinists and Arminians on various occasions.

Towards the close of the seventeenth century, a controversy was agitated amongst the English Dissenters, in which the one side, who were partial to the writings of Dr. Crisp, were charged with *Antinomianism*, and the other, who favored Mr. Baxter, were accused of Neonomianism. Mr. Daniel Williams, who was a principal writer on what was called the Neonomian side, after many things had been said, gives the following as a summary of his faith in reference to those subjects.—1. God has eternally elected a certain definite number of men whom he will infallibly save by Christ in that way prescribed by the Gospel. 2. These very elect are not personally justified until they receive Christ, and yield up themselves to him, but they remain condemned whilst unconverted to Christ. 3. By the ministry of the Gospel there is a serious offer of pardon and glory, upon the terms of the Gospel, to all that hear it; and God thereby requires them to comply with the said terms. 4. Ministers ought to use these and other Gospel benefits as motives, assuring men that if they believe they shall be justified; if they turn to God, they shall live; if they repent, their sins shall be blotted out; and whilst they *neglect* these duties, they cannot have a personal interest in these respective benefits. 5. It is by the power of the Spirit of Christ freely exerted, and not by the power of free-will, that the Gospel becomes effectual for the conversion of any soul to the obedience of faith. 6. When a man believes, yet it is not that very faith, and much less any other work, the matter of that righteousness for which a sinner is justified, *i. e.*, entitled to pardon, acceptance, and eternal glory, as righteous before God; and it is the imputed righteousness of Christ alone, for which the Gospel gives the believer a right to these and all saving blessings. who in this respect is justified by Christ's righteousness alone. By both this and the fifth head it appears that all boasting is excluded, and we are saved by free grace. 7. *Faith* alone receives the Lord Jesus and his righteousness, and the subject of this faith is a *convinced, penitent soul;* hence we are justified by faith alone, and yet the *impenitent* are not forgiven. 8. God has freely promised that all whom he predestinated to salvation shall not only savingly believe, but that he by his power shall preserve them from a *total* or a *final apostasy.* 9. Yet the believer, whilst he lives in this world, is to pass the time of his sojourning here with fear, because his warfare is not accomplished, and that it is true that, if he draw back, God will have no pleasure in him. Which with the like cautions God blesseth as means to the saints' perseverance, and these by ministers should be so urged. 10. The law of innocence, or moral law, is so in force still, as that every precept there-

of constitutes duty, even to the believer: every breach
thereof is a sin deserving of death: this law binds death
by its curse on every unbeliever, and the righteousness for
or by which we are justified before God, is a righteousness
(at least) adequate to that law which is Christ's alone righteousness; and this so imputed to the believer as that God
deals judicially with him according thereto. 11. Yet such
is the grace of the Gospel, that it promiseth in and by
Christ a freedom from the curse, forgiveness of sin, and
eternal life, to every sincere believer; which promise God
will certainly perform, notwithstanding the threatening of
the law.''

Dr. Williams maintains the conditionality of the covenant of grace; but admits with Dr. Owen, who also uses the
term *condition*, that " Christ undertook that those who were
to be taken into this covenant should receive grace enabling
them to comply with the terms of it, fulfil its conditions,
and yield the obedience which God required therein."

On this subject Dr. Williams further says, " The question is not whether the first (viz., regenerating) grace, by
which we are enabled to perform the condition, be absolutely given. This I affirm, though that be dispensed ordinarily in a due use of means, and in a way discountenancing
idleness, and fit encouragement given to the use of means."

The following objection, among others, was made by
several ministers in 1692, against Dr. William's *Gospel
Truth Stated*, &c. " To supply the room of the moral law,
vacated by him, he turns the Gospel into a new law, in
keeping of which we shall be justified for the sake of Christ's
righteousness, making qualifications and acts of ours a dis-
posing subordinate righteousness, whereby we become
capable of being justified by Christ's righteousness."

To this, among other things, he answers, " The difference is not, 1. Whether the Gospel be a new law in the

Socinian, Popish, or Arminian sense. This I deny. Nor,
2. Is faith, or any other grace or act of ours, any atonement for sin, satisfaction to justice, meriting qualification,
or any part of that righteousness for which we are justified
at God our Creator's bar. This I deny in places innumerable. Nor, 3. Whether the Gospel be a law more new
than is implied in the first promise to fallen Adam, proposed to Cain, and obeyed by Abel, to the differencing him
from his unbelieving brother. This I deny. 4. Nor whether
the Gospel be a law that allows sin, when it accepts such
graces as true, though short of perfection, to be the conditions of our personal interest in the benefits purchased by
Christ. This I deny. 5. Nor whether the Gospel be a
law, the promises whereof entitle the performers of its
conditions to the benefits as of debt. This I deny.

He goes on to say that the real difference is, that the
Gospel is a law, as commanding repentance, and promising
pardon to obedience, and threatening punishment to disobedience.

NONCONFORMISTS.

THIS sect is remarkable as having once included some
of the ablest, most eloquent and pious clergymen in England.
The Nonconformists were those who at certain periods refused to join the established church of England. Those in
England may be considered of three parts: 1. Such as absent
themselves from Divine worship in the established church
through total irreligion, and attend the service of no other
persuasion. 2. Such as absent themselves on the plea of
conscience; as Presbyterians, Independents, Baptists, etc.
3. Internal Nonconformists, or unprincipled clergymen,

who applaud and propagate doctrines quite inconsistent with several of those articles they promised on oath to defend. The word is generally used in reference to those ministers who were ejected from their livings by the Act of Uniformity, in 1662. The number of these was about two thousand. However some affect to treat these men with indifference, and suppose that their consciences were more tender than they need be, it must be remembered that they were men of as extensive learning, great abilities, and pious conduct, as ever appeared. Mr. Locke, if his opinion have any weight, calls them "worthy, learned, pious, orthodox divines, who did not throw themselves out of service, but were forcibly ejected." Mr. Bogue thus draws their character: "*As to their public ministration,*" he says, "they were orthodox, experimental, serious, affectionate, regular, faithful, able, and popular preachers. *As to their moral qualities,* they were devout and holy; faithful to Christ and the souls of men; wise and prudent; of great liberality and kindness; and strenuous advocates for liberty, civil and religious. *As to their intellectual qualities,* they were learned, eminent, and laborious." These men were driven from their houses, from the society of their friends, and exposed to the greatest difficulties. Their burdens were greatly increased by the Conventicle Act, whereby they were prohibited from meeting for any exercise of religion (above five in number) in any other manner than allowed by the liturgy or practice of the Church of England. For the first offence the penalty was three months' imprisonment, or pay five pounds; for the second offence, six months' imprisonment, or ten pounds; and for the third offence, to be banished to some of the American plantations for seven years, or pay one hundred pounds; and in case they returned, to suffer death without benefit of clergy. By virtue of this act, the jails were quickly filled with dissenting Protestants, and the trade of an informer was very gainful. So great was the severity of these times, says Neale, that they were afraid to pray in their families, if above four of their acquaintance, who came only to visit them, were present. Some families scrupled asking a blessing on their meat, if five strangers were at table.

But this was not all (to say nothing of the Test Act). In 1665, an act was brought into the House to banish them from their friends, commonly called the Oxford Five Mile Act, by which all dissenting ministers, on the penalty of forty pounds, who would not take an oath (that it was not lawful, upon any *pretence whatever*, to take arms against the king, etc.), were prohibited from coming within five miles of any city, town corporate, or borough, or any place where they had exercised their ministry, and from teaching any school. Some few took the oath; others could not, and consequently suffered the penalty.

In 1673, "the mouths of the high church pulpiteers were encouraged to open as loud as possible. One, in his sermon before the House of Commons, told them that the Nonconformists ought not to be tolerated, but to be cured by vengeance. He urged them to set fire to the faggot, and to teach them by scourges or scorpions, and open their eyes with gall."

Such were the dreadful consequences of this intolerant spirit, that it is supposed near eight thousand died in prison in the reign of Charles II. It is said that Mr. Jeremiah White had carefully collected a list of those who had suffered between Charles II. and the revolution, which amounted to sixty thousand. The same persecutions were carried on in Scotland; and there, as well as in England, many, to avoid persecution, fled from their country.

But, notwithstanding all these dreadful and furious attacks upon the Dissenters, they were not extirpated. Their

very persecution was in their favor. The infamous char
acters of their informers and persecutors; their piety,
zeal, and fortitude, no doubt, had influence on considerate
minds; and, indeed, they had additions from the established church, which "several clergymen in this reign
deserted as a persecuting church, and took their lot among
them." In addition to this, King James suddenly altered
his measures, granted a universal toleration, and preferred
Dissenters to places of trust and profit, though it was evidently with a view to restore Popery.

King William coming to the throne, the famous Toleration Act passed, by which they were exempted from suffering the penalties before mentioned, and permission given
them to worship God according to the dictates of their
own consciences. In the latter end of Queen Anne's
reign, they began to be a little alarmed. An act of Par
liament passed, called the Occasional Conformity Bill,
which prevented any person in office under the government
entering into a meeting-house. Another, called the Schism
Bill, had actually obtained the royal assent, which suffered
no Dissenters to educate their own children, but required
them to be put into the hands of Conformists; and which
forbade all tutors and schoolmasters being present at any
conventicle, or dissenting place of worship; but the very
day this iniquitous act was to have taken effect, the Queen
died (August 1, 1714).

But George I., being fully satisfied that these hardships
were brought upon the Dissenters for their steady adherence to the Protestant succession in his illustrious house,
against a Tory and Jacobite ministry who were paving the
way for a Popish pretender, procured the repeal of them
in the fifth year of his reign; though a clause was left
that forbade the mayor or other magistrate to go into any
meeting for religious worship with the ensigns of his office.

HUGUENOTS.

THIS term, which was applied to the Protestants in France in contempt, is of uncertain origin. In public documents, they were styled *Ceux de la religion prétendue réformée*, or *Religionnaires*.

The principles of Luther and Zwinglius had gained an entrance into France, during the reign of Francis I. (1515–47). The doctrines of Calvin spread still more widely, although Francis endeavored to suppress them by prohibiting Calvinistic books, and by penal laws, and, in some instances, by capital punishments.

Under Henry II., the successor of Francis, these doctrines made greater progress, in proportion as they were more violently persecuted. The opinions and influence of Queen Margaret of Navarre had no small share in this extension, and the parties at court contributed much to the bloody persecution of the Protestants. One party wished to enrich themselves by the estates of the heretics, who were executed or banished, and the other to gain the favor of the people by their punishment. The parties of the Bourbons and of the five princes of Guise, under the government of the weak Francis II., made use of this religious dispute, in order to advance their own political ends.

The Bourbons belonged to the Protestant party; and the Guises, in order to weaken, and, if possible, to destroy their rivals, continued the persecution of the heretics with fanatical fury. In every parliament there was a chamber established to examine and punish the Protestants, called by the people the *burning chamber* (*chambre ardente*),

19 *

because all convicted of heresy were burnt. The estates of those who fled were sold, and their children who remained behind were exposed to the greatest sufferings. But notwithstanding this persecution, the Protestants would not have thought of a rebellion, had not a prince of the blood encouraged them to it by the promise of his assistance.

In 1560 the conspiracy began. The discontented inquired of lawyers and theologians whether they could with a good conscience take arms against the Guises. The Protestant divines in Germany declared it proper to resist the tyranny of the Guises, if it were under the guidance and direction of a prince of the blood, and with the approbation of the majority in the States.

The malcontents having consulted upon the choice of a leader, all voices decided in favor of the brave prince Louis of Condé, who had conducted the whole affair, and gladly seized the opportunity to make himself formidable by the support of the Huguenots. The name of the leader was, however kept secret, and a Protestant gentleman of Perigord, John du Barry, *seigneur* of Renaudie, was appointed his deputy.

It was determined that a number of the Calvinists should appear on an appointed day before the king at Blois, to present a petition for the free exercise of their religion; and, in case this request was denied, as it was foreseen it would be, a chosen band of armed Protestants were to make themselves masters of the city of Blois, seize the Guises, and compel the king to name the Prince of Condé regent of the realm.

This plot was betrayed. The court left Blois, the military were summoned, and the greatest part of the Protestants who had armed themselves to carry the conspiracy into effect, were executed or imprisoned. Few of those who fell into the power of the court found mercy; and about 1200 expiated their offence with their lives.

The Guises now desired to establish the inquisition, but the wise chancellor, Michael de l'Hôpital, in order to avoid the greater evil, advised that all inquiries into the crime of heresy should be committed to the bishops, and that parliament should be prohibited from exercising any jurisdiction in matters of faith; and it was so ordered by the edict of Romorantin (1560).

In the reign of the next king, Charles IX., during whose minority the Queen mother, Catharine de Medici, was at the head of the government, the contest between the parties became yet more violent, and their contending interests were more and more used for a pretence to accomplish unholy designs, and it was only from motives of policy that the free exercise of their religion was secured to the Protestants by the Queen, in order to preserve the balance between the parties, by the edict of January (1562), so called. The Protestants thereby gained new courage; but their adversaries, dissatisfied with this ordinance, and regardless of decency, disturbed the Huguenots in their religious services. Bloody scenes were the result, and the massacre of Vassy (1562) was the immediate cause of the first civil war.

These religious wars desolated France almost to the end of the sixteenth century, and were only interrupted by occasional truces. The suffering which these wars brought upon the people is to be ascribed to the instability and bad policy of Queen Catharine de Medici, who exerted the most decided influence, not only over the feeble Charles IX., but likewise over the contemptible Henry III. She wished, in fact, for the extirpation of the Huguenots, and it was merely her intriguing policy which induced her, much to the vexation of the opposite party, to favour the

Protestants from time to time, and to grant them freedom of conscience. Always wavering between the two parties, she flattered herself with the expectation of holding them in check during peace, or of destroying the one by the other in war. Both parties were, therefore, generally dissatisfied with the court, and followed their own leaders.

A wild fanaticism seized the people. Heated with passion and religious hatred, they endeavored only to injure each other; and, with the exception of some party leaders, who made use of this excitement for the accomplishment of their own ambitious schemes, their only object was to acquire the superiority for their own creed by fire and sword.

The horrible effect of Catharine's policy was the massacre of St. Bartholomew's (1572), of which she and her son, her pupil in dissimulation, had laid the plan with their confidants. Shortly before the line of kings of the house of Valois had become extinct with Henry III., and the way was opened for the house of Bourbon, the head of which was the Protestant Henry, king of Navarre, the relations of the two parties became still more involved.

The feeble king found himself compelled to unite with the king of Navarre against the common enemy, as the intrigues of the ambitious Guises, who openly aimed at the throne, had excited the people against him to such a degree, that he was on the point of losing the crown.

After the assassination of Henry III., the king of Navarre was obliged to maintain a severe struggle for the vacant throne; and not until he had, by the advice of Sully, embraced the Catholic religion (1593), did he enjoy quiet possession of the kingdom.

Five years afterwards he secured to the Huguenots their civil rights by the edict of Nantes, which confirmed to them the free exercise of their religion, and gave them equal claims with the Catholics to all offices and dignities. They were also left in possession of the fortresses which had been ceded to them for their security.

This edict afforded them a means of forming a kind of republic within the kingdom, and such a powerful party, which had for a long time been obliged to be distrustful of the government, would always offer to the restless nobility a rallying point and a prospect of assistance.

Louis XIII., the weak and bigoted son of the liberal and magnanimous Henry IV., allowed himself to be influenced by his ambitious favorite, De Luines, and his confessor, against the Huguenots, who were able to offer a powerful resistance, as they had become very numerous in many provinces. But in the first religious war, which broke out in 1621, the Protestants lost the greatest part of their strong places, through the faithlessness or cowardice of the governors. Some of these, however, and among the rest Rochelle, remained to them, when, disunited among themselves and weary of war, they concluded a peace.

Rochelle enabled them to keep up a connection with England; and Richelieu, who aimed to make the royal power, which he exercised under the name of Louis, absolute, used every means to deprive the Protestants of this bulwark of their liberty, and thus destroy every remnant of a league which recalled the times when civil factions had so often weakened the royal power.

Rochelle fell into the hands of Louis, after an obstinate defence, in 1629; the Huguenots were obliged to surrender all their strong holds, and were thus left entirely at the mercy of the king. Freedom of conscience was indeed promised them, and Richelieu and his successor Mazarin did not disturb them in the enjoyment of it; but when Louis XIV. abandoned his voluptuous life for an affected devotion, he was led by his confessors and Madame de

Maintenon, to persecute the Protestants, for the purpose of bringing them back to the bosom of the true church.

In 1681, he deprived them of most of their civil rights, and, on the death of Colbert, who had generally opposed violent measures, he followed altogether the advice of his counsellors, who were in favor of persecution—his minister of war, Louvois, the chancellor Le Tellier, and the Jesuit La Chaise, his father confessor. Bodies of dragoons were sent into the southern provinces, where the Protestants were most numerous, to compel the unhappy inhabitants to abjure their faith.

To prevent the emigration of the Protestants, the frontiers were guarded with the utmost vigilance; yet more than 500,000 Huguenots fled to Switzerland, Germany, Holland, and England. Many, who could not escape, were obliged to renounce their faith.

Lists of Protestants who, it was pretended, had been converted, were sent to the king, and it was very easy for his flattering counsellors to persuade him that he had gained honor by having almost extirpated the Protestants in France. Under this erroneous supposition, he revoked the edict of Nantes, October 22, 1685. But he had still more than half a million of Protestant subjects, and this unjust and unwise revocation robbed France of a great number of useful and rich inhabitants, whose industry, wealth, and skill found a welcome reception in foreign countries.

But quiet was by no means restored in France. In the provinces between the Rhone and Garonne, the Protestants were yet very numerous, and the neighboring mountains of Cevennes afforded them shelter. There the Camisards maintained war for a long time, armed for the most part with clubs alone. The contest was not altogether unlike the war of La Vendée in later times.

After twenty years (1706), the government was finally obliged to come to terms with them; yet quiet was not perfectly restored. In the level country, especially at Nismes, a Protestant spirit still survived in secret; even the compassion of the Catholics was excited, and many persecutors of the Protestants became their defenders; and there were not wanting clergymen among the Huguenots, who were kept concealed.

In the reign of Louis XV., new but less severe measures were adopted against the Protestants, and, in 1746, they ventured to appear publicly in Languedoc and Dauphiny. By degrees, many voices were raised in favor of religious toleration. Montesquieu led the way; but Voltaire, shocked by the unhappy fate of John Calas, effected still more by his Essay on Toleration, in 1762.

From this time Protestants were no longer disturbed, yet they did not dare to make pretensions to public offices. The Revolution restored them all their civil rights, and they frequently laid out their hitherto secreted treasures in the purchase of the national domains. It was not therefore strange that, at the Restoration, they appeared attached to the former government, which had granted them privileges that they were fearful of losing under the new. Although they did not offer any opposition to the new order of things, yet troubles took place, which were attended with bloodshed, at Nismes and the vicinity; but these were suppressed by the judicious measures of the government.

On the revocation of the edict of Nantes, a considerable number of Protestants fled for refuge to America, most of whom settled in South Carolina. Dr. Ramsey, in his History of South Carolina, thus notices this little colony of Huguenots:

"The revocation of the edict of Nantes, fifteen years

subsequent to the settlement of Carolina, contributed much to its population. In it, soon after that event, were transplanted from France the stocks from which have sprung the respectable families of Bonneau, Bounetheau, Bordeaux, Benoist, Boiseau, Bocquet, Bacot, Chevalier, Cordes, Couterier, Chastaignier, Dupre, Delysle, Dubose, Dubois, Deveaux, Dutarque, De la Consilière, De Leiseline, Douxsaint, Du Pont, Du Bourdieu, D'Harriette, Faucheraud, Foissin, Faysoux, Gaillard, Gendron, Gignilliat, Guerard, Godin, Girardeau, Guerin, Gourdine, Horry, Huger, Jeannerette, Legare, Laurens, La Roche, Lenud, Lansac, Marion, Mazyck, Manigault, Mellichamp, Mouzon, Michau, Neufville, Prioleau,* Peronneau, Perdriau, Porcher, Postell, Peyre, Poyas, Ravenel, Royer, Simons, Sarazin, St. Julien, Serre, Trezevant.

QUAKERS,

A SECT which took its rise in England about the middle of the seventeenth century, and rapidly found its way into other countries in Europe, and into the English settlements in North America. The members of this society, we believe, called themselves at first *Seekers*, from their seeking the

---

* The Rev. Elias Prioleau, the founder of the eminently respectable family of that name in Carolina, migrated thither soon after the revocation of the edict of Nantes, and brought with him from France a considerable part of his Protestant congregation. He was the grandson of Anthoine Prioli, who was elected Doge of Venice in the year 1618. Many of his numerous descendants, who were born and constantly resided in or near Charleston, have approached or exceeded their seventieth year; and several have survived, or now survive, their eightieth.

truth; but after the society was formed, they assumed the appellation of Friends. The name of Quakers was given to them by their enemies, and though an epithet of reproach, seems to be stamped upon them indelibly. George Fox is supposed to be their first founder; but after the restoration, Penn and Barclay gave to their principles a more regular form.

The doctrines of their society have been variously represented; and some have thought and taken pains to prove them favorable to Socinianism. But, according to Penn, they believe in the Holy Three, or the trinity of the Father, Word, and Spirit, agreeably to the Scripture. In reply to the charge that they deny Christ to be God, Penn says "that it is a most untrue and uncharitable censure —that they truly and expressly own him to be so according to the Scripture." To the objection that they deny the human nature of Christ, he answers, "We never taught, said, or held so gross a thing, but believe him to be truly and properly man like us, sin only excepted." The doctrines of the fall, and the redemption by Christ, are, according to him, believed firmly by them; and he declares "that they own Jesus Christ as their sacrifice, atonement, and propitiation."

But we shall here state a further account of their principles and discipline, as extracted from a summary transmitted from one of their most respectable members.

They tell us that about the beginning of the seventeenth century, a number of men, dissatisfied with all the modes of religious worship then known in the world, withdrew from the communion of every visible church to seek the Lord in retirement. Among these was their *honorable elder, George Fox,* who, being quickened by the immediate touches of divine love, could not satisfy his apprehensions of duty to God without directing the people where to find the like

20

consolation and instruction.   In the course of his travels, he met with many seeking persons in circumstances similar to his own, and these readily received his testimony.   They then give us a short account of their sufferings and different settlements; they also vindicate Charles II. from the character of a persecutor; acknowledging that, though they suffered much during his reign, he gave as little countenance as he could to the severities of the legislature.   They even tell us that he exerted his influence to rescue their friends from the unprovoked and cruel persecutions they met with in New England; and they speak with becoming gratitute of the different acts passed in their favor during the reigns of William and Mary, and George I.   They then proceed to give us the following account of their doctrine: —

"We agree with other professors of the Christian name, in the belief of one eternal God, the Creator and Preserver of the universe: and in Jesus Christ his Son, the Messiah and mediator of the new covenant (Heb. xii. 24).

"When we speak of the gracious display of the love of God to mankind, in the miraculous conception, birth, life, miracles, death, resurrection, and ascension of our Saviour, we prefer the use of such terms as we find in Scripture; and, contented with that knowledge which divine wisdom hath *seen* meet to reveal, we attempt not to explain those mysteries which remain under the veil; nevertheless we acknowledge and assert the divinity of Christ, who is the wisdom and power of God unto salvation (1 Cor. i. 24).

"To Christ alone we give the title of the Word of God, (John i. 1), and not to the Scriptures, although we highly esteem these sacred writings, in subordination to the Spirit (2 Pet. i. 21) from which they were given forth; and we hold, with the apostle Paul, that they are able to make wise unto salvation, through faith, which is in Christ Jesus (2 Tim. iii. 15).

"We reverence those most excellent precepts which are recorded in Scripture to have been delivered by our great Lord; and we firmly believe that they are practicable, and binding on every Christian; and that in the life to come every man will be rewarded according to his works (Matt. xvi. 27). And, further, it is our belief that, in order to enable mankind to put in practice these sacred precepts, many of which are contradictory to the unregenerate will of man (John i. 9), every man coming into the world is endued with a measure of the light, grace, or good Spirit of Christ; by which, as it is attended to, he is enabled to distinguish good from evil, and to correct the disorderly passions and corrupt propensities of his nature, which mere reason is altogether insufficient to overcome. For all that belongs to man is fallible, and within the reach of temptation; but this divine grace, which comes by him who hath overcome the world (John xvi. 33), is, to those who humbly and sincerely seek it, an all-sufficient and present help in time of need. By this the snares of the enemy are detected, his allurements avoided, and deliverance is experienced through faith in its effectual operation; whereby the soul is translated out of the kingdom of darkness, and from under the power of Satan, unto the marvellous light and kingdom of the Son of God.

"Being thus persuaded that man, without the Spirit of Christ inwardly revealed, can do nothing to the glory of God, or to effect his own salvation, we think this influence especially necessary to the performance of the highest act of which the human mind is capable; even the worship of the Father of light and of spirits, in spirit and in truth: therefore we consider, as obstructions to pure worship, all forms which divert the attention of the mind from the

secret influence of this unction from the Holy One (1 John
ii. 20, 27).   Yet, although true worship is not confined to
time and place, we think it incumbent on Christians to meet
often together (Heb. x. 25), in testimony of their dependence on the heavenly Father, and for a renewal of their
spiritual strength : nevertheless, in the performance of worship, we dare not depend for our acceptance with him on
a formal repetition of the words and experiences of others ;
but we believe it to be our duty to lay aside the activity
of the imagination, and to wait in silence to have a true
sight of our condition bestowed upon us ; believing even a
single sigh (Rom. vii. 24) arising from such a sense of our
infirmities, and of the need we have of divine help, to be
more acceptable to God than any performances, however
specious, which originate in the will of man.

"From what has been said respecting worship, it follows
that the ministry we approve must have its origin from the
same source ; for that which is needful for man's own direction, and for his acceptance with God (Jer. xxiii. 30 to 32),
must be eminently so to enable him to be helpful to others.
Accordingly, we believe that the renewed assistance of the
light and power of Christ is indispensably necessary for
all true ministry, and that this holy influence is not at our
command, or to be procured by study, but in the free gift
of God to chosen and devoted servants.   Hence arises our
testimony against preaching for hire, in contradiction to
Christ's positive command, ' Freely ye have received, freely
give' (Matt. x. 8); and hence our conscientious refusal to
support such ministry by tithes, or other means.

"As we dare not encourage any ministry but that which
we believe to spring from the influence of the Holy Spirit,
so neither dare we attempt to restrain this influence to
persons of any condition in life, or to the male sex alone ;
but, as male and female are one in Christ, we allow such

of the female sex as we believe to be endued with a right qualification for the ministry, to exercise their gifts for the general edification of the church; and this liberty we esteem a peculiar mark of the Gospel dispensation, as foretold by the prophet Joel (Joel ii. 28, 29); and noticed by the apostle Peter (Acts ii. 16, 17).

"There are two ceremonies in use among most professors of the Christian name,—water baptism, and what is termed the Lord's Supper. The first of these is generally esteemed the essential means of initiation into the church of Christ; and the latter of maintaining communion with him. But as we have been convinced that nothing short of his redeeming power, invariably revealed, can set the soul free from the thraldom of sin, by this power alone we believe salvation to be effected. We hold that, as there is one Lord and one faith (Eph. iv. 5), so his baptism is one in nature and operation; that nothing short of it can make us living members of his mystical body; and that the baptism with water, administered by his forerunner John, belonged, as the latter confessed, to an inferior dispensation (John iii. 30).

"With respect to the other rite, we believe that communion between Christ and his church is not maintained by that nor any other external performance, but only by a real participation of his divine nature (1 Pet. ii. 4) through faith; that this is the supper alluded to in the Revelation (Rev. vii. 20): 'Behold I stand at the door and knock: if any man hear my voice, and open the door, I will come in to him, and will sup with him, and he with me;' and that where the substance is attained, it is unnecessary to attend to the shadow, which doth not confer grace, and concerning which opinions so different and animosities so violent have arisen.

"Now, as we thus believe that the grace of God, which
20 *

comes by Jesus Christ, is alone sufficient for salvation, we can neither admit that it is conferred on a few only, whilst others are left without it, nor, thus asserting its universality, can we limit its operation to a partial cleansing of the soul from sin, even in this life. We entertain worthier notions both of the power and goodness of our heavenly Father, and believe that he doth vouchsafe to assist the obedient to experience a total surrender of the natural will to the guidance of his pure, unerring Spirit, through whose renewed assistance they are enabled to bring forth fruits unto holiness, and to stand perfect in their present rank (Matt. v. 48; Eph. iv. 13; Col. iv. 12).

"There are not many of our tenets more generally known than our testimony against oaths, and against war. With respect to the former of these, we abide literally by Christ's positive injunction, delivered in his sermon on the mount, 'Swear not at all' (Matt. v. 34). From the same sacred collection of the most excellent precepts of moral and religious duty, from the example of our Lord himself (Matt. v. 39, 44, &c.; xxvi. 52, 53; Luke xxii. 51; John xviii. 11), and from the correspondent convictions of his Spirit in our hearts, we are confirmed in the belief that wars and fightings are in their origin and effects utterly repugnant to the Gospel, which still breathes peace and good-will to men. We also are clearly of the judgment that if the benevolence of the Gospel were generally prevalent in the minds of men, it would effectually prevent them from oppressing, much more from enslaving, their brethren (of whatever color or complexion), for whom, as for themselves, Christ died; and would even influence their conduct in their treatment of the brute creation, which would no longer groan, the victims of their avarice, or of their false ideas of pleasure.

"Some of our ideas have, in former times, as hath been

shown, subjected our friends to much suffering from government, though to the salutary purposes of government our principles are a security. They inculcate submission to the laws in all cases wherein conscience is not violated. But we hold that as Christ's kingdom is not of this world, it is not the business of the civil magistrate to interfere in matters of religion, but to maintain the external peace and good order of the community. We therefore think persecution, even in the smallest degree, unwarrantable. We are careful in requiring our members not to be concerned in illicit trade, nor in any manner to defraud the revenue.

" It is well known that the society, from its first appearance, has disused those names of the months and days, which, having been given in honor of the heroes or false gods of the heathen, originated in their flattery or superstition; and the custom of speaking to a single person in the plural number, as having arisen also from motives of adulation. Compliments, superfluity of apparel and furniture, outward shows of rejoicing and mourning, and the observation of days and times, we esteem to be incompatible with the simplicity and sincerity of a Christian life; and public diversions, gaming, and other vain amusements of the world, we cannot but condemn. They are a waste of that time which is given us for nobler purposes; and divert the attention of the mind from the sober duties of life, and from the reproofs of instruction by which we are guided to an everlasting inheritance.

"To conclude : although we have exhibited the several tenets which distinguish our religious society as objects of our belief, yet we are sensible that a true and living faith is not produced in the mind of man by his own effort, but is the free gift of God in Christ Jesus (Eph. ii. 8), nourished and increased by the progressive operation of his Spirit in our hearts, and our proportionate obedience (John

vii. 17). Therefore, although for the preservation of the testimonies given us to bear, and for the peace and good order of the society, we deem it necessary that those who are admitted into membership with us should be previously convinced of those doctrines which we esteem essential, yet we require no formal subscription to any articles, either as a condition of membership, or a qualification for the service of the church. We prefer the judging of men by their fruits, and depending on the aid of Him who, by his prophet, hath promised to be 'a spirit of judgment to him that sitteth in judgment.' (Is. xxviii. 6.) Without this, there is a danger of receiving numbers into outward communion, without any addition to that spiritual sheep-fold, whereof our blessed Lord declared himself to be both the door and the shepherd (John x. 7, 11); that is, such as know his voice and follow him in the paths of obedience.

"In the practice of discipline, we think it indispensable that the order recommended by Christ himself be invariably observed (Matt. xviii. 15, 17).

"To effect the salutary purposes of discipline, meetings were appointed at an early period of the society, which, from the times of their being held, were called quarterly meetings. It was afterwards found expedient to divide the districts of those meetings, and to meet more frequently, from whence arose monthly meetings, subordinate to those held quarterly. At length, in 1669, a yearly meeting was established, to superintend, assist, and provide rules for the whole, previously to which general meetings had been occasionally held.

"A monthly meeting is usually composed of several particular congregations, situated within a convenient distance from each other. Its business is to provide for the subsistence of the poor, and for the education of their offspring; to judge of the sincerity and fitness of persons appearing to be convinced of the religious principles of the society, and desiring to be admitted into membership; to excite due attention to the discharge of religious and moral duty; and to deal with disorderly members. Monthly meetings also grant to such of their members as remove into other monthly meetings certificates of their member-ship and conduct; without which they cannot gain membership in such meetings. Each monthly meeting is required to appoint certain persons, under the name of overseers, who are to take care that the rules of our discipline be put in practice; and when any case of complaint or disorderly conduct comes to their knowledge, to see that private admonition, agreeably to the gospel rule before mentioned, be given, previously to its being laid before the monthly meeting.

"When a case is introduced, it is usual for a small committee to be appointed to visit the offender, to endeavor to convince him of his error, and to induce him to forsake and condemn it. If they succeed, the person is by minute declared to have made satisfaction for the offence; if not, he is disowned as a member of the society.

"In disputes between individuals, it has long been the decided judgment of the society that its members should not sue each other at law. It therefore enjoins all to end their differences by speedy and impartial arbitration, agreeably to rules laid down. If any refuse to adopt this mode, or, having adopted it, to submit to the award, it is the direction of the yearly meeting that such be disowned.

"To monthly meetings also belongs the allowing of marriages; for our society hath always scrupled to acknowledge the exclusive authority of the priests in the solemnization of marriage. Those who intend to marry appear together, and propose their intention to the monthly meeting; and if not attended by their parents and guar-

dians, produce a written certificate of their consent, signed
in the presence of witnesses.   The meeting then appoints
a committee to inquire whether they be clear of other en-
gagements respecting marriage; and if at a subsequent
meeting, to which the parties also come and declare the
continuance of their intention, no objections be reported
they have the meeting's consent to solemnize their intended marriage.   This is done in a public meeting for
worship, towards the close whereof the parties stand up,
and solemnly take each other for husband and wife.   A
certificate of the proceedings is then publicly read, and
signed by the parties, and afterwards by the relations and
others as witnesses.   Of such marriage the monthly meeting keeps a record; as also of the births and burials of
its members.   A certificate of the date, of the name of
the infant, and of its parents, signed by those present at
the birth, is the subject of one of these last-mentioned
records; and an order for the interment, countersigned by
the grave-maker, of the other.   The naming of children
is without ceremony.   Burials are also conducted in a simple manner.   The body, followed by the relations and
friends, is sometimes, previously to interment, carried to a
meeting; and at the grave a pause is generally made; on
both which occasions it frequently falls out that one or
more friends present have somewhat to express for the edification of those who attend; but no religious rite is considered as an essential part of burial.

" Several monthly meetings compose a quarterly meeting.   At the quarterly meeting are produced written
answers from the monthly meetings to certain queries respecting the conduct of their members, and the meeting's
care over them.   The accounts thus received are digested
into one, which is sent, also in the form of answers to
queries, by representatives to the yearly meeting.   Ap-

peals from the judgment of monthly meetings are brought
to the quarterly meetings, whose business also it is to assist
in any difficult case, or where remissness appears in the
care of the monthly meetings over the individuals who
compose them. There are seven yearly meetings, viz.:
1. London, to which come representatives from Ireland;
2 New England; 3. New York; 4. Pennsylvania and
New Jersey; 5. Maryland; 6. Virginia; 7. The Carolinas
and Georgia.

"The yearly meeting has the general superintendence
of the society in the country in which it is established;
and, therefore, as the accounts which it receives discover
the state of inferior meetings, as particular exigencies require, or as the meeting is impressed with a sense of duty,
it gives its advice, making such regulations as appear to
be requisite, or excites to the observance of those already
made; and sometimes appoints committees to visit those
quarterly meetings which appear to be in need of immediate advice. Appeals from the judgment of quarterly
meetings are here finally determined; and a brotherly correspondence, by epistles, is maintained with other yearly
meetings.

"In this place it is proper to add, that, as we believe
women may be rightly called to the work of the ministry,
we also think that to them belongs a share in the support
of our Christian discipline; and that some parts of it
wherein their own sex is concerned, devolve on them with
peculiar propriety; accordingly they have monthly, quarterly, and yearly meetings of their own sex, held at the
same time, and in the same place with those of the men;
but separately, and without the power of making rules;
and it may be remarked, that during the persecutions
which in the last century occasioned the imprisonment of

so many of the men, the care of the poor often fell on the women, and was by them satisfactorily administered.

"In order that those who are in the situation of ministers may have the tender sympathy and counsel of those of either sex who, by their experience in the work of religion, are qualified for that service, the monthly meetings are advised to select such, under the denomination of elders. These, and ministers approved by their monthly meetings, have meetings peculiar to themselves, called meetings of ministers and elders; in which they have an opportunity of exciting each other to a discharge of their several duties, and of extending advice to those who may appear to be weak, without any needless exposure. Such meetings are generally held in the compass of each monthly, quarterly, and yearly meeting. They are conducted by rules prescribed by the yearly meeting, and have no authority to make any alteration or addition to them. The members of them unite with their brethren in the meetings for discipline, and are equally accountable to the latter for their conduct.

"It is to a meeting of this kind in London, called the second day's morning meeting, that the revisal of manuscripts concerning our principles, previously to publication, is intrusted by the yearly meeting; and also the granting, in the intervals of the yearly meeting, of certificates of approbation to such ministers as are concerned to travel in the work of the ministry in foreign parts, in addition to those granted by their monthly or quarterly meetings. When a visit of this kind doth not extend beyond Great Britain, a certificate from the monthly meeting of which the minister is a member, is sufficient; if to Ireland, the concurrence of the quarterly meeting is also required. Regulations of similar tendency obtain in other yearly meetings.

"The yearly meeting of London, in the year 1675, appointed a meeting to be held in that city, for the purpose of advising and assisting in cases of suffering for conscience' sake, which hath continued with great use to the society to this day. It is composed of friends, under the name of correspondents, chosen by the several quarterly meetings, and who reside in or near the society. The same meetings also appoint members of their own in the country as correspondents, who are to join their brethren in London on emergency. The names of all these correspondents, previously to their being recorded as such, are submitted to the approbation of the yearly meeting. Those of the men who are approved ministers are also members of this meeting, which is called the meeting for sufferings—a name arising from its original purpose, which is not yet become entirely obsolete.

"The yearly meeting has intrusted the meeting for sufferings with the care of printing and distributing books, and with the management of its stock; and, considered as a standing committee of the yearly meeting, it hath a general care of whatever may arise, during the intervals of that meeting, affecting the society, and requiring immediate attention, particularly of those circumstances which may occasion an application to government.

"There is not, in any of the meetings which have been mentioned, any president, as we believe that divine wisdom alone ought to preside; nor hath any member a right to claim pre-eminence over the rest. The office of clerk, with a few exceptions, is undertaken voluntarily by some member, as is also the keeping of the records. When these are very voluminous, and require a house for their deposit (as is the case in London, where the general records of the society in Great Britain are kept), a clerk is hired to have the care of them; but except a few clerks of this kind, and persons who have the care of meeting-houses, none receive any stipend or gratuity for their services in our religious society."

George Fox, the founder of this sect, was brought before two justices in Derbyshire, one of whom reviled him, and bade him *tremble* at the word of the Lord. From this circumstance arose the appellation *Quakers*, usually given to his followers; they call themselves *Friends*, from the scriptural salutation, "Our friends salute thee." In 1656 they came to America, and settled principally in Pennsylvania. They are opposed to the practice of taking oaths, and to war, in all its forms. They agree with the Baptists in denying the validity of infant baptism. They extend the privilege of preaching the gospel to females as well as to males. They have also peculiar notions in regard to dress, plainness and simplicity in language, etc.

Within a few years past, in this country, there has been a serious schism among the Quakers — a part professing the doctrines of Unitarianism, and called *Hicksites*, from their leader, the late Elias Hicks; the other portion adhering to the orthodox doctrines. It having been made a question which of them ought to be considered as *seceding* from the doctrines of the original sect, the yearly meeting of the Friends in London, May 20, 1829, sent forth an epistle containing a statement of their belief; from which it appears that they fully believe in the inspiration of the Scriptures, the supreme divinity of our Lord Jesus Christ, and in the atonement by his sufferings and death. By late reports, it appears that there are in the United States about 150,000 members of this society, of whom more than 50,000 are Hicksites; the remainder principally orthodox.

ARIANS.

ARIANS, followers of Arius, a presbyter of the church of Alexandria, about 315, who maintained that the Son of God was totally and essentially distinct from the Father; that he was the first and noblest of those beings whom God had created — the instrument, by whose subordinate operation he formed the universe; and, therefore, inferior to the Father both in nature and dignity; also, that the Holy Ghost was not God, but created by the power of the Son.

The Arians owned that the Son was the Word; but denied that Word to have been eternal. They held that Christ had nothing of man in him but the flesh, to which the λογος, or word, was joined, which was the same as the soul in us. The Arians were first condemned and anathematized by a council at Alexandria, in 320, under Alexander, bishop of that city, who accused Arius of impiety, and caused him to be expelled from the communion of the church; and afterwards by 380 fathers in the general council of Nice, assembled by Constantine, in 325. His doctrine, however, was not extinguished; on the contrary, it became the reigning religion, especially in the east.

Arius was recalled from banishment by Constantine in two or three years after the council of Nice, and the laws that had been enacted against him were repealed. Notwithstanding this, Athanasius, then bishop of Alexandria, refused to admit him and his followers to communion. This so enraged them, that, by their interest at court, they procured that prelate to be deposed and banished; but the church of Alexandria still refusing to admit Arius into their communion, the emperor sent for him to Constantinople; where upon delivering in a fresh confession of his faith in terms less offensive, the emperor commanded him to be received into their communion; but that very evening, it is said, Arius died as his friends were conducting him in triumph to the great church of Constantinople.

Arius, pressed by a natural want, stepped aside, but expired on the spot, his bowels gushing out. The Arian party, however, found a protector in Constantinus, who succeeded his father in the East. They underwent various revolutions and persecutions under succeeding emperors, till, at length, Theodosius the Great exerted every effort to suppress them. Their doctrine was carried, in the fifth century, into Africa, under the Vandals; and into Asia under the Goths. Italy, Gaul, and Spain, were also deeply infected with it; and towards the commencement of the sixth century, it was triumphant in many parts of Asia, Africa, and Europe; but it sunk almost at once, when the Vandals were driven out of Africa, and the Goths out of Italy by the arms of Justinian. However, it revived again in Italy, under the protection of the Lombards, in the seventh century, and was not extinguished till about the end of the eighth. Arianism was again revived in the West by Servetus, in 1531, for which he suffered death.

After this, the doctrine got footing in Geneva and in Poland; but at length degenerated in a great measure into Socinianism. Erasmus, it is thought, aimed at reviving it, in his commentaries on the New Testament; and the learned Grotius seems to lean that way. Mr. Whiston was one of the first divines who revived this controversy in the eighteenth century. He was followed by Dr. Clarke, who was chiefly opposed by Dr. Waterland. Those who hold the doctrine which is usually called *Low Arianism*, say that Christ pre-existed; but not as the eternal Logos of the Father, or as the being by whom he made the worlds, and had intercourse with the patriarchs, or as having any certain rank or employment whatever in the divine dispensations. In modern times, the term *Arian* is indiscriminately applied to those who consider Jesus simply subordinate to the Father. Some of them believe Christ to have been the creator of the world; but they all maintain that he existed previously to his incarnation, though in his pre-existent state they assign him different degrees of dignity. Hence the terms *High* and *Low Arian*.

ARMENIANS.

THE Armenians are the inhabitants of Armenia, whose religion is the Christian of the Eutychian sect; that is, they hold but one nature in Jesus Christ. They assert also the procession of the Holy Ghost from the Father only. They believe that Christ, at his descent into hell, freed the souls of the damned from thence, and reprieved them to the end of the world, when they shall be remanded to eternal flames. They believe that the souls of the righteous shall not be admitted to the beatific vision till after the resurrection, notwithstanding which they pray to departed saints, adore their pictures, and burn lamps before them. The Armenian clergy consist of patriarchs, archbishops, doctors, secular priests, and monks. The Armenian monks are of the order of St. Basil; and every Wednesday and Friday they eat neither fish, nor eggs, nor oil, nor anything made of milk; and during Lent they live upon nothing but roots. They have seven sacraments, baptism, confirmation, penance, the eucharist, extreme unction, orders, and matrimony. They admit infants to the communion at two or three months old. They seem to place the chief part of their religion in fastings and abstinences; and, among the clergy, the higher the degree, the lower they must live; insomuch, that it is said the archbishops live on nothing but pulse. They consecrate holy water but once a year, at which time every one fills a pot and carries it home, which brings in a considerable revenue to the church.

ARMINIANS.

THE Arminians are persons who follow the doctrines of Arminius, who was pastor at Amsterdam, and afterwards professor of divinity at Leyden. Arminius had been educated in the opinions of Calvin; but, thinking the doctrine of that great man with regard to free will, predestination, and grace, too severe, he began to express his doubts concerning them in the year 1591; and, upon further inquiry, adopted the sentiments of those whose religious system extends the love of the Supreme Being and the merits of Jesus Christ to all mankind. The Arminians are also called Remonstrants, because, in 1611, they presented a remonstrance to the states-general, wherein they state their grievances, and pray for relief.

The distinguishing *tenets* of the Arminians may be comprised in the five following articles relative to predestination, universal redemption, the corruption of man, conversion, and perseverance, viz.:

I. That God, from all eternity, determined to bestow salvation on those who he foresaw would persevere unto the end; and to inflict everlasting punishments on those who should continue their unbelief, and resist his divine succors; so that election was conditional, and reprobation in like manner the result of foreseen infidelity and persevering wickedness.

II. That Jesus Christ, by his sufferings and death, made an atonement for the sins of all mankind in general, and of every individual in particular; that, however, none but those who believe in him can be partakers of divine benefits.

III. That true faith cannot proceed from the exercise of our natural faculties and powers, nor from the force and operation of free will; since man, in consequence of his natural corruption, is incapable either of thinking or doing any good thing; and that, therefore, it is necessary, in order to his conversion and salvation, that he be regenerated and renewed by the operations of the Holy Ghost, which is the gift of God through Jesus Christ.

IV. That this divine grace or energy of the Holy Ghost begins and perfects everything that can be called good in man, and, consequently, all good works are to be attributed to God alone; that, nevertheless, this grace is offered to all, and does not force men to act against their inclinations, but may be resisted and rendered ineffectual by the perverse will of the impenitent sinner. Some modern Arminians interpret this and the last article with a greater latitude.

V. That God gives to the truly faithful, who are regenerated by his grace, the means of preserving themselves in this state. The first Arminians, indeed, had some doubt with respect to the closing part of this article; but their followers uniformly maintain "that the regenerate may lose true justifying faith, fall from a state of grace, and die in their sins."

After the appointment of Arminius to the theological chair at Leyden, he thought it his duty to avow and vindicate the principles which he had embraced; and the

freedom with which he published and defended tnem.
exposed`him to the resentment of those that adhered to
the theological system of Geneva, which then prevailed in
Holland; but his principal opponent was Gomar, his colleague. The controversy which was thus begun became
more general after the death of Arminius, in the year
1609, and threatened to involve the United Provinces in
civil discord. The Arminian tenets gained ground under
the mild and favorable treatment of the magistrates of
Holland, and were adopted by several persons of merit
and distinction. The Calvanists or Gomarists, as they
were now called, appealed to a national synod; accordingly, the synod of Dort convened, by order of the states-
general, in 1618; and was composed of ecclesiastic deputies from the United Provinces, as well as from the reformed churches of England, Hessia, Bremen, Switzerland,
and the Palatinate. The principal advocate in favor of
the Arminians was Episcopius, who at that time was professor of divinity at Leyden. It was first proposed to
discuss the principal subjects in dispute, that the Arminians
should be allowed to state and vindicate the grounds on
which their opinions were founded; but, some difference
arising as to the proper mode of conducting the debate,
the Arminians were excluded from the assembly, their
case was tried in their absence; and they were pronounced
guilty of pestilential errors, and condemned as corrupters
of the true religion. A curious account of the proceedings
of the above synod may be seen in a series of letters
written by Mr. John Hales, who was present on the
occasion.

In consequence of the above-mentioned decision, the
Arminians were considered as enemies to their country
and its established religion, and were much persecuted.
They were treated with great severity, and deprived of all

their posts and employments; their ministers were silenced, and their congregations were suppressed. The great Barneveldt was beheaded on a scaffold; and the learned Grotius, being condemned to perpetual imprisonment, fled, and took refuge in France.

After the death of Prince Maurice, who had been a violent partisan in favor of the Gomarists, in the year 1625, the Arminian exiles were restored to their former reputation and tranquillity; and, under the toleration of the state, they erected churches and founded a college at Amsterdam, appointing Episcopius the first theological professor. The Arminian system has very much prevailed in England since the time of Archbishop Laud, and its votaries in other countries are very numerous. It is generally supposed that a majority of the clergy in both the established churches of Great Britain favor the Arminian system, notwithstanding their articles are strictly Calvinistic. The name of Mr. John Wesley need hardly be mentioned here. Every one knows what an advocate he was for the tenets of Arminius, and the success he met with.

THE BAXTERIANS

ARE so called from the learned and pious Mr. Richard Baxter, who was born in the year 1615. His design was to reconcile Calvin and Arminius: for this purpose he formed a middle scheme between their systems. He taught that God had elected some, whom he is determined to save, without any foresight of their good works: and that others to whom the gospel is preached have common grace, which, if they improve, they shall obtain saving grace, according to the doctrine of Arminius. This denomination own, with Calvin, that the merits of Christ's death are to be applied to believers only; but they also assert that all men are in a state capable of salvation.

Mr. Baxter maintains that there may be a certainty of perseverance here, and yet he cannot tell whether a man may not have so weak a degree of saving grace as to lose it again.

In order to prove that the death of Christ has put all in a state capable of salvation, the following arguments are alleged by this learned author: — 1. It was the nature of all mankind which Christ assumed at his incarnation, and the sins of all mankind were the occasion of his suffering. — 2. It was to Adam, as the common father of lapsed mankind, that God made the promise (Gen. iii. 15). The conditional new covenant does equally give Christ, pardon, and life to all mankind, on condition of acceptance. The conditional grant is universal: *Whoever believeth shall be saved.* — 3. It is not to the elect only, but to all mankind, that Christ has commanded his ministers to proclaim his gospel, and offer the benefits of his procuring.

There are, Mr. Baxter allows, certain fruits of Christ's death which are proper to the elect only:—1. Grace eventually worketh in them true faith, repentance, conversion, and union with Christ as his living members. — 2. The actual forgiveness of sin as to the spiritual and eternal punishment. — 3. Our reconciliation with God, and adoption and right to the heavenly inheritance.—4. The Spirit of Christ to dwell in us and sanctify us, by a habit of divine love, Rom. viii. 9–13; Gal. v. 6.— 5. Employment in holy, acceptable service, and access in prayer, with a promise of being heard through Christ, Heb. ii. 5, 6; John xiv. 13. — 6. Well-grounded hopes of salvation, peace of conscience, and spiritual communion with the Church mystical in heaven and earth, Rom. v. 12; Heb.

xii. 22. — 7. A special interest in Christ and intercession with the Father, Rom. viii. 32, 33. 8. Resurrection unto life, and justification in judgment; glorification of the soul at death, and of the body at the resurrection, Phil. iii. 20, 21; 2 Cor. v. 1, 2, 3.

Christ has made a conditional deed of gift of these benefits to all mankind; but the elect only accept and possess them. Hence he infers that, though Christ never absolutely intended or decreed that his death should eventually put all men in possession of those benefits, yet he did intend and decree that all men should have a conditional gift of them by his death.

Baxter, it is said, wrote one hundred and twenty books, and had sixty written against him. Twenty thousand of his Call to the Unconverted were sold in one year. He told a friend that six brothers were converted by reading that Call. The eminent Mr. Elliott, of New England, translated this tract into the Indian tongue. A young Indian prince was so taken with it, that he read it with tears, and died with it in his hand.

SHAKERS.

A sect which was instituted about the year 1774, in England. Ann Lee, whom they style the Elect Lady, is the head of this party. They assert that she is the woman spoken of in the 12th chapter of Revelations, and that she speaks seventy-two tongues; and though those tongues are unintelligible to the living, she converses with the dead, who understand her language. They add further, that she is the mother of all the elect, and that she travails for the whole world; that, in fine, no blessing can descend to any person but only by and through her, and that in the way of her being possessed of their sins by their confessing and repenting of them, one by one, according to her direction. They vary in their exercises: their heavy dancing, as it is called, is performed by a perpetual springing from the house floor, about four inches up and down, both in the men's and women's apartments, moving about with extraordinary transport, singing sometimes one at a time, and sometimes more. This elevation affects the nerves, so that they have intervals of shuddering, as if they were in a violent fit of the ague. They sometimes clap their hands, and leap so high as to strike the joists above their heads. They throw off their outside garment in these exercises, and spend their strength very cheerfully this way: their chief speaker often calls for their attention, when they all stop, and hear some harangue, and then begin dancing again. They assert that their dancing is the token of the great joy and happiness of the Jerusalem state, and denotes the victory over sin. One of their most favorite exertions is turning round very swiftly for an hour or two. This, they say, is to show the great power of God. Such is the account which different writers have given us of this sect; but others observe that though, at first, they used these violent gesticulations, now they have "a regular, solemn, uniform *dance*, or genuflection, to a regular, solemn hymn, which is sung by the elders, and as regularly conducted as a proper band of music." See *New York Theol. Mag.* for Nov. and Dec. 1795.

SHAKERS IN THE UNITED STATES.

This society is sometimes called the *Millennial Church.* They are denominated *Shakers*, from the violent bodily commotions with which they are sometimes seized. In 1780, ten or twelve individuals came to this country from

England. In 1787, they formed themselves into a society at New Lebanon, New York, and established a community of goods in all respects. Their general employments are agriculture and the mechanic arts. They are remarkable for their neatness, sobriety, honesty, and harmlessness. Their peculiar manner of worship is by *dancing.* Societies of Shakers are formed at Alfred and New Gloucester, Me.; Canterbury and Enfield, N. H.; Shirley, Harvard, Tyringham, and Hancock, Mass.; Enfield, Conn.; Watervliet and New Lebanon, N. Y.; Union Village and Watervliet, Ohio; Pleasant Hill and South Union, Ky. Number of societies 16; preachers, 45; population, 5,400.

THEOPHILANTHROPISTS

ARE a sect of Deists who, in September, 1796, published at Paris a sort of catechism or directory for social worship, under the title of *Manuel des Theanthrophiles.* This religious breviary found favor; the congregation became numerous; and in the second edition of their Manuel they assumed the less harsh denomination of *Theophilanthropists, i. e.,* lovers of God and man. According to them, the temple the most worthy of the Divinity is the universe. Abandoned sometimes under the vault of heaven to the contemplation of the beauties of nature, they render its Author the homage of adoration and of gratitude. They nevertheless have temples erected by the hands of men, in which it is more commodious for them to assemble, to hear lessons concerning his wisdom. Certain moral inscriptions, a simple altar, on which they deposit a sign of gratitude for the benefits of the Creator, such flowers or fruits as the seasons afford, a tribute for the lectures and discourses, form the whole of the ornaments of their temples.

The first inscription, placed above the altar, recalls to remembrance the two religious dogmas which are the foundation of their moral.

First inscription.—We believe in the existence of God, in the immortality of the soul. *Second inscription.*—Worship God, cherish your kind, render yourselves useful to your country. *Third inscription.* — Good is everything which tends to the preservation or the perfection of man. Evil is everything which tends to destroy or deteriorate him. *Fourth inscription.*—Children, honor your fathers and mothers; obey them with affection, comfort their old age. Fathers and mothers, instruct your children. *Fifth inscription.*—Wives, regard your husbands, the chiefs of your houses. Husbands, love your wives, and render yourselves reciprocally happy.

From the concluding part of the *Manuel* of the Theophilanthropists, we may learn something more of their sentiments. "If any one ask you," say they, "what is the origin of your religion and of your worship, you can answer him thus: Open the most ancient books which are known, seek there what was the religion, what the worship of the first human beings of which history has preserved the remembrance. There you will see that their religion was what we now call *natural religion*, because it has for its principle even the Author of nature. It is he that has engraven it in the heart of the first human beings, in ours, in that of all the inhabitants of the earth; this religion, which consists in worshipping God and cherishing our kind, is what we express by one single word, that of *Theophilanthropy.* Thus our religion is that of our first parents; it is yours; it is ours; it is the universal religion. As to our worship, it is also that of our first fathers. See even in the most ancient writings, that the exterior signs by which they rendered their homage to the Creator were of great simplicity. They dressed for him an altar of earth; they offered him, in sign of their gratitude and of their submission, some of the productions which they held of his liberal hand. The fathers exhorted their children to virtue; they all encouraged one another, under the auspices of the Divinity, to the accomplishment of their duties. This simple worship the sages of all nations have not ceased to profess, and they have transmitted it down to us without interruption.

"If they yet ask you of whom 'you hold your mission, answer, we hold it of God himself, who, in giving us two arms to aid our kind, has also given us intelligence to mutually enlighten us, and the love of good to bring us together to virtue; of God, who has given experience and wisdom to the aged to guide the young, and authority to fathers to conduct their children.

"If they are not struck with the force of those reasons, do not farther discuss the subject, and do not engage yourself in controversies, which tend to diminish the love of our neighbors. Our principles are the Eternal Truth; they will subsist, whatever individuals may support or attack them, and the efforts of the wicked will not even prevail against them. Rest firmly attached to them, without attacking or defending any religious system; and remember that similar discussions have never produced good, and that they have often tinged the earth with the blood of men. Let us lay aside systems, and apply ourselves to doing good; it is the only road to happiness." So much for the divinity of the Theophilanthropists; a system entirely defective, because it wants the true foundation, — the word of God; the grand rule of all our actions, and the only basis on which our hopes and prospects of success can be built.

GNOSTICS.

THE Gnostics were ancient heretics, famous from the first rise of Christianity, principally in the east. It appears from several passages of Scripture, particularly 1 John ii. 18; 1 Tim. vi. 20; Col. ii. 8; that many persons were infected with the Gnostic heresy in the first century; though the sect did not render itself conspicuous, either for numbers or reputation, before the time of Adrian, when some writers erroneously date its rise. The name was adopted by this sect, on the presumption that they were the only persons who had the true *knowledge* of Christianity. Accordingly, they looked on all other Christians as simple, ignorant, and barbarous persons, who explained and interpreted the sacred writings in a low, literal, and unedifying signification. At first, the Gnostics were the only philosophers and wits of those times, who formed for themselves a peculiar system of theology, agreeable to the philosophy of Pythagoras and Plato; to which they accommodated all their interpretations of Scripture. But Gnostics afterwards became a generical name, comprehending divers sects and parties of heretics, who rose in the first centuries; and who, though they differed among themselves as to circumstances, yet all agreed in some common principles. They corrupted the doctrine of the Gospel by a profane mixture of the tenets of the oriental philosophy, concerning the origin of evil and the creation of the world, with its divine truths. Such were the Valentinians, Simonians, Carpocratians, Nicolaitans, &c.

Gnostic sometimes also occurs in a good sense, in the ancient ecclesiastical writers, particularly Clemens Alexandrinus, who in the person of his Gnostic describes the characters and qualities of a perfect Christian. This point he labors in the seventh book of his *Stromata*, where he shows that none but the Gnostic or learned person has any true religion. He affirms that, were it possible for the knowledge of God to be separated from eternal salvation, the Gnostic would make no scruple to choose the knowledge; and that if God would promise him impunity in doing anything that he has once spoken against, or offer him heaven on those terms, he would never alter a whit of his measures. In this sense the father uses Gnostics, in opposition to the heretics of the same name; affirming that the true Gnostic is grown old in the study of the holy Scripture, and that he preserves the orthodox doctrine of the apostles, and of the church; whereas the false Gnostic abandons all the apostolical traditions as imagining himself wiser than the apostles.

Gnostics was sometimes also more particularly used for the successors of the Nicolaitans and Carpocratians, in the second century, upon their laying aside the names of the first authors. Such as would be thoroughly acquainted with all their doctrines, reveries, and visions, may consult *St. Irenæus, Tertullian, Clemens Alexandrinus, Origen,* and *St. Epiphanius;* particularly the first of these writers, who relates their sentiments at large, and confutes them. Indeed he dwells more on the Valentinians than any other sect of Gnostics; but he shows the general principles whereon all their mistaken opinions were founded, and the method they followed in explaining Scripture. He accuses them of introducing into religion certain vain and ridiculous genealogies, i. e. a kind of divine processions or emanations, which had no other foundation but in their own wild imagination. The Gnostics confessed that these æons, or emanations, were nowhere expressly delivered in the sacred writings; but insisted that Jesus Christ had intimated them in parables to such as could understand them. They built their theology not only on the Gospels and the epistles of St. Paul, but also on the law of Moses and the prophets. These last were peculiarly serviceable to them, on account of the allegories and allusions with which they abound, which are capable of different interpretations, though their doctrine concerning the creation of the world by one or more inferior beings of an evil or imperfect nature, led them to deny the divine authority of the books of the Old Testament, which contradicted this idle fiction, and filled them with an abhorrence of Moses and the religion he taught; alleging that he was actuated by the malignant author of this world, who consulted his own glory and authority, and not the real advantage of men. Their persuasion that evil resided in matter, as its centre and source, made them treat the body with contempt, discourage marriage, and reject the doctrine of the resurrection of the body, and its reunion with the immortal spirit. Their notion that malevolent genii presided in nature, and occasioned diseases and calamities, wars and desolations, induced them to apply themselves to the study of magic, in order to weaken the powers, or suspend the influence of these malignant agents. The Gnostics considered Jesus Christ as the Son of God, and inferior to the Father, who came into the world for the rescue and happiness of miserable mortals, oppressed by matter and evil beings; but they rejected our Lord's humanity, on the principle that everything corporeal is essentially and intrinsically evil; and therefore the greatest part of them denied the reality of his sufferings. They set a great value on the beginning of the Gospel of St. John, where they fancied they saw a great deal of their æons, or emanations, under the terms, the *word*, the *life*, the *light*, &c. They divided all nature into three kinds of beings, viz.: *hylic,*

or material; *psychic*, or animal; and *pneumatic*, or spiritual. On the like principle they also distinguished three
sorts of men; *material, animal,* and *spiritual.* The first,
who were material, and incapable of knowledge, inevitably
perished, both soul and body; the third, such as the
Gnostics themselves pretended to be, were all certainly
saved; the psychic, or animal, who were the middle
between the other two, were capable either of being saved
or damned, according to their good or evil actions. With
regard to their moral doctrines and conduct, they were
much divided. The greatest part of this sect adopted very
austere rules of life, recommended rigorous abstinence, and
prescribed severe bodily mortifications, with a view of
purifying and exalting the mind. However, some maintained that there was no moral difference in human actions;
and thus confounding right with wrong, they gave a loose
rein to all the passions, and asserted the innocence of following blindly all their motions, and of living by their
tumultuous dictates. They supported their opinions and
practice by various authorities; some referred to fictitious
and apocryphal writings of Adam, Abraham, Zoroaster,
Christ, and his apostles; others boasted that they had
deduced their sentiments from secret doctrines of Christ,
concealed from the vulgar; others affirmed that they
arrived at superior degrees of wisdom by an innate vigor
of mind; and others asserted that they were instructed in
these mysterious parts of theological science by Theudas,
a disciple of St. Paul, and by Matthias, one of the friends
of our Lord. The tenets of the ancient Gnostics were
revived in Spain, in the fourth century. by a sect called
the Priscillianists. At length the name *Gnostic,* which
originally was glorious, became infamous, by the idle
opinions and dissolute lives of the persons who bore it.

HUSSITES,

A PARTY of reformers, the followers of John Huss.—John Huss. from whom the Hussites take their name, was born in a little village in Bohemia, called Huss, and lived at Prague in the highest reputation, both on account of the sanctity of his manners and the purity of his doctrine. He was distinguished by his uncommon erudition and eloquence; and performed at the same time the functions of professor of divinity in the university, and of ordinary pastor in the church of that city. He adopted the senti ments of Wickliffe and the Waldenses; and, in the year 1407. began openly to oppose and preach against divers errors in doctrine, as well as corruptions in point of disci- pline, then reigning in the Church. Huss likewise endea- vored to the utmost of his power to withdraw the univer- sity of Prague from the jurisdiction of Gregory XII., whom the king of Bohemia had hitherto acknowledged as the true and lawful head of the Church. This occasioned a violent quarrel between the incensed Archbishop of Prague and the zealous Reformer, which the latter inflamed and augmented from day to day, by his pathetic exclama- tions against the court of Rome, and the corruption that prevailed among the sacerdotal order.

There were other circumstances that contributed to inflame the resentment of the clergy against him. He adopted the philosophical opinions of the Realists, and vehemently opposed and even persecuted the Nominalists, whose number and influence were considerable in the Uni- versity of Prague. He also multiplied the number of his enemies in the year 1408, by procuring through his own credit, a sentence in favor of the Bohemians, who disputed with the Germans concerning the number of suffrages which their respective nations were entitled to in all matters that were carried by election in this university. In consequence of a decree obtained in favor of the former, which restored them to their constitutional right of three suffrages, usurped by the latter, the Germans withdrew from Prague, and in the year 1409, founded a new academy at Leipsic. This event no sooner happened than Huss began to inveigh, with greater freedom than he had done before, against the vices and corruptions of the clergy; and to recommend in a public manner the writings and opinions of Wickliffe, as far as they related to the papal hierarchy, the despotism of the court of Rome, and the corruption of the clergy. Hence, an accusation was brought against him, in the year 1410, before the tribunal of John XXIII., by whom he was solemnly expelled from the communion of the Church. Notwithstanding this sentence of excommunication, he proceeded to expose the Romish Church with a fortitude and zeal that were almost universally applauded.

This eminent man, whose piety was equally sincere and fervent, though his zeal was perhaps too violent, and his prudence not always circumspect, was summoned to appear before the Council of Constance. Secured, as he thought from the rage of his enemies by the safe-conduct granted him by the Emperor Sigismund for his journey to Constance, his residence in that place, and his return to his own country, John Huss obeyed the order of the Council, and appeared before it to demonstrate his innocence, and to prove that the charge of his having deserted the Church of Rome was entirely groundless. However, his enemies so far prevailed, that by the most scandalous breach of public faith, he was cast into prison, declared a heretic, because he refused to plead guilty against the dictates of his conscience, in obedience to the Council, and burnt alive in 1415; a punishment which he endured with unparalleled magnanimity and resolution.   When he came to the place of execution, he fell on his knees, sang portions of psalms, looked steadfastly towards heaven, and repeated these words : " Into Thy hands, O Lord, do I commit my spirit ; Thou hast redeemed me, O most good and faithful God. Lord Jesus Christ assist and help me, that with a firm and present mind, by Thy most powerful grace I may undergo this most cruel and ignominious death, to which I am condemned for preaching the truth of Thy most holy gospel." When the chain was put upon him at the stake, he said, with a smiling countenance, " My Lord Jesus Christ was bound with a harder chain than this for my sake, and why should I be ashamed of this old rusty one ?"   When the fagots were piled up to his very neck, the Duke of Bavaria was officious enough to desire him to abjure.   " No," says Huss, " I never preached any doctrine of an evil tendency ; and what I taught with my lips I seal with my blood."   He said to the executioner, "Are you going to burn a goose ?   In one century you will have a *swan* you can neither roast nor boil."   If he were prophetic, he must have meant Luther, who had a swan for his arms.   The fire was then applied to the fagots ; when the martyr sang a hymn, with so loud and cheerful a voice, that he was heard through all the cracklings of the combustibles and the noise of the multitude.   At last his voice was cut short, after he had uttered, " Jesus Christ, thou Son of the living God, have mercy upon me," and he was consumed in a most miserable manner.   The Duke of Bavaria ordered the executioner to throw all the martyr's clothes into the flames ; after which his ashes were carefully collected, and cast into the Rhine.

But the cause in which this eminent man was engaged did not die with him. His disciples adhered to their master's doctrines after his death, which broke out into an open war. John Ziska, a Bohemian knight, in 1420, put himself at the head of the Hussites, who were now become a very considerable party, and threw off the despotic yoke of Sigismund, who had treated their brethren in the most barbarous manner. Ziska was succeded by Procopius, in the year 1424. Acts of barbarity were committed on both sides; for, notwithstanding the irreconcilable opposition between the religious sentiments of the contending parties, they both agreed in this one horrible principle, that it was innocent and lawful to persecute and extirpate with fire and sword the enemies of the true religion; and such they reciprocally appeared to each other. These commotions in a great measure subsided by the interference of the Council of Basil, in the year 1433.

The Hussites, who were divided into two parties, viz. the Calixtines and the Taborites, spread over all Bohemia and Hungary, and even Silesia and Poland; and there are, it is said, some remains of them still subsisting in those parts.

HUTCHINSONIANS.

HUTCHINSONIANS, the followers of John Hutchinson, who was born in Yorkshire, in 1674. In the early part of his life he served the Duke of Somerset in the capacity of steward; and in the course of his travels from place to place, employed himself in collecting fossils. We are told that the large and noble collection bequeathed by Dr. Woodward to the University of Cambridge was actually made by him, and even unfairly obtained from him. In 1724, he published the first part of his curious book, called *Moses' Principia*, in which he ridiculed Dr. Woodward's Natural History of the Earth, and exploded the doctrine of gravitation established in Newton's Principia. In 1727, he published a second part of Moses' Principia, containing the principles of the Scripture philosophy. From this time to his death, he published a volume every year or two, which, with the manuscripts he left behind, were published in 1748, in 12 volumes, 8vo. On the Monday before his death, Dr. Mead urged him to be bled; saying, pleasantly, "I will soon send you to Moses," meaning his studies; but Mr. Hutchinson, taking it in the literal sense, answered, in a muttering tone, "I believe, doctor, you will;" and was so displeased, that he dismissed him for another physician; but he died in a few days after, August 28, 1737.

It appears to be a leading sentiment of this denomination, that all our ideas of divinity are formed from the ideas in nature, — that nature is a standing picture, and Scripture an application of the several parts of the picture, to draw out to, as the great things of God, in order to reform our mental conceptions. To prove this point, they allege that the Scriptures declare *the invisible things of God from the formation of the world are clearly seen, being understood by the things which are made; even his eternal power and Godhead*, (Rom. i. 20). *The heavens must declare God's righteousness and truth in the congregation of the saints*, (Ps. lxxxix. 5.) And, in short, the whole system of nature, in one voice of analogy, declares and gives us ideas of his glory, and shows us his handiwork. We cannot have any ideas of invisible things till they are pointed out to us by revelation; and as we cannot know them immediately, such as they are in themselves, after the manner in which we know sensible objects, they must be communicated to us by the mediation of such things as we already comprehend. For this reason the Scripture is found to have a language of its own, which does not consist of words, but of signs or figures taken from visible things; in consequence of which, the world we now see becomes a sort of commentary on the mind of God, and explains the world in which we believe. The doctrines of the Christian faith are attested by the whole natural world; they are recorded in a language which has never been confounded; they are written in a text which shall never be corrupted. .

The Hutchinsonians maintain that the great mystery of the Trinity is conveyed to our understanding by ideas of sense; and that the created substance of the air, or heaven, in its threefold agency of fire, light, and spirit, is the enigma of the one essence or one Jehovah in three persons. The unity of essence is exhibited by its unity of substance; the trinity, of conditions, fire, light, and spirit. Thus the one substance of the air, or heaven, in its three conditions, shows the unity in trinity; and its three conditions in or of one substance, the trinity in unity. For (says this denomination) if we consult the writings of the Old and New Testament, we shall find the persons of the Deity represented under the names and characters of the three material agents, fire, light, and spirit, and their actions expressed by the actions of these their emblems. The Father is called a consuming fire; and his judicial proceedings are spoken of in words which denote the several actions of fire. *Jehovah is a consuming fire; our God is a consuming fire,* (Deut. iv. 24; Heb. xii. 29). The Son has the name of light, and his purifying actions and offices are described by words which denote the actions and offices of light. *He is the true light, which lighteth*

23

every man that cometh into the world, (John i. 9; Mal. iv. 2).
The Comforter has the name of Spirit; and his animating
and sustaining offices are described by words, for the
actions and offices of the material spirit. His actions in
the spiritual economy are agreeable to his type in the
natural economy; such as inspiring, impelling, driving,
leading, (Matt. ii. 1). The philosophic system of the
Hutchinsonians is derived from the Hebrew Scriptures.
The truth of it rests on these suppositions: 1. That the
Hebrew language was formed under Divine inspiration,
either all at once, or at different times, as occasion required; and that the Divine Being had a view in construct-
ing it, to the various revelations which he in all succeeding
times should make in that language; consequently, that its
words must be the most proper and determinate to convey
such truths as the Deity, during the Old Testament dispensation, thought fit to make known to the sons of men.
Further than this, that the inspired penmen of those ages
at least were under the guidance of heaven in the choice
of words for recording what was revealed to them: therefore, that the Old Testament, if the language be rightly
understood, is the most determinate in its meaning of any
other book under heaven. 2. That whatever is recorded
in the Old Testament is strictly and literally true, allowing
only for a few common figures of rhetoric; that nothing
contrary to truth is accommodated to vulgar apprehensions.

In proof of this, the Hutchinsonians argue in this manner.
The primary and ultimate design of revelation is indeed
to teach men divinity; but in subserviency to that, geography, history, and chronology, are occasionally introduced; all which are allowed to be just and authentic.
There are also innumerable references to things of nature,
and descriptions of them. If, then, the former are just,
and to be depended on, for the same reason the latter

ought to be esteemed philosophically true. Further, they think it not unworthy of God, that he should make it a secondary end of his revelation to unfold the secrets of his works; as the primary was to make known the mysteries of his nature, and the designs of his grace, that men might thereby be led to admire and adore the wisdom and goodness which the great Author of the universe has displayed throughout all his works. And as our minds are often referred to natural things for ideas of spiritual truths, it s of great importance, in order to conceive aright of divine matters, that our ideas of the natural things referred to be strictly just and true.

Mr. Hutchinson found that the Hebrew Scriptures had some capital words, which he thought had not been duly considered and understood; and which, he has endeavored to prove, contain in their radical meaning the greatest and most comfortable truths. The *cherubim* he explains to be a hieroglyphic of Divine construction, or a sacred image, to describe, as far as figures could go, the humanity united to Deity; and so he treats of several other words of similar import. From all which he concluded, that the rites and ceremonies of the Jewish dispensation were so many delineations of Christ, in what he was to be, to do, and to suffer; that the early Jews knew them to be types of his actions and sufferings; and, by performing them as such, were so far Christians both in faith and practice.

The Hutchinsonians have, for the most part, been men of devout minds, zealous in the cause of Christianity, and untainted with heterodox opinions, which have so often divided the church of Christ. The names of Romaine, Bishop Horne, Parkhurst, and others of this denomination, will be long esteemed, both for the piety they possessed, and the good they have been the instruments of promoting amongst mankind.

ICONOCLASTES.

ICONOCLASTES, or Iconoclastæ, breakers of images — a name which the Church of Rome gives to all who reject the use of images in religious matters. The word is Greek, formed from εικων, *image*, and χλασϵιν, *rumpere*, "to break." In this sense not only the reformed, but some of the eastern churches, are called *iconoclastes*, and esteemed by them heretics, as opposing the worship of the images of God and the saints, and breaking their figures and representations in churches.

The opposition to images began in Greece, under the reign of Bardanes, who was created emperor of the Greeks a little after the commencement of the eighth century, when the worship of them became common. But the tumults occasioned by it were quelled by a revolution, which, in 713, deprived Bardanes of the imperial throne. The dispute, however, broke out with redoubled fury under Leo the Isaurian, who issued an edict in the year 726, abrogating, as some say, the worship of images; and ordering all the images, except that of Christ's crucifixion, to be removed out of the churches; but, according to others this edict only prohibited the paying to them any kind of adoration or worship. This edict occasioned a civil war, which broke out in the islands of the Archipelago, and, by the suggestions of the priests and monks, ravaged a part of Asia, and afterwards reached Italy. The civil commotions and insurrections in Italy were chiefly promoted by the Roman pontiffs, Gregory I. and II. Leo was excommunicated; and his subjects in the Italian provinces violated their allegiance, and rising in arms, either massacred or banished all the emperor's deputies and officers. In consequence of these proceedings, Leo assembled a council at Constantinople in 730, which degraded Germanus, bishop of that city, who was a patron of images; and he ordered all the images to be publicly burnt, and inflicted a variety of punishments upon such as were attached to that idolatrous worship. Hence arose two factions, one of which adopted the adoration and worship of images, and on that account was called *iconoduli* or *iconolatræ;* and the other maintained that such worship was unlawful, and that nothing was more worthy the zeal of Christians than to demolish and destroy those statues and pictures which were the occasion of this gross idolatry; and hence they were distinguished by the titles of *iconomachi* (from εικων, *image,* and μαχω, *I contend*), and *iconoclastæ.* The zeal of Gregory II. in favor of image worship was not only imitated, but even surpassed, by his successor, Gregory III.; in consequence of which the Italian provinces were torn from the Grecian empire. Constantine, called Copronymus, in 764 convened a council at Constantinople, regarded by the Greeks as the seventh œcumenical council, which solemnly condemned the worship and usage of images. Those who, notwithstanding the decree of the council, raised commotions in the state, were severely punished, and new laws were enacted to set bounds to the violence of monastic rage. Leo IV., who was declared emperor in 755, pursued the same measures, and had recourse to the coercive influence of penal laws, in order to extirpate idolatry out of the Christian Church. Irene, the wife of Leo, poisoned her husband in 780; assumed the reins of the empire during the minority of her son Constantine; and in 786 summoned a council at Nice, in Bithynia, known by the name of the *Second Nicene Council,* which *abrogated* the laws and decrees against the new idolatry, restored the worship of images and of the cross, and denounced severe punishments against those who maintained that God was the only object of religious adoration. In this contest the Britons, Germans, and Gauls were of opinion that images might be lawfully continued in churches; but they considered the worship of them as highly injurious, and offensive to the Supreme Being. Charlemagne distinguished himself as a mediator in this controversy; he ordered four books concerning images to be composed, refuting the reasons urged by the Nicene bishops to justify the worship of images, which he sent to Adrian, the Roman pontiff, in 790, in order to engage him to withdraw his approbation of the decrees of the last Council of Nice. Adrian wrote an answer; and in 794, a council of 300 bishops, assembled by Charlemagne at Frankfort-on-the-Maine, confirmed the opinion contained in the four books, and solemnly condemned the worship of images.

In the Greek Church, after the banishment of Irene, the controversy concerning images broke out anew, and was carried on by the contending parties, during the half of the ninth century, with various and uncertain success. The Emperor Nicephorus appears, upon the whole, to have been an enemy to this idolatrous worship. His successor, Michael Curopalates, surnamed *Rhangabe*, patronized and encouraged it. But the scene changed on the accession of Leo, the Armenian, to the empire, who assembled a council at Constantinople, in 812, that abolished the decrees of the Nicene Council. His successor Michael, surnamed *Balbus*, disapproved of the worship of images, and his son Theophilus treated them with great severity. However, the Empress Theodora, after his death, and during the minority of her son, assembled a council at Constantinople in 842, which reinstated the decrees of the Second Nicene

Council, and encouraged image worship by a law. The council held at the same place under Protius, in 879, and reckoned by the Greeks the eighth general council, confirmed and renewed the Nicene decrees. In commemoration of this council, a festival was instituted by the superstitious Greeks, called the *Feast of Orthodoxy*. The Latins were generally of opinion that images might be suffered, as the means of aiding the memory of the faithful, and of calling to their remembrance the pious exploits and virtuous actions of the persons whom they represented; but they detested all thoughts of paying them the least marks of religious homage or adoration. The Council of Paris, assembled in 824 by Louis the Meek, resolved to allow the use of images in the churches, but severely prohibited rendering them religious worship; nevertheless, towards the conclusion of this century, the Gallican clergy began to pay a kind of religious homage to the images of saints, and their example was followed by the Germans and other nations. However, the Iconoclastes still had their adherents among the Latins; the most eminent of whom was Claudius, Bishop of Turin, who, in 823, ordered all images, and even the cross, to be cast out of the churches, and committed to the flames; and he wrote a treatise, in which he declared both against the use and worship of them. He condemned relics, pilgrimages to the Holy Land, and all voyages to the tombs of saints; and to his writings and labors it was owing that the city of Turin, and the adjacent country, was for a long time after his death much less infected with superstition than the other parts of Europe. The controversy concerning the sanctity of images was again revived by Leo, Bishop of Chalcedon, in the 11th century, on occasion of the Emperor Alexius's converting the figures of silver that adorned the portals of the churches into money, in order to supply the exigencies of the state. The bishop obstinately maintained that he had been guilty of sacrilege, and published a treatise, in which he affirmed that in these images there resided an inherent sanctity, and that the adoration of Christians ought not to be confined to the persons represented by these images, but extend to the images themselves. The emperor assembled a council at Constantinople, which determined that the images of Christ and of the saints were to be honored only with a relative worship; and that the invocation and worship were to be addressed to the saints only, as the servants of Christ, and on account of their relation to him as their master. Leo, dissatisfied with these absurd and superstitious decisions, was sent into banishment. In the western church, the worship of images was disapproved, and opposed by several considerable parties, as the Petrobrussians, Albigenses, Waldenses, etc.; till at length this idolatrous practice was abolished in many parts of the Christian world by the Reformation.

WICKLIFFITES,

THE followers of the famous John Wickliffe, called "the first reformer," who was born in Yorkshire in the year 1324. He attacked the jurisdiction of the pope and the bishops. He was for this summoned to a council at Lambeth, to give an account of his doctrines: but being countenanced by the duke of Lancaster, was both times dismissed without condemnation. Wickliffe, therefore, continued to spread his new principles as usual, adding to them doctrines still more alarming; by which he drew after him a great number of disciples. Upon this, William Courtnay, archbishop of Canterbury, called another council in 1382, which condemned twenty-four propositions of Wickliffe and his disciples, and obtained a declaration of Richard II. against all who should preach them; but while these proceedings were agitating, Wickliffe died at Lutterworth, leaving many works behind him for the establishment of his doctrines. He was buried in his own church at Lutterworth, in Leicestershire, where his bones were suffered to rest in peace till the year 1428, when by an order from the pope, they were taken up and burnt. Wickliffe was doubtless a very extraordinary man, considering the times in which he lived. He discovered the absurdities and imposition of the church of Rome, and had the honesty and resolution to promulgate his opinions, which a little more support would probably have enabled him to establish; they were evidently the foundation of the subsequent Reformation.

WILKINSONIANS,

THE followers of Jemima Wilkinson, who was born in Cumberland, R. I. In October, 1776, she asserted that she was taken sick, and actually died, and that her soul went to heaven, where it still continues. Soon after her body was reanimated with the spirit and power of Christ, upon which she set up as a public teacher; and declared she had an immediate revelation for all she delivered, and was arrived to a state of absolute perfection. It is also said she pretended to foretell future events, to discern the secrets of the heart, and to have the power of healing diseases; and if any per-

son who had made application to her was not healed, she
attributed it to his want of faith. She asserted that those
who refused to believe these exalted things concerning her,
will be in the state of the unbelieving Jews, who rejected
the counsel of God against themselves; and she told her
hearers that was the eleventh hour, and the last call of
mercy that ever should be granted them : for she heard an
inquiry in heaven, saying, "Who will go and preach to a
dying world?" or words to that import; and she said she
answered, "Here am I—send me;" and that she left the
realms of light and glory, and the company of the heavenly
host, who are continually praising and worshipping God,
in order to descend upon earth, and pass through many
sufferings and trials for the happiness of mankind. She
assumed the title of the universal friend of mankind ; hence
her followers distinguish themselves by the name of Friends

WALDENSES,

OR Valdenses, a sect of reformers, who made their first
appearance about the year 1160. They were most numerous about the valleys of Piedmont; and hence, some say,
they were called Valdenses, or Vaudois, and not from Peter
Valdo, as others suppose. Mosheim, however, gives this
account of them : he says, that Peter, an opulent merchant
of Lyons, surnamed *Valdensis*, or *Validisius*, from Vaux,
or Waldum, a town in the marquisate of Lyons, being extremely zealous for the advancement of true piety and
Christian knowledge, employed a certain priest, called
Stephanus de Evisa, about the year 1160, in translating,
from Latin into French, the four Gospels, with other books

of holy Scripture, and the most remarkable sentences of the ancient doctors, which were so highly esteemed in this century. But no sooner had he perused these sacred books with a proper degree of attention, than he perceived that the religion which was now taught in the Roman church differed totally from that which was originally inculcated by Christ and his apostles. Struck with this glaring contradiction between the doctrines of the pontiffs and the truths of the Gospel, and animated with zeal, he abandoned his mercantile vocation, distributed his riches among the poor (whence the Waldenses were called *poor men of Lyons*), and, forming an association with other pious men, who had adopted his sentiments and his turn of devotion, he began, in the year 1180, to assume the quality of a public teacher, and to instruct the multitude in the doctrines and precepts of Christianity.

Soon after Peter had assumed the exercise of his ministry, the archbishop of Lyons, and the other rulers of the church in that province, vigorously opposed him. However, their opposition was unsuccessful; for the purity and simplicity of that religion which these good men taught, the spotless innocence that shone forth in their lives and actions, and the noble contempt of riches and honors which was conspicuous in the whole of their conduct and conversation, appeared so engaging to all such as had any sense of true piety, that the number of their followers daily increased. They accordingly formed religious assemblies, first in France, and afterwards in Lombardy; from whence they propagated their sect throughout the other provinces of Europe with incredible rapidity, and with such invincible fortitude, that neither fire nor sword, nor the most cruel inventions of merciless persecution, could damp their zeal, or entirely ruin their cause.

The attempts of Peter Waldus and his followers were

neither emplc yed nor designed to introduce new doctrines into the church, nor to propose new articles of faith to Christians. All they aimed at was, to reduce the form of ecclesiastical government, and the manners both of the clergy and people, to that amiable simplicity and primitive sanctity that characterized the apostolic ages, and which appear so strongly recommended in the precepts and injunctions of the Divine Author of our holy religion. In consequence of this design, they complained that the Roman church had degenerated, under Constantine the Great, from its primitive purity and sanctity. They denied the supremacy of the Roman pontiff, and maintained that the rulers and ministers of the church were obliged, by their vocation, to imitate the poverty of the apostles, and to procure for themselves a subsistence by the work of their hands. They considered every Christian as, in a certain measure, qualified and authorized to instruct, exhort, and confirm the brethren in their Christian course; and demanded the restoration of the ancient penitential discipline of the church, *i. e.*, the expiation of transgressions by prayer, fasting, and alms, which the newly-invented doctrine of indulgences had almost totally abolished. They at the same time affirmed that every pious Christian was qualified and entitled to prescribe to the penitent the kind or degree of satisfaction or expiation that their transgressions required; that confession made to priests was by no means necessary, since ·the humble offender might acknowledge his sins and testify his repentance to any true believer, and might expect from such the counsel and admonition which his case demanded. They maintained that the power of delivering sinners from the guilt and punishment of their offences belonged to God alone; and that indulgences, of consequence, were the criminal inventions of sordid avarice. They looked upon the prayers and other ceremonies that were instituted in behalf of the dead, as vain, useless, and absurd, and denied the existence of departed souls in an intermediate state of purification; affirming that they were immediately, upon their separation from the body, received into heaven, or thrust down to hell. These and other tenets of a like nature, composed the system of doctrine propagated by the Waldenses. It is evident that the ancient Waldenses denied the obligation of infant baptism, and that others rejected water baptism entirely; but Wall has labored to prove that infant baptism was generally practised among them.

Their rules of practice were extremely austere; for they adopted as the model of their moral discipline the sermon of Christ on the mount, which they interpreted and explained in the most rigorous and literal manner; and consequently prohibited and condemned in their society all wars, and suits of law, and all attempts towards the acquisition of wealth; the inflicting of capital punishments, self-defence against unjust violence, and oaths of all kinds.

During the greatest part of the seventeenth century, those of them who lived in the valleys of Piedmont, and who had embraced the doctrine, discipline, and worship of the church of Geneva, were oppressed and persecuted in the most barbarous and inhuman manner by the ministers of Rome. This persecution was carried on with peculiar marks of rage and enormity in the years 1655, 1656, and 1696, and seemed to portend nothing less than the total extinction of that unhappy nation. The most horrid scenes of violence and bloodshed were exhibited in this theatre of papal tyranny; and the few Waldenses that survived were indebted for their existence and support to the intercession made for them by the English and Dutch governments, and also by the Swiss cantons, who solicited the clemency of the duke of Savoy on their behalf.

GREEK CHURCH.

THE Greek Church comprehends in its bosom a considerable part of Greece, the Grecian Isles, Wallachia, Moldavia, Egypt, Abyssinia, Nubia, Libya, Arabia, Mesopotamia, Syria, Cilicia, and Palestine, which are all under the jurisdiction of the patriarchs of Constantinople, Alexandria, Antioch, and Jerusalem. If to these we add the whole of the Russian empire in Europe, great part of Siberia in Asia, Astracan, Casan, and Georgia, it will be evident that the Greek church has a wider extent of territory than the Latin, with all the branches which have sprung from it; and that it is with great impropriety that the church of Rome is called by her members the *catholic* or universal church. That in these widely distant countries the professors of Christianity are agreed in every minute article of belief, it would be rash to assert; but there is certainly such an agreement among them, with respect both to faith and to discipline, that they mutually hold communion with each other, and are, in fact, but one church. It is called the Greek church, in contradistinction to the Latin or Roman church; as also the Eastern, in distinction from the Western church. We shall here present the reader with a view of its rise, tenets, and discipline.

The Greek church is considered as a separation from the Latin. In the middle of the ninth century, the controversy relating to the procession of the Holy Ghost (which had been started in the sixth century) became a point of great importance, on account of the jealousy and ambition which were at that time blended with it. Photius, the patriarch of Constantinople, being advanced to that see in the room of Ignatius, whom he procured to be

deposed, was solemnly excluded by pope Nicholas, in a
council held at Rome, and his ordination declared null and
void The Greek emperor resented this conduct of the
pope, who defended himself with great spirit and resolution. Photius, in his turn, convened what he called an
œcumenical council, in which he pronounced sentence of
excommunication and deposition against the pope, and got
it subscribed by twenty-one bishops and others, amounting
in number to a thousand. This occasioned a wide breach
between the sees of Rome and Constantinople. However,
the death of the emperor Michael, and the deposition of
Photius, subsequent thereupon, seemed to have restored
peace; for the emperor Basil held a council at Constantinople in the year 869, in which entire satisfaction was
given to pope Adrian; but the schism was only smothered
and suppressed a while. The Greek church had several
complaints against the Latin; particularly it was thought
a great hardship for the Greeks to subscribe to the definition of a council according to the Roman form, prescribed
by the pope, since it made the church of Constantinople
dependent on that of Rome, and set the pope above an
œcumenical council; but, above all, the pride and haughti-
ness of the Roman court gave the Greeks a great distaste;
and as their deportment seemed to insult his imperial
majesty, it entirely alienated the affections of the emperor
Basil. Towards the middle of the eleventh century,
Michael Cerularius, patriarch of Constantinople, opposed
the Latins with respect to their making use of unleavened
bread in the eucharist, their observation of the Sabbath,
and fasting on Saturdays, charging them with living in
communion with the Jews. To this, pope Leo IX. replied,
and, in his apology for the Latins, declaimed very warmly
against the false doctrine of the Greeks, interposing,
at the same time, the authority of his see. He likewise,

by his legates, excommunicated the patriarch in the church of Santa Sophia, which gave the last shock to the reconciliation attempted a long time after, but to no purpose; for from that time the hatred of the Greeks to the Latins, and of the Latins to the Greeks, became insuperable, insomuch that they have continued ever since separated from each other's communion.

The following are some of the chief tenets held by the Greek church:—They disown the authority of the pope, and deny that the church of Rome is the true catholic church. They do not baptize their children till they are three, four, five, six, ten, nay, sometimes eighteen years of age: baptism is performed by trine immersion. They insist that the sacrament of the Lord's Supper ought to be administered in both kinds, and they give the sacrament to children immediately after baptism. They grant no indulgences, nor do they lay any claim to the character of infallibility, like the church of Rome. They deny that there is any such place as purgatory; notwithstanding they pray for the dead, that God would have mercy on them at the general judgment. They practise the invocation of saints; though, they say, they do not invoke them as deities, but as intercessors with God. They exclude confirmation, extreme unction, and matrimony, out of the seven sacraments. They deny auricular confession to be a Divine precept, and say it is only a positive injunction of the church. They pay no religious homage to the eucharist. They administer the communion in both kinds to the laity, both in sickness and in health, though they have never applied themselves to their confessors; because they are persuaded that a lively faith is all which is requisite for the worthy receiving of the Lord's Supper. They maintain that the Holy Ghost proceeds only from the Father, and not from the Son. They believe in predestination. They admit of no images in relief or embossed work, but use paintings and sculptures in copper or silver. They approve of the marriage of priests, provided they enter into that state before their admission into holy orders. They condemn all fourth marriages. They observe a number of holy days, and keep four fasts in the year more solemn than the rest, of which the fast in Lent, before Easter, is the chief. They believe the doctrine of consubstantiation, or the union of the body of Christ with the sacramental bread.

Since the Greeks became subject to the Turkish yoke, they have sunk into the most deplorable ignorance, in consequence of the slavery and thraldom under which they groan; and their religion is now greatly corrupted. It is, indeed, little better than a heap of ridiculous ceremonies and absurdities. The head of the Greek church is the patriarch of Constantinople, who is chosen by the neighboring archbishops and metropolitans, and confirmed by the emperor or grand vizier. He is a person of great dignity, being the head and director of the Eastern church. The other patriarchs are those of Jerusalem, Antioch, and Alexandria. Mr. Tournefort tells us that the patriarchates are now generally set to sale and bestowed upon those who are the highest bidders. The patriarchs, metropolitans, archbishops, and bishops, are always chosen from among the caloyers, or Greek monks. The next person to a bishop, among the clergy, is an archimandrite, who is the director of one or more convents, which are called mandren; then come the abbot, the arch-priest, the priest, the deacon, the under-deacon, the chanter, and the lecturer. The secular clergy are subject to no rules, and never rise higher than high-priest. The Greeks have few nunneries, but a great many convents of monks, who are

24 *

all priests, and (students excepted) obliged to follow some handicraft employment, and lead a very austere life.

The Russians adhere to the doctrine and ceremonies of the Greek church, though they are now independent of the patriarch of Constantinople. The Russian church, indeed, may be reckoned the first, as to extent of empire; yet there is very little of the power of vital religion among them. The *Roskolniki*, or, as they now call themselves, the *Starovertzi*, were a sect that separated from the church of Russia about 1666; they affected extraordinary piety and devotion, a veneration for the letter of the Holy Scriptures, and would not allow a priest to administer baptism who had that day tasted brandy. They harbored many follies and superstitions, and have been greatly persecuted; but, perhaps, there will be found among them "some that shall be counted to the Lord for a generation." Several settlements of German Protestants have been established on the Wolga. The Moravians also have done good in Livonia, and the adjacent isles in the Baltic under the Russian government.

MAHOMETANISM

Is the system of religion formed and propagated by Mahomet, and still adhered to by his followers. It is professed by the Turks and Persians, by several nations among the Africans, and many among the East Indians.

Mahomet was born in the reign of Anushirwan the Just, emperor of Persia, about the end of the sixth century of the Christian era. He came into the world under some disadvantages. His father Abd'allah was a younger son of Abd'almotalleb; and dying very young, and in his father's lifetime, left his widow and infant son in very mean circumstances, his whole subsistence consisting but of five camels and one Ethiopian she-slave. Abd'almotalleb was therefore obliged to take care of his grandchild Mahomet; which he not only did during his life, but at his death enjoined his eldest son Abu Taleb, who was brother to Abd'allah by the same mother, to provide for him for the future; which he very affectionately did, and instructed him in the business of a merchant, which he followed: and to that end he took him into Syria when he was but thirteen. He afterwards recommended him to Khadijah, a noble and rich widow, for her factor; in whose service he behaved himself so well, that, by making him her husband, she soon raised him to an equality with the richest in Mecca.

After he began by this advantageous match to live at his ease, it was, that he formed the scheme of establishing a new religion, or, as he expressed it, of replanting the only true and ancient one, professed by Adam, Noah, Abraham, Moses, Jesus, and all the prophets, by destroying the gross idolatry into which the generality of his countrymen had fallen, and weeding out the corruptions and superstitions which the latter Jews and Christians had, as he thought, introduced into their religion, and reducing it to its original purity, which consisted chiefly in the worship of one God.

Before he made any attempt abroad, he rightly judged that it was necessary for him to begin with the conversion of his own household. Having therefore retired with his family, as he had done several times before, to a cave in Mount Hara, he there opened the secret of his mission to his wife Khadijah; and acquainted her that the angel Gabriel had just before appeared to him, and told him that he was appointed the apostle of God: he also repeated to her a passage which he pretended had been revealed to him by the ministry of the angel, with those other circumstances of this first appearance which are related by the Mahometan writers. Khadijah received the news with great joy, swearing by Him in whose hands her soul was, that she trusted he would be the prophet of his nation; and immediately communicated what she had heard to her cousin Warakah Ebn Nawfal, who, being a Christian, could write in the Hebrew character, and was tolerably well versed in the Scriptures; and he readily came into her opinion, assuring her that the same angel who had formerly appeared unto Moses, was now sent to Mahomet. The first overture the prophet made was in the month of Ramadan, in the fortieth year of his age, which is therefore usually called the year of his mission.

Encouraged by so good a beginning, he resolved to proceed, and try for some time what he could do by private persuasion, not daring to hazard the whole affair by exposing it too suddenly to the public. He soon made proselytes of those under his own roof, viz. his wife Khadijah, his servant Zeid Ebn Haretha, to whom he gave his freedom on that occasion (which afterwards became a rule to his followers), and his cousin and pupil Ali, the son of Abu Taleb, though then very young; but this last, making no account of the other two, used to style himself the *first of believers*. The next person Mahomet applied to was Abd'allah Ebn Abi Kohafa, surnamed *Abu Becr*, a man of great authority among the Koreish, and one whose interest he well knew would be of great service to him, as it soon appeared; for Abu Becr being gained over, prevailed also on Othman Ebn Affan, Abd'alraham Ebn Awf, Saad Ebn Abbi Wakkus, At Zobeir al Awam, and Telha Ebn Obeidalla, all principal men of Mecca, to follow his example. These men were six chief companions, who, with a

few more, were converted in the space of three years; at
the end of which, Mahomet having, as he hoped, a sufficient interest to support him, made his mission no longer
a secret, but gave out that God had commanded him to
admonish his near relations; and in order to do it with
more convenience and prospect of success, he directed Ali
to prepare an entertainment, and invited the sons and descendants of Abd'almotalleb, intending then to open his
mind to them. This was done, and about forty of them
came; but Abu Laheb, one of his uncles, making the company break up before Mahomet had an opportunity of
speaking, obliged him to give them a second invitation the
next day; and when they were come, he made them the
following speech: "I know no man in all Arabia who can
offer his kindred a more excellent thing than I now do to
you: I offer you happiness, both in this life, and in that
which is to come: God Almighty hath commanded me to
call you unto him. Who, therefore, among you, will be
assistant to me herein, and become my brother and my
vicegerent?" All of them hesitating and declining the
matter, Ali at length rose up, and declared that he would
be his assistant, and vehemently threatened those who
should oppose him. Mahomet upon this embraced Ali
with great demonstrations of affection, and desired all who
were present to hearken to and obey him as his deputy; at
which the company broke out into a great laughter, telling
Abu Taleb that he must now pay obedience to his son.

This repulse, however, was so far from discouraging
Mahomet, that he began to preach in public to the people,
who heard him with some patience, till he came to upbraid
them with the idolatry, obstinacy, and perverseness of
themselves and their fathers, which so highly provoked
them, that they declared themselves his enemies, and
would soon have procured his ruin, had he not been pro-

tected by Abu Taleb.   The chief of the Koreish warmly
solicited this person to desert his nephew, making frequent
remonstrances against the innovations he was attempting:
which proving ineffectual, they at length threatened him
with an open rupture if he did not prevail on Mahomet to
desist.   At this Abu Taleb was so far moved that he
earnestly dissuaded his nephew from pursuing the affair
any further, representing the great danger that he and his
friends must otherwise run.   But Mahomet was not to be
intimidated; telling his uncle plainly, *that if they set the
sun against him on his right hand, and the moon on his
left, he would not leave his enterprise;* and Abu Taleb,
seeing him so firmly resolved to proceed, used no further
arguments, but promised to stand by him against all his
enemies.

The Koreish, finding they could prevail neither by fair
words nor menaces, tried what they could do by force and
ill treatment; using Mahomet's followers so very injuri-
ously, that it was not safe for them to continue at Mecca
any longer; whereupon Mahomet gave leave to such of
them as had no friends to protect them to seek for refuge
elsewhere.   And accordingly, in the fifth year of the prophet's mission, sixteen of them, four of whom were women,
fled into Ethiopia; and among them Othman Ebn Affan,
and his wife Rakiah, Mahomet's daughter.   This was the
first flight; but afterwards several others followed them,
retiring one after another, to the number of eighty-three
men and eighteen women, besides children.   These refu-
gees were kindly received by the Najashi, or king of Ethiopia, who refused to deliver them up to those whom the
Koreish sent to demand them, and, as the Arab writers
unanimously attest, even professsed the Mahometan religion.

In the sixth year of his mission, Mahomet had the pleasure of seeing his party strengthened by the conversion of his uncle Hamza, a man of great valor and merit; and of Omar Ebn al Kattab, a person highly esteemed, and once a violent opposer of the prophet. As persecution generally advances rather than obstructs the spreading of a religion, Islamism made so great a progress among the Arab tribes, that the Koreish, to suppress it effectually, if possible, in the seventh year of Mahomet's mission, made a solemn league or covenant against the Hashemites and the family of Abd'almotalleb, engaging themselves to contract no marriage with any of them, and to have no communication with them; and to give it the greater sanction, reduced it to writing, and laid it up in the Caaba. Upon this, the tribe became divided into two factions; and the family of Hashem all repaired to Abu Taleb, as their head; except only Abd'al Uzza, surnamed the *Abu Laheb*, who, out of inveterate hatred to his nephew and his doctrine, went over to the opposite party, whose chief was Abu Sosian Ebn Harb, of the family of Ommeya.

The families continued thus at variance for three years; but in the tenth year of his mission, Mahomet told his uncle Abu Taleb, that God had manifestly showed his disapprobation of the league which the Koreish had made against them, by sending a worm to eat out every word of the instrument except the name of *God*. Of this accident Mahomet had probably some private notice; for Abu Taleb went immediately to the Koreish, and acquainted them with it; offering, if it proved false, to deliver his nephew up to them; but, in case it were true, he insisted that they ought to lay aside their animosity, and annul the league they had made against the Hashemites. To this they acquiesced; and going to inspect the writing, to their great astonishment found it to be as Abu Taleb had said; and the league was thereupon declared void.

In the same year Abu Taleb died at the age of above fourscore, and it is the general opinion that he died an infidel; though others say that, when he was at the point of death he embraced Mahometanism, and produce some passages out of his poetical compositions to confirm their assertion. About a month, or, as some write, three days, after the death of this great benefactor and patron, Mahomet had the additional mortification to lose his wife Khadijah, who had so generously made his fortune. For which reason this year is called the *year of mourning.*

On the death of these two persons, the Koreish began to be more troublesome than ever to their prophet, and especially some who had formerly been his intimate friends; insomuch that he found himself obliged to seek for shelter elsewhere, and first pitched upon Tayef, about sixty miles east from Mecca, for the place of his retreat. Thither, therefore, he went, accompanied by his servant Zeid, and applied himself to two of the chief of the tribe of Thakif, who were the inhabitants of that place; but they received him very coldly. However, he stayed there a month; and some of the more considerate and better sort of men treated him with a little respect; but the slaves and inferior people at length rose against him; and bringing him to the wall of the city, obliged him to depart and return to Mecca, where he put himself under the protection of Al Motaam Ebn Ali.

This repulse greatly discouraged his followers. However, Mahomet was not wanting to himself, but boldly continued to preach to the public assemblies at the pilgrimage, and gained several proselytes; and, among them, six of the inhabitants of Yathreb, of the Jewish tribe of Khazraj; who, on their return home, failed not to speak much in recommendation of their new religion, and exhorted their fellow-citizens to embrace the same.

In the twelfth year of his mission it was that Mahomet gave out that he had made his night journey from Mecca to Jerusalem, and thence to heaven, so much spoken of by all that write of him. Dr. Prideaux thinks he invented it either to answer the expectations of those who demanded some miracle as a proof of his mission; or else, by pretending to have conversed with God, to establish the authority of whatever he should think fit to leave behind by way of oral tradition, and make his sayings to serve the same purpose as the oral law of the Jews. But it does not appear that Mahomet himself ever expected so great a regard should be paid to his sayings as his followers have since done; and seeing he all along disclaimed any power of performing miracles, it seems rather to have been a fetch of policy to raise his reputation, by pretending to have actually conversed with God in heaven, as Moses had heretofore done in the mount, and to have received several institutions immediately from him, whereas, before, he contented himself with persuading them that he had all by the ministry of Gabriel.

However, this story seemed so absurd and incredible, that several of his followers left him upon it; and had probably ruined the whole design, had not Abu Beer vouched for his veracity, and declared that if Mahomet affirmed it to be true, he verily believed the whole. Which happy incident not only retrieved the prophet's credit, but increased it to such a degree, that he was secure of being able to make his disciples swallow whatever he pleased to impose on them for the future. And this fiction, notwithstanding its extravagance, was one of the most artful contrivances Mahomet ever put in practice, and what chiefly contributed to the raising of his reputation to that great height to which it afterwards arrived.

In this year, called by the Mahometans the *accepted*

year, twelve men of Yathreb or Medina, of whom ten were of the tribe of Khazraj, and the other two of that of Aws, came to Mecca, and took an oath of fidelity to Mahomet at Al Akaba, a hill on the north of that city. This oath was called the *woman's oath;* not that any women were present at this time, but because a man was not thereby obliged to take up arms in defence of Mahomet or his religion; it being the same oath that was afterwards exacted of the women, the form of which we have in the Koran, and is to this effect, viz.: That they should renounce all idolatry; and that they should not steal, nor commit fornication, nor kill their children (as the pagan Arabs used to do when they apprehended they should not be able to maintain them), nor forge calumnies; and that they should obey the prophet in all things that were reasonable. When they had solemnly engaged to all this, Mahomet sent one of his disciples named *Masab Ebn Omair* home with them, to instruct them more fully in the grounds and ceremonies of his new religion.

Masab, being arrived at Medina, by the assistance of those who had been formerly converted, gained several proselytes, particularly Osed Ebn Hodeira, a chief man of the city, and Saad Ebn Moadh, prince of the tribe of the Aws; Mahometanism spreading so fast, that there was scarce a house wherein there were not some who had embraced it.

The next year, being the thirteenth of Mahomet's mission, Masab returned to Mecca, accompanied by seventy-three men and two women of Medina who had professed Islamism, besides some others who were as yet unbelievers. On their arrival they immediately sent to Mahomet, and offered him their assistance, of which he was now in great need; for his adversaries were by this time grown so powerful in Mecca, that he could not stay there much longer without imminent danger. Wherefore he accepted their proposal, and met them one night, by appointment, at Al Akaba above mentioned, attended by his uncle Al Abbas; who, though he was not then a believer, wished his nephew well, and made a speech to those of Medina; wherein he told them that, as Mahomet was obliged to quit his native city and seek an asylum elsewhere, and they had offered him their protection, they would do well not to deceive him: that if they were not firmly resolved to defend, and not betray him, they had better declare their minds, and let him provide for his safety in some other manner. Upon their protesting their sincerity, Mahomet swore to be faithful to them, on condition that they should protect him against all insults as heartily as they would their own wives and families. They then asked him what recompense they were to expect, if they should happen to be killed in his quarrel? He answered, Paradise. Whereupon they pledged their faith to him, and so returned home after Mahomet had chosen twelve out of their number, who were to have the same authority among them as the twelve apostles of Christ had among his disciples.

Hitherto Mahomet had propagated his religion by fair means; so that the whole success of his enterprise before his flight to Medina must be attributed to persuasion only, and not to compulsion. For before this second oath of fealty or inauguration at Al Akaba, he had no permission to use any force at all; and in several places of the Koran, which he pretended were revealed during his stay at Mecca, he declares his business was only to preach and admonish; that he had no authority to compel any person to embrace his religion; and that, whether people believe or not, was none of his concern, but belonged solely unto God. And he was so far from allowing his followers to use force, that he exhorted them to bear patiently those injuries which were offered them on account of their faith; and, when persecuted himself, he chose rather to quit the place of his birth, and retire to Medina, than to make any resistance. But this great passiveness and moderation seem entirely owing to his want of power, and the great superiority of his opposers, for the first twelve years of his mission; for no sooner was he enabled, by the assistance of those of Medina, to make head against his enemies, than he gave out, that God had allowed him and his followers to defend themselves against the infidels; and at length, as his forces increased, he pretended to have the divine leave even to attack them, and destroy idolatry, and set up the true faith by the sword; finding by experience, that his designs would otherwise proceed very slowly, if they were not utterly overthrown; and knowing, on the other hand, that innovaters, when they depend solely on their own strength, and can compel, seldom run any risk; from whence, says Machiavel, it follows that all the armed prophets have succeeded, and the unarmed ones have failed. Moses, Cyrus, Theseus, and Romulus, would not have been able to establish the observance of their institution for any length of time, had they not been armed. The first passage of the Koran which gave Mahomet the permission of defending himself by arms, is said to have been that in the twenty-second chapter; after which, a great number to the same purpose were revealed.

Mahomet, having provided for the security of his companions, as well as his own, by the league offensive and defensive which he had now concluded with those of Medina, directed them to repair thither, which they accordingly did; but himself, with Abu Becr and Ali, staid behind, having not yet received the divine permission, as he pretended, to leave Mecca. The Koreish, fearing the consequence of this new alliance, began to think it absolutely necessary to prevent Mahomet's escape to Medina; and having held a council thereon, after several milder expedients had been rejected, they came to a resolution that he should be killed; and agreed that a man should be chosen out of every tribe for the execution of this design; and that each man should have a blow at him with his sword, that the guilt of his blood might fall equally on all the tribes, to whose united power the Hashemites were much inferior, and therefore durst not attempt to revenge their kinsman's death.

This conspiracy was scarce formed, when, by some means or other, it came to Mahomet's knowledge, and he gave out that it was revealed to him by the angel Gabriel, who had now ordered him to retire to Medina. Whereupon, to amuse his enemies, he directed Ali to lie down in his place, and wrap himself up ir his green cloak, which he did; and Mahomet escaped miraculously, as they pretended, to Abu Becr's house, unperceived by the conspirators, who had already assembled at the prophet's door. They, in the meantime, looking through the crevice, and seeing Ali, whom they took to be Mahomet himself, asleep, continued watching there till morning, when Ali arose, and they found themselves deceived.

From Abu Becr's house Mahomet and he went to a cave in mount Thur, to the southeast of Mecca, accompanied only by Amor Ebn Foheirah, Abu Becr's servant, and Abd'allah Ebn Oreitah, an idolater whom they had hired for a guide. In this cave they lav hid three days, to avoid the search of their enemies; which they very narrowly escaped, and not without the assistance of more miracles than one; for some say that the Koreish were struck with blindness, so that they could not find the cave; others, that after Mahomet and his companions were got in, two pigeons laid their eggs at the entrance, and a spider covered

25 *

the mouth of the cave with her web, which made them look
no further.   Abu Beer, seeing the prophet in such imminent danger, became very sorrowful; whereupon Mahomet
comforted him with these words, recorded in the Koran:
Be not grieved, for God is with us.   Their enemies being
retired, they left the cave, and set out for Medina by a
by-road; and having fortunately, or, as the Mahometans
tell us, miraculously, escaped some who were sent to pur-
sue them, arrived safely at that city; whither Ali followed them in three days, after he had settled some affairs
at Mecca.

Mahomet being securely settled at Medina, and able not
only to defend himself against the insults of his enemies,
but to attack them, began to send out small parties to make
reprisals on the Koreish; the first party consisting of no
more than nine men, who intercepted and plundered a
caravan belonging to that tribe, and in the action took two
prisoners.   But what established his affairs very much, and
was the foundation on which he built all his succeeding
greatness, was the gaining of the battle of Bedr, which was
fought in the second year of the Hegira, and is so famous
in the Mahometan history.   Some reckon no less than
twenty-seven expeditions, wherein Mahomet was personally
present, in nine of which he gave battle, besides several
other expeditions in which he was not present.   His forces
he maintained partly by the contributions of his followers
for this purpose, which he called by the name of *zacat*, or
alms, and the paying of which he very artfully made one
main article of his religion: and partly by ordering a fifth
part of the plunder to be brought into the public treasury
for that purpose, in which matter he likewise pretended to
act by the divine direction.

In a few years, by the success of his arms, notwithstanding he sometimes came off with the worst, he considerably

raised his credit and power. In the sixth year of the Hegira he set out with 1400 men to visit the temple of Mecca, not with any intent of committing hostilities, but in a peaceable manner. However, when he came to Al Hodeibiya, which is situated partly within and partly without the sacred territory, the Koreish sent to let him know that they would not permit him to enter Mecca, unless he forced his way: whereupon he called his troops about him, and they all took a solemn oath of fealty or homage to him, and he resolved to attack the city; but those of Mecca sending Arwa Ebn Masun, prince of the tribe of Thakif, as their ambassador, to desire peace, a truce was concluded between them for ten years, by which any person was allowed to enter into a league either with Mahomet, or with the Koreish, as he thought fit.

In the seventh year of the Hegira, Mahomet began to think of propagating his religion beyond the bounds of Arabia, and sent messengers to the neighboring princes, with letters to invite them to Mahometanism. Nor was this project without some success: Khosru Parviz, then king of Persia, received his letter with great disdain, and tore it in a passion, sending away the messenger very abruptly; which, when Mahomet heard, he said, *God shall tear his kingdom.* And soon after a messenger came to Mahomet from Badhan, king of Yaman, who was a dependent on the Persians, to acquaint him that he had received orders to send him to Khosru. Mahomet put off his answer till the next morning, and then told the messenger it had been revealed to him that night that Khosru was slain by his son Shiruyeh: adding, that he was well assured his new religion and empire should rise to as great a height as that of Khosru: and therefore bid him advise his master to embrace Mahometanism. The messenger being returned, Badhan in a few days received a letter from Shiruyeh, in-

forming him of his father's death, and ordering him to give
the prophet no further disturbance.   Whereupon Badhan,
and the Persians with him, turned Mahometans.

The emperor Heraclius, as the Arabian historians assure
us, received Mahomet's letter with great respect, laying it
on his pillow, and dismissed the bearer honorably.   And
some pretend that he would have professed this new faith,
had he not been afraid of losing his crown.

Mahomet wrote to the same effect to the king of Ethiopia, though he had been converted before, according to the
Arab writers; and to Mokawkas, governor of Egypt, who
gave the messenger a very favorable reception, and sent
several valuable presents to Mahomet, and among the rest
two girls, one of whom, named Mary, became a great favorite with him.   He also sent letters of the like purport to
several Arab princes; particularly one to Al Hareth Ebn
Abi Shamer, king of Ghassan, who, returning for answer
that he would go to Mahomet himself, the prophet said,
May his kingdom perish!   Another to Hawdha Ebn Ali,
king of Yamama, who was a Christian, and, having some
time before professed Islamism, had lately returned to his
former faith: this prince sent back a very rough answer,
upon which Mahomet cursing him, he died soon after; and
a third to Al Mondar Ebn Sawa, king of Bahrein, who
embraced Mahometanism, and all the Arabs of that country
followed his example.

The eighth year of the Hegira was a very fortunate
year to Mahomet.   In the beginning of it Khaled Ebn al
Walid and Amru Ebn al As, both excellent soldiers, the
first of whom afterwards conquered Syria and other countries, and the latter Egypt, became proselytes to Mahometanism.   And soon after the prophet sent 3000 men against
the Grecian forces, to revenge the death of one of his ambassadors, who, being sent to the governor of Bosra on the

same errand as those who went to the above-mentioned princes, was slain by an Arab of the tribe of Ghassan, at Muta, a town in the territory of Balka, in Syria, about three days' journey eastward from Jerusalem, near which town they encountered. The Grecians being vastly superior in number (for, including the auxiliary Arabs, they had an army of 100,000 men), the Mahometans were repulsed in the first attack, and lost successively three of their generals, viz., Zeid Ebn Haretha, Mahomet's freedman; Jassar, the son of Abu Taleb; and Abdalia Ebn Rawalia: but Khaled Ebn al Walid, succeeding to the command, overthrew the Greeks with great slaughter, and brought away abundance of rich spoil: on occasion of which action Mahomet gave him the title of *Seif min soyuf Allah*, "one of the swords of God."

In this year also Mahomet took the city of Mecca, the inhabitants whereof had broken the truce concluded on two years before; for the tribe of Beer, who were confederates with the Koreish, attacking those of Kozaah, who were allies of Mahomet, killed several of them, being supported in the action by a party of the Koreish themselves. The consequence of this violation was soon apprehended, and Abu Sosian himself made a journey to Medina on purpose to heal the breach and renew the truce, but in vain; for Mahomet, glad of this opportunity, refused to see him; whereupon he applied to Abu Beer and Ali; but they giving him no answer, he was obliged to return to Mecca as he came.

Mahomet immediately gave orders for preparations to be made that he might surprise the Meccans while they were unprovided to receive him: in a little time he began his march thither; and by the time he came near the city, his forces were increased to ten thousand men. Those of Mecca not being in a condition to defend themselves against so formidable an army, surrendered at discretion, and Abu Sosian saved his life by turning Mahometan. About twenty-eight of the idolaters were killed by a party under the command of Khaled; but this happened contrary to Mahomet's orders, who, when he entered the town, pardoned all the Koreish on their submission, except only six men and four women, who were more obnoxious than ordinary (some of them having apostatized), and were solemnly proscribed by the prophet himself; but of these no more than one man and one woman were put to death, the rest obtaining pardon on their embracing Mahometanism, and one of the women making her escape.

The remainder of this year Mahomet employed in destroying the idols in and around Mecca, sending several of the generals on expeditions for that purpose, and to invite the Arabs to Islamism; wherein it is no wonder if they now met with success.

The next year, being the ninth of the Hegira, the Mahometans call the *year of embassies;* for the Arabs had been hitherto expecting the issue of the war between Mahomet and the Koreish; but as soon as that tribe, the principal of the whole nation, and the genuine descendants of Ishmael, whose prerogatives none offered to dispute, had submitted, they were satisfied that it was not in their power to oppose Mahomet; and therefore began to come in to him in great numbers, and to send embassies to make their submissions to him, both to Mecca, while he staid there, and also to Medina, whither he returned this year. Among the rest, five kings of the tribe of Hamyar professed Mahometanism, and sent ambassadors to notify the same.

In the tenth year Ali was sent into Yaman to propagate the Mahometan faith there; and, as it is said, converted the whole tribe of Hamdan in one day. Their example was quickly followed by all the inhabitants of that province, except only those of Najran, who, being Christians, chose rather to pay tribute.

Thus was Mahometanism established, and idolatry rooted out, even in Mahomet's lifetime (for he died the next year), throughout all Arabia, except only Yamama, where Moseilama, who set up also as a prophet, as Mahomet's competitor, had a great party, and was not reduced till the kalifat of Abu Beer; and the Arabs being then united in one faith, and under one prince, found themselves in a condition of making those conquests which extended the Mahometan faith over so great a part of the world.

1. *Tenets of the Mahometans.*—The Mahometans divide their religion into two general parts, faith and practice; of which the first is divided into six distinct branches: Belief in God, in his angels, in his Scriptures, in his prophets, in the resurrection and final judgment, and in God's absolute decrees. The points relating to practice are prayer, with washings, etc., alms, fasting, pilgrimage to Mecca, and circumcision.

Of the Mahometan Faith.—1. That both Mahomet, and those among his followers who are reckoned orthodox, had and continue to have just and true notions of God and his attributes, appears so plain from the Koran itself, and all the Mahometan divines, that it would be loss of time to refute those who suppose the God of Mahomet to be different from the true God, and only a fictitious deity or idol of his own creation.

2. The existence of angels and their purity, are absolutely required to be believed in the Koran; and he is reckoned an infidel who denies there are such beings, or hates any of them, or asserts any distinction of sexes among them. They believe them to have pure and subtle bodies, created of fire; that they neither eat nor drink,

nor propagate their species; that they have various forms
and offices, some adoring God in different postures, others
singing praises to him, or interceding for mankind.   They
hold that some of them are employed in writing down the
actions of men; others in carrying the throne of God,
and other services.

3. As to the Scriptures, the Mahometans are taught by
the Koran that God, in divers ages of the world, gave
revelations of his will in writing to several prophets, the
whole and every one of which it is absolutely necessary
for a good Moslem to believe.   The number of these sacred
books were, according to them, one hundred and four; of
which ten were given to Adam, fifty to Seth, thirty to
Edris or Enoch, ten to Abraham; and the other four,
being the Pentateuch, the Psalms, the Gospel, and the
Koran, were successively delivered to Moses, David, Jesus,
and Mahomet; which last being the seal of the prophets,
those revelations are now closed, and no more are to be
expected.   All these divine books, except the four last,
they agree to be now entirely lost, and their contents unknown; though the Sabians have several books which they
attribute to some of the antediluvian prophets.   And of
those four, the Pentateuch, Psalms, and Gospel, they say,
have undergone so many alterations and corruptions, that
though there may possibly be some part of the true word
of God therein, yet no credit is to be given to the present
copies in the hands of the Jews and Christians.

4. The number of the prophets which have been from
time to time sent by God into the world, amounts to no
less than 224,000, according to one Mahometan tradition,
or to 124,000, according to another; among whom 313
were apostles, sent with special commissions to reclaim
mankind from infidelity and superstition; and six of them
brought new laws or dispensations, which successively ab-

rogated the preceding; these were Adam, Noah, Abraham, Moses, Jesus, and Mahomet. All the prophets in general the Mahometans believe to have been free from great sins and errors of consequence, and professors of one and the same religion — that is, Islamism — notwithstanding the different laws and institutions which they observed. They allow of degrees among them, and hold some of them to be more excellent and honorable than others The first place they give to the revealers and establishers of new dispensations, and the next to the apostles.

In this great number of prophets they not only reckon divers patriarchs and persons named in Scripture, but not recorded to have been prophets (wherein the Jewish and Christian writers have sometimes led the way), as Adam, Seth, Lot, Ishmael, Nun, Joshua, etc., and introduce some of them under different names, as *Enoch*, *Heber*, and *Jethro*, who are called in the Koran *Edris*, *Hud*, and *Shoaib;* but several others whose very names do not appear in Scripture (though they endeavor to find some persons there to fix them on), as Saleh, Khedr, Dhu'lkefl, etc

5. The belief of a general resurrection and a future judgment.

The time of the resurrection the Mahometans allow to be a perfect secret to all but God alone; the angel Gabriel himself acknowledging his ignorance on this point, when Mahomet asked him about it. However, they say the approach of that day may be known from certain signs which are to precede it.

After examination is past (the account of which is too long and tedious for this place), and every one's works weighed in a just balance, they say that mutual retaliation will follow, according to which every creature will take vengeance one of another, or have satisfaction made them for the injuries which they have suffered. And, since there will then be no other way of returning like for like, the manner of giving this satisfaction will be by taking away a proportional part of the good works of him who offered the injury, and adding it to those of him who suffered it. Which being done, if the angels (by whose ministry this is to be performed) say, *Lord, we have given to every one his due, and there remaineth of this person's good works so much as equalleth the weight of an ant*, God will, of his mercy, cause it to be doubled unto him, that he may be admitted into Paradise; but if, on the contrary, his good works be exhausted, and there remain evil works only, and there be any who have not yet received satisfaction from him, God will order that an equal weight of their sins be added unto his, that he may be punished for them in their stead, and he will be sent to hell laden with both. This will be the method of God's dealing with mankind. As to brutes, after they shall have likewise taken vengeance of one another, he will command them to be changed into dust; wicked men being reserved to more grievous punishment, so that they shall cry out, on hearing this sentence passed on the brutes, *Would to God that we were dust also!* As to the genii, many Mahometans are of opinion that such of them as are true believers, will undergo the same fate as the irrational animals, and have no other reward than the favor of being converted into dust; and for this they quote the authority of their prophet.

The trials being over, and the assembly dissolved, the Mahometans hold that those who are to be admitted into Paradise will take the right hand way, and those who are destined into hell fire will take the left; but both of them must first pass the bridge called in Arabic *Al Sirat*, which, they say, is laid over the midst of hell, and describe to be finer than a hair, and sharper than the edge of a sword;

so that it seems very difficult to conceive how any one shall be able to stand upon it; for which reason most of the sect of the Motazalites reject it as a fable; though the orthodox think it a sufficient proof of the truth of this article, that it was seriously affirmed by him who never asserted a falsehood, meaning their prophet; who, to add to the difficulty of the passage, has likewise declared tha this bridge is beset on each side with briers and hooked thorns, which will, however, be no impediment to the good; for they shall pass with wonderful ease and swiftness, like lightning, or the wind, Mahomet and his Moslems leading the way; whereas the wicked, what with the slipperiness and extreme narrowness of the path, the entangling of the thorns, and the extinction of the light which directed the former to Paradise, will soon miss their footing, and fall down headlong into hell, which is gaping beneath them.

As to the punishment of the wicked, the Mahometans are taught that hell is divided into seven stories or apartments, one below another, designed for the reception of as many distinct classes of the damned.

The first, which they call *Jehenan*, they say will be the receptacle of those who acknowledged one God, that is, the wicked Mahometans; who, after having been punished according to their demerits, will at length be released; the second, named *Ladka*, they assign to the Jews; the third, named *Al Hotama*, to the Christians; the fourth, named *Al Sair*, to the Sabians; the fifth, named *Sakar*, to the Magians; the sixth, named *Al Jahin*, to the idolaters; and the seventh, which is the lowest and worst of all, and is called *Al Hawyat*, to the hypocrites, or those who outwardly professed some religion, but in their hearts were of none. Over each of these apartments they believe there will be set a guard of angels, nineteen in number, to whom the damned will confess the just judgment

of God, and beg them to intercede with him for some alle-
viation of their pain, or that they may be delivered by
being annihilated.

Mahomet has, in his Koran and traditions, been very
exact in describing the various torments of hell, which,
according to him, the wicked will suffer, both from intense
heat and excessive cold. We shall, however, enter into
no detail of them here, but only observe that the degrees
of these pains will also vary in proportion to the crimes
of the sufferer, and the apartment he is condemned to;
and that he who is punished the most lightly of all will be
shod with shoes of fire, the fervor of which will cause his
skull to boil like a cauldron. The condition of these unhappy wretches, as the same prophet teaches, cannot be
properly called either *life* or *death ;* and their misery will
be greatly increased by their despair of being ever delivered from that place, since, according to that frequent
expression in the Koran, *they must remain therein forever.*
It must be remarked, however, that the infidels alone will
be liable to eternity of damnation; for the Moslems, or
those who have embraced the true religion, and have been
guilty of heinous sins, will be delivered thence after they
shall have expiated their crimes by their sufferings. The
time which these believers shall be detained there, according to a tradition handed down from their prophet, will not
be less than nine hundred years, nor more than seven
thousand. And, as to the manner of their delivery, they
say that they shall be distinguished by the marks of pros-
tration on those parts of their bodies with which they used
to touch the ground in prayer, and over which the fire will
therefore have no power; and that being known by this
characteristic, they will be released by the mercy of God,
at the intercession of Mahomet and the blessed; whereupon those who shall have been dead will be restored to

life, as has been said; and those whose bodies shall have contracted any sootiness or filth from the flames and smoke of hell, will be immersed in one of the rivers of Paradise, called the *River of Life*, which will wash them whiter than pearls.

The righteous, as the Mahometans are taught to believe, having surmounted the difficulties, and passed the sharp bridge above mentioned, before they enter Paradise, will be refreshed by drinking at the *pond* of their prophet, who describes it to be an exact square, of a month's journey in compass; its water, which is supplied by two pipes from *Al Cawthay*, one of the rivers of Paradise, being whiter than milk or silver, and more odoriferous than musk, with as many cups set around it as there are stars in the firmament; of which water, whoever drinks will thirst no more forever. This is the first taste which the blessed will have of their future and now near-approaching felicity.

Though Paradise be so very frequently mentioned in the Koran, yet it is a dispute among the Mahometans, whether it be already created, or to be created hereafter; the Motazalites and some other sectaries asserting, that there is not at present any such place in nature, and that the Paradise which the righteous will inhabit in the next life will be different from that from which Adam was expelled. However, the orthodox profess the contrary, maintaining that it was created even before the world, and describe it, from their prophet's traditions, in the following manner:—

They say it is situated above the seven heavens (or in the seventh heaven,) and next under the throne of God; and, to express the amenity of the place, tell us, that the earth of it is of the finest wheat-flour, or of the purest musk, or, as others will have it, of saffron; that its stones are pearls and jacinths, the walls of its buildings enriched with gold and silver, and that the trunks of all its trees are of gold; among which the most remarkable is the tree called *tuba*, or the tree of happiness. Concerning this tree, they fable that it stands in the palace of Mahomet, though a branch of it will reach to the house of every true believer; that it will be laden with pomegranates, grapes, dates, and other fruits, of surprising bigness, and of tastes unknown to mortals. So that, if a man desire to eat of any particular kind of fruit, it will immediately be presented him; or, if he choose flesh, birds ready dressed will be set before him, according to his wish. They add that the boughs of this tree will spontaneously bend down to the hand of the person who would gather of its fruits, and that it will supply the blessed not only with food, but also with silken garments, and beasts to ride on ready saddled and bridled, and adorned with rich trappings, which will burst forth from its fruits; and that this tree is so large, that a person mounted on the fleetest horse would not be able to gallop from one end of its shade to the other in one hundred years.

As plenty of water is one of the greatest additions to the pleasantness of any place, the Koran often speaks of the rivers of Paradise as a principal ornament thereof; some of these rivers, they say, flow with water, some with milk, some with wine, and others with honey; all taking their rise from the root of the tree tuba.

But all these glories will be eclipsed by the resplendent and ravishing girls of Paradise, called, from their large black eyes, *Hur al oyun*, the enjoyment of whose company will be a principal felicity of the faithful. These, they say, are created not of clay, as mortal women are, but of pure musk; being, as their prophet often affirms in his Koran, free from all natural impurities, defects, and inconveniences incident to the sex; of the strictest modesty, and secluded from public view in pavilions of hollow pearls, so large, that, as some traditions have it, one of them will be no less than four parasangs (or, as others say, sixty miles) long, and as many broad.

The name which the Mahometans usually give to this happy mansion is *al Jannat*, or, "the Garden;" and sometimes they call it, with an addition, *Jannat al Ferdaws*, "the Garden of Paradise;" *Jannat Adan*, "the Garden of Eden," (though they generally interpret the word *Eden* not according to its acceptation in Hebrew, but according to its meaning in their own tongue, wherein it signifies "a settled or perpetual habitation;") *Jannat al Mawa*, "the Garden of Abode;" *Jannat al Maim*, "the Garden of Pleasure," and the like; by which several appellations some understand so many different gardens, or at least places of different degrees of felicity, (for they reckon no less than one hundred such in all,) the very meanest whereof will afford its inhabitants so many pleasures and delights, that one would conclude they must even sink under them, had not Mahomet declared that, in order to qualify the blessed for a full enjoyment of them, God will give to every one the abilities of one hundred men.

6. God's absolute decree and predestination both of good and evil. The orthodox doctrine is, that whatever hath or shall come to pass in this world, whether it be good, or whether it be bad, proceedeth entirely from the Divine will, and is irrevocably fixed and recorded from all eternity in the preserved table; God having secretly predetermined not only the adverse and prosperous fortune of every person in this world, in the most minute particulars, but also his faith or infidelity, his obedience or disobedience, and consequently his everlasting happiness or misery after death; which fate or predestination it is not possible by any foresight or wisdom to avoid.

II. *Religious practice.* 1. The first point is *prayer,*
under which are also comprehended those legal washings
or purifications which are necessary preparations thereto.

For the regular performance of the duty of prayer
among the Mahometans, it is requisite, while they pray,
to turn their faces towards the temple of Mecca; the
quarter where the same is situated being, for that reason,
pointed out within their mosques by a niche, which they
call *al Mehrab ;* and without, by the situation of the doors
opening into the galleries of the steeples; there are also
tables calculated for the ready finding out their Keblah,
or part towards which they ought to pray, in places where
they have no other direction.

2. *Alms* are of two sorts, *legal* and *voluntary.* The
legal alms are of indispensable obligation, being commanded
by the law, which directs and determines both the portion
which is to be given, and of what things it ought to consist;
but the *voluntary alms* are left to every one's liberality, to
give more or less as he shall see fit. The former kind of
alms some think to be properly called *zacat,* and the latter,
sadakat, though this name be also frequently given to the
legal alms. They are called *zacat,* either because they
increase a man's store by drawing down a blessing thereon,
and produce in his soul the virtue of liberality ; or because
they *purify* the remaining part of one's substance from
pollution, and the soul from the filth of avarice ; and
sadakat, because they are a proof of a man's sincerity in
the worship of God. Some writers have called the legal
alms *tithes;* but improperly, since in some cases they fall
short, and in others exceed that proportion.

3. *Fasting* is a duty of so great moment, that Mahomet
used to say it was *the gate of religion,* and that the *odor
of the mouth of him who fasteth is more grateful to God
than that of musk;* and Al Ghazali reckons fasting *one*

fourth part of the faith. According to the Mahometan divines, there are three degrees of fasting: 1. The restraining the belly and other parts of the body from satisfying their lusts. 2. The restraining the ears, eyes, tongue, hands, feet, and other members from sin. 3. The fasting of the heart from worldly cares, and restraining the thought from everything besides God.

4. The pilgrimage to Mecca is so necessary a point of practice, that according to a tradition of Mahomet, he who dies without performing it, may as well die a Jew or a Christian; and the same is expressly commanded in the Koran.

III. *Causes of the success of Mahometanism.* — The rapid success which attended the propagation of this new religion was owing to causes that are plain and evident, and must remove, or rather prevent our surprise, when they are attentively considered. The terror of Mahomet's arms, and the repeated victories which were gained by him and his successors, were, no doubt, the irresistible arguments that persuaded such multitudes to embrace his religion, and submit to his dominion. Besides, his law was artfully and marvellously adapted to the corrupt nature of man; and, in a most particular manner, to the manners and opinions of the Eastern nations, and the vices to which they were naturally addicted; for the articles of faith which it proposed were few in number, and extremely simple; and the duties it required were neither many nor difficult, nor such as were incompatible with the empire of appetites and passions. It is to be observed farther, that the gross ignorance under which the Arabians, Syrians, Persians, and the greatest part of the Eastern nations, labored at this time, rendered many an easy prey to the artifice and eloquence of this bold adventurer. To these causes of the progress of Mahometanism, we may add the bitter dissensions and cruel animosities that reigned among the Christian sects, particularly the Greeks, Nestorians, Eutychians, and Monophysites; dissensions that filled a great part of the East with carnage, assassinations, and such detestable enormities, as rendered the very name of Christianity odious to many. We might add here, that the Monophysites and Nestorians, full of resentment against the Greeks, from whom they had suffered the bitterest and most injurious treatment, assisted the Arabians in the conquest of several provinces, into which, of consequence, the religion of Mahomet was afterwards introduced. Other causes of the sudden progress of that religion will naturally occur to such as consider attentively its spirit and genius, and the state of the world at this time.

IV. *Subversion of Mahometanism.* — Of things yet to come it is difficult to say anything with precision. We have, however, some reason to believe, from the aspect of Scripture prophecy, that, triumphant as this sect has been, it shall at last come to nought. As it arose as a scourge to Christendom about the time that Antichrist obtained a temporal dominion, so it is not improbable but they will have their downfall nearly at the same period. The ninth chapter of Revelations seems to refer wholly to this imposture; "the four angels were loosed," says the prediction, 15th verse, "which were prepared for an hour, and a day, and a month, and a year, for to slay the third part of men." This period, in the language of prophecy, makes 391 years, which being added to the year when the four angels were loosed, will bring us down to 1844, or thereabouts, for the final destruction of the Mahometan empire. It must be confessed, however, that though the event is certain, the exact time cannot be easily ascertained.

JEWS.

THE name Jews is a name derived from the patriarch Judah, and given to the descendants of Abraham by his grandson Jacob. We shall here present the reader with as comprehensive a view of this singular people as we can.

1. *History of the Jews.*—The Almighty promised Abraham that he would render his seed extremely numerous: this promise began to be fulfilled in Jacob's twelve sons. In about two hundred and fifteen years they increased in Egypt from seventy to between two and three millions, men, women, and children. While Joseph lived, they were kindly used by the Egyptian monarchs; but soon after, from a suspicion that they would become too strong for the natives, they were condemned to slavery; but the more they were oppressed, the more they grew. The midwives and others were therefore ordered to murder every male infant at the time of its birth; but they shirking the horrible task, everybody was then ordered to destroy the male children wherever they found them.

After they had been thus oppressed for about one hundred years, and on the very day that finished the four hundred and thirtieth year from God's first promise of a seed to Abraham, and about four hundred years after the birth of Isaac, God, by terrible plagues on the Egyptians, obliged them to liberate the Hebrews under the direction of Moses and Aaron. Pharaoh pursued them with a mighty army; but the Lord opened a passage for them through the Red Sea; and the Egyptians, in attempting to follow them, were drowned. After this, we find them in a dry and barren desert, without any provision for their journey; but God supplied them with water from a rock, and manna and quails from heaven. A little after they routed the Amalekites, who fell on their rear. In the wilderness God delivered them the law, and confirmed the authority of Moses. Three thousand of them were cut off for worshipping the golden calf; and for loathing the manna, they were punished with a month's eating of flesh, till a plague broke out among them; and for their rash belief of the ten wicked spies, and the contempt of the promised land, God had entirely destroyed them, had not Moses' prayers prevented. They were condemned, however, to wander in the desert till the end of forty years, till that whole generation, except Caleb and Joshua, should be cut off by death. Here they were often punished for their rebellion, idolatry, whoredom, &c. God's marvellous favors, however, were still continued in conducting and supplying them with meat; and the streams issuing from the rock of Meribah followed their camp about thirty-nine years, and their clothes never waxed old.

On their entrance into Canaan, God ordered them to cut off every idolatrous Canaanite; but they spared vast numbers of them, who enticed them to wickedness, and were sometimes God's rod to punish them. For many ages they had enjoyed little prosperity, and often relapsed into awful idolatry, worshipping Baalim and Ashtaroth. Micah and the Danites introduced it not long after Joshua's death. About this time the lewdness of the men of Gibeah occasioned a war of the eleven tribes against their brethren of Benjamin; they were twice routed by the Benjamites, and forty thousand of them were slain. In the third, however, all the Benjamites were slain, except six hundred. Vexed for the loss of a tribe, the other Hebrews provided wives for these six hundred, at the expense of slaying most of the inhabitants of Jabesh Gilead.

Their relapses into idolatry also brought on them repeated turns of slavery from the heathen among or around
them. See books of Judges and Samuel. Having been
governed by judges for about three hundred and forty
years after the death of Joshua, they took a fancy to have
a king. Saul was their first sovereign, under whose reign
they had perpetual struggles with the Ammonites, Moabites, and Philistines. After about seven years' struggling
between the eleven tribes that clave to Ishbosheth, the son
of Saul, and the tribe of Judah, who erected themselves
into a kingdom under David, David became sole monarch.
Under him they subdued their neighbors, the Philistines,
Edomites, and others ; and took possession of the whole
dominion which had been promised them, from the border
of Egypt to the banks of the Euphrates. Under Solomon
they had little war ; when he died, ten of the Hebrew
tribes formed a kingdom of Israel, or Ephraim, for themselves, under Jeroboam, the son of Nebat, in opposition to
the kingdom of Judah and Benjamin, ruled by the family
of David. The kingdom of Israel, Ephraim, or the ten
tribes, had never so much as one pious king ; idolatry was
always their established religion. The kingdom of Judah
had pious and wicked sovereigns by turns, though they
often relapsed into idolatry, which brought great distress
upon them. See books of Samuel, Kings, and Chronicles.
Not only the kingdom of Israel, but that of Judah, was
brought to the very brink of ruin after the death of Jeho-
shaphat.

After various changes, sometimes for the better and
sometimes for the worse, the kingdom of Israel was ruined
two hundred and fifty four years after its erection, by So,
king of Egypt, and Halmanaser, king of Assyria, who invaded it, and destroyed most of the people. Judah was
invaded by Sennacherib; but Hezekiah's piety and Isaiah's

27

prayer were the means of their preservation; but under Manasseh, the Jews abandoned themselves to horrid impiety; for which they were punished by Esarhaddon, king of Assyria, who invaded and reduced the kingdom, and carried Manasseh prisoner to Babylon. Manasseh repented, and the Lord brought him back to his kingdom, where he promoted the reformation; but his son Amon defaced all. Josiah, however, again promoted it, and carried it to a higher pitch than in the reigns of David and Solomon. After Josiah was slain by Pharaoh Necho, king of Egypt, the people returned to idolatry, and God gave them up to servitude to the Egyptians and Chaldeans. The fate of their kings, Jehoas, Jehoiakim, Jehoiachin, and Zedekiah, was unhappy. Provoked by Zedekiah's treachery, Nebuchadnezzar invaded the kingdom, murdered vast numbers, and reduced them to captivity.

Thus the kingdom of Judah was ruined, A. M. 3416, about three hundred and eighty-eight years after its division from that of the ten tribes. In the seventieth year from the begun captivity, the Jews, according to the edict of Cyrus, king of Persia, who had overturned the empire of Chaldea, returned to their own country. See Nehemiah, Ezra. Vast numbers of them, who had agreeable settlements, remained in Babylon. After their return they rebuilt the temple and city of Jerusalem, put away their strange wives, and renewed their covenant with God.

About 3490, or 3546, they escaped the ruin designed them by Haman. About 3653, Darius Ochus, king of Persia, ravaged part of Judea, and carried off a great many prisoners. When Alexander was in Canaan, about 3670, he confirmed to them all their privileges; and having built Alexandria, he settled vast numbers of them there. About fourteen years after, Ptolemy Lagus, the Greek king of Egypt, ravaged Judea, and carried one hundred thousand prisoners to Egypt, but used them kindly, and assigned them many places of trust. About eight years after, he transported another multitude of Jews to Egypt, and gave them considerable privileges. About the same time, Seleucus Nicator, having built about thirty new cities in Asia, settled in them as many Jews as he could: and Ptolemy Philadelphus, of Egypt, about 3720, bought the freedom of all the Jew slaves in Egypt. Antiochus Epiphanes, about 3834, enraged with them for rejoicing at the report of his death, and for the peculiar form of their worship, in his return from Egypt, forced his way into Jerusalem, and murdered forty thousand of them; and about two years after he ordered his troops to pillage the cities of Judea, and murder the men, and sell the women and children for slaves. Multitudes were killed, and ten thousand prisoners carried off; the temple was dedicated to Olympius, an idol of Greece, and the Jews exposed to the basest treatment. Mattathias, the priest, with his sons, chiefly Judas, Jonathan, and Simon, who were called Maccabees, bravely fought for their religion and liberties. Judas, who succeeded his father about 3840, gave Nicanor and the king's troops a terrible defeat, regained the temple and dedicated it anew, restored the daily worship, and repaired Jerusalem, which was almost in a ruinous heap. After his death, Jonathan and Simon, his brethren, successively succeeded him; and both wisely and bravely promoted the welfare of the Church and State. Simon was succeeded by his son Hircanus, who subdued Idumea and reduced the Samaritans. In 3899 he was succeeded by his son Janneus, who reduced the Philistines, the country of Moab, Ammon, Gilead, and part of Arabia. Under these three reigns alone the Jewish nation was independent after the captivity. After the death of the widow of Janneus, who governed nine years, the nation was almost ruined by civil broils. In 3939, Aristobulus invited the Romans to assist him against Hircanus, his elder brother. The country was quickly reduced, and Jerusalem taken by force; and Pompey and a number of his officers, pushed their way into the sanctuary, if not into the Holy of Holies, to view the furniture thereof. Nine years after, Crasses, the Roman general, pillaged the temple of its valuables. After Judea had for more than thirty years been a scene of ravage and blood, and twenty-four of which had been oppressed by Herod the Great, Herod got himself installed in the kingdom. About twenty years before our Saviour's birth, he, with the Jew's consent, began to build the temple. About this time the Jews had hopes of the Messiah; and about A. M. 4000, Christ actually came, whom Herod (instigated by the fear of losing his throne) sought to murder. The Jews, however, a few excepted, rejected the Messiah, and put him to death. The sceptre was now wholly departed from Judah; and Judea, about twenty-seven years before, reduced to a province. The Jews, since that time, have been scattered, contemned, persecuted, and enslaved among all nations, not mixed with any in the common manner, but have remained as a body distinct by themselves.

2. *Sentiments of the Jews.*—The Jews commonly reckon but fourteen articles of their faith. Maimonides, a famous Jewish rabbi, reduced them to this number when he drew up their confession about the end of the eleventh century, and it was generally received. All the Jews are obliged to live and die in the profession of these thirteen articles, which are as follows;—1. That God is the creator of all things; that He guides and supports all creatures; that He has done everything; and that He still acts, and shall act during the whole eternity.—2. That God is one; there

is no unity like his. He alone hath been, is, and shall be eternally our God. — 3. That God is incorporeal, and cannot have any material properties; and no corporeal essence can be compared with him. — 4. That God is the beginning and end of all things, and shall eternally subsist. — 5. That God alone ought to be worshipped, and none beside Him is to be adored. — 6. That whatever has been taught by the prophets is true. — 7. That Moses is the head and father of all contemporary doctors, of those who lived before, or shall live after him.—8. That the law was given by Moses. — 9. That the law shall never be altered, and that God will give no other. —10. That God knows all the thoughts and actions of men.—11. That God will regard the works of all those who have performed what he commands, and punish those who have transgressed his laws.—12. That the Messiah is to come, though he tarry a long time.—13. That there shall be a resurrection of the dead when God shall see fit.

The modern Jews adhere still as closely to the Mosaic dispensation, as their dispersed and despised condition will permit them. Their service consists chiefly in reading the law in their synagogues, together with a variety of prayers. They use no sacrifices since the destruction of the Temple. They repeat blessings and particular praises to God, not only in their prayers, but on all accidental occasions, and in almost all their actions. They go to prayers three times a day in their synagogues. Their sermons are not made in Hebrew, which few of them now perfectly understand, but in the language of the country where they reside. They are forbidden all vain swearing, and pronouncing any of the names of God without necessity. They abstain from meats prohibited by the Levitical law; for which reason, whatever they eat must be dressed by Jews, and after a manner peculiar to themselves. As soon as a child can speak,

27 *

they teach him to read and translate the Bible into the language of the country where they live. In general they observe the same ceremonies which were practised by their ancestors, in the celebration of the passover. They acknowledge a two-fold law of God, a written and an unwritten one; the former is contained in the Pentateuch, or five books of Moses; the latter, they pretend, was delivered by God to Moses, and handed down from him by oral tradition, and now to be received as of equal authority with the former. They assert the perpetuity of their law, together with its perfection. They deny the accomplishment of the prophecies in the person of Christ; alleging that the Messiah is not yet come, and that he will make his appearance with the greatest worldly pomp and grandeur, subduing all nations before him, and subjecting them to the house of Judah. Since the prophets have predicted his mean condition and sufferings, they confidently talk of two Messiahs; one Ben-Ephraim, whom they grant to be a person of a mean and afflicted condition in this world; and the other, Ben-David, who shall be a victorious and powerful prince

The Jews pray for the souls of the dead, because they suppose there is a paradise for the souls of good men, where they enjoy glory in the presence of God. They believe that the souls of the wicked are tormented in hell with fire and other punishments; that some are condemned to be punished in this manner forever, while others continue only for a limited time; and this they call *purgatory*, which is not different from hell in respect of the place, but of the duration. They suppose no Jew, unless guilty of heresy, or certain crimes specified by the rabbins, shall continue in purgatory above a twelvemonth; and that there are but few who suffer eternal punishment.

Almost all the modern Jews are Pharisees, and are as much attached to tradition as their ancestors were; and assert that whoever rejects the oral law deserves death. Hence they entertain an implacable hatred to the Caraites, who adhere to the text of Moses, rejecting the rabbinistical interpretation.

There are still some of the Sadducees in Africa, and in several other places; but they are few in number: at least there are but very few who declare openly for these opinions.

There are to this day some remains of the ancient sect of the Samaritans, who are zealous for the law of Moses, but are despised by the Jews, because they receive only the Pentateuch, and observe different ceremonies from theirs. They declare they are no Sadducees, but acknowledge the spirituality and immortality of the soul. There are numbers of this sect at Gaza, Damascus, Grand Cairo, and in some other places of the east; but especially at Sichem, now called Naplouse, which is risen out of the ruins of the ancient Samaria, where they sacrificed not many years ago, having a place for this purpose on Mount Gerizim.

David Levi, a learned Jew, who in 1796 published "Dissertations on the Prophecies of the Old Testament," observes in that work that Deism and infidelity have mad such large strides in the world, that they have at length reached even to the Jewish nation; many of whom are at this time so greatly infected with scepticism, by reading Bolingbroke, Hume, Voltaire, &c., that they scarcely believe in a revelation; much less have they any hope in their future restoration.

3. *Calamities of the Jews.*—All history cannot furnish us with a parallel to the calamities and miseries of the Jews; rapine and murder, famine and pestilence, within; fire and sword, and all the terrors of war, without. Our Saviour wept at the foresight of these calamities; and it is almost impossible for persons of any humanity to read the account

without being affected.   The predictions concerning them
were remarkable, and the calamities that came upon them
were the greatest the world ever saw. Deut. xxviii., xxix.;
Matt. xxiv.   Now, what heinous sin was it that could be
the cause of such heavy judgments?   Can any other be
assigned than what the Scripture assigns?   1 Thess. ii.
15, 16. "They both killed the Lord Jesus and their own
prophets, and persecuted the apostles: and so filled up
their sins, and wrath came upon them to the uttermost."
It is hardly possible to consider the nature and extent of
their sufferings, and not conclude the Jews' own impreca
tion to be singularly fulfilled upon them.   Matt. xxvii. 25.
" His blood be on us and our children."   At Cesarea twenty
thousand of the Jews were killed by the Syrians in their
mutual broils.   At Damascus ten thousand unarmed Jews
were killed; and at Bethshan the heathen inhabitants
caused their Jewish neighbors to assist them against their
brethren, and then murdered thirty thousand of these in
habitants.   At Alexandria the Jews murdered multitudes
of the heathens, and were murdered in their turn to about
fifty thousand.   The Romans under Vespasian invaded the
country, and took the cities of Galilee, Chorazen, Beth-
saida, Capernaum, &c., where Christ had been especially
rejected, and murdered numbers of the inhabitants.   At
Jerusalem the scene was most wretched of all.   At the
passover, when there might be two or three millions of
people in the city, the Romans surrounded it with troops,
trenches, and walls, that none might escape.   The three
different factions within murdered one another.   Titus, one
of the most merciful generals that ever breathed, did all in
his power to persuade them to an advantageous surrender,
but they scorned every proposal.   The multitudes of un-
buried carcases corrupted the air, and produced a pestilence.   The people fed on one another; and even ladies,

it is said, broiled their sucking infants, and ate them. After a siege of six months, the city was taken. They murdered almost every Jew they met with. Titus was bent to save the Temple, but could not: there were six thousand Jews who had taken shelter in it, all burnt or murdered! The outcries of the Jews, when they saw it, were most dreadful: the whole city, except three towers and a small part of the wall, were razed to the ground, and the foundations of the temple and other places were ploughed up. Soon after the forts of Herodian and Macheron were taken, the garrison of Massada murdered themselves rather than surrender. At Jerusalem alone, it is said, one million one hundred thousand perished by sword, famine, and pestilence. In other places we hear of two hundred and fifty thousand that were cut off, besides vast numbers sent to Egypt to labor as slaves. About fifty years after, the Jews murdered about five hundred thousand of the Roman subjects, for which they were severely punished by Trajan. About 130, one Barocaba pretended that he was the Messiah, and raised a Jewish army of two hundred thousand, who murdered all the heathens and Christians who came in their way; but he was defeated by Adrian's forces. In this war, it is said, about sixty thousand Jews were slain and perished. Adrian built a city on Mount Calvary, and erected a marble statue of swine over the gate that led to Bethlehem. No Jew was allowed to enter the city, or to look to it at a distance, under pain of death. In 360, they began to rebuild their city and temple; but a terrible earthquake and flames of fire issuing from the earth, killed the workmen, and scattered their materials. Nor till the seventh century durst they so much as creep over the rubbish to bewail it, without bribing the guards. In the third, fourth, and fifth centuries, there were many of them furiously harassed and murdered. In the sixth century, twenty thousand of them were slain, and as many taken and **sold** for slaves. In 602, they were severely punished for their horrible massacre of the Christians at Antioch. In Spain, in 700, they were ordered to be enslaved. In the eighth and ninth centuries, they were greatly derided and abused: in some places they were made to wear leathern girdles, and ride without stirrups on asses and mules. In France and Spain they were much insulted. In the tenth, eleventh, and twelfth centuries, their miseries rather increased: they were greatly persecuted in Egypt. Besides what they suffered in the East by the Turkish and sacred war, it is shocking to think what multitudes of them the eight crusades murdered in Germany, Hungary, Lesser Asia, and elsewhere. In France, multitudes were burnt. In England, in 1020, they were banished; and at the coronation of Richard I. the mob fell upon them, and murdered a great many of them. About one thousand and five hundred of them were burnt in the palace in the city of York, which they set fire to themselves, after killing their wives and children. In the thirteenth and fourteenth centuries their condition was no better. In Egypt, Canaan, and Syria, the crusaders still harassed them. Provoked with their mad running after pretended Messiahs, Caliph Nasser scarce left any of them alive in his dominions of Mesopotamia. In Persia, the Tartars murdered them in multitudes. In Spain, Ferdinand persecuted them furiously. About 1349, the terrible massacre of them at Toledo forced many of them to murder themselves, or change their religion. About 1253, many were murdered, and others banished from France, but in 1275 recalled. In 1320 and 1330, the crusades of the fanatic shepherds, who wasted the south of France, massacred them; besides fifteen hundred that were murdered on another occasion. In 1358, they were totally banished from France, since which few of them have entered that country. In 1291, king Edward expelled them from England, to the number of one hundred and sixty thousand. In the fifteenth, sixteenth, and seventeenth centuries, their miseries continued. In Persia they have been terribly used: from 1663 to 1666, the murder of them was so universal, that but a few escaped to Turkey. In Portugal and Spain, they have been miserably handled. About 1392, six or eight hundred thousand were banished from Spain. Some were drowned in their passage to Africa, some died by hard usage, and many of their carcasses lay in the fields till the wild beasts devoured them. In Germany they have endured many hardships. They have been banished from Bohemia, Bavaria, Cologne, Nuremberg, Augsburgh, and Vienna: they have been terribly massacred in Moravia, and plundered in Bonn and Bamberg. Except in Portugal and Spain, their present condition is generally tolerable. In Holland, Poland, and at Frankfort and Hamburgh, they have their liberty. They have repeatedly, but till lately in vain, attempted to obtain a naturalization in England, and other nations among whom they are scattered

4. *Preservation of the Jews.*—" The preservation of the Jews," says Basnage, "in the midst of the miseries which they have undergone during 1700 years, is the greatest prodigy that can be imagined. Religions depend on temporal prosperity; they triumph under the protection of a conqueror: they languish and sink with sinking monarchies. Paganism, which once covered the earth, is extinct. The Christian church, glorious in its martyrs, yet was considerably diminished by the persecutions to which it was exposed; nor was it easy to repair the breaches in it made by those acts of violence. But here we behold a church hated and persecuted for 1700 years, and yet sustaining itself, and widely extended. Kings have often employed the severity of edicts and the hand of executioners to ruin it. The seditious mul-

titudes, by murders and massacres, have committed out-
rages against it still more violent and tragical. Princes
and people, Pagans, Mahometans, Christians, disagreeing
in so many things, have united in the design of extermi-
nating it, and have not been able to succeed. The *bush
of Moses*, surrounded with flames, ever burns, and is never
consumed. The Jews have been expelled, in different times,
from every part of the world, which hath only served to
spread them in all regions. From age to age they have
been exposed to misery and persecution; yet still they
subsist, in spite of the ignominy and the hatred which hath
pursued them in all places, whilst the greatest monarchies
are fallen, and nothing remains of them besides the name.

"The judgments which God has exercised upon this
people are terrible, extending to the men, the religion, and
the very land in which they dwelt. The ceremonies essential to their religion can no more be observed; the ritual
law, which cast a splendor on the national worship, and
struck the pagans so much that they sent their presents
and their victims to Jerusalem, is absolutely fallen, for
they have no temple, no altar, no sacrifices. Their land
itself seems to lie under a never-ceasing curse. Pagans,
Christians, Mohammedans, in a word, almost all nations,
have by turns seized and held Jerusalem. To the Jew
only hath God refused the possession of this small tract
of ground, so supremely necessary for him, since he ought
to worship on this mountain. A Jewish writer hath affirmed that it is long since any Jew has been seen settled
near Jerusalem; scarcely can they purchase there six feet
of land for a burying-place.

"In all this there is no exaggeration: I am only point-
ing out known facts; and, far from having the least design
to raise an odium against the nation from its miseries, I
conclude that it ought to be looked upon as one of those

prodigies which we admire without comprehending ; since, in spite of evils so durable, and a patience so long exercised, it is preserved by a particular providence. The Jew ought to be weary of expecting a Messiah who so unkindly disappoints his vain hopes; and the Christian ought to have his attention and his regard excited towards men whom God preserves, for so great a length of time, under calamities which would have been the total ruin of any other people."

5. *Number and Dispersion of the Jews.*—They are looked upon to be as numerous at present as they were formerly in the land of Canaan. Some have rated them at three millions, and others more than double that number. Their dispersion is a remarkable particular in this people. They swarm all over the east, and are settled, it is said, in the remotest parts of China. The Turkish empire abounds with them. There are more of them at Constantinople and Salonichi than in any other place. They are spread through most of the nations of Europe and Africa, and many families of them are established in the West Indies; not to mention whole nations bordering on Prester John's country, and some discovered in the inner parts of America, if we may give any credit to their own writers. Their being always in rebellions (as Addison observes) while they had the Holy Temple in view, has excited most nations to banish them. Besides, the whole people are now a race of such merchants as are wanderers by profession; and at the same time are in most, if not in all places, incapable of holding either lands or offices, that might engage them to make any part of the world their home. In addition to this, we may consider what providential reasons may be assigned for their numbers and dispersion. Their firm adherence to their religion, and being dispersed all over the earth, has furnished every age

28

and every nation with the strongest arguments for the
Christian faith; not only as these very particulars are
foretold of them, but as they themselves are the deposita-
ries of these and all other prophecies which tend to their
own confusion and the establishment of Christianity.
Their number furnishes us with a sufficient cloud of witnesses that attest the truth of the Bible, and their dispersion spreads these witnesses through all parts of the world.

6. *Restoration of Jews.* — From the declarations of
Scripture, we have reason to suppose the Jews shall be
called to a participation of the blessings of the gospel
(Rom. xi.; 2 Cor. iii. 16; Hos. i. 11); and some suppose
shall return to their own land (Hos. iii. 5; Is. lxv. 17,
etc.; Ezek. xxxvi). As to the time, some think about
1866 or 2016; but this, perhaps, is not so easy to determine altogether, though it is probable it will not be before
the fall of Antichrist and the Ottoman empire. Let us,
however, avoid putting stumbling-blocks in their way. If
we attempt anything for their conversion, let it be with
peace and love. Let us, says one, propose Christianity to
them, as Christ proposed it to them. Let us lay before
them their own prophecies. Let us show them their accomplishment in Jesus. Let us applaud their hatred of
idolatry. Let us show them the morality of Jesus in our
lives and tempers. Let us never abridge their civil liberty,
nor ever try to force their consciences.

UNITED BRETHREN IN CHRIST.

THIS large and respectable society is frequently mistaken for the Moravians, but is entirely distinct from them, being founded, near the close of the eighteenth century, by REV. WM. OTTERBEIN, a learned minister of the German Reformed Church. Mr. Otterbein was born in Germany, but came to this country in 1752. Not long afterward, impressed by the study of the Scriptures with the need of the New Birth, taught by Christ as the source of all spiritual life, he first sought that blessing for himself; and, having found it, began earnestly to enforce its necessity upon others, however familiar they might be, as he had been, with the religion of forms and education. Numbers of professing Christians were soon roused from apathy and false security, to an active interest in spiritual things. Meetings were appointed on week evenings, not only for preaching, but for prayer and religious conversation—things common now, but then counted "strange things," among his denomination. Otterbein also adopted and spread the new idea that all true Christians, of whatever name, should unite at the Lord's table. For these innovations on established order, the Synod called him to account, tried him, and though it never formally excommunicated him, nearly every pulpit was henceforth closed against him.

Though sorely pained at these proceedings, Mr. Otterbein was not silenced or dismayed. He resorted to the fields and private houses; even the barn was welcome as a place to preach the Gospel. He travelled extensively, and success attended his labors. Many joined him from other denominations, and such was the concord between them, that they agreed to take the name they now bear, of "United Brethren in Christ."

Mr. Asbury, sent out to this country by Mr. Wesley to form churches, labored in company with them for some time, they preaching in German, and he in English. Hence they were called "German Methodists," though they preferred an organization of their own. Some steps were taken to this end in 1789, at a conference held in Baltimore, Md., but nothing effectual was done until 1800, when an organization was formed, and Otterbein and Martin Bochm were chosen the first superintendents or Bishops.

The society throve rapidly, both in preachers and people, though not as rapidly as the Methodist Episcopal Church, being confined for a number of years to the German population. Their "Discipline" was adopted in their General Conference at Mount Pleasant, Pa., in 1815. They are distinguished by no new doctrines, but by an organization in which the ministers and people have, in the main, an equal proportion of power, and the rulers hold office only by the authority and consent of the governed. In this freedom they are chiefly distinguished from their Methodist Episcopal brethren.

Their ecclesiastical courts consist, like theirs, of Quarterly, Annual, and General Conferences; and their officers of ordained elders, who alone exercise the functions of the ministry; class leaders; stewards, who attend to the pecuniary wants of the ministers; preachers in charge, who must have the oversight of one circuit; presiding elders; and bishops, who have the general superintendence of the whole Church. Their ministry is earnest, quiet, and. perseveringly devoted to the salvation of souls.

They allow, but do not enjoin, the washing of feet They oppose all secret societies, intemperance, and slavery, and are zealous in supporting Missions.

In 1870, they had 40 Conferences, 3924 churches, 1634 ministers, and 118,055 members.

PELAGIANS.

PELAGIANISM is that theological view which denies the total corruption of men, attributed to the fall of Adam (original sin), and declares man's natural capacity sufficient for the exercise of Christian duties and virtues, provided he have but an earnest purpose to do well. It does not exclude faith in divine assistance towards man's improvement, but believes this assistance will be granted to those only who strive to improve themselves. This view was broached by the English monk Pelagius, who, in the fifth century, resided in Rome, with the reputation of great learning and an unspotted life, and fled from that city when it was taken by the Goths, in 409, with his friend Cœlestus, to Sicily, and thence to Africa, where Augustine declared him a heretic; in which several African synods concurred. Pelagius travelled to Jerusalem, and there closed his life in tranquillity, in the year 420, at the age of ninety years. The philosophical soundness and noble frankness of his writings, together with his own great virtue in a time of universal and deep-rooted corruption, procured many adherents to his opinions, which at all times have been considered, by some of the purest and most reflecting men, as the only ones worthy of the Deity. He never attempted to found a heretical or dissenting sect, yet the Pelagians, whose views were formally condemned at the Council of Ephesus, in 431, and the Semi-Pelagians, founded by John Cassianus at Marseilles (died in 435), who somewhat modified the orthodox dogma of the utter insufficiency of man's nature for virtue, occupy a very important place in ecclesiastical history.

28 *

EUTYCHIANS.

THE Eutychians were a sect of Christians which began in the east in the fifth century. Eutyches, its reputed founder, though the opinions attributed to him are said to have existed before (*de Eutychianismo ante Eutychen*, by Christ. Aug. Selig, and also Assemani, *Bibliotheca Orientalis*, tom. i., p. 219), was a monk who lived near Constantinople, and had a great reputation for austerity and sanctity. He was already advanced in years when he came out of his retirement, A. D. 448, in order to oppose the Nestorians, who were accused of teaching " that the divine nature was not incarnate in, but only attendant on, Jesus, being superadded to his human nature after the latter was formed ;" an opinion, however, which Nestorius himself had disavowed. In his zeal for opposing the error ascribed to the Nestorians, Eutyches ran into the opposite extreme of saying that in Christ there was " only one nature, that of the incarnate Word," his human nature having been absorbed in a manner by his divine nature.

Eusebius, Bishop of Dorylæum, who had already opposed the Nestorians, denounced Eutyches before a council assembled at Constantinople by Flavianus, bishop of that city. That assembly condemned Eutyches, who, being supported by friends at the court of Theodosius II., appealed to a general council, which was soon after convoked by the emperor at Ephesus, A. D. 449, under the presidency of Dioscorus, Bishop of Alexandria, and successor to the famous Cyril, who had himself broached a doctrine very similar to that of Eutyches.

The majority of the council tumultuously acquitted Eutyches, and condemned Flavianus; the bishops opposed to him were obliged to escape, and Flavianus was cruelly scourged by the soldiers. It was, in short, a scene of disgraceful violence, which earned for the Council of Ephesus the name of "a meeting of robbers."

Flavianus appealed to Leo the Great, Bishop of Rome, who, in his answer, condemned the doctrine of Eutyches, but could not obtain of Theodosius the convocation of another council. After the death of that emperor, his successor, Marcianus, convoked a council at Chalcedon, A. D. 451, which is reckoned as the fourth œcumenical council of the Church, and which the Pope's legates attended. By this assembly the acts of the Council of Ephesus were annulled, Dioscorus was deposed and banished, and Eutyches, who had already been banished by the emperor, was again condemned, and deprived of his sacerdotal office.

The doctrine was at the same time expounded that "in Christ two distinct natures are united in one person, and that without any change, mixture, or confusion." Eutyches died in exile; but several monks, especially in Syria, continued the schism, and having found a protectress in the Empress Eudocia, the widow of Theodosius, who was living in Palestine, they became more daring, and excited the people against the partisans of the Council of Chalcedon, whom they stigmatized as Nestorians. The emperor was obliged to send troops to repress these disorders.

The doctrine of Eutyches was perpetuated in the east under certain modifications, or rather quibbling of words, which caused the sect to be subdivided under various names, all, however, comprehended under the general name of Monophysites, or believers in one nature. In the sixth century a fresh impulse was given to the Eutychian doctrine by one Jacob, a monk, surnamed Baradæus, who reconciled the various divisions of the Monophysites throughout the east, and spread their tenets through Syria, Armenia, Mesopotamia, and Egypt, found supporters among several prelates (among others in the Bishop of Alexandria), and died himself Bishop of Edessa, A. D. 588. He was considered as the second founder of the Monophysites, who assumed from him the name of Jacobites, under which appellation they still constitute a very numerous church, equally separate from the Greek, the Roman or Latin, and the Nestorian churches. The Armenians and the Copts are Jacobites, and so are likewise many Syrian Christians in contradistinction to the Melchites, who belong to the Greek Church. Jacobite congregations are found in Mesopotamia.

The Monothelites who appeared in the seventh century have been considered as an offshoot of the Eutychians or Monophysites, though they pretended to be quite unconnected with them. They admitted the two natures in Christ, explaining that after the union of the two into one person, there was in him only one will and one operation. This was an attempt to conciliate the Monophysites with the orthodox church, and it succeeded for a time. It was approved of by many eastern prelates, and even by Pope Honorius I., in two epistles to Sergius, patriarch of Constantinople, which are found in the Acts of the Councils But the successors of Honorius condemned the Monothelites, and Martin I., in a bull of excommunication, A. D. 649, consigned them and their patrons (meaning the Emperor Constans, who protected them) " to the devil and his angels." Constans, indignant at this, caused his exarch in Italy to arrest Martin, and send him prisoner to the Chersonesus. At last, under Constantine, who succeeded Constans, the Council of Constantinople, which is the sixth œcumenical council, A. D. 680, condemned the Monothelites, and with them Pope Honorius himself.

FIFTH MONARCHY MEN,

A SECT of religionists, whose distinguishing tenet was a belief in the fifth universal monarchy, of which Jesus Christ was to be the head, while the saints, under his personal sovereignty, should possess the earth. They appeared in England towards the close of the Protectorate; and in 1660, a few months after the Restoration, they broke out into a serious tumult in London under their leader Venner, in which many of them lost their lives, some being killed by the military, and others afterwards executed. Several Fifth Monarchy Men also suffered death in 1662, on a charge (most probably unfounded) of having conspired to kill the King and the Duke of York, to seize the Tower, etc. They are the same who were sometimes called Millenarians, their notion being that the reign of Christ upon earth was to last for a thousand years. They seem also, from the extravagance and violence of conduct into which they occasionally broke out, to have been confounded, in the popular imagination, with the old Anabaptists of Münster.

FRATRICELLI.

FRATRICELLI, or Little Brethren, also called *Fratres de paupere vitâ*, a religious sect which arose in Italy towards the end of the thirteenth century. They were Franciscan monks, who separated themselves from the grand community of St. Francis, with the intention of obeying the laws of their founder in a more rigorous manner than they were observed by the other Franciscans. They accordingly renounced every kind of property, both common and individual, and begged from door to door their daily subsistence, alleging that neither Christ nor his Apostles had any possessions, either individual or in common; and that these were the models which St. Francis had commanded them to imitate. They went about clothed in rags, declaiming against the vices of the Pope and the bishops, and foretold the reformation of the Church and the restoration of the true gospel of Christ, by the real followers of St. Francis. As the Franciscan order acknowledges for its companions a set of men who observe the third rule prescribed by St. Francis, and were therefore commonly called Tertiarii; so likewise the order of the Fratricelli, who were anxious to be considered as the only true followers of St. Francis, had a great number of Tertiarii attached to their cause. These Tertiarii, or half-monks, were called in Italy *Bizochi* or *Bocazoi*, in France *Beguins*, in Germany *Begwards* or *Beghards*. This last appellation was generally applied to them. The Tertiarii differed from the Fratricelli, not in their opinions, but only in their manner of living. The Fratricelli were real monks, subject to the rule of St. Francis, whilst the Bizo-

chi or Beghards, as well as the Franciscan Tertiarii, excepting their dirty habits, and certain maxims and observances which they followed in compliance with the rules
of their patron saint, lived after the manner of other
men, and were therefore considered as laymen. The Beghards were divided into two classes, the *perfect* and the
imperfect. The first lived on alms, abstained from marriage, and had no fixed dwellings ; the second had houses,
wives, and possessions, and were engaged in the common
avocations of life like other people. Pope Celestin V.
was favorably disposed to the Fratricelli, and permitted
them to constitute themselves into a separate order. They
were submissive to that Pope, but they violently opposed
his successor, Boniface VIII., and subsequent Popes who
persecuted their sect. The Fratricelli were accused of
great enormities, and persecuted by the court of Rome ;
but they found protection from princes, nobles, and towns,
who respected them on account of the austerity of their
devotion. The Fratricelli did not always submit with the
meekness of the first Christian martyrs to their persecutors, but frequently opposed force to force, and even put
to death some inquisitors in Italy. This sect continued
during the fourteenth century, and spread as far as Bohemia, Silesia, and Poland. The members of it were most
severely persecuted in the fifteenth century, and many of
them fled from France to England and Ireland. All the
persecutions directed against the sect did not, however,
extinguish it; and some remnants of it existed till the
Reformation of Luther, whose doctrines they embraced.
Their name is supposed to have been derived from *Fratri-
cellus* or *Fraterculus*, an Italian nickname which was applied in the middle ages to all persons who, without belonging to any religious order, assumed a sanctimonious
appearance.

PIETISTS.

PIETISTS is the name given in the seventeenth century to a kind of German Methodists or Evangelicals, who, being members of the Lutheran Church, were dissatisfied with the cold dogmatism of the generality of its clergy, and felt the want of a revival of religious feeling and of practical piety and charity. Without separating themselves from the church, they instituted meetings called "Collegia Pietatis," from which the denomination of Pietists was derived. Philip Jacob Spener, a divine of the Lutheran Church, who was preacher at Frankfort, and afterwards at Dresden and Berlin, was the chief promoter of these meetings, which began about 1670. He wrote several ascetic works, and died in 1705. A spirit similar to that of the Pietists of Germany has arisen in our own times in the Swiss and French Protestant churches, and the promoters of it, after suffering considerable annoyance from the less religious part of the community, have succeeded in effecting a revival of evangelical doctrines and practice. They have been styled in derision "Momiers" (from *momerie*, mummery), a name which the great majority of them are far from deserving.

MANICHÆANS.

THE Manichæans were an heretical Christian sect, who derived their name from Mani, as he is called by the Persians and Arabians, or Manes or Manichæus, according to the Greek and Roman writers. The particulars of the

life and death of this individual are variously reported by
the Greek and Oriental writers; but it appears from all
accounts that he was a native of Persia, or at least brought
up in that country; that he was well acquainted with the
doctrines of the Magi; that he attempted to amalgamate
the Persian religion with Christianity; and that after
meeting with considerable success, he was eventually put
to death by Varanes I., king of Persia. It is difficult to
determine the exact time at which the doctrines of Mani
were first promulgated in the Roman empire; but they do
not appear to have been known before the end of the third
century or the beginning of the fourth.

The Manichæans believed, like the Magi, in two eternal
principles, from which all things proceed, namely, light
and darkness, which are respectively subject to the
dominion of two beings, one the god of good, and the other
the god of evil. They also believed that the first parents
of the human race were created by the god of darkness
with corrupt and mortal bodies, but that their souls formed
part of that eternal light which was subject to the god of
light. They maintained that it was the great object of
the government of the god of light to deliver the captive
souls of men from their corporeal prisons, and that with
this view he created two sublime beings, Christ and the
Holy Ghost, and sent Christ into the world, clothed with
the shadowy form of a human body, and not with the real
substance, to teach mortals how to deliver the rational
soul from the corrupt body, and to overcome the power of
malignant matter. Referring to the promise of Christ
shortly before his crucifixion, which is recorded by John
(xvi. 7–15), that he would send to his disciples the Comforter, "who would lead them into all truth," the Manichæans maintained that this promise was fulfilled in the
person of Mani, who was sent by the god of light to declare

to all men the doctrine of salvation, without concealing any of its truths under the veil of metaphor, or under any other covering. Mani also taught that those souls which obeyed the laws delivered by Christ, as explained by himself the Comforter, and struggled against the lusts and appetites of a corrupt nature, would, on their death, be delivered from their sinful bodies, and, after being purified by the sun and moon, would ascend to the regions of light; but that those souls which neglected to struggle against their corrupt natures would pass after death into the bodies of animals or other beings, until they had expiated their guilt. Their belief in the evil of matter led them to deny the doctrine of the resurrection.

Mani entirely rejected the authority of the Old Testament, which he had said was the word of the god of darkness, whom the Jews had worshipped in the place of the god of light. He asserted that the books of the New Testament had been grossly interpolated; and that they were not all written by the persons whose names they bear. The doctrines of the sect were contained in four works, said to have been written by Mani himself, which were entitled respectively "Mysteries," "Chapters," "Gospel," and "Treasury;" but we know little or nothing of their contents.

Bower, in the second volume of his "History of the Popes," has attempted to prove that the Manichæans were addicted to immoral practices; but this opinion has been ably controverted by Beausobre and Lardner, who have shown that they were, on the contrary, exceedingly rigorous and austere in their mode of life.

The disciples of Mani were divided into two classes, one of which was called the *Elect*, and the other *Hearers*. The former were bound to abstain from animal food, wine, and all sensual enjoyments; the latter were considered as imperfect and feeble Christians, and were not obliged to submit to such a severe mode of life. The ecclesiastical constitution of the Manichæans consisted of twelve apostles and a president, who represented Christ; of seventy-two bishops, who also represented the seventy-two disciples of Christ; and of presbyters and deacons, as in the Catholic church.

The Manichæans never appear to have been very numerous, but they were spread over almost all parts of the Christian world. Numerous treatises were written against them, the most important of which were by Eusebius of Cæsarea, Eusebius of Emesa, Serapion of Thumis, Athanasius of Alexandria, George and Apollinarius of Laodicea, and Titus of Bostra. Much valuable information concerning this sect may be found in the writings of Augustine, who was for nine years a zealous supporter of the Manichæan doctrines.

The Paulicians are generally considered to be a branch of the Manichæan sect, and are supposed to have appeared first in the seventh century in Armenia, and to have derived their name from Paul, a zealous preacher of the doctrines of Mani. But this is an error. See appendix.

In the sixth century the Manichæan doctrines are said to have spread very widely in Persia. They continued to have supporters, under their new name of Paulicianism, till a very late period in ecclesiastical history. About the middle of the eighth century, the emperor Constantine, surnamed Copronymus, transplanted from Armenia a great number of Paulicians to Thrace; where they continued to exist even after the capture of Constantinople by the Turks. In the eleventh and twelfth centuries, the doctrines of the Paulicians were introduced into Italy and France, and met with considerable success.

MARCIONITES.

THE Marcionites were a religious sect of the second and third centuries of our æra, so called from their teacher Marcion, a native of Sinope and a priest, who adopted the old Oriental belief of two independent, eternal, co-existing principles, one evil and the other good. He endeavored to apply this doctrine to Christianity, asserting that our souls are emanations of the good principle, but our bodies and the whole visible world are the creation of the evil genius, who strives to chain down our spiritual nature by corporeal fetters, so as to make the soul forget its pure and noble origin. He further maintained that the law of Moses, with its threats and promises of things terrestrial, was a contrivance of the evil principle in order to bind men still more to the earth; but that the good principle, in order to dissipate these delusions, sent Jesus Christ, a pure emanation of itself, giving him a corporeal appearance and a semblance of bodily form, in order to remind men of their intellectual nature, and that they cannot expect to find happiness until they are reunited to the principle of good from which they are derived. Marcion and his disciples condemned all pleasures which are not spiritual; they taught that it was necessary to combat every impulse that attaches us to the visible world; they condemned marriage, and some of them even regretted the necessity of eating of the fruits of the earth, which they believed to have been created by the evil principle. The Marcionites spread far in the East, and especially in Persia. The chief opponent of Marcion was Tertullianus, who wrote a book to refute his doctrines.

MARONITES.

MARONITES is the name of a community of Christians belonging to the Western or Roman church, and living on Mount Lebanon. They are the neighbors of, and allied to, and in some places mixed with the Druses, and, like them, independent, in great measure, of the Turkish power. The Maronites occupy the valleys and fastnesses of the principal ridge of Lebanon east of Beyroot and Tripoli, and they extend inland as far as the Bekaa, or plain between the Libanus and Anti-Libanus, where they are mixed with the Druses, though they do not intermarry with them. The town of Zhaklé, in the valley of Bekaa, contains between ten and twelve thousand inhabitants, chiefly Maronites.

There are also many Maronites at Beyroot and Tripoli, but the tract of country in which the great bulk of the Maronites reside is called Kesrouan. It extends along the ridge of Libanus from the Nahr el Kelb, a stream which enters the sea twelve miles north of Beyroot, to the Nahr el Kebir, which enters the sea north of Tripoli, near the island of Ruad, the ancient Aradus, on which side the Maronites border on the Nosaïris, or Ansarieh, who extend to the northward towards Latakieh, and the Ismaelians, who live farther inland, near the banks of the Orontes. To the eastward, the Maronites have for neighbors the Metualis, a tribe of independent Moslems, of the sect of Ali, who live under their own emir, and occupy the belad or district of Baalbek and part of the Anti-Libanus; and on the south they border on the territory of the Druses. with whom they form one political body, being subject to the Emir Beschir, in so far as they join him when he calls

29 *

them to arms for the common defence, and pay him their share of the tribute, which the emir paid formerly to the Porte, and now pays to the pasha of Egypt. But in their internal concerns the Maronites are governed by their own sheiks, of whom there is one in every village, from whose decision there is an appeal to the bishops, who have great authority; and in some cases to the emir of the Druses, and his divan or council.

The clergy are very numerous; the secular parish clergy are married, as in the Greek church; but the regular clergy, who are said to amount to 20,000, and are distributed among about 200 convents, follow the rule of St. Anthony, and are bound by vows of chastity and obedience. The Maronite monks are not idle; they cultivate the land belonging to their convents, and live by its produce. Every convent is a farm. The convents are under the jurisdiction of bishops, of whom there is one in every large village. The bishops are under the obligation of celibacy. The bishops collectively elect the patriarch, who is confirmed by the pope, and who resides at the convent of Kanobin, in a valley of the Libanus, south-east of Tripoli, where there is a printing-press, which furnishes the elementary books for the use of the Maronite schools.

Not far from Kanobin is the large village of Eden, ten miles above which, and high up the Libanus, is the famed clump of old cedars, called the "Cedars of Solomon," of large dimensions, but now reduced to seven in number (Lamartine, *Voyage en Orient;* Richardson), not including the younger and smaller ones. Dr. Richardson measured the trunk of one of the old trees, and found it thirty-two feet in circumference. The whole clump of old and young trees may be walked round in about half an hour. Old cedars are not found in any other part of Libanus.

At the opposite or southern extremity of the Kesrouan

is the handsome convent of Antoura, which is the residence of the papal legate and of some European missionaries. Near it is a convent of Maronite nuns.

The Maronites derive their name from a monk of the name of Maro, who, in the fifth century, collected a number of followers, and founded several convents in these mountains. When the Monothelite heresy prevailed in the East in the seventh century, and was favored by the court of Constantinople, many Christians who did not embrace its tenets took refuge in the fastnesses of Libanus, around the convents, and thus the name of Maronites was assumed by the population of the mountains. This is the account of the Maronites themselves; others pretend that the Maronites were Monothelites, who took refuge in the Libanus after the Emperor Anastasius II. had condemned and proscribed their sect, in the beginning of the eighth century. Joseph Simonius Assemani, and his friend Ambarach, better known as Father Benedetti, have defended the Maronites from the charge of Monothelitism. Ambarach translated from the Arabic into Latin the work of Stephen, patriarch of Antioch, concerning the origin and liturgy of the Maronites. In 1736, at a great synod held at Marhanna, the Maronite church formally acknowledged the canons of the Council of Trent, but they retained the mass in the Syriac language, and the marriage of the priests. Before that time they received the sacrament under both forms, as in the Greek church. At mass the priest turns towards the congregation and reads the gospel of the day in Arabic, which is the vulgar tongue.

The Maronite population is said to be above 200,000 individuals, and to contain between thirty and forty thousand men fit for military service. Every Maronite is armed, and they are all soldiers in case of need. Volney reckoned them, in 1784, at 120,000, but the population has been rapidly increasing since that time. Their language is Arabic, and by their appearance and habits they belong to the Arabian race. They are a fine-looking people, high-spirited, civil, and hospitable, especially towards European travellers, and perfectly honest. Robbery and other acts of violence are hardly known among them. They are altogether an interesting race, full of vigor, and perhaps destined with the Druses to act an important part in the future vicissitudes of Syria. (Jowett, Light, Lamartine, and other travellers in Syria.)

There is at Rome, on the Quirinal Mount, a convent of Maronite monks, who perform the service of the mass in the Syriac language, according to the liturgy of their country. This church was founded by Pope Gregory XIII., and is dedicated to St. John. The monastery serves as a college for young Maronites who come to Rome to study and take orders, after which they return to their own country. It is one of those exotic colonies which give a peculiar interest to the city of Rome.

The ceremonies of these Maronites of Rome on great festivals, their chanting in Syriac, and their curious musical instruments, are described by the Abbé Richard, in his "Voyage en Italie."

CALVINISTS.

THE followers of the religious doctrine and Church government instituted by Calvin. Calvin published his system in his "Christian Institutes," in the year 1536; but it does not appear to have obtained the name of Calvinism, nor its supporters the name of Calvinists, till the conference of Poissy, in 1561. The reformer was not

Engraved by A. B. Walter.

John Calvin

himself present at that assembly, being prevented from attending by his local duties and the ill state of his health; but we see from his correspondence with Beza, the deputy from Geneva, how deep was his interest in its proceedings, and that nothing was done on the part of the reformers without his knowledge and advice. In the debate which took place on the Augsburg Confession, the points of difference between the Lutherans and Calvinists were drawn out; and they were such as that from thenceforth the latter became known as a distinct sect under that denomination.

The tenets of Calvinism respect the doctrines of the Trinity, predestination, or particular election and reprobation, original sin, particular redemption, effectual or irresistible grace in regeneration, justification by faith, and the perseverance of Saints; together also with the government and discipline of the Church, the nature of the eucharist, and the qualification of those entitled to partake of it. The great leading principles of the system, however, are the absolute decrees of God, the spiritual presence of Christ in the eucharist, and the independence of the Church.

Calvinism was, perhaps, like Lutheranism, exemplified first at Strasburg; where, in the year 1538, Calvin established a French church on his own plan. But it was at Geneva the system was seen in all its vigor; and from thence it spread into France, Germany, Prussia, the United Provinces, England and Scotland. To this last place it was carried by Knox, the disciple and intimate correspondent of Calvin; and as within the little territory of Geneva there was neither room nor need for the parochial sessions, presbyteries, provincial synods, and general assembly, into which the presbyterial government expands itself in a large community, we shall briefly advert to its leading features

in Scotland, as it appeared there in the lifetime of Knox.
We shall thus, indeed, see the Church of Scotland in its
infancy; but, at the same time, — and it is this we have
chiefly in view,—we shall thus, perhaps, have the best idea
of the matured opinions of the great reformer.

The Confession of Faith, ratified by the Scotch parliament in 1560, declares * that by the sin of our first parents,
"commonly called original sin, the image of God was
utterly defaced in man, and he and his posterity of nature
became enemies of God, slaves to Satan, and servants unto
sin; insomuch that death everlasting has had, and shall
have, power and dominion over all that have not been, are
not, or shall not be, regenerated from above, which regeneration is wrought by the power of the Holy Ghost working
in the hearts of the elect of God an assured faith in the
promise of God revealed in his word; that "from the
eternal and immutable decree of God all our salvation
springs and depends;" "God of mere grace electing us in
Christ Jesus his Son before the foundation of the world
was laid;" and that "our faith and the assurance of the
same proceeds not from flesh and blood, that is to say,
from our natural powers within us, but is the inspiration
of the Holy Ghost;" "who sanctifies us and brings us in
all verity by his own operation, without whom we should
remain for ever enemies to God and ignorant of his son
Christ Jesus; for of nature we are so dead, so blind, and
so perverse, that neither can we feel when we are pricked,
see the light when it shines, nor assent to the will of God
when it is revealed, unless the spirit of the Lord Jesus
quicken that which is dead, remove the darkness from our
minds, and bow our stubborn hearts to the obedience of
his blessed will;" "so that the cause of good works we

---

* We have here modernized the spelling.

confess to be not our free will, but the spirit of the Lord Jesus, who, dwelling in our hearts by true faith, brings forth such works as God has prepared for us to walk in;" and "whoso boast themselves of the merits of their own works, or put their trust in works of supererogation, boast themselves in that which is not, and put their trust in damnable idolatry." It further admits that "we now, in the time of the evangel, have two chief sacraments only," to wit, Baptism and the Lord's Supper; by the former of which, "we are ingrafted in Christ Jesus to be made par-takers of his justice, by which our sins are covered and remitted;" and in the latter it is asserted there is a real though only spiritual presence of Christ, and "in the sup-per rightly used, Christ Jesus is joined with us, that he becomes very nourishment and food of our souls." The marks of a true church are said to be the true preaching of the word of God, the right administration of the sacra-ments, and ecclesiastical discipline rightly administered as the word of God prescribes. The polity or constitution of the Church, however, is not detailed; this was done in the "Book of discipline" drawn up by Knox and his brethren. The highest Church judicatory is the General Assembly, composed of representatives from the others, which are provincial synods, presbyteries, and kirk ses-sions. The officers of the Church are pastors or ministers, doctors or teachers, and lay elders, to which are to be added lay deacons, for the care of the poor. Among the clergy there is a perfect parity of jurisdiction and autho-rity, and in the Church courts clergy and laity have equal voices. The minister and the elder indeed are both *pres-byters* — the one a preaching presbyter, and the other a ruling presbyter; and it will be remembered that when Bucer expressed his approbation of the episcopal hierarchy of England, Calvin said it was only another papacy. Another principle, recognised alike by Calvin and the reformers of Scotland, was the education of the people; which both seem to have regarded as the rock upon which the Reformed Church should be built; and in Scotland, as was fit, this foundation was as broad as the building, it being meant that, besides the universities of the kingdom, there should be in every district a parish church and a parish school.

MOLINISTS.

LOUIS MOLINA, born at Cuença in Castile, entered the order of Jesuits in 1553. He studied at Coimbra, became a learned divine, and taught theology for twenty years in the college of Evora. He died at Madrid in the year 1600. He wrote commentaries upon Thomas Aquinas, and a treatise "De Justitia et Jure;" but the work which has rendered his name famous as the head of a school of theology is his book " De Concordia Gratiæ et Liberi Arbitrii," printed at Lisbon in 1568, with an appendix to it, published after. In this work Molina undertook the task of reconciling the free-will of man with the foreknowledge of God and predestination. He observed that the early fathers who had preceded the heresy of Pelagius had defined predestination as being the foreknowledge of God from all eternity of the use which each individual would make of his free-will; but St. Augustine, who had to oppose the Pelagians, who granted too much to free-will, spoke of predestination in a more absolute and restricted sense. Molina says that man requires grace in order to do good, but that God never fails to grant this grace to those who ask it with fervor.

He also asserts that man has it in his power to answer, or not, to the calling of grace.

The opinions of Molina, which were adopted, enlarged, and commented upon by the Jesuits, and strongly opposed by the Dominicans, gave rise to the long disputes concerning grace and free-will. The partisans of Molina were called Molinists, and their antagonists Thomists, from Thomas Aquinas, the favorite divine of the Dominican order. Already in Molina's lifetime his opinions were stigmatized as savoring of Pelagianism. After numerous disputations, Pope Paul V., in 1609, forbade both Jesuits and Dominicans from reviving the controversy. But soon after Jansenius, bishop of Ypres, wrote a book in which he discussed the question concerning grace after the manner of St. Augustine. His book was denounced by the Jesuits, and thus the dispute began afresh between the Molinists and the Jansenists. Pascal, in his second "Lettre Provinciale," gives an account of the state of the controversy in his time. He says that "the Jesuits pretend that there is a sufficient grace imparted unto all men, and subordinate to their free-will, which can render it active or inactive, while the Jansenists maintain that the only sufficient grace is that which is efficacious, that is to say, which determines the will to act effectively. The Jesuits support the 'sufficient grace,' the Jansenists the 'efficacious grace.'"

Molina must not be confounded with *Molinos (Michael)*, a Spanish clergyman of the seventeenth century, who was the founder of the theory of piety and devotion called Quietism, of which Fenelon and Madame Guyon were distinguished supporters.

30

MONTANISTS,

OR CATAPHRYGIANS, were a sect of Christians, which arose
in Phrygia about 171 A. D. They were called Montanists
from their leader Montanus, and Cataphrygians or Phry-
gians, from the country in which they first appeared.

Of the personal history of Montanus little is known.
He is said to have been born at Ardaba, a village in Mysia,
and to have been only a recent convert when he first made
pretensions to .ne character of a prophet. His principal
associates were two prophetesses, named Prisca or Priscilla,
and Maximilla. According to some of the ancient writers,
Montanus was believed by his followers to be the Paraclete,
or Holy Spirit. Probably this is an exaggeration, but it
is certain that he claimed divine inspiration for himself and
his associates. They delivered their prophecies in an
ecstasy, and their example seems to have introduced into
the church the practice of appealing to visions in favor of
opinions and actions, of which practice Cyprian and others
availed themselves to a great extent. Tertullian, who belonged to this sect, informs us that these revelations related only to points of discipline, and neither affected the
doctrines of religion nor superseded the authority of Scripture. The doctrines of Montanus agreed in general with
those of the Catholic Church, but some of his followers appear to have embraced the Sabellian heresy. The Montanists were chiefly distinguished from other Christians by
the austerity of their manners and the strictness of their
discipline. They condemned second marriages, and practised fasts. They maintained that all flight from persecution was unlawful, and that the Church had no power to
forgive great sins committed after baptism. They held the

doctrine of the personal reign of Christ on earth at the Millennium. They are accused by some of the early writers of celebrating mysteries attended by deeds of cruelty and lewdness, but it appears quite certain that these charges are unfounded.

The Montanists were warmly opposed by the writers of the Catholic party, though they were once countenanced for a short time by a bishop of Rome, whose name is unknown, but who is supposed by some to have been Victor. Tertullian wrote several works in defence of their opinions.

The sect was numerous, and lasted a considerable time. They still existed in the time of Augustin and Jerome, the latter of whom wrote against them.

MUGGLETONIANS.

THE Mugggletonians were a sect of Christians which arose in England in the year 1651. The leaders of this sect were Lodowicke Muggleton, a journeyman tailor, and John Reeve, who asserted that they had been appointed by an audible voice from God, as the last and greatest prophets of Jesus Christ, that they were the two witnesses mentioned in the 11th chapter of the Revelations, and that they had power to bless or damn to all eternity whomsoever they pleased. They published a great number of works, and obtained many followers. The chief writers against them were the Quakers, and among these, George Fox and Wm. Penn. On the 17th of January, 1676, Muggleton was tried at the Old Bailey, and convicted of blasphemy. He died on the 14th of March, 1697, at the age of 88.

It is impossible here to give a full account of the strange

doctrines of this sect. The chief articles of their creed
appear to have been, that God has the real body of a man,
that the Trinity is only a variety of names of God, that
God himself came down to earth, and was born as a man
and suffered death, and that during this time Elias was
his representative in heaven. They held very singular
and not very intelligible doctrines concerning angels and
devils. According to them the soul of man is inseparably
united with the body, with which it dies and will rise
again.

A complete collection of the works of Reeve and Muggleton, together with other Muggletonian tracts, was published by some of their modern followers, in 3 vols. 4to.,
1832. Among the works written against them are the following: "The New Witnesses proved Old Heretics," by
William Penn, 4to., 1672; "A True Representation of the
Absurd and Mischievous Principles of the Sect commonly
known by the name of Muggletonians," 4to., London, 1694.

FLAGELLANTS,

(From the Latin *flagellare*, to beat,) the name of a sect in
the 13th century, who thought that they could best expiate
their sins by the severe discipline of the scourge. Rainer,
a hermit of Perugia, is said to have been its founder, in
1260. He soon found followers in nearly all parts of Italy.
Old and young, great and small, ran through the cities,
scourging themselves, and exhorting to repentance. Their
number soon amounted to 10,000, who went about, led by
priests bearing banners and crosses. They went in thousands from country to country, begging alms. In 1261,

they broke over the Alps in crowds into Germany, showed themselves in Alsatia, Bavaria, Bohemia, and Poland, and found there many imitators. In 1296, a small band of Flagellants appeared in Strasburg, who, with covered faces, whipped themselves through the city, and at every church. The princes and higher clergy were little pleased with this new fraternity, although it was favored by the people. The shameful public exposure of the person by the Flagellants offended good manners; their travelling in such numbers afforded opportunity for seditious commotions, and irregularities of all sorts; and their extortion of alms was a severe tax upon the peaceful citizen. On this account, both in Germany and in Italy, several princes forbade these expeditions of the Flagellants. The kings of Poland and Bohemia expelled them with violence from their states, and the bishops strenuously opposed them. In spite of this, the society continued under another form, in the fraternities of the *Beghards*, in Germany and France, and in the beginning of the fifteenth century, among the *Brothers of the Cross*, so numerous in Thuringia (so called from wearing on their clothes a cross on the breast and on the back), of whom 91 were burnt at once at Sangershausen, in 1414. The council assembled at Constance, between 1414 and 1418, was obliged to take decisive measures against them. Since this time nothing more has been heard of a fraternity of this sort.

Flagellation has almost always been used for the punishment of crimes. Its application as a means of religious penance is an old Oriental custom, admitted into Christianity partly because self-torture was considered salutary as mortifying the flesh, and partly because both Christ and the apostles underwent scourging. From the first century of Christianity, religious persons sought to atone for their sins, and to move an impartial Judge to compassion and

pardon by voluntary bodily torture.   Like the abbot Re-
gino, at Prum, in the 10th century, many chose to share
in the sufferings of Christ, in order to make themselves the
more certain of forgiveness through him.   It became general in the 11th century, when Peter Damiani of Ravenna,
abbot of the Benedictine monastery of Santa Croce d'Avel-
lano, near Gubbio, in Italy, afterwards cardinal bishop of
Ostia, zealously recommended scourging as an atonement
for sin, to Christians generally, and, in particular, to the
monks.   His own example, and the fame of his sanctity,
rendered his exhortations effective.   Clergy and laity, men
and women, began to torture themselves with rods and
thongs and chains.   They fixed certain times for the inflic-
tion of this discipline upon themselves.   Princes caused
themselves to be scourged naked by their father confessors.
Louis IX. constantly carried with him, for this purpose, an
ivory box, containing five small iron chains, and exhorted
his father confessor to scourge him with severity.   He likewise gave similar boxes to the princes and princesses of his
house, and to other pious friends, as marks of his peculiar
favor.   The wild expectation of being purified from sin by
flagellation, prevailed throughout Europe in the last half
of the 13th century.   "About this time," says the monk
of Padua, in his chronicles of the year 1260, "when all
Italy was filled with vice, the Perugians suddenly entered
upon a course never before thought of; after them the
Romans. and at length all Italy.   The fear of Christ exerted
upon the people so strong an influence, that men of noble
and ignoble birth, old and young, traversed the streets of
the city naked, yet without shame.   Each carried a scourge
in his hand, with which he drew forth blood from his tortured body, amidst sighs and tears, singing, at the same
time, penitential psalms, and entreating the compassion of
the Deity.   Both by day and night, and even in the coldest

winters, by hundreds and thousands, they wandered through cities and churches, streets and villages, with burning wax candles. Music was then silent, and the song of love echoed no more; nothing was heard but atoning lamentations. The most unfeeling could not refrain from tears; discordant parties were reconciled; usurers and robbers hastened to restore their unlawful gains; criminals, before unsuspected, came and confessed their crimes, &c." But these penances soon degenerated into noisy fanaticism and a sort of trade. The penitents united into fraternities called the *Flagellants* (described above), of which there were branches in Italy, France, and Germany. After the council of Constance (1414–18), both clergy and laity by degrees became disgusted with flagellation. The Franciscan monks in France (Cordeliers) observed the practice longest. It is not to be wondered at, that a custom so absurd was so long maintained, when we remember the great advantages which the sufferers promised themselves. In the opinion of men in the middle ages, flagellation was equivalent to every sort of expiation for past sins, imposed by the father confessors. 3000 strokes, and the chanting of 30 penitential psalms, were sufficient to cancel the sins of a year; 30,000 strokes, the sins of 10 years, &c. An Italian widow, in the 11th century, boasted that she had made expiation by voluntary scourging for 100 years, for which no less than 300,000 stripes were requisite. The opinion was prevalent, likewise, that, however great the guilt, by self-inflicted pain, hell might be escaped, and the honor of peculiar holiness acquired. By this means, flagellation gained a charm in the sight of the guilty and ambitious, which raised them above the dread of corporeal suffering, till the conceits of hypocrisy vanished before the clearer light of civilization and knowledge.

ANABAPTISTS.

ANABAPTISTS are those who maintain that baptism ought always to be performed by immersion. The word is compounded of ανα, "anew," and βαπτιστης, "a Baptist;" signifying that those who have been baptized in their infancy ought to be baptized *anew*. It is a word which has been indiscriminately applied to Christians of very different principles and practices. The English and Dutch Baptists do not consider the word as at all applicable to their sect; because those persons whom they baptize they consider as never having been baptized before, although they have undergone what they term the ceremony of sprinkling in their infancy.

The Anabaptists of Germany, besides their notions concerning baptism, depended much upon certain ideas which they entertained concerning a perfect church establishment, pure in its members, and free from the institutions of human policy. The most prudent part of them considered it possible, by human industry and vigilance, to purify the church; and seeing the attempts of Luther to be successful, they hoped that the period was arrived in which the church was to be restored to this purity. Others, not satisfied with Luther's plan of reformation, undertook a more perfect plan, or, more properly, a visionary enterprise, to found a new church, entirely spiritual and divine.

This sect was soon joined by great numbers, whose characters and capacities were very different. Their progress was rapid; for, in a very short space of time, their discourses, visions, and predictions, excited great commotions in a great part of Europe. The most pernicious faction of all those which composed this motley multitude, was that which pretended that the founders of this *new* and *perfect* church were under a divine impulse, and were armed against all opposition by the power of working miracles. It was this faction that, in the year 1521, began their fanatical work under the guidance of Munzer, Stubner, Storick, etc. These men taught that, among Christians, who had the precepts of the gospel to direct, and the Spirit of God to guide them, the office of magistracy was not only unnecessary, but an unlawful encroachment on their spiritual liberty; that the distinctions occasioned by birth, rank, or wealth should be abolished; that all Christians, throwing their possessions into one stock, should live together in that state of equality which becomes members of the same family; that, as neither the laws of nature, nor the precepts of the New Testament, had prohibited polygamy, they should use the same liberty as the patriarchs did in this respect.

They employed, at first, the various arts of persuasion in order to propagate their doctrines, and related a number of visions and revelations with which they pretended to have been favored from above; but when they found that this would not avail, and that the ministry of Luther and other reformers was detrimental to their cause, they then madly attempted to propagate their sentiments by force of arms. Munzer and his associates, in the year 1525, put themselves at the head of a numerous army, and declared war against all laws, governments, and magistrates of every kind, under the chimerical pretext that Christ himself was now to take the reins of all government into his hands; but this seditious crowd was routed and dispersed by the Elector of Saxony and other princes, and Munzer, their leader, put to death.

Many of his followers, however, survived, and propagated their opinions through Germany, Switzerland, and Holland. In 1533, a party of them settled at Munster, under two leaders of the names of Matthias and Bockholdt. Having made themselves masters of the city, they deposed the magistrates, confiscated the estates of such as had escaped, and deposited the wealth in a public treasury for common use. They made preparations for the defence of the city; invited the Anabaptists in the Low Countries to assemble at Munster, which they called Mount Sion, that from thence they might reduce all the nations of the earth under their dominion. Matthias was soon cut off by the Bishop of Munster's army, and was succeeded by Bockholdt, who was proclaimed by a special designation of heaven, as the pretended King of Sion, and invested with legislative powers like those of Moses. The city of Munster, however, was taken after a long siege, and Bockholdt punished with death.

It must be acknowledged that the true rise of the insurrections of this period ought not to be attributed to religious opinions. The first insurgents groaned under severe oppressions, and took up arms in defence of their civil liberties; and of these commotions the Anabaptists seem rather to have availed themselves, than to have been the prime movers. That a great part were Anabaptists seems indisputable; at the same time, it appears from history that a great part also were Roman Catholics, and a still greater part of those who had scarcely any religious principles at all. Indeed, when we read of the vast numbers that were concerned in these insurrections, of whom it is reported that 100,000 fell by the sword, it appears reasonable to conclude that they were not all Anabaptists.

It is but justice to observe also, that the Baptists of our time have nothing in common with this sect. They profess an equal aversion to all principles of rebellion on the one hand, and to enthusiasm on the other.

ANTINOMIANS.

ANTINOMIANS are those who maintain that the law is of no use or obligation under the gospel dispensation. or who held doctrines that clearly supersede the necessity of good works. The Antinomians took their name from John Agricola, about the year 1538, who taught that the law is no way necessary under the gospel; that good works do not promote our salvation, nor ill ones hinder it; that repentance is not to be preached from the decalogue, but only from the gospel.

This sect sprang up in England during the protectorate of Cromwell, and extended their system of libertinism much farther than Agricola did. Some of them, it is said, maintained that if they should commit any kind of sin, it would do them no hurt, nor in the least affect their eternal state; and that it is one of the distinguishing characters of the elect, that they cannot do anything displeasing to God. It is necessary, however, to observe here, and candor obliges us to confess, that there have been others, who have been styled Antinomians, who cannot, strictly speaking, be ranked with these men; nevertheless, the unguarded expressions they have advanced, the bold positions they have laid down, and the double construction which might so easily be put upon many of their sentences, have led some to charge them with Antinomian principles.

For instance, when they have asserted justification to be eternal, without distinguishing between the secret determination of God in eternity and the execution of it in time; when they have spoken lightly of good works, or asserted that believers have nothing to do with the law of God, without fully explaining what they mean; when they assert that God is not angry with his people for their sins, nor in any sense punishes them for them, without distinguishing between fatherly correction and vindictive punishment; these things, whatever be the private sentiments of those who advance them, have a tendency to injure the minds of many. It has been alleged that the principal thing they have had in view was to counteract those legal doctrines which have so much abounded among the self-righteous; but granting this to be true, there is no occasion to run from one extreme to another. Had many of those writers proceeded with more caution, been less dogmatical, more explicit in the explanation of their sentiments, and possessed more candor towards those who differed from them, they would have been more serviceable to the cause of truth and religion.

JUMPERS.

JUMPERS, persons so called from the practice of jumping during the time allotted for religious worship. This singular practice began, it is said, in the western part of Wales, about the year 1760. It was soon after defended by Mr. William Williams, (the Welsh poet, as he is sometimes called,) in a pamphlet, which was patronized by the abettors of jumping in religious assemblies. Several of the more zealous itinerant preachers encouraged the people to cry out *gogoniant* (the Welsh word for glory,) amen. &c., &c.; to put themselves in violent agitations; and, finally, to jump until they were quite exhausted, so as often to be obliged to fall down on the floor or field, where this kind of worship was held.

LABADISTS.

THE Labadists were so called from their founder, John Labadie, a native of France. He was originally in the Romish communion; but leaving that, he became a member of the reformed church, and performed with reputation the ministerial functions in France, Switzerland, and Holland. He at length erected a new community, which resided successively at Middleburg, in Zealand, Amsterdam, Hervorden, and at Altona, where he died about 1674. After his death, his followers removed their wandering community to Wiewert, in the district of North Holland, where it soon fell into oblivion. If we are to judge of the Labadists by their own account, they did not differ from the reformed church so much in their tenets and doctrines as in their manners and rules of discipline; yet it seems that Labadie had some strange notions. Among other things, he maintained that God might and did, on certain occasions, deceive men; that the faithful ought to have all things in common; that there is no subordination or distinction of rank in the true church; that in reading the Scriptures greater attention should be paid to the internal inspiration of the Holy Spirit than to the words of the text; that the observation of Sunday was a matter of indifference; that the contemplative life is a state of grace and union with God, and the very height of perfection.

31

MYSTICS.

MYSTICS, a sect distinguished by their professing pure, sublime, and perfect devotion, with an entire disinterested love of God, free from all selfish considerations. The authors of this mystic science, which sprung up towards the close of the third century, are not known; but the principles from which it was formed are manifest. Its first promoters proceeded from the known doctrine of the Platonic school, which was also adopted by Origen and his disciples, that the divine nature was diffused through all human souls; or that the faculty of reason, from which proceed the health and vigor of the mind, was an emanation from God into the human soul, and comprehended in it the principles and elements of all truth, human and divine. They denied that men could, by labor or study, excite this celestial flame in their breasts; and therefore they disapproved highly of the attempts of those who, by definitions, abstract theorems, and profound speculations, endeavored to form distinct notions of truth, and to discover its hidden nature.

On the contrary, they maintained that silence, tranquillity, repose, and solitude, accompanied with such acts as might tend to extenuate and exhaust the body, were the means by which the hidden and internal word was excited to produce its latent virtues, and to instruct men in the knowledge of divine things. For thus they reasoned: — Those who behold with a noble contempt all human affairs; who turn away their eyes from terrestrial vanities, and shut all the avenues of the outward senses against the contagious influences of a material world, must necessarily return to God when the spirit is thus disengaged from the impediments that prevented that happy union; and in this blessed frame they not only enjoy inexpressible raptures from their communion with the Supreme Being, but are also invested with the inestimable privilege of contemplating truth undisguised and uncorrupted in its native purity, while others behold it in a vitiated and delusive form.

The number of the Mystics increased in the fourth century, under the influence of the Grecian fanatic, who gave himself out for Dionysius, the Areopagite disciple of St. Paul, and probably lived about this period; and by pretending to higher degrees of perfection than other Christians, and practising greater austerity, their cause gained ground, especially in the eastern provinces, in the fifth century.

A copy of the pretended works of Dionysius was sent by Balbus to Lewis the Meek, in the year 824, which kindled the oily flame of mysticism in the western provinces, and filled the Latins with the most enthusiastic admiration of this new religion. In the twelfth century these Mystics took the lead in their method of expounding the Scriptures. In the thirteenth century they were the most formidable antagonists of the schoolmen; and, towards the close of the fourteenth, many of them resided and propagated their tenets almost in every part of Europe. They had, in the fifteenth century, many persons of distinguished merit in their number; and in the sixteenth century, previous to the Reformation, if any sparks of real piety subsisted under the despotic empire of superstition, they were only to be found among the Mystics.

The celebrated Madame Bourignon, and tne amiable Fenelon, archbishop of Cambray, were of this sect. Dr. Haweis, in speaking of the Mystics, Church History, vol. iii. p. 47, thus observes: "Among those called Mystics, I am persuaded some were found who loved God out of a pure heart fervently; and though they were ridiculed and reviled for proposing a disinterestedness of love without other motives, and as professing to feel in the enjoyment of the temper itself an abundant reward, their holy and heavenly conversation will carry a stamp of real religion upon it."

As the late Rev. William Law, who was born in 1687, makes a distinguished figure among the modern Mystics, a brief account of the outlines of his system may, perhaps, be entertaining to some readers. He supposed that the material world was the very region which originally belonged to the fallen angels. At length the light and spirit of God entered into the chaos, and turned the angels' ruined kingdom into a paradise on earth. God then created man, and placed him there. He was made in the image of the triune God, a living mirror of the divine nature, formed to enjoy communion with Father, Son, and Holy Ghost, and live on earth as the angels do in heaven. He was endowed with immortality, so that the elements of this outward world could not have any power of acting on his body; but by his fall he changed the light, life, and spirit of God for the light, life, and spirit of the world. He died the very day of his transgression to all the influences and operations of the Spirit of God upon him, as we die to the influences of this world when the soul leaves the body; and all the influences and operations of the elements of this life were open in him, as they were in any animal, at his birth into this world; he became an earthly creature, subject to the dominion of this outward world, and stood only in the highest rank of animals. But the goodness of God would not leave man in this condition; redemption from it was immediately granted, and the bruiser of the serpent brought the light,

life, and spirit of heaven, once more into the human nature
All men, in consequence of the redemption of Christ, have
in them the first spark, or seed, of the divine life, as a
treasure hid in the centre of our souls, to bring forth, by
degrees, a new birth of that life which was lost in Paradise.
No son of Adam can be lost, only by turning away from
the Saviour within him. The only religion which can save
us, must be that which can raise the light, life, and Spirit
of God in our souls. Nothing can enter into the vegetable
kingdom till it have the vegetable life in it, or be a member
of the animal kingdom till it have the animal life. Thus
all nature joins with the Gospel in affirming that no man
can enter into the kingdom of heaven till the heavenly life
is born in him. Nothing can be our righteousness or
recovery but the divine nature of Jesus Christ derived to
our souls.

ABYSSINIAN CHURCH,

THAT which is established in the empire of Abyssinia.
They are a branch of the Copts, with whom they agree
in admitting only one nature in Jesus Christ, and rejecting
the Council of Chalcedon; whence they are also called
Monophysites and Eutychians.

The Abyssinian Church is governed by a Bishop, styled
Abuna. They have canons also, and monks. The emperor has a kind of supremacy in ecclesiastical matters.
The Abyssinians have at divers times expressed an inclination to be reconciled to the see of Rome; but rather
from interested views than from any other motive. They
practice circumcision on females, as well as males. They
eat no meats prohibited by the law of Moses. They ob-

serve both Saturday and Sunday sabbaths. Women are obliged to the legal purifications. Brothers marry their brother's wives, &c.

On the other hand they celebrate the Epiphany with peculiar festivity; have four Lents; pray for the dead; and invoke angels. Images in painting they venerate, but abhor all those in relievo, except the cross. They admit the apocryphal books and the canons of the apostles, as well as the apostolical constitutions, for genuine. They allow of divorce, which is easily granted among them, and by the civil judge; nor do their civil laws prohibit polygamy. They have, at least, as many miracles and legends of saints as the Romish Church. They hold that the soul of man is not created; because, say they, God finished all his works on the sixth day.

Thus we see that the doctrines and ritual of this sect form a strange compound of Judaism and Christianity, ignorance and superstition. Some, indeed, have been at a loss to know whether they are most Christians or Jews; it is to be feared, however, that there is little beside the name of Christianity among them.

ADAMITES,

A sect that sprang up in the second century. Epiphanius tells us that they were called Adamites from their pretending to be re-established in the state of innocence, such as Adam was at the moment of his creation, whence they ought to imitate him in going naked. They detested marriage; maintaining that the conjugal union would never have taken place upon earth had sin been unknown. This obscure and ridiculous sect did not last long. It was,

however, revived with additional absurdities, in the twelfth
century. About the beginning of the fifteenth century,
these errors spread in Germany and Bohemia; it found
also some partisans in Poland, Holland, and England.
They assembled in the night; and, it is said, one of the
fundamental maxims of their society was contained in the
following verse:

> Jura, perjura, secretum prodere noli.
> Swear, forswear, and reveal not the secret.

ALBIGENSES.

ALBIGENSES (Albigeois); a name common to several
sects, particularly the Cathari and Waldenses, who agreed
in opposing the dominion of the Roman hierarchy, and
endeavoring to restore the simplicity of primitive Christianity. They had increased very much towards the close
of the twelfth century, in the south of France, about Toulouse and Albi, and were denominated by the crusaders
Albigenses from the district Albigeois (territory of Albi),
where the army of the cross, called together by Pope
Innocent III., attacked them in 1209. The assassination
of the papal legate and inquisitor, Peter of Castelnau,
while occupied in extirpating these heretics in the territory of the Count Raymond of Toulouse, occasioned this
war, which is important as the first which the Romish
Church waged against heretics within her own dominions.
It was carried on with a degree of cruelty which cast a
deep shade over the Roman clergy, as their real object
appeared to be to deprive the Count of Toulouse of his
possessions, on account of his tolerating the heretics. It
was in vain that this powerful prince had suffered a dis-

graceful penance and flagellation from the legate Milo, and
obtained the papal absolution by great sacrifices. The
legates, Arnold, Abbot of Citeaux, and Milo, took Beziers,
the capital of his nephew Roger, by storm, and put all the
inhabitants (about 60,000), without any distinction of
creed, to the sword. Simon de Montfort, the military
leader of the crusade, under the legates, was equally severe towards other places in the territory of Raymond and
his allies, of whom Roger died in a prison, and Peter I.,
king of Arragon, in battle. The lands taken were presented by the Church, as a reward for his services, to the
Count of Montfort, who, however, on account of the
changing fortune of war, never obtained the quiet possession of them; he was killed by a stone, at the siege of
Toulouse, in 1218. The legates prevailed on his son
Amalric to cede his claims to the king of France. The
papal indulgences attracted from all provinces of France
new crusaders, who continued the war, and, even after
the death of Raymond VI., in 1222, under excommunication, his son, Raymond VII., was obliged, notwithstanding
his readiness to do penance, to defend his inheritance till
1229 against the legates and Louis VIII. of France, who
fell, in 1226, in a campaign against the heretics. After
hundreds of thousands had fallen on both sides, and the
most beautiful parts of Provence and Upper Languedoc had
been laid waste, a peace was made, by the terms of which
Raymond was obliged to purchase his absolution with a large
sum of money, to cede Narbonne, with several estates, to
Louis IX., and make his son-in-law, a brother of Louis, heir
of his other lands. The pope suffered these provinces to
come into the possession of the king of France, in order
to bind him more firmly to his interests, and force him to
receive his inquisitors. The heretics were now delivered
up to the proselyting zeal of the Dominicans, and to the

courts of the inquisition; and these new auxiliaries, which priestcraft had acquired during the war, employed their whole power to bring the remainder of the Albigenses to the stake, and made even the converts feel the irreconcilable anger of the Church, by heavy fines and personal punishments. The name of the Albigenses disappeared after the middle of the thirteenth century; but fugitives of their party formed, in the mountains of Piedmont and in Lombardy, what is called the *French Church*, which was continued through the Waldenses, to the times of the Hussites and the Reformation.

PANTHEISTS.

PANTHEISM, a philosophical species of idolatry, leading to atheism, in which the universe was considered as the Supreme God. Who was the inventor of this absurd system, is perhaps not known, but it was of early origin, and differently modified by different philosophers. Some held the universe to be one immense animal, of which the incorporeal soul was properly their god, and the heavens and the earth the body of that god; whilst others held but one substance, partly active, and partly passive, and therefore looked upon the visible universe as the only *Numen*. The earliest Grecian pantheists of whom we read was Orpheus, who called the world the *body of God*, and its several parts his members, making the whole universe one *divine animal*. According to Cudworth, Orpheus and his followers believed in the immaterial soul of the world: therein agreeing with Aristotle, who certainly held that God and matter are co-eternal: and that there is some such union between them,

Y

as subsists between the souls and bodies of men. An institution, embodying sentiments nearly of this kind. was set on foot early in the last century, in England, by a society of philosophical idolaters, who called themselves *Pantheists*, because they professed the worship of All Nature as their deity. They had Mr. John Toland for their secretary and chaplain. Their liturgy was in Latin; an English translation was published in 1751, from which the following sentiments are extracted: "The ethereal fire environs all things, and is therefore supreme. The æther is a reviving fire: it rules all things, it disposes all things. In it is soul, mind, prudence. This fire is Horace's particle of divine breath, and Virgil's *inwardly* nourishing spirit. All things are comprised in an intelligent nature." This force they call the soul of the world; as also, a mind of perfect wisdom, and, consequently, God. Vanini, the Italian philosopher, was nearly of this opinion: his god was nature. Some very learned and excellent remarks are made on this error by Mr. Boyle, in his discourse on the vulgarly received notion of nature.

SECOND ADVENTISTS.

SECOND ADVENTISTS: (sometimes called MILLERITES and MILLENNARIANS,) those who hold, in opposition to the general opinion, that the Second Coming of Christ will *precede* the Millennium, and is necessary to introduce it. On the nature of the Millennium, its antecedents, consequences, and the signs of its approach, they differ widely among themselves; but they all agree that it will be ushered in by the Second Advent of the Son of God, and be distinguished as the period of his personal reign on the earth. Some go so far as to fix the time; but others content themselves with saying that it is at the door.

This pre-millennial view of the Second Advent is therefore the characteristic mark of this denomination, although they seldom are embodied as a distinct sect, but are found in all denominations, more or less.

They strenuously contend that their view rests upon the literal interpretation of the prophecies; that it was the general belief of the earliest Christians, and forms an essential and powerful element of practical Christianity. They insist that the ordinary view of the Millennium as a spiritual reign of righteousness and peace, preceding the personal coming of Christ, and followed by a brief but terrible Apostacy, which calls down the Son of God to judgment (Rev. xx.), is of modern date; that it unsettles the principles of interpretation, and deadens the spiritual life of believers.

It is but just to say that all these arguments have been soberly met and acutely answered by some of the ablest writers on Prophecy, particularly by Dr. Brown of Edinburgh.

In the last century Dr. John Gill and Rev. A. M. Toplady advocated the doctrine of Christ's personal reign. Bishop Newton does not go so far as to give an opinion, while President Edwards, Archibald McLean, and Andrew Fuller, after long investigation, decided in favor of the spiritual reign of Christ in the Millennium. Mr. Fuller's last thoughts on this subject were written within a few months of his death.

Since that time Rev. Edward Irving, Dr. Cumming, George Gilfillan, Mr. Bickersteth, and other clergymen of the Church of England, have revived the doctrine of the Premillennial Advent abroad. In this country it has found many zealous and able advocates, among whom we may name William Miller, II. L. Hastings, and D. T. Taylor. Men of standing and scholarship in evangelical denominations, are found maintaining substantially the same views of the Second Advent, unmixed with the errors and extravagance charged upon those previously named. Dr. Lord of New York, and Drs. Seiss, Newton, Duffield and others of Philadelphia, have long sustained this doctrine through the periodical press. The last named gentlemen, in the first issue of their work (Jan. 1863), drew out astatement of their belief in twelve propositions, and in the fourth number (April 1863), one of the editors gave a more formal and elaborate Theory of the Millennium. Our space will not permit us to introduce them here, though in all our previous statements we have kept them in view.

The only point of real difference between the Second Adventists and their opponents—the main pivot on which every thing turns—is this: Will the future Personal Advent of Christ—that blessed hope so often set before us in the Scriptures—precede, or follow the promised Millennium?

Both parties equally believe in the certainty and glory of the Second Advent of Christ in person to judge the world, all representations to the contrary notwithstanding. All alike expect it, but in different time, order, and effects. It is a pure question of Biblical Interpretation. The question involves, in all its extent, the complete compass and harmony of the Prophecies of Scripture, which, proceeding from one Omniscient Mind, can never conflict in meaning when properly understood. It is not probable that a matter of this high and solemn moment has really been left in darkness. The clearness of Divine Revelation is usually in proportion to its importance to mankind. But of the day and hour of the Second Advent, Christ himself assures us no man knoweth. It is not a thing revealed, or to be ascertained by any searching of the Scriptures. It is purposely kept secret, that all may watch; yet it will come at last as a snare, suddenly and unexpectedly, to the men of the latest generation, the scoffers of the last days. Matt. xxiv. 36–51. Luke xviii. 8. 1 Thess. v. 1–6. 2 Pet. iii. 1- 12. Rev. xx. 7–15

SOCINIANS.

THE Socinians are so called from Faustus Socinus, who died in Poland in 1604. There were two who bore the name Socinus, uncle and nephew, and both disseminated the same doctrine; but it is the nephew who is generally considered as the founder of this sect. They maintain " that Jesus Christ was a mere man, who had no existence before he was conceived by the Virgin Mary; that the Holy Ghost is no distinct person; but that the Father is truly and properly God. They own that the name of God is given in the Holy Scriptures to Jesus Christ, but contend that it is only a deputed title, which, however, invests him with a great authority over all created beings. They deny the doctrines of satisfaction and imputed righteousness, and say that Christ only preached the truth to mankind, set before them in himself an example of heroic virtue, and sealed his doctrines with his blood. Original sin and absolute predestination they esteem scholastic chimeras. Some of them likewise maintain the sleep of the soul, which, they say, becomes insensible at death, and is raised again with the body at the resurrection, when the good shall be established in the possession of eternal felicity, while the wicked shall be consigned to a fire that will not torment them eternally, but for a certain duration proportioned to their demerits."

There is some difference, however, between ancient and modern Socinians. The latter, indignant at the name Socinian, have appropriated to themselves that of Unitarians, and reject the notions of a miraculous conception and the worship of Christ; both which were held by Socinus. Dr. Priestley has labored hard in attempting to defend this doctrine of the Unitarians; but Dr. Horsley, Bishop of Rochester, has ably refuted the doctor in his Theological Tracts, which are worthy the perusal of every Christian, and especially every candidate for the ministry.

Dr. Price agreed with the Socinians in the main, yet his system was somewhat different. He believed in the pre-existence of Christ, and likewise that he was more than a human being; and took upon him human nature for a higher purpose than merely revealing to mankind the will of God, and instructing them in their duty and in the doctrines of religion.

The Socinians flourished greatly in Poland about the year 1551; and J. Siemienius, palatine of Podolia, built purposely for their use the city of Racow. A famous catechism was published, called the Racovian Catechism; and their most able writers are known by the title of the *Polones Fratres*, or Polonian Brethren. Their writings were republished together, in the year 1656, in one great collection, consisting of six volumes in folio, under the title of Bibliotheca Fratrum.

SANDEMANIANS.

THE Sandemanians are a sect that originated in Scotland about the year 1728, where it is, at this time, distinguished by the name of Glassites, after its founder, Mr. John Glass, who was a minister of the established church in that kingdom; but, being charged with a design of subverting the national covenant, and sapping the foundation of all national establishments, by maintaining that *the kingdom of Christ is not of this world*, was expelled from the synod by the Church of Scotland. His sentiments are fully explained in a tract, published at that time, entitled " The Testimony of the King of Martyrs," and preserved in the first volume of his works. In consequence of Mr. Glass' expulsion, his adherents formed themselves into churches, conformable, in their institution and discipline, to what they apprehended to be the plan of the first churches recorded in the New Testament. Soon after the year 1755, Mr. Robert Sandeman, an elder in one of these churches in Scotland, published a series of letters addressed to Mr. Hervey, occasioned by his Theron and Aspasia, in which he endeavors to show that *his* notion of faith is contradictory to the Scripture account of it, and could only serve to lead men, professedly holding the doctrines called Calvinistic, to establish their own righteousness upon their frames, feelings, and acts of faith. In these letters Mr. Sandeman attempts to prove that justifying faith is no more than a simple belief of the truth, or the divine testimony passively received by the understanding; and that this divine testimony carries in itself sufficient ground of hope to every one who believes it, without anything

wrought in us, or done by us, to give it a particular direc
tion to ourselves.

Some of the popular preachers, as they were called, had
taught that it was of the essence of faith to believe that
Christ is ours; but Mr. Sandeman contended that that
which is believed in true faith is *the truth*, and what would
have been the truth, though we had never believed it.
They dealt largely in calls and invitations to repent and
believe in Christ in order to forgiveness; but he rejects
the whole of them, maintaining that the gospel contained
no offer but that of evidence, and that it was merely a
record or *testimony* to be credited.   They had taught that
though acceptance with God, which included the forgiveness of sins, was merely on account of the imputed righteousness of Christ, yet that no one was accepted of God,
nor forgiven, till he repented of his sin, and received
Christ as the only Saviour; but he insists that there is
acceptance with God through Christ for sinners, while
such, or before "any act, exercise, or exertion of their
minds whatsoever;" consequently before repentance; and
that "a passive belief of this quiets the guilty conscience,
begets hope, and so lays the foundation for love." It is
by this passive belief of the truth that we, according to
Mr. Sandeman, are justified, and that boasting is excluded.
If any act, exercise, or exertion of the mind were necessary to our being accepted of God, he conceives there
would be whereof to glory; and justification by faith could
not be opposed, as it is in Rom. iv. 4, 6, to justification by
works.

The authors to whom Mr. Sandeman refers, under the
title of "popular preachers," are Flavel, Boston, Guthrie,
the Erskines, etc., whom he has treated with acrimony and
contempt. "I would be far," says he, "from refusing
even to the popular preachers themselves what they so

much grudge to others—the benefit of the one instance of
a hardened sinner finding mercy at last; for I know of no
sinners more hardened, none greater destroyers of mankind, than they." There have not been wanting writers,
however, who have vindicated these ministers from his in
vectives and have endeavored to show that Mr. Sandeman's
notion of faith, by excluding all exercise or concurrence
of the will with the gospel way of salvation, confounds
the faith of devils with that of Christians, and so is calculated to deceive the souls of men. It has also been observed, that though Mr. Sandeman admits of the acts of
faith and love as fruits of believing the truth, yet, "all his
godliness consisting (as he acknowledges to Mr. Pike) *in
love to that which first relieved him,*" it amounts to nothing
but self-love. And as self-love is a stranger to all those
strong affections expressed in the 109th Psalm towards the
law of God, he cannot admit of them as the language of a
good man, but applies the whole psalm to Christ, though
the person speaking acknowledges that "before he was
afflicted, he went astray." Others have thought that from
the same principle it were easy to account for the bitterness, pride, and contempt which distinguish the system;
for self-love, say they, is consistent with the greatest aver
sion to all beings divine or human, excepting so far as they
become subservient to us.

The chief opinion and practices in which this sect differs
from other Christians, are their weekly administration of
the Lord's Supper; their love feasts, of which every member is not only allowed but required to partake, and which
consist of their dining together at each other's houses in
the interval between the morning and afternoon service.
Their kiss of charity used on this occasion at the admis
sion of a new member, and at other times when they deem
it necessary and proper; their weekly collection before

32*

the Lord's Supper, for the support of the poor, and defraying other expenses; mutual exhortation; abstinence from blood and things strangled; washing each other's feet, when, as a deed of mercy, it might be an expression of love, the precept concerning which, as well as other precepts, they understand literally; community of goods, so far as that every one is to consider all that he has in his possession and power liable to the calls of the poor and the church; and the unlawfulness of laying up treasures upon earth, by setting them apart for any distant, future, and uncertain use. They allow of public and private diversions, so far as they are unconnected with circumstances really sinful; but apprehending a lot to be sacred, disapprove of lotteries, playing at cards, dice, etc.

They maintain a plurality of elders, pastors or bishops, in each church; and the necessity of the presence of two elders in every act of discipline, and at the administration of the Lord's Supper.

In the choice of these elders, want of learning, and engagement in trade, are no sufficient objection, if qualified according to the instructions given to Timothy and Titus; but second marriages disqualify for the office; and they are ordained by prayer and fasting, imposition of hands, and giving the right hand of fellowship.

In their discipline they are strict and severe, and think themselves obliged to separate from the communion and worship of all such religious societies as appear to them not to profess the simple truth for their only ground of hope, and who do not walk in obedience to it. We shall only add, that in every transaction they esteem unanimity to be absolutely necessary.

In the year 1764, Mr. Sandeman, having accepted an invitation from some persons in America, who had read his writings and professed a strong attachment to them, to

come and settle among them, sailed for New England
There is reason to believe that he was much disappointed
in the persons who had invited him over, and in the expectations he had formed generally respecting America.
Dissensions began to arise, soon after his arrival, between
the colonies and mother country. Mr. Sandeman's principles led him to avow the most implicit allegiance to the
latter, which rendered him obnoxious to the colonists; his
days were imbittered; his prospects of usefulness in a
great measure blighted; and, after collecting a few small
societies, he ended his life at Danbury, in Connecticut,
Fairfield County, in the year 1771. Since his death,
there has appeared from his pen, "The Honor of Marriage opposed to all Impurities;" "An Essay on Solomon's
Song;" "On the Sign of the Prophet Jonah," etc., etc.,
all of which may be read with profit.

NECESSARIANS.

NECESSARIANS, an appellation which may be given to
all who maintain that moral agents act from necessity.

Necessity signifies whatever is done by a cause or
power that is irresistible, in which sense it is opposed to
freedom. Man is a necessary agent, if all his actions be
so determined by the causes preceding each action, that
not one past action could possibly not have come to pass,
or have been otherwise than it hath been, nor one future
action can possibly not come to pass, or be otherwise than
it shall be. On the other hand, it is asserted that he is a
free agent, if he be able, at any time, under the causes
and circumstances he then is, to do different things; or,

in other words, if he be not unavoidably determined in
every point of time by the circumstances he is in, and the
causes he is under, to do any one thing he does, and not
possibly to do any other thing. Whether man is a necessary or a free agent, is a question which has been debated
by writers of the first eminence. Hobbes, Collins, Hume,
Leibnitz, Kaims, Hartley, Priestley, Edwards, Crombie,
Toplady, and Belsham, have written on the side of necessity; while Clarke, King, Law, Reid, Butler, Price,
Bryant, Wollaston, Horsley, Beattie, Gregory, and But-
terworth, have written against it. To state all their arguments in this place, would take up too much room; suffice
it to say, that the Anti-necessarians suppose that the doctrine of necessity charges God as the author of sin; that
it takes away the freedom of the will, renders man unaccountable, makes sin to be no evil, and morality or virtue
to be no good; precludes the use of means, and is of the
most gloomy tendency. The Necessarians deny these
to be legitimate consequences, and observe that the Deity
acts no more immorally in decreeing vicious actions, than
in permitting all those irregularities, which he could so
easily have prevented. The difficulty is the same on each
hypothesis. All necessity, say they, doth not take away
freedom. The actions of a man may be at one and the
same time free and necessary too. It was infallibly certain that Judas would betray Christ, yet he did it voluntarily. Jesus Christ necessarily became a man, and died,
yet he acted freely. A good man doth naturally and
necessarily love his children, yet voluntarily. It is part
of the happiness of the blessed to love God unchangeably,
yet freely, for it would not be their happiness if done by
compulsion. Nor does it, says the Necessarian, render
man unaccountable, since the Divine Being does no injury
to his rational faculties; and man, as his creature, is

answerable to him; besides, he has a right to do what he will with his own. That necessity doth not render actions less morally good, is evident; for if necessary virtue be neither moral nor praiseworthy, it will follow that God himself is not a moral being, because he is a necessary one; and the obedience of Christ cannot be good, because it was necessary. Further, say they, necessity does not preclude the use of means; for means are no less appointed than the end. It was ordained that Christ should be delivered up to death; but he could not have been betrayed without a betrayer, nor crucified without crucifiers. That it is not a gloomy doctrine, they allege, because nothing can be more consolatory than to believe that all things are under the direction of an all-wise Being; that his kingdom ruleth over all, and that he doth all things well. So far from its being inimical to happiness, they suppose there can be no solid true happiness without the belief of it; that it inspires gratitude, excites confidence, teaches resignation, produces humility, and draws the soul to God. It is also observed, that to deny necessity is to deny the foreknowledge of God, and to wrest the sceptre from the hand of the Creator, and to place that capricious and undefinable principle—the self-determining power of man—upon the throne of the universe. Besides, say they, the Scripture places the doctrine beyond all doubt, Job xxiii. 13, 14, ; xxxiv. 29; Prov. xvi. 4; Is. xlv. 7; Acts xiii. 48; Eph. i. 11; 1 Thess. iii. 3; Matt. x. 29, 30, xviii. 7; Luke xxiv. 26; John vi. 37.

LOLLARDS.

THE Lollards were a religious sect, differing in many points from the Church of Rome, which arose in Germany about the beginning of the fourteenth century; so called, as many writers have imagined, from Walter Lollard, who began to dogmatize in 1315, and was burned at Cologne; though others think that Lollard was no surname, but merely a term of reproach applied to all heretics who concealed the poison of error under the appearance of piety.

The monk of Canterbury derives the origin of the word lollard among us from *lolium*, "a tare," as if the Lollards were the tares sown in Christ's vineyard. Abelly says, that the word signifies "praising Gôd," from the German *loben*, "to praise," and *herr*, "lord;" because the Lollards employed themselves in travelling about from place to place, singing psalms and hymns. Others, much to the same purpose, derive *lollhard, lulhard,* or *lollert, lullert,* as it was written by the ancient Germans, from the old German word, *lullen, lollen,* or *lallen,* and the termination *hard*, with which many of the High Dutch words end. *Lollen* signifies, "to sing with a low voice," and therefore lollard is a singer, or one who frequently sings; and in the vulgar tongue of the Germans it denotes a person who is continually praising God with a song, or singing hymns to his honor.

The Alexians or Cellites were called *Lollards,* because they were public singers, who made it their business to inter the bodies of those who died of the plague, and sang a dirge over them in a mournful and indistinct tone, as they carried them to the grave. The name was afterwards assumed by persons that dishonored it; for we find among those Lollards who made extraordinary pretences to religion, and spent the greatest part of their time in meditation, prayer, and such acts of piety, there were many abominable hypocrites, who entertained the most ridiculous opinions, and concealed the most enormous vices under the specious mask of this extraordinary profession Many injurious aspersions were therefore propagated against those who assumed this name by the priests and monks; so that, by degrees, any person who covered heresies or crimes under the appearance of piety was called a *Lollard.* Thus the name was not used to denote any one particular sect, but was formerly common to all persons or sects who were supposed to be guilty of impiety towards God or the church, under an external profession of great piety. However, many societies, consisting both of men and women, under the name of Lollards, were formed in most parts of Germany and Flanders, and were supported partly by their manual labors, and partly by the charitable donations of pious persons. The magistrates and inhabitants of the towns where these brethren and sisters resided, gave them particular marks of favor and protection, on account of their great usefulness to the sick and needy. They were thus supported against their malignant rivals, and obtained many papal constitutions, by which their institute was confirmed, their persons exempted from the cognizance of the inquisitor, and subjected entirely to the jurisdiction of the bishops; but as these measures were insufficient to secure them from molestation, Charles, duke of Burgundy, in the year 1472, obtained a solemn bull from pope Sextus IV., ordering that the Cellites or Lollards should be ranked among the religious orders, and delivered from the jurisdiction of the bishops. And pope Julius II. granted them still greater privileges, in the year

1506. Mosheim informs us, that many societies of this kind are still subsisting at Cologne, and in the cities of Flanders, though they have evidently departed from their ancient rules.

Lollard and his followers rejected the sacrifice of the mass, extreme unction, and penances for sin; arguing that Christ's sufferings were sufficient. He is likewise said to have set aside baptism, as a thing of no effect; and repentance as not absolutely necessary, &c. In England, the followers of Wickliffe were called, by way of reproach, *Lollards*, from the supposition that there was some affinity between some of their tenets; though others are of opinion that the English Lollards came from Germany.

JESUITS.

JESUITS, or the Society of Jesus, a famous religious order of the Roman Church, founded by Ignatius Loyola, a Spanish knight, in the sixteenth century. The plan which this fanatic formed of its constitution and laws, was suggested, as he gave out, by the immediate inspiration of Heaven. But, notwithstanding this high pretension, his design met at first with violent opposition. The Pope, to whom Loyola had applied for the sanction of his authority to confirm the institution, referred his petition to a committee of cardinals. They represented the establishment to be unnecessary as well as dangerous, and Paul refused to grant his approbation of it. At last, Loyola removed all his scruples, by an offer which it was impossible for any Pope to resist. He proposed that, besides the three vows of poverty, of chastity, and of monastic obedience, which are common to all the orders of regulars, the members of his society should take a fourth vow of obedience to the Pope, binding themselves to go whithersoever he should command for the service of religion, and without requiring anything from the Holy See for their support. At a time when the Papal authority had received such a shock by the revolt of so many nations from the Romish Church, at a time when every part of the popish system was attacked with so much violence and success, the acquisition of a body of men, thus peculiarly devoted to the see of Rome, and whom it might set in opposition to all its enemies, was an object of the highest consequence. Paul. instantly perceiving this, confirmed the institution of the Jesuits by his bull, granted the most ample privileges to the members of the society, and appointed Loyola to be the first general of the order. 1640 The event justified Paul's discernment in expecting such beneficial consequences to the see of Rome from this institution. In less than half a century, the society obtained establishments in every country that adhered to the Roman Catholic Church; its power and wealth increased amazingly; the number of its members became great; their character as well as accomplishments were still greater; and the Jesuits were celebrated by the friends and dreaded by the enemies of the Romish faith, as the most able and enterprising order in the church.

2. *Jesuits, object of the Order of.*—The primary object of almost all the monastic orders is to separate men from the world, and from any concern in its affairs. In the solitude and silence of the cloister, the monk is called to work out his salvation by extraordinary acts of mortification and piety. He is dead to the world, and ought not to mingle in its transactions. He can be of no benefit to mankind but by his example and by his prayers. On the contrary, the

Jesuits are taught to consider themselves as formed for action. They are chosen soldiers, bound to exert themselves continually in the service of God, and of the Pope, his vicar on earth. Whatever tends to instruct the ignorant, whatever can be of use to reclaim or oppose the enemies of the Holy See, is their proper object. That they may have full leisure for this active service, they are totally exempted from those functions, the performance of which is the chief business of other monks. They appear in no processions; they practise no rigorous austerities; they do not consume one-half of their time in the repetition of tedious offices; but they are required to attend to all the transactions of the world, on account of the influence which these may have upon religion : they are directed to study the disposition of persons in high rank, and to cultivate their friendship; and by the very constitution and genius of the order, a spirit of action and intrigue is infused into all its members.

3. *Jesuits, peculiarities of their policy and government.* —Other orders are to be considered as voluntary associations, in which, whatever affects the whole body, is regulated by the common suffrage of all its members. But Loyola, full of the ideas of implicit obedience, which he had derived from his military profession, appointed that the government of his order should be purely monarchical. A general chosen for life, by deputies from the several provinces, possessed power that was supreme and independent, extending to every person and to every case. To his commands they were required to yield not only outward obedience, but to resign up to him the inclinations of their own wills, and the sentiments of their own understandings. Such a singular form of policy could not fail to impress its character on all the members of the order, and to give a peculiar force to all its operations. There has not been,

perhaps, in the annals of mankind, any example of such a perfect despotism exercised, not over monks shut up in the cells of a convent, but over men dispersed among all the nations of the earth. As the constitutions of the order vest in the general such absolute dominion over all its members, they carefully provide for his being perfectly informed with respect to the character and abilities of his subjects. Every novice who offers himself for a candidate for entering into the order, is obliged to manifest his conscience to the superior, or a person appointed by him; and is required to confess not only his sins and defects, but to discover the inclinations, the passions, and the bent of the soul. This manifestation must be renewed every six months. Each member is directed to observe the words and actions of the novices, and they are bound to disclose everything of importance concerning them to the superior. In order that the scrutiny into their character may be as complete as possible, a long noviciate must expire, during which they pass through the several gradations of rank in the society; and they must have attained the full age of thirty-three years before they can be admitted to take the final vows by which they become professed members. By these various methods, the superiors, under whose immediate inspection the novices are placed, acquire a thorough knowledge of their disposition and talents; and the general, by examining the registers kept for this purpose, is enabled to choose the instruments which his absolute power can employ in any service for which he thinks meet to destine them.

4. *Jesuits, progress of the power and influence of.*—As it was the professed intention of this order to labor with unwearied zeal in promoting the salvation of men, this engaged them, of course, in many active functions. From their first institution, they considered the education of youth as their peculiar province: they aimed at being spiritual

guides and confessors; they preached frequently, in order
to instruct the people; they set out as missionaries to convert unbelieving nations. Before the expiration of the sixteenth century, they had obtained the chief direction of the
education of youth in every Catholic country in Europe.
They had become the confessors of almost all its monarchs;
a function of no small importance in any reign, but, under
a weak prince, superior to that of minister. They were
the spiritual guides of almost every person eminent for
rank or power; they possessed the highest degree of confidence and interest with the papal court, as the most zealous
and able champions for its authority; they possessed, at
different periods, the direction of the most considerable
courts in Europe; they mingled in all affairs, and took part
in every intrigue and revolution. But while they thus
advanced in power, they increased also in wealth: various
expedients were devised for eluding the obligation of the vow
of poverty. Besides the sources of wealth common to all
the regular clergy, the Jesuits possessed one which was
peculiar to themselves. Under the pretext of promoting
the success of their missions, and of facilitating the support of their missionaries, they obtained a special license
from the court of Rome, to trade with the nations which
they labored to convert; in consequence of this, they engaged in an extensive and lucrative commerce, both in the
East and West Indies; they opened warehouses in different
parts of Europe, in which they vended their commodities.
Not satisfied with trade alone, they imitated the example
of other commercial societies, and aimed at obtaining settlements. They acquired possession, accordingly, of the
large and fertile province of Paraguay, which stretches
across the southern continent of America, from the bottom
of the mountains of Potosi to the confines of the Spanish
and Portuguese settlements on the banks of the river De la

Plata. Here, indeed, it must be confessed, they were of service : they found the inhabitants in a state little different from that which takes place among men when they first begin to unite together ; strangers to the arts ; subsisting precariously by hunting or fishing ; and hardly acquainted with the first principles of subordination and government. The Jesuits set themselves to instruct and civilize these savages : they taught them to cultivate the ground, build houses, and brought them to live together in villages, &c. They made them taste the sweets of society, and trained them to arts and manufactures.   Such was their power over them, that a few Jesuits presided over some hundred thousand Indians.   But even in this meritorious effort of the Jesuits for the good of mankind, the genius and spirit of their order was discernible : they plainly aimed at establishing in Paraguay an independent empire, subject to the society alone, and which, by the superior excellence of its constitution and police, could scarcely have failed to extend its dominion over all the southern continent of America. With this view, in order to prevent the Spaniards and Portuguese in the adjacent settlements from acquiring any dangerous influence over the people within the limits of the province subject to the society, the Jesuits endeavored to inspire the Indians with hatred and contempt of these nations ; they cut off all intercourse between their subjects and the Spanish or Portuguese settlements.   When they were obliged to admit any person in a public character from the neighboring governments, they did not permit him to have any conversation with their subjects ; and no Indian was allowed even to enter the house where these strangers resided, unless in the presence of a Jesuit.   In order to render any communication between them as difficult as possible, they industriously avoided giving the Indians any knowledge of the Spanish or any other European language.

33 *

but encouraged the different tribes which they had civilized to acquire a certain dialect of the Indian tongue, and labored to make that the universal language throughout their dominions. As all these precautions, without military force, would have been insufficient to have rendered their empire secure and permanent, they instructed their subjects in the European art of war, and formed them into bodies completely armed, and well disciplined.

5. *Jesuits, pernicious effects of this order on civil society.*—Though it must be confessed that the Jesuits cultivated the study of ancient literature, and contributed much towards the progress of polite learning; though they have produced eminent masters in every branch of science, and can boast of a number of ingenious authors; yet, unhappily for mankind, their vast influence has been often exerted with the most fatal effects. Such was the tendency of that discipline observed by the society in forming its members, and such the fundamental maxims in its constitution, that every Jesuit was taught to regard the interest of the order as the capital object to which every consideration was to be sacrificed. As the prosperity of the order was intimately connected with the preservation of the papal authority, the Jesuits, influenced by the same principle of attachment to the interest of their society, have been the most zealous patrons of those doctrines which tend to exalt ecclesiastical power on the ruins of civil government. They have attributed to the court of Rome a jurisdiction as extensive and absolute as was claimed by the most presumptuous pontiffs in the dark ages. They have contended for the entire independence of ecclesiastics on the civil magistrates. They have published such tenets concerning the duty of opposing princes who were enemies of the Catholic faith, as countenanced the most atrocious crimes, and tended to dissolve all the ties which connect subjects

with their rulers. As the order derived both reputation and authority from the zeal with which it stood forth in defence of the Romish Church against the attacks of the reformers, its members, proud of this distinction, have considered it as their peculiar function to combat the opinions, and to check the progress of the Protestants. They have made use of every art, and have employed every weapon against them. They have set themselves in opposition to every gentle or tolerating measure in their favor. They have incessar tly stirred up against them all the rage of ecclesiastical and civil persecution. Whoever recollects the events which have happened in Europe during two centuries, will find that the Jesuits may justly be considered as responsible for most of the pernicious effects arising from that corrupt and dangerous casuistry, from those extravagant tenets concerning ecclesiastical power, and from that intolerant spirit which have been the disgrace of the Church of Rome throughout that period, and which have brought so many calamities upon society.

6. *Jesuits, downfall in Europe.* — Such were the laws, the policy, and the genius of this formidable order; of which, however, a perfect knowledge has only been attainable of late. Europe had observed for two centuries the ambition and power of the order; but while it felt many fatal effects of these, it could not fully discern the causes to which they were to be imputed. It was unacquainted with many of the singular regulations in the political constitution or government of the Jesuits, which formed the enterprising spirit of intrigue that distinguished its members, and elevated the body itself to such a height of power. It was a fundamental maxim with the Jesuits, from their first institution, not to publish the rules of their order : these they kept concealed as an impenetrable mystery. They never communicated them to strangers, nor

even to the greater part of their own members; they refused to produce them when required by courts of justice;
and, by a strange solecism in policy, the civil power in
different countries authorized or connived at the establishment of an order of men, whose constitution and laws were
concealed with a solicitude which alone was a good reason
for having excluded them. During the prosecutions which
have been carried on against them in Portugal and France,
the Jesuits have been so inconsiderate as to produce the
mysterious volumes of their institute. By the aid of these
authentic records, the principles of their government may
be delineated, and the sources of their power investigated,
with a degree of certainty and precision which, previous
to that event, it was impossible to attain.

The pernicious effects of the spirit and constitution of
this order rendered it early obnoxious to some of the
principal powers in Europe, and gradually brought on its
downfall. There is a remarkable passage in a sermon
preached at Dublin by Archbishop Brown, so long ago as
the year 1551, and which may be considered as almost
prophetic. It is as follows: "But there are a new fraternity of late sprung up, who call themselves Jesuits, which
will deceive many, much after the Scribes and Pharisees'
manner. Amongst the Jews they shall strive to abolish
the truth, and shall come very near to do it. For these
sorts will turn themselves into several forms; with the
heathen, a heathenist; with the atheist, an atheist; with
the Jews, a Jew; with the reformers, a reformade; purposely to know your intentions, your minds, your hearts,
and your inclinations, and thereby bring you at last to be
like the fool that said in his heart, there was no God.
These shall be spread over the whole world, shall be admitted into the councils of princes, and they never the
wiser; charming of them, yea, making your princes reveal

their hearts, and the secrets therein, and yet they not perceive it; which will happen from falling from the law of God, by neglect of fulfilling the law of God, and by winking at their sins; yet, in the end, God, to justify his law, shall suddenly cut off this society, even by the hand of those who have most succored them, and made use of them; so that at the end they shall become odious to all nations. They shall be worse than Jews, having no resting place upon earth; and then shall a Jew have more favor than a Jesuit." This singular passage seems to be accomplished. The Emperor Charles V. saw it expedient to check their progress in his dominions; they were expelled England by proclamation, 2 James I., in 1604; Venice in 1606; Portugal in 1759; France in 1764: Spain and Sicily in 1767; and totally suppressed and abolished by Pope Clement XIV., in 1773.

In 1801 the society was restored in Russia by the Emperor Paul; and in 1804, by King Ferdinand, in Sardinia. In August, 1814, a bull was issued by Pope Pius VII., restoring the order to all their former privileges, and calling upon all Catholic princes to afford them protection and encouragement.

HOPKINSIANS.

THE Hopkinsians were so called from the Rev. Samuel Hopkins, D. D., an American divine, who in his sermons and tracts has made several additions to the sentiments first advanced by the celebrated Jonathan Edwards, late president of New Jersey College.

The following is a summary of the distinguished tenets

of the Hopkinsians, together with a few of the reasons they bring forward in support of their sentiments.

1. That all true virtue, or real holiness, consists in disinterested benevolence.   The object of benevolence is universal being, including God and all intelligent creatures. It wishes and seeks the good of every individual, so far as is consistent with the greatest good of the whole, which is comprised in the glory of God and the perfection and happiness of his kingdom.   The law of God is the standard of all moral rectitude or holiness.   This is reduced into love to God, and our neighbor as ourselves, and universal good-will comprehends all the love to God, our neighbor and ourselves, required in the divine law, and therefore must be the whole of holy obedience.   Let any serious person think what are the particular branches of true piety; when he has viewed each one by itself, he will find that disinterested friendly affection is its distinguishing characteristic.   For instance, all the holiness in pious fear, which distinguishes it from the fear of the wicked, consists in love. Again—holy gratitude is nothing but good-will to God and our neighbor, in which we ourselves are included; and correspondent affection, excited by a view of the good-will and kindness of God.   Universal good-will also implies the whole of the duty we owe to our neighbor, for justice, truth, and faithfulness, are comprised in universal benevolence; so are temperance and chastity.   For an undue indulgence of our appetites and passions is contrary to benevolence, as tending to hurt ourselves or others; and so opposite to the general good, and the divine command, in which all the crime of such indulgence consists.   In short, all virtue is nothing but benevolence acted out in its proper nature and perfection; or love to God and our neighbor, made perfect in all its genuine exercises and expressions.

2. That all sin consists in selfishness.   By this is meant

an interested, selfish affection, by which a person sets him-self up as supreme, and the only object of regard; and nothing is good or lovely in his view, unless suited to pro-mote his own private interest. This self-love is, in its whole nature, and every degree of it, enmity against God: it is not subject to the law of God, and is the only affection that can oppose it. It is the foundation of all spiritual blindness, and therefore the source of all the open idolatry in the heathen world, and false religion under the light of the Gospel; all this is agreeable to that self-love which opposes God's true character. Under the influence of this principle, men depart from truth; it being itself the great-est practical lie in nature, as it sets up that which is com-paratively nothing above universal existence. Self-love is the source of all profaneness and impiety in the world, and of all pride and ambition among men, which is nothing but selfishness, acted out in this particular way. This is the foundation of all covetousness and sensuality, as it blinds people's eyes, contracts their hearts, and sinks them down, so that they look upon earthly enjoyments as the greatest good. This is the source of all falsehood, injustice, and oppression, as it excites mankind by undue methods to in-vade the property of others. Self-love produces all the violent passions; envy, wrath, clamor, and evil speaking: and everything contrary to the divine law is briefly com-prehended in this fruitful source of all iniquity, self-love.

3. That there are no promises of regenerating grace made to the doings of the unregenerate. For as far as men act from self-love, they act from a bad end: for those who have no true love to God, really do no duty when they attend on the externals of religion. And as the unregene-rate act from a selfish principle, they do nothing which is commanded: their impenitent doings are wholly opposed to repentance and conversion; therefore not implied in the

command to repent, &c.; so far from this, they are altogether disobedient to the command. Hence it appears that there are no promises of salvation to the doings of the unregenerate.

4. That the impotency of sinners, with respect to believing in Christ, is not natural, but moral; for it is a plain dictate of common sense, that natural impossibility excludes all blame. But an unwilling mind is universally considered as a crime, and not as an excuse, and is the very thing wherein our wickedness consists. That the impotence of the sinner is owing to a disaffection of heart, is evident from the promises of the Gospel. When any object of good is proposed and promised to us upon asking, it clearly evinces that there can be no impotence in us with respect to obtaining it, beside the disapprobation of the will; and that inability which consists in disinclination, never renders anything improperly the subject of precept or command.

5. That, in order to faith in Christ, a sinner must approve in his heart of the divine conduct, even though God should cast him off forever; which, however, neither implies love of misery, nor hatred of happiness. For if the law is good, death is due to those who have broken it. The Judge of all the earth cannot but do right. It will bring everlasting reproach upon his government to spare us, considered merely as in ourselves. When this is felt in our hearts, and not till then, we shall be prepared to look to the free grace of God, through the redemption which is in Christ, and to exercise faith in his blood, *who is set forth to be a propitiation to declare God's righteousness, that he might be just, and yet be the justifier of him who believeth in Jesus.*

6. That the infinitely wise and holy God has exerted his omnipotent power in such a manner as he purposed should

be followed with the existence and entrance of moral evil into the system. For it must be admitted on all hands, that God has a perfect knowledge, foresight, and view of all possible existences and events. If that system and scene of operation, in which moral evil should never have existed, was actually preferred in the divine mind, certainly the Deity is infinitely disappointed in the issue of his own operations. Nothing can be more dishonorable to God than to imagine that the system which is actually formed by the divine hand, and which was made for his pleasure and glory, is yet not the fruit of wise contrivance and design

7. That the introduction of sin is, upon the whole, for the general good. For the wisdom and power of the Deity are displayed in carrying on designs of the greatest good; and the existence of moral evil has undoubtedly occasioned a more full, perfect, and glorious discovery of the infinite perfections of the divine nature, than could otherwise have been made to the view of creatures. If the extensive manifestations of the pure and holy nature of God, and his infinite aversion to sin, and all his inherent perfections, in their genuine fruits and effects, is either itself the greatest good, or unnecessarily contains it, it must necessarily follow that the introduction of sin is for the greatest good.

8. That repentance is before faith in Christ.—By this is not intended, that repentance is before a speculative belief of the being and perfections of God, and of the person and character of Christ; but only that true repentance is previous to a saving faith in Christ, in which the believer is united to Christ, and entitled to the benefits of his mediation and atonement. That repentance is before faith, in this sense, appears from several considerations. 1. As repentance and faith respect different objects, so they are distinct exercises of the heart; and therefore one not only may, but must be prior to the other. 2. There may be

genuine repentance of sin without faith in Christ, but there cannot be true faith in Christ without repentance of sin; and since repentance is necessary in order to faith in Christ, it must necessarily be prior to faith in Christ. 3. John the Baptist, Christ and his apostles, taught that repentance is before faith. John cried, *Repent, for the kingdom of heaven is at hand;* intimating that true repentance was necessary in order to embrace the Gospel of the kingdom. Christ commanded, *Repent ye, and believe the Gospel.* And Paul preached *repentance toward God, and faith toward our Lord Jesus Christ.*

9. That though men became sinners by Adam, according to a divine constitution, yet they have and are accountable for no sins but personal: for, 1. Adam's act, in eating the forbidden fruit, was not the *act* of his posterity; therefore they did not sin at the same time he did. 2. The sinfulness of that act could not be *transferred* to them afterwards, because the sinfulness of an act can no more be transferred from one person to another than an act itself 3. Therefore Adam's act, in eating the forbidden fruit, was not the *cause*, but only the *occasion* of his posterity's being sinners. God was pleased to make a constitution, that, if Adam remained holy through his state of trial, his posterity should in consequence be holy also; but if he sinned, his posterity should in consequence be sinners likewise. Adam sinned, and now God brings his posterity into the world sinners. *By* Adam's sin we are become sinners, not *for* it; his sin being only the *occasion,* not the *cause* of our committing sins.

10. That though believers are justified *through* Christ's righteousness, yet his righteousness is not *transferred* to them. For, 1. Personal righteousness can no more be transferred from one person to another, than personal sin. 2. If Christ's personal righteousness were transferred to

believers, they would be as perfectly holy as Christ; and so stand in no need of forgiveness. 3. But believers are not conscious of having Christ's personal righteousness, but feel and bewail much indwelling sin and corruption. 4. The Scripture represents believers as receiving only the *benefits* of Christ's righteousness in justification, or their being pardoned and accepted for Christ's righteousness' sake, and this is the proper Scripture notion of imputation. Jonathan's righteousness was imputed to Mephibosheth, when David showed kindness to him for his father Jonathan's sake.

The Hopkinsians warmly contend for the doctrine of the divine decrees, that of particular election, total depravity, the special influences of the Spirit of God in regeneration, justification by faith alone, the final perseverance of the saints, and the consistency between entire freedom and absolute dependence; and therefore claim it as their just due, since the world will make distinctions, to be called Hopkinsian Calvinists.

ERASTIANS.

THE Erastians are so called from Erastus, a German divine of the sixteenth century. The pastoral office, according to him, was only persuasive, like a professor of science over his students, without any power of the keys annexed. The Lord's Supper and other ordinances of the Gospel were to be free and open to all. The minister might dissuade the vicious and unqualified from the communion; but might not refuse it, or inflict any kind of censure; the punishment of all offences, either of a civil or religious nature, being referred to the civil magistrate.

DANCERS.

THE Dancers were a sect which sprung up about 1373, in Flanders, and places about. It was their custom all of a sudden to fall a dancing, and, holding each other's hands, to continue thereat, till, being suffocated with the extraordinary violence, they fell down breathless together. During these intervals of vehement agitation they pretended they were favored with wonderful visions. Like the Whippers, they roved from place to place, begging their victuals, holding their secret assemblies, and treating the priesthood and worship of the church with the utmost contempt. Thus we find, as Dr. Haweis observes, that the French Convulsionists and Welch Jumpers have had predecessors of the same stamp. There is nothing new under the sun.

DAVIDISTS.

THE Davidists were the adherents of David George, a native of Delft, who, in 1525, began to preach a new doctrine, publishing himself to be the true Messiah; and that he was sent of God to fill heaven, which was quite empty for want of people to deserve it. He is likewise said to have denied the existence of angels, good and evil, and to have disbelieved the doctrine of a future judgment. He rejected marriage with the Adamites; held with Manes, that the soul was not defiled by sin; and laughed at the self-denial so much recommended by Jesus Christ.

Such were his principal errors. He made his escape from Delft, and retired first into Friesland, and then to Basil, where he changed his name, assuming that of John Bruck, and died in 1556. He left some disciples behind him, to whom he promised that he would rise again at the end of three years. Nor was he altogether a false prophet herein; for the magistrates of that city being informed, at the three years' end, of what he had taught, ordered him to be dug up, and burnt, together with his writings, by the common hangman.

COCCEIANS.

THE Cocceians were a denomination which arose in the seventeenth century; so called from John Cocceius, professor of divinity in the university of Leyden. He represented the whole history of the Old Testament as a mirror, which held forth an accurate view of the transactions and events that were to happen in the church under the dispensation of the New Testament, and unto the end of the world. He maintained that by far the greatest part of the ancient prophecies foretold Christ's ministry and mediation, and the rise, progress, and revolutions of the church, not only under the figure of persons and transactions, but in a literal manner, and by the very sense of the words used in these predictions; and laid it down as a fundamental rule of interpretation, that the words and phrases of Scripture are to be understood in every sense of which they are susceptible, or, in other words, that they signify in effect everything that they can possibly signify.

Cocceius also taught, that the covenant made between

God and the Jewish nation, by the ministry of Moses, was of the same nature as the new covenant, obtained by the mediation of Jesus Christ. In consequence of this general principle, he maintained that the ten commandments were promulgated by Moses, not as a rule of obedience, but as a representation of the covenant of grace — that when the Jews had provoked the Deity by their various transgressions, particularly by the worship of the golden calf, the severe and servile yoke of the ceremonial law was added to the decalogue, as a punishment inflicted on them by the Supreme Being in his righteous displeasure — that this yoke, which was painful in itself, became doubly so on account of its typical signification; since it admonished the Israelites from day to day of the imperfection and uncertainty of their state, filled them with anxiety, and was a perpetual proof that they had merited the righteous displeasure of God, and could not expect, before the coming of the Messiah, the entire remission of their iniquities — that indeed good men, even under the Mosaic dispensation, were immediately after death made partakers of everlasting glory; but that they were nevertheless, during the whole course of their lives, far removed from that firm hope and assurance of salvation, which rejoices the faithful under the dispensation of the Gospel — and that their anxiety flowed naturally from this consideration, that their sins, though they remained unpunished, were not pardoned; because Christ had not as yet offered himself up a sacrifice to the Father, to make an entire atonement for them.

COLLEGIANS.

COLLEGIANS, or Collegiants, a sect formed among the Arminians and Anabaptists in Holland, about the beginning of the seventeenth century; so called because of their colleges or meetings twice every week, where every one, females excepted, has the same liberty of expounding the Scriptures, praying, &c. They are said to be all either Arians or Socinians; they never communicate in the college, but meet twice a year, from all parts of Holland, at Rhinsbergh, (whence they are also called *Rhinsberghers*) a village two miles from Leyden, where they communicate together; admitting every one that presents himself, professing his faith in the divinity of the Holy Scriptures, and resolution to live suitably to their precepts and doctrines, without regard to his sect or opinion. They have no particular ministers, but each officiates as he is disposed. They baptize by immersion.

BEREANS.

THE Bereans are a sect of Protestant Dissenters from the Church of Scotland, who take their title from and profess to follow the example of the ancient Bereans, in building their system of faith and practice upon the Scriptures alone, without regard to any human authority whatever.

As to the *origin* of this sect, we find that the Bereans first assembled as a separate society of Christians, in the city of Edinburgh, in the autumn of 1773, and soon after in the parish of Fettercairn. The opponents of the Berean doctrines allege that the new system of faith would never have been heard of, had not Mr. Barclay, the founder of it, been disappointed of a settlement in the Church of Scotland. But the Bereans, in answer to this charge, appeal not only to Mr. Barclay's doctrine, uniformly preached in the church of Fettercairn, and many other places in that neighborhood, for fourteen years before that benefice became vacant, but likewise to two different treatises, containing the same doctrines, published by him about ten or twelve years before that period. They admit, indeed, that previous to May, 1773, when the general assembly, by sustaining the king's presentation in favor of Mr. Foote, excluded Mr. Barclay from succeeding to the church of Fettercairn (notwithstanding the almost unanimous desire of the parishioners), the Bereans had not left the established church, nor attempted to erect themselves into a distinct society; but they add, that this was by no means necessary on their part, until by the assembly's decision they were in danger of being not only deprived of his instructions, but of being scattered as sheep without a shepherd. And they add, that it was Mr. Barclay's open and public avowal, both from the pulpit and the press, of those peculiar sentiments which now distinguish the Bereans, that was the first and principal, if not the only cause of the opposition set on foot against his settlement in Fettercairn.

The Bereans agree with the great majority of Christians respecting the doctrine of the Trinity, which they hold as a fundamental article; and they also agree in a great measure with the professed principles of both the established churches respecting predestination and election, though they allege that these doctrines are not consistently taught in either church. But they differ from the majority of all sects of Christians in various other important particulars, such as, 1. Respecting our knowledge of the Deity. Upon this subject they say, the majority of professed Christians stumble at the very threshold of revelation; and, by admitting the doctrine of natural religion, natural conscience, natural notices, etc., not founded upon revelation, or derived from it by tradition, they give up the cause of Christianity at once to the infidels; who may justly argue, as Mr. Paine in fact does in his Age of Reason, that there is no occasion for any revelation or word of God, if man can discover his nature and perfections from his works alone. But this the Bereans argue is beyond the natural powers of human reason; and therefore our knowledge of God is from revelation alone, and that without revelation man would never have entertained an idea of his existence. 2. With regard to faith in Christ, and assurance of salvation through his merits, they differ from almost all other sects whatsoever. These they reckon inseparable, or rather the same, because (say they) "God hath expressly declared, he that believeth shall be saved; and therefore it is not only absurd but impious, and in a manner calling God a liar, for a man to say, I believe the gospel, but have doubts, nevertheless, of my own salvation." With regard to the various distinctions and definitions that have been given of different kinds of faith, they argue that there is nothing incomprehensible or obscure in the meaning of this word as used in Scripture; but that as faith, when applied to human testimony, signifies neither more nor less than the mere simple belief of that testimony as true, upon the authority of the testifier, so, when applied to the testimony of God, it signifies precisely "the belief of his testimony, and resting upon his veracity alone, without any kind of collateral support from concurrence of any

other evidence or testimony whatever." And they insist
that, as this faith is the gift of God alone, so the person
to whom it is given is as conscious of possessing it as the
being to whom God gives life is of being alive; and therefore he entertains no doubts either of his faith or his consequent salvation through the merits of Christ, who died
and rose again for that purpose. In a word, they argue
that the gospel would not be what it is held forth to be,
glad tidings of great joy, if it did not bring full personal
assurance of eternal salvation to the believer; which assurance, they insist, is the present infallible privilege and
portion of every individual believer of the gospel. 3.
Consistently with the above definition of faith, they say
that the sin against the Holy Ghost, which has alarmed
and puzzled so many in all ages, is nothing else but unbelief; and that the expression "it shall not be forgiven
neither in this world nor that which is to come," means
only that a person dying in infidelity would not be forgiven, neither under the former dispensation by Moses
(the then *present* dispensation, kingdom, or government
of God), nor under the gospel dispensation which, in respect of the Mosaic, was a kind of future world or king-
lom to come. 4. The Bereans interpret a great part of
the Old Testament prophecies, and in particular the whole
of the Psalms, excepting such as are merely historical or
laudatory, to be typical or prophetical of Jesus Christ, his
sufferings, atonement, mediation, and kingdom; and they
esteem it a gross perversion of these Psalms and prophecies to apply them to the experiences of private Christians.
In proof of this, they not only urge the words of the apostle, that no prophecy is of any private interpretation, but
they insist that the whole of the quotations from the ancient prophecies in the New Testament, and particularly
those from the Psalms, are expressly applied to Christ.

In this opinion many other classes of Protestants agree with them. 5. Of the absolute all-superintending sovereignty of the Almighty, the Bereans entertain the highest idea, as well as of the uninterrupted exertion thereof over all his works, in heaven, earth, and hell, however unsearchable by his creatures. A God without election, they argue, or choice in all his works, is a God without existence, a mere idol, a nonentity. And to deny God's election, purpose, and express will in all his works, is to make him inferior to ourselves.

As to their *practice* and *discipline*, they consider infant baptism as a divine ordinance, instituted in the room of circumcision; and think it absurd to suppose that infants, who, all agree, are admissible to the kingdom of God in heaven, should nevertheless be incapable of being admitted into his visible church on earth. They commemorate the Lord's Supper generally once a month; but as the words of the institution fix no particular period, they sometimes celebrate it oftener, and sometimes at more distant periods, as it may suit their general convenience. They meet every Lord's day for the purpose of preaching, praying, and exhorting to love and good works. With regard to admission and exclusion of members, their method is very simple: when any person, after hearing the Berean doctrines, professes his belief and assurance of the truths of the gospel, and desires to be admitted into their communion, he is cheerfully received upon his profession, whatever may have been his former manner of life. But if such a one should afterwards draw back from his good profession or practice, they first admonish him, and, if that has no effect, they leave him to himself. They do not think that they have any power to deliver a backsliding brother to Satan; that text, and other similar passages, such as, " Whatsoever ye shall bind on earth shall be bound in heaven," etc., they consider as restricted to the apostles, and to the inspired testimony alone, and not to be extended to any church on earth, or any number of churches or of Christians, whether decided by a majority of votes, or by unanimous voices. Neither do they think themselves authorized, as a Christian church, to inquire into each other's political opinions, any more than to examine into each other's notions of philosophy. They both recommend and practise, as a Christian duty, submission to lawful authority; but they do not think that a man, by becoming a Christian, or joining their society, is under any obligation by the rules of the gospel to renounce his right of private judgment upon matters of public or private importance. Upon all such subjects they allow each other to think and act as each may see it his duty; and they require nothing more of the members than a uniform and steady profession of the apostolic faith, and a suitable walk and conversation.

It is said that their doctrine has found converts in various places of Scotland, England, and America; and that they have congregations in Edinburgh, Glasgow, Paisley, Stirling, Crieff, Dundee, Arbroath, Montrose, Fettercairn, Aberdeen, and other towns in Scotland, as well as in London, and various places in England.

AGNOETÆ.

AGNOETÆ (from αγνοεω, "to be ignorant of,"), a sect which appeared about 370. They called in question the omniscience of God; alleging that he knew things past only by memory, and things future only by an uncertain prescience. There arose another sect of the same name in the sixth century, who followed Themistius, deacon of Alexandria. They maintained that Christ was ignorant of certain things, and particularly of the time of the day of judgment. It is supposed they built their hypothesis on that passage in Mark xiii. 32:—"Of that day and that hour knoweth no man; no, not the angels which are in heaven, neither the Son, but the Father." The meaning of which most probably is, that this was not known to the Messiah himself in his human nature, or by virtue of his unction, as any part of the mysteries he was to reveal; for, considering him as God, he could not be ignorant of anything.

ALBANENSES.

ALBANENSES, a denomination which commenced about the year 796. They held, with the Gnostics and Mani-cheans, two principles, the one of good and the other of evil. They denied the divinity and even the humanity of Jesus Christ; asserting that he was not truly man, did not suffer on the cross, die, rise again, nor really ascend into heaven. They rejected the doctrine of the resurrection, affirmed that the general judgment was past, and that hell torments were no other than the evils we feel and suffer in this life. They denied free-will, did not admit original sin, and never administered baptism to infants. They held that a man can give the Holy Spirit of himself, and that it is unlawful for a Christian to take an oath.

This denomination derived their name from the place where their spiritual ruler resided.

35

LATITUDINARIANS.

LATITUDINARIAN, a person not conforming to any particular opinion or standard, but of such moderation as to suppose that people will be admitted into heaven, although of different persuasions. The term was more especially applied to those pacific doctors in the seventeenth century, who offered themselves as mediators between the more violent Episcopalians and the rigid Presbyterians and Independents, respecting the forms of Church government, public worship, and certain religious tenets, more especially those that were debated between the Arminians and Calvinists. The chief leaders of these Latitudinarians were Hales and Chillingworth; but More, Cudworth, Gale, Whitchcot, and Tillotson were also among the number. These men, although firmly attached to the Church of England, did not go so far as to look upon it as of *divine institution;* and hence they maintained, that those who followed other forms of government and worship, were not on that account to be excluded from their communion. As to the doctrinal part of religion, they took the system of Episcopius for their model, and, like him, reduced the fundamental doctrines of Christianity to a few points; and by this manner of proceeding they endeavored to show the contending parties that they had no reason to oppose each other with such animosity and bitterness, since the subjects of their debates were matters of an indifferent nature with respect to salvation. They met, however, with opposition for their pains, and were branded as Atheists and Deists by some, and as Socinians by others; but upon the restoration of Charles II., they were raised to the first dignities of the Church, and were held in considerable esteem.

ORIGENISTS.

THE Origenists were a denomination which appeared in
the third century, who derived their opinions from the
writings of Origen, a presbyter of Alexandria, and a man
of vast and uncommon abilities, who interpreted the divine
truths of religion according to the tenor of the Platonic
philosophy. He alleged that the source of many evils lies
in adhering to the literal and external part of Scripture;
and that the true meaning of the sacred writers was to be
sought in a mysterious and hidden sense, arising from the
nature of things themselves.

The principal tenets ascribed to Origen, together with a
few of the reasons made use of in their defence, are comprehended in the following summary:—

1. That there is a pre-existent state of human souls.
For the nature of the soul is such as to make her capable
of existing eternally, backward as well as forward, because
her spiritual essence, as such, makes it impossible that she
should, either through age or violence, be dissolved; so
that nothing is wanting to her existence but the good pleasure of him from whom all things proceed. And if, according to the Platonic scheme, we assign the production
of all things to the exuberant fulness of life in the Deity,
which, through the blessed necessity of his communicative
nature, empties itself into all possibilities of being, as into
so many capable receptacles, we must suppose her existence in a sense necessary, and in a degree co-eternal with
God.

2. That souls were condemned to animate mortal bodies
in order to expiate faults they had committed in a pre-

existent state; for we may be assured, from the infinite goodness of their Creator, that they were at first joined to the purest matter, and placed in those regions of the universe which were most suitable to the purity of essence they then possessed. For that the souls of men are an order of essentially incorporate spirits, their deep immersion into terrestrial matter, the modification of all their operations by it, and the heavenly body promised in the gospel, as the highest perfection of our renewed nature, clearly evince. Therefore, if our souls existed before they appeared inhabitants of the earth, they were placed in a purer element, and enjoyed far greater degrees of happiness. And certainly He, whose overflowing goodness brought them into existence, would not deprive them of their felicity, till by their mutability they rendered themselves less pure in the whole extent of their powers, and became disposed for the susception of such a degree of corporeal life as was exactly answerable to their present disposition of spirit. Hence it was necessary that they should become terrestrial men.

3. That the soul of Christ was united to the Word before the incarnation. For the Scriptures teach us that the soul of the Messiah was created before the beginning of the world, Phil. ii. 5, 7. This text must be understood of Christ's human soul, because it is unusual to propound the Deity as an example of humility in Scripture. Though the humanity of Christ was so God-like, he emptied himself of this fulness of life and glory, *to take upon him the form of a servant.* It was this Messiah who conversed with the patriarchs under a human form; it was he who appeared to Moses upon the Holy Mount; it was he who spoke to the prophets under a visible appearance; and it is he who will at last come in triumph upon the clouds to restore the universe to its primitive splendor and felicity.

4. That at the resurrection of the dead we shall be clothed with ethereal bodies. For the elements of our terrestrial compositions are such as almost fatally entangle us in vice, passion, and misery. The purer the vehicle the soul is united with, the more perfect is her life and operations. Besides, the Supreme Goodness who made all things, assures us he made all things best at first, and therefore his recovery of us to our lost happiness (which is the design of the gospel) must restore us to our better bodies and happier habitations, which is evident from 1 Cor. xv. 49; 2 Cor. v. 1; and other texts of Scripture.

5. That, after long periods of time, the damned shall be released from their torments, and restored to a new state of probation. For the Deity has such reserves in his gracious providence, as will vindicate his sovereign goodness and wisdom from all disparagement. Expiatory pains are a part of his adorable plan; for this sharper kind of favor has a righteous place in such creatures as are by nature mutable. Though sin has extinguished or silenced the divine life, yet it has not destroyed the faculties of reason and understanding, consideration and memory, which will serve the life which is most powerful. If, therefore, the vigorous attraction of the sensual nature be abated by a ceaseless pain, these powers may resume the sense of a better life and nature. As in the material system there is a gravitation of the less bodies towards the greater, there must of necessity be something analogous to this in the intellectual system; and since the spirits created by God are emanations and streams from his own abyss of being, and as self-existent power must needs subject all beings to itself, the Deity could not but impress upon her intimate natures and substances a central tendency towards himself; an essential principle of re-union to their great original.

35 *

6. That the earth, after its conflagration, shall become habitable again, and be the mansion of men and animals, and that in eternal vicissitudes. For it is thus expressed in Isaiah: *Behold I make new heavens and a new earth, &c.*, and in Heb. i. 10, 12, *Thou, Lord, in the beginning hast laid the foundations of the earth; as a vesture shalt thou change them, and they shall be changed, &c.* Where there is only a change the substance is not destroyed, this change being only as that of a garment worn out and decaying. The fashion of the world passes away like a turning scene, to exhibit a fresh and new representation of things; and if only the present dress and appearance of things go off, the substance is supposed to remain entire.

PETROBRUSSIANS.

PETROBRUSSIANS, a sect founded about the year 1110, in Languedoc and Provence, by Peter de Bruys, who made the most laudable attempts to reform the abuses and to remove the superstitions that disfigured the beautiful simplicity of the Gospel; though not without a mixture of fanaticism. The following tenets were held by him and his disciples:—1. That no persons whatever were to be baptized before they were come to the full use of their reason. 2. That it was an idle superstition to build churches for the service of God, who will accept of a sincere worship wherever it is offered; and that, therefore, such churches as had already been erected, were to be pulled down and destroyed. 3. That the crucifixes, as instruments of superstition, deserved the same fate. 4. That the real body and blood of Christ were not exhibited in the eucharist, but were merely represented in that ordinance. 5. That the oblations, prayers, and good works of the living, could be in no respect advantageous to the dead. The founder of this sect, after a laborious ministry of twenty years, was burnt in the year 1130, by an enraged populace set on by the clergy, whose traffic was in danger from the enterprising spirit of this new reformer.

PAULIANISTS.

THE Paulianists were a sect so called from their founder, Paulus Samosatenus, a native of Samosata, elected bishop of Antioch in 262. His doctrine seems to have amounted to this: that the Son and the Holy Ghost exist in God in the same manner as the faculties of reason and activity do in man; that Christ was born a mere man; but that the reason or wisdom of the Father descended into him, and by him wrought miracles upon earth, and instructed the nations; and, finally, that on account of this union of the Divine Word with the man Jesus, Christ might, though improperly, be called God. It is also said that he did not baptize in the name of the Father, and the Son, &c.; for which reason the council of Nice ordered those baptized by him to be re-baptized. Being condemned by Dionysius Alexandrinus in a council, he abjured his errors to avoid deposition; but soon after he resumed them, and was actually deposed by another council in 269. He may be considered as the father of the modern Socinians; and his errors are severely condemned by the council of Nice, whose creed differs a little from that now used under the same name in the church of England. The creed agreed upon by the Nicene fathers with a view to the errors of Paulus Samosatenus concludes thus : "But those who say there was a time when he was not, and that he was not before he was born, the catholic and apostolic church anathematize."

PAULICIANS.

THE Paulicians were a branch of the ancient Manichees, so called from their founder, one Paulus, an Armenian, in the seventh century, who, with his brother John, both of Samosata, formed this sect : though others are of opinion that they were thus called from another Paul, an Armenian by birth, who lived under the reign of Justinian II. In the seventh century, a zealot, called Constantine, revived this drooping sect, which had suffered much from the violence of its adversaries, and was ready to expire under the severity of the imperial edicts, and that zeal with which they were carried into execution. The Paulicians, however, by their number, and the countenance of the emperor Nicephorus, became formidable to all the East. But the cruel rage of persecution, which had for some years been suspended, broke forth with redoubled violence under the reigns of Michael Curopalates, and Leo the Armenian, who inflicted capital punishment on such of the Paulicians as refused to return into the bosom of the church. The empress Theodora, tutoress of the emperor Michael, in 845, would oblige them either to be converted, or to quit the empire; upon which several of them were put to death, and more retired among the Saracens; but they were neither all exterminated nor banished.

U₁ on this, they entered into a league with the Saracens, and choosing for their chief an officer of the greatest resolution and valor, whose name was Carbeus, they declared against the Greeks a war, which was carried on for fifty years with the greatest vehemence and fury. During these commotions, some Paulicians, towards the conclusion of this century, spread abroad their doctrines among the Bulgarians: many of them, either from a principle of zeal for the propagation of their opinions, or from a natural desire of flying from the persecution which they suffered under the Grecian yoke, retired about the close of the eleventh century from Bulgaria and Thrace, and formed settlements in other countries. Their first migration was into Italy; whence, in process of time, they sent colonies into almost all the other provinces of Europe, and formed gradually a considerable number of religious assemblies, who adhered to their doctrine, and who were afterwards persecuted with the utmost vehemence by the Roman pontiffs. In Italy they were called *Patarini*, from a certain place called *Pataria*, being a part of the city of Milan, where they held their assemblies; and *Gathari*, or *Gazari*, from Gazaria, or the Lesser Tartary. In France they were called *Albigenses*, though their faith differed widely from that of the Albigenses whom Protestant writers generally vindicate. The first religious assembly the Paulicians had formed in Europe, is said to have been discovered at Orleans in 1017, under the reign of Robert, when many of them were condemned to be burnt alive. The ancient Paulicians, according to Photius, expressed the utmost abhorrence of Manes and his doctrine. The Greek writers comprise their errors under the six following particulars:—1. They denied that this inferior and visible world is the production of the Supreme Being; and they distinguish the Creator of the world and of human

2 B

bodies from the Most High God, who dwells in the heavens; and hence some have been led to conceive that they were a branch of the Gnostics rather than of the Manichæans. 2. They treated contemptuously the Virgin Mary, or, according to the usual manner of speaking among the Greeks, they refused to adore and worship her. 3. They refused to celebrate the institution of the Lord's Supper. 4. They loaded the cross of Christ with contempt and reproach, by which we are only to understand that they refused to follow the absurd and superstitious practice of the Greeks, who paid to the pretended wood of the cross a certain sort of religious homage. 5. They rejected, after the example of the greatest part of the Gnostics, the books of the Old Testament, and looked upon the writers of that sacred history as inspired by the Creator of this world, and not by the Supreme God. 6. They excluded presbyters and elders from all part in the administration of the church.

LIBERTINES.

THE Libertines were a religious sect which arose in the year 1525, whose principal tenets were, that the Deity was the sole operating cause in the mind of man, and the immediate author of all human actions; that, consequently, the distinctions of good and evil, which had been established with regard to those actions, were false and groundless, and that men could not, properly speaking, commit sin; that religion consisted in the union of the spirit, or rational soul, with the Supreme Being; that all those who had attained this happy union, by sublime contemplation and elevation of mind, were then allowed to indulge, without exception or restraint, their appetites or passions; that all their actions and pursuits were then perfectly innocent; and that, after the death of the body, they were to be united to the Deity. They likewise said that Jesus Christ was nothing but a mere *je ne scai quoi*, composed of the spirit of God and the opinion of men. These maxims occasioned their being called *Libertines*, and the word has been used in an ill sense ever since. This sect spread principally in Holland and Brabant Their leaders were one Quintin, a Picard, Pockesius, Ruffus, and another, called Chopin, who joined with Quintin, and became his disciple. They obtained footing in France through the favor and protection of Margaret, Queen of Navarre, and sister to Francis I., and found patrons in several of the reformed churches.

The Libertines of Geneva were a cabal of rakes rather than fanatics; for they made no pretence to any religious system, but pleaded only for the liberty of leading voluptuous and immoral lives. This cabal was composed of a certain number of licentious citizens, who could not bear the severe discipline of Calvin. There were also among them several who were not only notorious for their dissolute and scandalous manner of living, but also for their atheistical impiety and contempt of all religion. To this odious class belonged one Gruet, who denied the divinity of the Christian religion, the immortality of the soul, the difference between moral good and evil, and rejected with disdain the doctrines that are held most sacred among Christians; for which impieties he was at last brought before the civil tribunal, in the year 1550, and condemned to death.

INGHAMITES,

A DENOMINATION of Calvinistic Dissenters, who are the followers of B. Ingham, Esq., who in the last century was a character of great note in the north of England. About the year 1735, Mr. Ingham was at Queen's College, with Mr. Hervey and other friends, but soon afterwards adopted the religious opinions and zeal of Wesley and Whitfield. We do not know the cause of his separation from these eminent men; but it seems in a few years afterwards he became the leader of numerous societies, distinct from the Methodists. They received their members by *lot*, and required them to declare before the church their *experience*, that the whole society might judge of the gracious change which had been wrought upon their hearts. It happened in a few years, that some individuals who were much respected, and who applied for admission, instead of speaking of their own attainments, or the comfortable impression on their minds, which they only considered as productive of strife and vainglory, declared their only hope was the finished work of Jesus Christ; as to themselves they were sensible of their own vileness. Such confessions as this threw the congregation into some confusion, which was considerably increased when they found that, on their having recourse as usual to the *lot*, that there were votes against their admission, which was considered as a rejection from the Lord. On this they were led to examine more particularly both their church order and doctrines. After this time, Mr. Ingham became much more orthodox in his sentiments, and new-modelled his churches. The book which he published is in general well thought of by the Independents. He contends very strongly for salvation by the imputation of Christ's righteousness; and as to doctrine, the chief point wherein the Inghamites differ from the Independents is respecting the Trinity. The common manner of speaking of the Divine Three as distinct persons, they decisively condemn. They do not consider a plurality of elders as necessary in a church to administer the Lord's Supper. In other respects they much esteem the writings of Mr. R. Sandeman. Their numbers have not been so numerous since they became more strict in their public worship.

HATTEMISTS.

THIS is the name of a modern Dutch sect, so called from Pontian Van Hattem, a minister in the province of Zealand, towards the close of the last century, who, being addicted to the sentiments of Spinosa, was on that account degraded from his pastoral office. The Verschorists and Hattemists resemble each other in their religious systems, though they never so entirely agreed as to form one communion. The founders of these sects deduced from the doctrine of absolute decrees a system of fatal and uncontrollable necessity; they denied the difference between moral good and evil, and the corruption of human nature; from whence they farther concluded, that mankind were under no sort of obligation to correct their manners, to improve their minds, or to obey the divine laws; that the whole of religion consisted not in acting, but in suffering; and that all the precepts of Jesus Christ are reducible to this one, *that we bear with cheerfulness and patience the*

36

events that happen to us through the divine will, and make it our constant and only study to maintain a permanent tranquillity of mind. Thus far they agreed; but the Hattemists further affirmed, that Christ made no expiation for the sins of men by his death; but had only suggested to us, by his mediation, that there was nothing in us that could offend the Deity: this, they say, was Christ's manner of justifying his servants, and presenting them blameless before the tribunal of God. It was one of their distinguished tenets, that God does not punish men *for* their sins, but *by* their sins. These two sects, says Mosheim, still subsist, though they no longer bear the name of their founders.

EUNOMIANS.

THE Eunomians were a sect in the fourth century. They were a branch of Arians, and took their name from Eunomius, bishop of Cyzicus. Cave, in his *Historia Literaria,* vol. i. p. 223, gives the following account of their faith: "There is one God, uncreated and without beginning; who has nothing existing before him, for nothing can exist before what is uncreated; nor with him, for what is uncreated must be one; nor in him, for God is a simple and uncompounded being. This one simple and eternal being is God, the creator and ordainer of all things: first, indeed, and principally of his only begotten Son; and then through him of all other things. For God begat, created, and made the Son only by his direct operation and power, before all things, and every other creature; not producing, however, any being like himself, or imparting any of his own proper substance to the Son; for God is immortal, uniform, indivisible; and therefore cannot communicate any part of his own proper substance to another. He alone is unbegotten; and it is impossible that any other being should be formed of an unbegotten substance. He did not use **his** own substance in begetting the Son, but his will only; nor did he beget him in the likeness of his substance, but according to his own good pleasure; he then created the Holy Spirit, the first and greatest of all spirits, by his own power, in deed and operation mediately; yet by the immediate power and operation of the Son. After the Holy Spirit, he created all other things, in heaven and in earth, visible and invisible, corporeal and incorporeal, mediately by himself, by the power and operation of the Son, &c." The reader will evidently see how near these tenets are to those of Arianism.

EUCHITES.

THE Euchites, or Euchitæ, were a sect of ancient heretics, who were first formed into a religious body towards the end of the fourth century, though their doctrine and discipline subsisted in Syria, Egypt, and other eastern countries, before the birth of Christ: they were thus called because they prayed without ceasing, imagining that prayer alone was sufficient to save them. They were a sort of mystics, who imagined, according to the oriental notion, that two souls resided in man, the one good and the other evil; and who were zealous in expelling the evil soul or demon, and hastening the return of the good Spirit of God by contemplation, prayer, and singing of hymns. They also embraced opinions nearly resembling the Manichean doctrine, and which they derived from the tenets of the oriental philosophy.   The same denomination was used in the twelfth century to denote certain fanatics who infested the Greek and Eastern churches, and who were charged with believing a double Trinity, rejecting wedlock, abstain ing from flesh, treating with contempt the sacraments of baptism and the Lord's Supper, and the various branches of external worship, and placing the essence of religion solely in external prayer; and maintaining the efficacy of perpetual supplications to the Supreme Being for expelling an evil being or genius, which dwelt in the breast of every mortal.   This sect is said to have been founded by a person called *Lucopetrus*, whose chief disciple was named *Tychicus*. By degrees it became a general and invidious appellation for persons of eminent piety, and zeal for genuine Christianity, who opposed the vicious practices and insolent tyranny of the priesthood, much in the same manner as the Latins comprehended all the adversaries of the Roman pontiff under the general terms of Albigenses and Waldenses.

EBIONITES,

The Ebionites were ancient heretics, who rose in the church in the very first age thereof, and formed themselves into a sect in the second century, denying the divinity of Jesus Christ.   Origen takes them to have been so called from the Hebrew word *ebion*, which in that languoge signifies *poor;* because, says he, they were poor in sense and wanting understanding.   Eusebius, with a view to the same etymology, is of opinion they were thus called, as having poor thoughts of Jesus Christ, taking him for no more than a mere man. It is more probable the Jews gave this appellation to the Christians in general out of contempt; because, in the first times, there were few but poor people that embraced the Christian religion.

The Ebionites were little else than a branch of the Nazarenes, only that they altered and corrupted, in many things, the purity of the faith held among the first adherents to Christianity. For this reason, Origen distinguishes two kinds of Ebionites in his answer to Celsus: the one believed that Jesus Christ was born of a virgin; and the other, that he was born after the manner of other men. The first were orthodox to everything, except that to the Christian doctrine they joined the ceremonies of the Jewish law, with the Jews, Samaritans, and Nazarenes, together with the traditions of the Pharisees. They differed from the Nazarenes, however, in several things, chiefly as to what regards the authority of the sacred writings; for the Nazarenes received all for Scripture contained in the Jewish canon; whereas the Ebionites rejected all the prophets, and held the very names of David, Solomon, Isaiah, Jeremiah, and Ezekiel, in abhorrence. They also rejected all St. Paul's epistles, whom they treated with the utmost disrespect. They received nothing of the Old Testament but the Pentateuch. They agreed with the Nazarenes, in using the Hebrew Gospel of St. Matthew, otherwise called the Gospel of the twelve apostles; but they corrupted their copy in abundance of places; and particularly had left out the genealogy of our Saviour, which was preserved entire in that of the Nazarenes, and even in those used by the Corinthians.

Besides the Hebrew Gospel of St. Matthew, the Ebionites had adopted several other books under the title of St. James, John, and the other apostles; they also made use

of the travels of St. Peter, which are supposed to have been
written by St. Clement; but had altered them so, that there
was scarce anything of truth left in them. They even made
that saint tell a number of falsehoods, the better to authorize their own practices.

DONATISTS.

THE Donatists were ancient schismatics, in Africa so
denominated from their leader, Donatus. They had their
origin in the year 311, when, in the room of Mensurius,
who died in that year, on his return to Rome, Cecilian was
elected bishop of Carthage, and consecrated, without the
concurrence of the Numidian bishops, by those of Africa
alone, whom the people refused to acknowledge, and to
whom they opposed Majorinus, who accordingly was ordained by Donatus, bishop of Casæ Nigræ.

They were condemned in a council held at Rome, two
years after their separation; and afterwards in another at
Arles, the year following; and again at Milan, before Constantine the Great, in 316, who deprived them of their
churches, and sent their seditious bishops into banishment,
and punished some of them with death. Their cause was
espoused by another Donatus, called the *Great*, the principal bishop of that sect, who, with numbers of his followers, was exiled by order of Constans. Many of them were
punished with great severity. However, after the accession
of Julian to the throne in 362, they were permitted to return, and restored to their former liberty.

Gratian published several edicts against them, and in 377
deprived them of their churches, and prohibited all their

assemblies. But, notwithstanding the severities they suffered, it appears that they had a very considerable number of churches towards the close of this century; but at this time they began to decline on account of a schism among themselves, occasioned by the election of two bishops in the room of Parmenian, the successor of Donatus: one party elected Primian, and were called *Primianists*; and another, Maximinian, and were called *Maximinianists*. Their decline was also precipitated by the zealous opposition of St. Augustine, and by the violent measures which were pursued against them by order of the emperor Honorius, at the solicitation of two councils held at Carthage, the one in 404, and the other in 411. Many of them were fined, their bishops were banished, and some put to death.

This sect revived and multiplied under the protection of the Vandals, who invaded Africa in 427, and took possession of this province; but it sunk again under new severities, when their empire was overturned, in 534. Nevertheless, they remained in a separate body till the close of this century, when Gregory, the Roman pontiff, used various methods for suppressing them: his zeal succeeded, and there are few traces to be found of the Donatists after this period. They were distinguished by other appellations, as *Circumcelliones*, *Montenses* or *Mountaineers*, *Campetes*, *Rupites*, &c. They held three councils, that of Cita in Numidia, and two at Carthage.

The Donatists, it is said, held that baptism conferred out of the church, that is, out of their sect, was null; and accordingly they re-baptized those who joined their party from other churches, they also re-ordained their ministers. Donatus seems likewise to have embraced the doctrine of the Arians; though St. Augustine affirms that the Donatists in this point kept clear of the errors of their leader.

DEISTS.

THE Deists are a class of people whose distinguishing character it is not to profess any particular form or system of religion, but only to acknowledge the existence of a God, and to follow the light and law of Nature, rejecting revelation and opposing Christianity. The name of Deists seems to have been first assumed as the denomination of a party, about the middle of the sixteenth century, by some gentlemen in France and Italy, who were desirous of thus disguising their opposition to Christianity by a more honorable appellation than that of atheists. Viret, an eminent reformer, mentions certain persons in his epistle dedicatory, prefixed to the second volume of his *Instruction Chrétienne*, published in 1553, who called themselves by a new name, that of Deists. These, he tells us, professed to believe in God, but showed no regard to Jesus Christ, and considered the doctrines of the apostles and evangelists as fables and dreams. He adds, that they laughed at all religion, though they outwardly conformed to the religion of those with whom they lived, or whom they wished to please, or feared to offend. Some, he observed, professed to believe the immortality of the soul; others denied both this doctrine and that of providence.

Many of them were considered as persons of acute and subtle genius, and took pains in disseminating their notions. The Deists hold that, considering the multiplicity of religions, the numerous pretences to revelation, and the precarious arguments generally advanced in proof thereof, the best and surest way is to return to the simplicity of nature, and the belief of one God; which is the only truth agreed to by all nations. They complain that the freedom of thinking and reasoning is oppressed under the yoke of religion, and that the minds of men are tyrannized over by the necessity imposed upon them of believing inconceivable mysteries ; and contend that nothing should be required to be assented to or believed but what their reason clearly conceives.

The distinguishing character of modern Deists is, that they discard all pretences to revelation as the effects of imposture or enthusiasm. They profess a regard for natural religion, though they are far from being agreed in their notions concerning it.

They are classed by some of their own writers into mortal and immortal Deists — the latter acknowledging a future state, and the former denying it, or representing it as very uncertain. Dr. Clarke distinguishes four sorts of Deists : 1. Those who pretend to believe the existence of an eternal, infinite, independent, intelligent Being, who made the world, without concerning himself in the government of it. 2. Those who believe the being and natural providence of God, but deny the difference of actions as morally good or evil, resolving it into the arbitrary constitution of human laws; and therefore they suppose that God takes no notice of them. With respect to both these classes, he observes, that their opinions can consistently terminate in nothing but downright atheism. 3. Those who, having right apprehensions concerning the nature, attributes, and all-governing providence of God, seem also to have some notion of his moral perfections; though they consider them as transcendant, and such in nature and degree, that we can form no true judgment, nor argue with any certainty concerning them ; but they deny the immortality of human souls, alleging that men perish at death, and that the present life is the whole of human existence. 4. Those who believe the existence, perfections, and providence of God, the obligations of natural religion, and a state of future retribution, on the evidence of the light of Nature, without a divine revelation; such as these, he says, are the only true Deists; but their principles, he apprehends, should lead them to embrace Christianity, and therefore he concludes that there is now no consistent scheme of Deism in the world.

The first Deistical writer of any note that appeared in England was Herbert, Baron of Cherbury. He lived and wrote in the seventeenth century. His book *De Veritate* was first published at Paris, in 1624. This, together with his book *De Causis Errorum*, and his treatise *De Religione Laici*, were afterwards published in London. His celebrated work, *De Religione Gentilium*, was published at Amsterdam, in 1663, in 4to., and in 1700 in 8vo.; and an English translation of it was published at London in 1705.

As he was one of the first that formed Deism into a system, and asserted the sufficiency, universality, and absolute perfection of natural religion, with a view to discard all extraordinary revelation as useless and needless, we shall subjoin the five fundamental articles of this universal religion. They are these: 1. There is one supreme God. 2. That he is chiefly to be worshipped. 3. That piety and virtue are the principal part of his worship. 4. That we must repent of our sins; and if we do so, God will pardon them. 5. That there are rewards for good men and punishments for bad men, both here and hereafter. A number of advocates have appeared in the same cause; and however they may have differed among themselves, they have been agreed in their attempts at invalidating the evidence and authority of divine revelation. We might mention Hobbes, Blount, Toland, Collins, Woolston, Tindal, Morgan, Chubb, Lord Bolingbroke, Hume, Gibbon, Paine, and some add Lord Shaftesbury to the number. Among foreigners, Voltaire, Rousseau, Condorcet, and many other celebrated French authors, have rendered themselves conspicuous by their Deistical writings. "But," as one observes, "the friends of Christianity have no reason to regret the free and unreserved discussion which their religion has undergone. Objections have been stated and urged in their full force, and as fully answered; arguments and raillery have been repelled; and the controversy between Christians and Deists has called forth a great number of excellent writers, who have illustrated both the doctrines and evidences of Christianity in a manner that will ever reflect honor on their names, and be of lasting service to the cause of genuine religion, and the best interests of mankind.

SUBLAPSARIANS.

SUBLAPSARIANS are those who hold that God permitted the first man to fall into transgression, without absolutely predetermining his fall; or that the decree of predestination regards man as fallen, by an abuse of that freedom which Adam had, into a state in which all were to be left to necessary and unavoidable ruin, who were not exempted from it by predestination.

SUPRALAPSARIANS.

THE Supralapsarians are persons who hold that God, without any regard to the good or evil works of men, has resolved, by an eternal decree, *supra lapsum*, antecedently to any knowledge of the fall of Adam, and independently of it, to save some and reject others: or, in other words, that God intended to glorify his justice in the condemnation of some, as well as his mercy in the salvation of others; and for that purpose, decreed that Adam should necessarily fall.

Dr. Gill gives us the following account of Supralapsarianism. The question which he proposes to discuss, is, " Whether men were considered in the mind of God in the decree of election as fallen or unfallen, as in the corrupt mass through the fall, or in the pure mass of creatureship, previous to it, and as to be created?" There are some who think that the latter, so considered, were the objects of election in the divine mind. These are called Supralapsarians, though of these some are of opinion that man was considered as to be created or creatable, and others as created but not fallen. The former seems best, that of the vast number of individuals which came up in the divine mind whom his power could create, those whom he meant to bring into being he designed to glorify himself by them in some way or other. The decree of election respecting any part of them may be distinguished into the decree of the end and the decree of the means. The decree of the end respecting some is either subordinate to their eternal happiness, or ultimate, which is more properly the end, the glory of God; and if both are put together, it is a state of everlasting communion with God, for the glorifying of the riches of his grace. The decree of the means includes the decree to create men to permit them to fall, to recover them out of it through redemption by Christ, to sanctify them by the grace of the Spirit, and completely save them; and which are not to be reckoned as materially many decrees, but as making one formal decree; or they are not to be considered as subordinate, but as co-ordinate means, and as making up one entire complete medium: for it is not to be supposed that God decreed to create man, that he might permit him to fall, in order to redeem, sanctify, and save him; but he decreed all this that he might glorify his grace, mercy, and justice. And in this way of considering the decrees of God, they think that they sufficiently obviate and remove the slanderous calumny cast upon them with respect to the other branch of predestination, which leaves men in the same state when others are chosen, and that for the glory of God. Which calumny is that, according to them, God made man to damn him; whereas, according to their real sentiments, God decreed to make man, and made man neither to damn him nor save him, but for his own glory, which end is answered in them some way or other. Again, they argue that the end is first in view before the means, and the decree of the end is, in order of nature, before the decree of the means; and what is first in intention, is last in execution. Now, as the glory of God is last in execution, it must be first in intention, wherefore men must be considered in the decree of the end as not yet created and fallen; since the creation and permission of sin belong to the decree of the means, which in order of nature is after the decree of the end. And they add to this, that if God first decreed to create man, and suffered him to fall, and then out of the fall chose some to grace and glory, he must decree to create man without an end, which is to make

God to do what no wise man would; for when a man is about to do anything, he proposes an end, and then contrives and fixes on ways and means to bring about that end. They think also that this way of conceiving and speaking of these things best expresses the sovereignty of God in them, as declared in the 9th of Romans, where he is said to will such and such things, for no other reason but because he wills them.

The opponents of this doctrine consider, however, that it is attended with insuperable difficulties. We demand, say they, an explanation of what they mean by this principle, " God hath made all things for his own glory." If they mean that justice requires a creature to devote himself to the worship and glorifying of his Creator, we grant it; if they mean that the attributes of God are displayed in all his works, we grant this too; but if the proposition be intended to affirm that God had no other view in creating men, so to speak, than his own interest, we deny the proposition, and affirm that God created men for their own happiness, and in order to have subjects upon whom he might bestow favors.

We desire to be informed, in the next place, say they, how it can be conceived that a determination to damn millions of men can contribute to the glory of God? We easily conceive that it is for the glory of divine justice to punish guilty men: but to resolve to damn men without the consideration of sin, to create them that they might sin, to determine that they should sin in order to their destruction, is what seems to us more likely to tarnish the glory of God than to display it.

Again, we demand how, according to this hypothesis, it can be conceived that God is not the author of sin? In the general scheme of our churches, God only permits men to sin, and it is the abuse of liberty that plunges man into misery: even this principle, all lenified as it seems, is yet subject to a great number of difficulties; but in this scheme God wills sin to produce the end he proposed in creating the world, and it was necessary that men should sin: God created them for that. If this be not to make God the author of sin, we must renounce the most distinct and clear ideas.

Again, we require them to reconcile this system with many express declarations of Scripture, which inform us that *God would have all men to be saved.* How doth it agree with such pressing entreaties, such cutting reproofs, such tender expostulations, as God discovers in regard to the unconverted? Matt. xxiii. 37.

Lastly, we desire to know, how is it possible to conceive a God, who being in the actual enjoyment of perfect happiness, incomprehensible and supreme, could determine to add this decree, though useless to his felicity, to create men without number for the purpose of confining them for ever in the chains of darkness, and burning them for ever in unquenchable flames.

RELLYANISTS.

The Rellyanists, or Rellyan Universalists are the followers of Mr. James Relly. He first commenced his ministerial character in connection with Mr. Whitefield, and was received with great popularity. Upon a change of his views, he encountered reproach, and was pronounced by many as an enemy to godliness. He believed that Christ, as a Mediator, was so united to mankind, that his actions were theirs, his obedience and sufferings theirs;

and, consequently, that he has as fully restored the whole
human race to the divine favor, as if all had obeyed and
suffered in their own persons; and upon this persuasion
he preached a finished salvation, called by the apostle
Jude, " The common salvation."

Many of his followers are removed to the world of
spirits, but a branch still survives. They are not observers
of ordinances, such as water-baptism and the sacrament;
professing to believe only in one baptism, which they call
an immersion of the mind or conscience into truth by the
teaching of the Spirit of God; and by the same Spirit
they are enabled to feed on Christ as the bread of life,
professing that in and with Jesus they possess all things.
They inculcate and maintain good works for necessary
purposes; but contend that the principal and only work
which ought to be attended to, is the doing of real good
without religious ostentation; that to relieve the miseries
and distresses of mankind, according to our ability, is
doing more real good than the superstitious observance of
religious ceremonies.

In general, they appear to believe that there will be a
resurrection to life, and a resurrection to condemnation; that
believers only will be among the former, who as first fruits,
and kings and priests, will have part in the first resurrection, and shall reign with Christ in his kingdom of the
millennium; that unbelievers who are after raised, must
wait the manifestation of the Saviour of the world, under
that condemnation of conscience which a mind in darkness
and wrath must necessarily feel; that believers, called
kings and priests, will be made the medium of communication to their condemned brethren, and like Joseph to his
brethren, though he spoke roughly to them, in reality over-
flowed with affection and tenderness; that ultimately every
knee shall bow, and every tongue confess that in the Lord

they have righteousness and strength; and thus every enemy shall be subdued to the kingdom and glory of the Great Mediator. A Mr. Murray belonging to this society emigrated to America, and preached these sentiments at Boston and elsewhere. Mr. Relly published several works, the principal of which were, "Union," "The Trial of Spirits," "Christian Liberty," "One Baptism," "The Salt of Sacrifice," "Antichrist Resisted," "Letters on Universal Salvation," "The Cherubimical Mystery."

MONOPHYSITES.

MONOPHYSITES is (from μονος, *solus*, and φυσις, *natura*,) a general name given to all those sectaries in the Levant who only own one nature in Jesus Christ; and who maintain that the divine and human nature of Jesus Christ were so united as to form only one nature, yet without any change, confusion, or mixture of the two natures.

The *Monophysites*, however, properly so called, are the followers of Severus, a learned monk of Palestine, who was created patriarch of Antioch, in 513, and Petrus Fullensis.

The Monophysites were encouraged by the emperor Anastasius, but suppressed by Justin and succeeding emperors. However, this sect was restored by Jacob Baradæus, an obscure monk, insomuch that when he died bishop of Edessa, A. D. 588, he left it in a most flourishing state in Syria, Mesopotamia, Armenia, Egypt, Nubia, Abyssinia, and other countries. The laborious efforts of Jacob were seconded in Egypt and the adjacent countries by Theodosius, bishop of Alexandria; and he became so

famous, that all the Monophysites of the East considered
him as their second parent and founder, and are to this
day called *Jacobites*, in honor of their new chief.

The Monophysites are divided into two sects or parties,
the one African and the other Asiatic; at the head of the
latter is the patriarch of Antioch, who resides for the most
part in the monastery of St. Athanias, near the city of Mer-
din; the former are under the jurisdiction of the patriarch
of Alexandria, who generally resides at Grand Cairo, and
are subdivided into Cophts and Abyssinians.   From the
fifteenth century downwards, all the patriarchs of the
Monophysites have taken the name of *Ignatius*, in order
to show that they are the lineal successors of Ignatius,
who was bishop of Antioch in the first century, and con
sequently the lawful patriarch of Antioch.   In the seventeenth century, a small body of Monophysites, in Asia,
abandoned for some time the doctrine and institution of
their ancestors, and embraced the communion of Rome;
but the African Monophysites, notwithstanding that
poverty and ignorance which exposed them to the seduc-
tions of sophistry and gain, stood firm in their principles,
and made an obstinate resistance to the promises, presents,
and attempts employed by the papal missionaries to bring
them under the Roman yoke; and in the eighteenth century, those of Asia and Africa have persisted in their
refusal to enter into the communion of the Romish church,
notwithstanding the earnest entreaties and alluring offers
that have been made from time to time by the pope's
legates, to conquer their inflexible constancy.

MONOTHELITES.

MONOTHELITES, (compounded of μονος, "single," and and θελημα, θελω, volo, "I will,") an ancient sect, which sprung out of the Eutychians; thus called, as only allowing of one will in Jesus Christ.

The opinion of the Monothelites had its rise in 630, and had the emperor Heraclius for an adherent; it was the same with that of the acephalous Severians. They allowed of two wills in Christ, considered with regard to the two natures; but reduced them to one by reason of the union of the two natures, thinking it absurd that there should be two free wills in one and the same person. They were condemned by the sixth general council in 680, as being supposed to destroy the perfection of the humanity of Jesus Christ, depriving it of will and operation. Their sentiments were afterwards embraced by the Maronites.

CARMATHITES.

CARMATHITES, the followers of a noted impostor in the ninth century, who endeavored to overthrow all the foundations of Mussulmanism. Carmath their prophet was a person of great austerity of life; and said that God had commanded him to pray not *five* times, with the Mussulmans, but *fifty* times a day. To comply with this, they often neglected their business; they ate many things forbidden by the law of Mahomet, and believed that angels were their guides in all their actions, and that the demons or ghosts are their enemies.

SADDUCEES.

THE Sadducees were a famous sect among the Jews; so called, it is said, from their founder Sadoc. It began in the time of Antigonus, of Socho, president of the Sanhedrim at Jerusalem, and teacher of the law in the principal divinity school of that city. Antigonus having often, in his lectures, inculcated to his scholars that they ought not to serve God in a servile manner, but only out of filial love and fear, two of his scholars, Sadoc and Baithus, thence inferred that there were no rewards at all after this life; and, therefore, separating from the school of their master, they thought there was no resurrection nor future state, neither angel nor spirit, Matt. xii. 23; Acts xxiii. 8. They seem to agree greatly with the Epicureans; differing, however, in this, that though they denied a future state, yet they allowed the power of God to create the world; whereas the followers of Epicurus denied it. It is said also, they rejected the Bible, except the Pentateuch; denied predestination; and taught that God had made man absolute master of all his actions, without assistance to good, or restraint from evil.

SAMARITANS.

THE Samaritans were an ancient sect among the Jews, whose origin was in the time of King Rehoboam, under whose reign the people of Israel were divided into two distinct kingdoms, that of Judah and that of Israel. The capital of the kingdom of Israel was Samaria, whence the

Israelites took the name of Samaritans. Shalmaneser, king of Assyria, having besieged and taken Samaria, carried away all the people captives into the remotest parts of his dominions, and filled their place with Babylonians, Cutheans, and other idolaters. These, finding that they were exposed to wild beasts, desired that an Israelitish priest might be sent among them to instruct them in the ancient religion and customs of the land they inhabited. This being granted them, they were delivered from the plague of wild beasts, and embraced the law of Moses, with which they mixed a great part of their ancient idolatry. Upon the return of the Jews from the Babylonish captivity, it appears that they had entirely quitted the worship of their idols. But though they were united in religion, they were not so in affection with the Jews; for they employed various calumnies and stratagems to hinder their rebuilding the temple of Jerusalem; and when they could not prevail, they erected a temple on Mount Gerizim in opposition to that on Jerusalem. See 2 Kings xvii.; Ezra iv., v., vi. The Samaritans at present are few in number, but pretend to great strictness in their observation of the law of Moses. They are said to be scattered; some at Damascus, some at Gaza, and some at Grand Cairo, in Egypt.

MELCHITES.

MELCHITES, the name given to the Syriac, Egyptian, and other Christians of the Levant. The Melchites, excepting some few points of little or no importance, which relate only to ceremonies and ecclesiastical discipline, are, in every respect, professed Greeks; but they are governed by a particular patriarch, who assumes the title of Patriarch of Antioch. They celebrate mass in the Arabian language. The religious among the Melchites follow the rule of St. Basil, the common rule of all the Greek monks.

CERINTHIANS.

THE Cerinthians were ancient heretics, who denied the deity of Jesus Christ; so named from Cerinthus. They believed that he was a mere man, the son of Joseph and Mary; but that in his baptism a celestial virtue descended on him in the form of a dove; by means whereof he was consecrated by the Holy Spirit, made Christ, and wrought so many miracles; that, as he received it from heaven, it quitted him after his passion, and returned to the place whence it came; so that Jesus, whom they called a *pure man*, really died and rose again; but that Christ, who was distinguished from Jesus, did not suffer at all. It was partly to refute this sect that St. John wrote his Gospel They received the Gospel of St. Matthew, to countenance their doctrine of circumcision; but they omitted the genealogy. They discarded the epistles of St. Paul, because that apostle held circumcision abolished.

LUCIANISTS.

LUCIANISTS, or Lucanists, a sect so called from Lucianus, or Lucanus, a heretic of the second century, being a disciple of Marcion, whose errors he followed, adding some new ones to them. Epiphanius says he abandoned Mar cion, teaching that people ought not to marry, for fear of enriching the Creator; and yet other authors mention, that he held this error in common with Marcion and other Gnostics. He denied the immortality of the soul, asserting it to be material.

There was another sect of Lucianists, who appeared some time after the Arians. They taught that the Father had been a Father always, and that he had the name even before he had begot the Son, as having in him the power and faculty of generation; and in this manner they accounted for the eternity of the Son.

LUCIFERIANS.

LUCIFERIANS, a sect who adhered to the schism of Lucifer, Bishop of Cagliari, in the fourth century, who was banished by the Emperor Constantius, for having defended the Nicene doctrine concerning the three persons in the Godhead. It is said also that they believed the soul to be corporeal, and to be transmitted from the father to the children. The Luciferians were numerous in Gaul, Spain, Egypt, &c. The occasion of this schism was, that Lucifer would not allow any acts he had done to be abolished. There were but two Luciferian bishops, but a great number of priests and deacons. The Luciferians bore a great aversion to the Arians.

GALILEANS.

THE Galileans were a sect of the Jews which arose in Judea, some years after the birth of our Saviour. They sprang from one Judas, a native of Gaulam, in Upper Galilee, upon the occasion of Augustus appointing the people to be mustered, which they looked upon as an instance of servitude which all true Israelites ought to oppose. They pretended that God alone should be owned as master and lord, and in other respects were of the opinion of the Pharisees; but as they judged it unlawful to pray for infidel princes, they separated themselves from the rest of the Jews, and performed their sacrifices apart. As our Saviour and his apostles were of Galilee, they were suspected to be of the sect of the Galileans; and it was on this principle, as St. Jerome observes, that the Pharisees laid a snare for him, asking, Whether it were lawful to give tribute to Cæsar? that in case he denied it, they might have an occasion of accusing him.

SABELLIANS.

THE Sabellians were a sect in the third century that embraced the opinions of Sabellius, a philosopher of Egypt, who openly taught that there is but one person in the Godhead.

The Sabellians maintained that the Word and the Holy Spirit are only virtues, emanations, or functions of the Deity; and held that he who is in heaven is the Father of all things; that he descended into the Virgin, became a child, and was born of her as a son; and that, having accomplished the mystery of our salvation, he diffused himself on the apostles in tongues of fire, and was then enominated the *Holy Ghost*. This they explained by mparing God to the sun; the illuminated virtue or quality of which was the Word, and its warming virtue the Holy Spirit. The Word, they taught, was darted, like a divine ray, to accomplish the work of redemption; and that, being re-ascended to heaven, the influences of the Father were communicated after a like manner to the apostles.

MATERIALISTS.

THE Materialists were a sect in the ancient church, composed of persons who, being prepossessed with that maxim in philosophy, "*ex nihilo nihil fit*," out of nothing nothing can arise, had recourse to an eternal matter, on which they supposed God wrought in the creation, instead of admitting Him alone as the sole cause of the existence of all things. Tertullian vigorously opposed them in his treatise against Hermogenes, who was one of their number.

Materialists are also those who maintain that the soul of man is material, or that the principle of perception and thought is not a substance distinct from the body, but the result of corporeal organization. There are others called by this name, who have maintained that there is nothing but matter in the universe.

The followers of the late Dr. Priestley are considered as Materialists, or Philosophical Necessarians. According to the doctor's writing, he believed—

38

1. That man is no more than what we now see of him; his being commences at the time of his conception, or perhaps at an earlier period. The corporeal and mental faculties, inhering in the same substance, grow, ripen, and decay together; and whenever the system is dissolved, it continues in a state of dissolution, till it shall please that Almighty Being, who called it into existence, to restore it to life again. For if the mental principle were, in its own nature, immaterial and immortal, all its peculiar faculties would be so too; whereas we see that every faculty of the mind, without exception, is liable to be impaired, and even to become wholly extinct, before death. Since, therefore, all the faculties of the mind, separately taken, appear to be mortal, the substance, or principle, in which they exist, must be pronounced mortal too. Thus we might conclude that the body was mortal, from observing that all the separate senses and limbs were liable to decay and perish.

This system gives a real value to the doctrine of the resurrection from the dead, which is peculiar to revelation; on which alone the sacred writers build all our hope of future life; and it explains the uniform language of the Scriptures, which speak of one day of judgment for all mankind, and represent all the rewards of virtue, and all the punishments of vice, as taking place at that awful day, and not before. In the Scriptures the heathens are represented as without hope, and all mankind as perishing at death, if there be no resurrection of the dead.

The Apostle Paul asserts, in 1 Cor. xv. 16, that *if the dead rise not, then is not Christ risen; and if Christ be not raised, your faith is vain, ye are yet in your sins: then they also who are fallen asleep in Christ are perished.* And again, verse 32: *If the dead rise not, let us eat and drink, for to-morrow we die.* In the whole discourse, he does not even mention the doctrine of happiness or misery without the body.

If we search the Scriptures for passages expressive of the state of man at death, we find such declarations as expressly exclude any trace of sense, thought, or enjoyment. See Ps. vi. 5; Job xiv. 7, etc.

2. That there is some fixed law of nature respecting the will, as well as the other powers of the mind, and everything else in the constitution of nature; and consequently that it is never determined without some real or apparent cause foreign to itself; *i. e.*, without some motive or choice; or that motives influence us in some definite and invariable manner, so that every volition, or choice, is constantly regulated and determined by what precedes it; and this constant determination of mind, according to the motives presented to it, is what is meant by its *necessary determination.* This being admitted to be the fact, there will be a necessary connection between all things past, present, and to come, in the way of proper cause and effect, as much in the intellectual as in the natural world; so that, according to the established laws of nature, no event could have been otherwise than it *has been* or *is to be,* and therefore all things past, present, and to come, are precisely what the Author of Nature really intended them to be, and has made provision for.

To establish this conclusion, nothing is necessary but that, throughout all nature, the same consequences should invariably result from the same circumstances. For, if this be admitted, it will necessarily follow, that at the commencement of any system, since the several parts of it and their respective situations were appointed by the Deity, the first change would take place according to a certain rule established by himself, the result of which would be a new situation; after which the same laws continuing, another change would succeed, according to the same rules, and so on forever; every new situation invariably leading to another, and every event, from the commencement to the termination of the system, being strictly connected; so that, unless the fundamental laws of the system were changed, it would be impossible that any event should have been otherwise than it was. In all these cases, the circumstances preceding any change are called the causes of that change; and since a determinate event or effect constantly follows certain circumstances or causes, the connection between cause and effect is concluded to be invariable, and therefore necessary.

It is universally acknowledged, that there can be no effect without an adequate cause. This is even the foundation on which the only proper argument for the being of a God rests. And the Necessarian asserts that if, in any given state of mind, with respect both to dispositions and motives, two different determinations, or volitions, be possible, it can be on no other principle than that one of them should come under the description of an effect without a cause; just as if the beam of balance might incline either way, though loaded with equal weights. And if anything whatever, even a thought in the mind of man, could arise without an adequate cause, anything else, the mind itself, or the whole universe, might likewise exist without an adequate cause.

This scheme of philosophical necessity implies a chain of causes and effects established by infinite wisdom, and terminating in the greatest good of the whole universe; evils of all kinds, natural and moral, being admitted, as far as they contribute to that end, or are in the nature of things inseparable from it. Vice is productive not of good, but of evil to us, both here and hereafter, though good may result from it to the whole system; and according to the fixed laws of nature, our present and future happiness necessarily depend on our cultivating good dispositions.

This scheme of philosophical necessity is distinguished from the Calvinistic doctrine of predestination in the following particulars:

1. No Necessarian supposes that any of the human race will suffer eternally, but that future punishments will answer the same purpose as temporal ones are found to do; all of which tend to good, and are evidently admitted for that purpose. Upon the doctrine of necessity, also, the most indifferent actions of men are equally necessary with the most important; since every volition, like any other effect, must have an adequate cause depending upon the previous state of the mind, and the influence to which it is exposed.

2. The Necessarian believes that his own dispositions and actions are the necessary and sole means of his present and future happiness; so that, in the most proper sense of the words, it depends entirely on himself whether he be virtuous or vicious, happy or miserable.

3. The Calvinistic system entirely excludes the popular notion of free will, viz.: the liberty or power of doing what we please, virtuous or vicious, as belonging to every person, in every situation; which is perfectly consistent with the doctrine of philosophical necessity, and indeed results from it.

4 The Necessarian believes nothing of the posterity of Adam's sinning in him, and of their being liable to the wrath of God on that account; or the necessity of an infinite Being making atonement for them by suffering in their stead, and thus making the Deity propitious to them. He believes nothing of all the actions of any man being necessarily sinful; but, on the contrary, thinks that the very worst of men are capable of benevolent intentions in

many things that they do; and likewise that very good men are capable of falling from virtue, and consequently of sinking into final perdition. Upon the principles of the Necessarian, also, all late repentance, and especially after long and confirmed habits of vice, is altogether and necessarily ineffectual; there not being sufficient time left to produce a change of disposition and character, which can only be done by a change of conduct of proportionably long continuance.

In short, the three doctrines of Materialism, Philosophical Necessity, and Socinianism, are considered as equally. parts of one system. The scheme of Necessity is the immediate result of the materiality of man; for mechanism is the undoubted consequence of materialism, and that man is wholly material, is eminently subservient to the proper or mere humanity of Christ. For if no man have a soul distinct from his body, Christ, who in all other respects appeared as a man, could not have a soul which had existed before his body; and the whole doctrine of the pre-existence of souls, of which the opinion of the pre-existence of Christ is a branch, will be effectually overturned.

JACOBITES.

THE Jacobites are a sect of Christians in Syria and Mesopotamia; so called, either from Jacob, a Syrian, who lived in the reign of the Emperor Mauritius, or from one Jacob, a monk, who flourished in the year 550.

The Jacobites are of two sects, some following the rites of the Latin church, and others continuing separated from the church of Rome. There is also a division among the latter, who have two rival patriarchs. As to their belief, they hold but one nature in Jesus Christ; with respect to purgatory, and prayers for the dead, they are of the same opinion with the Greeks and other eastern Christians. They consecrate unleavened bread at the eucharist, and are against confession, believing that it is not of divine institution.

JANSENISTS.

THE Jansenists were a sect of the Roman Catholics in France, who followed the opinions of Jansenius (bishop of Ypres, and doctor of divinity of the universities of Louvain and Douay,) in relation to grace and predestination.

In the year 1640, the two universities just mentioned, and particularly father Molina and father Leonard Celsus, thought fit to condemn the opinions of the Jesuits on grace and free-will. This having set the controversy on foot, Jansenius opposed to the doctrine of the Jesuits the sentiments of St. Augustine, and wrote a treatise on grace, which he intituled *Augustinus*. This treatise was attacked by the Jesuits, who accused Jansenius of maintaining dangerous and heretical opinions; and afterwards, in 1642, obtained of pope Urban VIII. a formal condemnation of the treatise written by Jansenius; when the partisans of Jansenius gave out that this bull was spurious, and composed by a person entirely devoted to the Jesuits. After the death of Urban VIII., the affair of Jansenism began to be more warmly controverted, and gave birth to a great number of polemical writings concerning grace; and what occasioned some mirth, were the titles which each party gave to their writings: one writer published the *Torch of*

St. Augustine ; another found *Snuffers for St. Augustine's Torch ;* and father Veron formed *A Gag for the Jansenists,* &c. In the year 1650, sixty-eight bishops of France subscribed a letter to pope Innocent X., to obtain an inquiry into and condemnation of the five following propositions, extracted from Jansenius's Augustinus. 1. Some of God's commandments are impossible to be observed by the righteous, even though they endeavor with all their power to accomplish them. 2. In the state of corrupted nature, we are incapable of resisting inward grace. 3. Merit and demerit, in a state of corrupted nature, do not depend on a liberty which excludes necessity, but on a liberty which excludes constraint. 4. The Semipelagians admitted the necessity of an inward preventing grace for the performance of each particular act, even for the beginning of faith; but they were heretics in maintaining that this grace was of such a nature that the will of man was able either to resist or obey it. 5. It is Semipelagianism to say that Jesus Christ died, or shed his blood, for all mankind in general.

In the year 1652, the pope appointed a congregation for examining into the dispute relative to grace. In this congregation Jansenius was condemned; and the bull of condemnation, published in May, 1653, filled all the pulpits in Paris with violent outcries and alarms against the Jansenists. In the year 1656, pope Alexander VII. issued another bull, in which he condemned the five propositions of Jansenius. However, the Jansenists affirmed that these propositions were not to be found in this book; but that some of his enemies having caused them to be printed on a sheet, inserted them in the book, and thereby deceived the pope. At last Clement XI. put an end to the dispute by his constitution of July 17, 1705, in which, after having recited the constitutions of his predecessors in relation to this affair, he declared, " That, in order to pay a proper obedience to the papal constitutions concerning the present question, it is necessary to receive them with a respectful silence." The clergy of Paris, the same year, approved and accepted this bull, and none dared to oppose it. This is the famous bull *Unigenitus*, so called from its beginning with the words *Unigenitus Dei Filius*, &c., which has occasioned so much confusion in France.

It was not only on account of their embracing the doctrines of Augustine that the Jesuits were so embittered against them; but that which offended the Jesuits, and the other creatures of the Roman pontiff, was their strict piety and severe moral discipline. The Jansenists cried out against the corruptions of the church of Rome, and complained that neither its doctrines nor morals retained any traces of their former purity. They reproached the clergy with an universal depravation of sentiments and manners, and an entire forgetfulness of the dignity of their character and the duties of their vocation; they censured the licentiousness of the monastic orders, and insisted upon the necessity of reforming their discipline according to the rules of sanctity, abstinence, and self-denial, that were originally prescribed by their respective founders. They maintained, also, that the people ought to be carefully instructed in all the doctrines and precepts of Christianity; and that, for this purpose, the Holy Scriptures and public liturgies should be offered to their perusal in their mother tongue; and, finally, they looked upon it as a matter of the highest moment to persuade all Christians that true piety did not consist in the observance of pompous rites, or in the performance of external acts of devotion, but in inward holiness and divine love.

Notwithstanding the above-mentioned sentiments, the

Jansenists have been accused of superstition and fanaticism; and, on account of their severe discipline and practice, have been denominated *Rigorists*. It is said that they made repentance consist chiefly in those voluntary sufferings which the transgressor inflicted upon himself, in proportion to the nature of his crimes and the degree of his guilt. They tortured and macerated their bodies by painful labor, excessive abstinence, continual prayer, and contemplation; nay, they carried these austerities, it is said, to so high a pitch, as to place merit in them, and to consider those as the *sacred victims of repentance* who had gradually put an end to their days by their excessive abstinence and labor. Dr. Haweis, however, in his Church History, (vol. iii. p. 46,) seems to form a more favorable opinion of them. "I do not," says he, "readily receive the accusations that Papists or Protestants have objected to them as over-rigorous and fanatic in their devotion; but I will admit many things might be blameable; a tincture of popery might drive them to push monkish austerities too far, and secretly to place some merit in mortification, which they in general disclaimed; yet, with all that can be said, surely the root of the matter was in them. When I read Jansenius, or his disciples Pascal or Quesnel, I bow before such distinguished excellencies, and confess them my brethren; shall I say my fathers? Their principles are pure and evangelical; their morals founded upon the apostles and prophets; and their zeal to amend and convert, blessed with eminent success '

FRENCH PROPHETS.

They first appeared in Dauphiny and Vivarais. In the year 1688, five or six hundred Protestants of both sexes gave themselves out to be prophets, and inspired of the Holy Ghost. They soon became so numerous, that there were many thousands of them inspired. They were people of all ages and sexes without distinction, though the greatest part of them were boys and girls from six or seven to twenty-five years of age. They had strange fits, which came upon them with tremblings and faintings as in a swoon, which made them stretch out their arms and legs, and stagger several times before they dropped down. They struck themselves with their hands, they fell on their backs, shut their eyes, and heaved with their breasts. They remained a while in trances, and, coming out of them with twitchings, uttered all which came in their mouths. They said they saw the heavens open, the angels, paradise, and hell. Those who were just on the point of receiving the spirit of prophecy, dropped down not only in the assemblies, crying out *mercy*, but in the fields, and in their own houses. The least of their assemblies made up four or five hundred, and some of them amounted to even three or four thousand persons. When the prophets had for a while been under agitations of body, they began to prophesy. The burden of their prophecies was—*Amend your lives; repent ye: the end of all things draws nigh!* The hills resounded with their loud cries for mercy, and imprecations against the priests, the church, the pope, and against the anti-christian dominion, with predictions of the approaching fall of popery. All they said at these times was heard and received with reverence and awe

In the year 1706, three or four of these prophets come
over into England, and brought their prophetic spirit along
with them, which discovered itself in the same ways and
manners, by ecstacies, and agitations, and inspirations
under them, as it had done in France; and they propagated the like spirit to others, so that before the year was
out, there were two or three hundred of these prophets in
and about London, of both sexes, of all ages, men, women,
and children; and they had delivered, under inspiration,
four or five hundred prophetic warnings.

The great things they pretended by their spirit was, to
give warning of the *near approach of the kingdom of God,
the happy times of the church, the millennium state.* Their
message was (and they were to proclaim it as heralds to the
Jews, and every nation under heaven, beginning at England), that the grand jubilee, the acceptable year of the
Lord, the accomplishment of those numerous Scriptures
concerning the *new heaven* and the *new earth,* the *kingdom
of the Messiah,* the *marriage of the Lamb,* the *first resurrection,* or *the new Jerusalem descending from above,* were
now even at the door; that this great operation was to be
wrought on the part of man by spiritual arms only, proceeding from the mouths of those who should, by inspiration, or the mighty gift of the Spirit, be sent forth in great
numbers; to labor in the vineyard; that this mission of his
servants should be witnessed to by signs and wonders from
heaven, by a deluge of judgments on the wicked universally
throughout the world, as famine, pestilence, earthquakes,
&c.; that the extermination angels shall root out the tares,
and there shall remain upon the earth only good corn; and
the works of men being thrown down, there shall be but
one Lord, one faith, one heart, one voice among mankind.
They declared that all the great things they spoke of would

be manifest over the whole earth within the term of three years.

These prophets also pretended to the gift of languages, of discerning the secrets of the heart, the gift of ministration of the same spirit to others by the laying on of the hands, and the gift of healing. To prove they were really inspired by the Holy Ghost, they alleged the complete joy and satisfaction they experienced, the spirit of prayer, which was poured forth upon them, and the answer of their prayer to God.

CIRCONCELLIONES.

THE Circoncelliones were a species of fanatics, so called because they were continually rambling round the houses in the country. They took their rise among the Donatists, in the reign of the Emperor Constantine. It is incredible what ravages and cruelties they committed in Africa, through a long series of years. They were illiterate, savage peasants, who understood only the Punic language.

Intoxicated with a barbarous zeal, they renounced agriculture, professed continence, and assumed the title of "Vindicators of justice, and protectors of the oppressed." To accomplish their mission, they enfranchised slaves, scoured the roads, forced masters to alight from their chariots, and run before their slaves, whom they obliged to mount in their place; and discharged debtors, killing the creditors if they refused to cancel their bonds. But the chief objects of their cruelty were the Catholics, and especially those who had renounced Donatism.

At first, they used no swords, because God had forbidden

the use of one to Peter; but they were armed with clubs, which they called the *clubs of Israel*, and which they handled in such a manner as to break a man's bones without killing him immediately, so that he languished a long time, and then died. When they took away a man's life at once, they looked upon it as a favor. They became less scrupulous afterwards, and made use of all sorts of arms. Their shout was, *Praise be to God*. These words in their mouths were the signal of slaughter, more terrible than the roaring of a lion. They had invented an unheard-of punishment, which was, to cover with lime, diluted with vinegar, the eyes of those unhappy wretches whom they had crushed with blows and covered with wounds, and to abandon them in that condition.

Never was a stronger proof of what horrors superstition can beget in minds destitute of knowledge and humanity. These brutes, who had made a vow of chastity, gave themselves up to wine, and all sorts of impurities; running about with women and young girls as drunk as themselves, whom they called *sacred virgins*, and who often carried proofs of their incontinence. Their chief took the name of *chief of the saints*. After having glutted themselves with blood, they turned their rage upon themselves, and sought death with the same fury with which they gave it to others. Some scrambled up to the tops of rocks, and cast themselves down headlong in multitudes; others burned themselves, or threw themselves into the sea.

Those who proposed to acquire the title of martyrs, published it long before; upon which they were feasted and fattened like oxen for the slaughter: after these preparations, they set out to be destroyed. Sometimes they gave money to those whom they met, and threatened to murder them if they did not make them martyrs.

Theodoret gives an account of a stout young man, who,

meeting with a troop of these fanatics, consented to kill them, provided he might bind them first; and having by this means put it out of their power to defend themselves, whipped them as long as he was able, and then left them tied in that manner. Their bishops pretended to blame them, but in reality made use of them to intimidate such as might be tempted to forsake their sect; they even honored them as saints. They were not, however, able to govern these furious monsters; and more than once found themselves under the necessity of abandoning them, and even of imploring the assistance of the secular power against them.

The Counts Ursacius and Taurinus were employed to quell them; they destroyed a great number of them, of whom the Donatists made as many martyrs. Ursacius, who was a Catholic, and a religious man, having lost his life in an engagement with the barbarians, the Donatists did not fail to triumph in his death, as an effect of the vengeance of heaven. Africa was the theatre of these bloody scenes during a great part of Constantine's life.

COPHTS

COPHTI, Cophts, or Copti, a name given to the Christians of Egypt who are of the sect of the Jacobites. The Cophts have a patriarch, who resides at Cairo; but he takes his title from Alexandria. He has no archbishop under him, but eleven or twelve bishops. The rest of the clergy, whether secular or regular, are composed of the orders of St. Anthony, St. Paul, St. Macarius, who have each their monasteries. Besides the orders of priests, deacons, and sub-deacons, the Cophts have likewise archi-mandrites, or abbots; the dignity whereof they confer with all the prayers and ceremonies of a strict ordination.

By a custom of six hundred years' standing, if a priest elected bishop be not already archimandrite, that dignity must be conferred on him before episcopal ordination. The second person among the clergy after the patriarch, is the titular patriarch of Jerusalem, who also resides at Cairo. To him belongs the government of the Cophtic Church during the vacancy of the patriarchal see. To be elected patriarch, it is necessary the person have lived all his life in continence. To be elected bishop the person must be in the celibate; or if he have been married, it must not be above once.

The priests and inferior ministers are allowed to be married before ordination; but not forced to it, as some have observed. They have a great number of deacons, and even confer the dignity frequently on their children. None but the lowest rank among the people commence ecclesiastics; whence arises that excessive ignorance found among them; yet the respect of the laity towards the clergy is very extraordinary. The monastic life is in great esteem among them; to be admitted into it, there is always required the consent of the bishop.

The religious Cophts, it is said, make a vow of perpe-tual chastity; renounce the world, and live with great austerity in deserts; they are obliged to sleep in their clothes and their girdle, on a mat stretched on the ground; and to prostrate themselves every evening one hundred and fifty times with their face and breast on the ground. They are all, both men and women, of the lowest class of the people, and live on alms. The nunneries are properly hospitals, and few enter but widows reduced to beggary.

BASILIDIANS.

THE Basilidians were a denomination in the second century, from Basilides, chief of the Egyptian Gnostics. He acknowledged the existence of one supreme God, perfect in goodness and wisdom, who produced from his own substance seven beings, or *aions*, of a most excellent nature. Two of these *aions*, called Dynamis and Sophiz (i. e., *power* and *wisdom*), engendered the angels of the highest order. These angels formed a heaven for their habitation, and brought forth other angelic beings, of a nature somewhat inferior to their own. Many other generations of angels followed these. New heavens were also created, until the number of angelic orders and of their respective heavens, amounted to three hundred and sixty-five, and thus equalled the days of the year. All these are under the empire of an omnipotent Lord, whom Basilides called *Abraxas.*

The inhabitants of the lowest heavens, which touched upon the borders of the eternal, malignant, and self-animated matter, conceived the design of forming a world from that confused mass, and of creating an order of beings to people it. This design was carried into execution, and was approved by the Supreme God, who, to the animal life with which only the inhabitants of this new world were at first endowed, added a reasonable soul, giving at the same time to the angels the empire over them.

These angelic beings, advanced to the government of the world which they had created, fell by degrees from their original purity, and soon manifested the fatal marks of their depravity and corruption. They not only endeavored to efface in the minds of men their knowledge of the Supreme Being, that they might be worshipped in his stead, but also began to war against each other, with an ambitious view to enlarge every one the bounds of his respective dominion. The most arrogant and turbulent of all these angelic spirits was that which presided over the Jewish nation. Hence the Supreme God, beholding with compassion the miserable state of rational beings, who groaned under the contest of these jarring powers, sent from heaven his son *Nus*, or Christ, the chief of the *aions*, that, joined in a substantial union with the man Jesus, he might restore the knowledge of the Supreme God, destroy the empire of those angelic natures which presided over the world, and particularly that of the arrogant leader of the Jewish people. The God of the Jews, alarmed at this, sent forth his ministers to seize the man Jesus, and put him to death. They executed his commands; but their cruelty could not extend to Christ, against whom their efforts were vain. Those souls, who obey the precepts of the Son of God, shall, after the dissolution of their mortal frame, ascend to the Father, while their bodies return to the corrupt mass of matter whence they were formed. Disobedient spirits, on the contrary, shall pass successively into other bodies.

CHRISTIANS OF ST. JOHN.

THE Christians of St. John, a sect of Christians very numerous in Balfara, and the neighboring towns: they formerly inhabited along the river Jordan, where St. John baptized, and it was from thence they had their name. They hold an anniversary feast of five days, during which they all go to the bishop, who baptizes them with the baptism of St. John. Their baptism is also performed in rivers, and that only on Sundays; they have no notion of tne third person in the Trinity; nor have they any canonical book, but abundance full of charms, &c. Their bishoprics descend by inheritance as our estates do, though they have the ceremony of an election.

CHRISTIANS OF ST. THOMAS.

THE Christians of St. Thomas were a sort of Christians in a peninsula of India on this side the Gulf; they inhabit chiefly at Cranganor, and the neighboring country; these admit of no images, and receive only the cross, to which they pay a great veneration. They affirm that the souls of the saints do not see God till after the day of judgment; they acknowledge but three sacraments, viz., baptism, orders, and the eucharist: they make no use of holy oils in the administration of baptism, but, after the ceremony, anoint the infant with an unction composed of oil and walnuts, without any benediction. In the eucharist they consecrate with little cakes made of oil and salt, and instead of wine, make use of water in which raisins have been infused.

In the Asiatic Researches of the Society instituted in Bengal, may be found an enlarged account of the Christians of St. Thomas, which was laid before that society by F. Wrede, Esq. See also *Monthly Magazine* for 1804, p. 60, and Dr. Kerr's Report to Lord Bentinck, on the state of the Christians inhabiting the kingdom of Cochin and Travancore.

ANTISABBATARIANS.

THE Antisabbatarians are a modern religious sect, who deny the necessity of observing the Sabbath Day. Their chief arguments are, 1. That the Jewish Sabbath was only of ceremonial, not of moral obligation; and consequently, is abolished by the coming of Christ. 2. That no other Sabbath was appointed to be observed by Christ or his apostles. 3. That there is not a word of *Sabbath-breaking* in all the New Testament. 4. That no command was given to Adam or Noah to keep any Sabbath. And, 5. That, therefore, although Christians are commanded "not to forsake the assembling of themselves together," they ought not to hold one day more holy than another.

ATHEISTS.

AN Atheist is one who denies the existence of God:—this is called speculative atheism. Professing to believe in God, and yet acting contrary to this belief, is called practical atheism. Absurd and irrational as atheism is, it has had its votaries and martyrs. In the seventeenth century, Spinosa, a foreigner, was its noted defender. Lucilio Vanini, a native of Naples, also publicly taught atheism in France; and being convicted of it at Toulouse, was condemned and executed in 1619. It has been questioned, however, whether any man ever seriously adopted such a principle. The pretensions to it have been generally

founded on pride or affectation. The open avowal of athe
ism by several of the leading members of the French convention seems to have been an extraordinary moral phenomenon. This, however, as we have seen, was too vague
and uncomfortable a principle to last long. Archbishop
Tillotson justly observes that speculative atheism is unreasonable upon five accounts. 1. Because it gives no tolerable account of the existence of the world. 2. It does not
give any reasonable account of the universal consent of
mankind in this apprehension, that there is a God. 3. It
requires more evidence for things than they are capable
of giving. 4. The atheist pretends to know that which no
man can know. 5. Atheism contradicts itself. Under the
first of these he thus argues: "I appeal to any man of
reason whether anything can be more unreasonable than
obstinately to impute an effect to chance, which carries in
the very face of it all the arguments and characters of a
wise design and contrivance. Was ever any considerable
work, in which there was required a great variety of parts,
and a regular and orderly disposition of those parts, done
by chance? Will chance fit means to ends, and that in
ten thousand instances, and not fail in any one? How
often might a man, after he had jumbled a set of letters in
a bag, fling them out upon the ground before they would
fall into an exact poem; yea, or so much as make a good
discourse in prose? And may not a little book be as easily
made by chance as the great volume of the world? How
long might a man be in sprinkling colors upon canvas with
a careless hand, before they would happen to make the
exact picture of a man? And is a man easier made by
chance than his picture? How long might twenty thousand
blind men who should be sent out from several remote parts
of England, wander up and down before they would all
meet upon Salisbury plain, and fall into rank and file in

the exact order of an army? And yet this is much more easy to be imagined than how the innumerable blind parts of matter should rendezvous themselves into a world. A man that sees Henry the Seventh's chapel at Westminster might with as good reason maintain (yea, with much better, considering the vast difference betwixt that little structure and the huge fabric of the world) that it was never contrived or built by any means, but that the stones did by chance grow into those curious figures into which they seem to have been cut and graven; and that upon a time (as tales usually begin) the materials of that building, the stone, mortar, timber, iron, lead, and glass, happily met together, and very fortunately ranged themselves into that delicate order in which we see them, now so close compacted, that it must be a very great chance that parts them again. What would the world think of a man that should advance such an opinion as this, and write a book for it? If they would do him right, they ought to look upon him as mad; but yet with a little more reason than any man can have to say, that the world was made by chance, or that the first men grew up out of the earth as plants do now. For, can anything be more ridiculous, and against all reason, than to ascribe the production of men to the first fruitfulness of the earth, without so much as one instance and experiment, in any age or history, to countenance so monstrous a supposition? The thing is, at first sight, so gross and palpable, that no discourse about it can make it more apparent. And yet, these shameful beggars of principles give this precarious account of the original of things; assume to themselves to be the men of reason, the great wits of the world, the only cautious and wary persons that hate to be imposed upon, that must have convincing evidence for everything, and can admit of nothing without a clear demonstration of it."

GUEBERS, OR FIRE-WORSHIPPERS.

GUEBERS, or Guebres, or Gauers (i. e., infidels); the
fire-worshippers in Persia; in India called *Parsees*. They
call themselves *Behendie*, or followers of the true faith,
and live chiefly in the deserts of Caramania, towards the
Persian gulf, and in the province Yerd Keram. These
people, who are but little known, are laborious and temperate cultivators of the ground. The manners of the Guebers
are mild. They drink wine, eat all kinds of meat, marry
but one wife, and live chastely and temperately. Divorce
and polygamy are prevented by their religion; but if a
wife remains barren during the first nine years of marriage,
the husband may take a second wife. They worship one
Supreme Being, whom they call the *Eternal Spirit*, or
Yerd. The sun, moon, and planets, they believe to be
peopled with rational beings, acknowledge light as the
primitive cause of the good, darkness as that of evil, and
worship fire, as it is said, from which they have received
their name. But they themselves say, that they do not
worship fire, but only find in it an image of the incomprehensible God; on which account they offer up their prayers
before a fire, and maintain one uninterruptedly burning
on holy places, which their prophet Zoroaster, they say,
kindled 4000 years ago. Their holy book is called *Zend-
Avesta*. One of the peculiarities of the Guebers is, that
they do not bury their dead, but expose the bodies upon
the towers of their temples, to be devoured by birds.
They observe which part the birds first eat, from which
they judge of the fate of the deceased.

NESTORIANS,

A SECT of ancient Christians, still subsisting in some parts of Asia, whose distinguishing tenet is that Mary is not the mother of God. They take their name from Nestorius, Bishop of Constantinople, whose doctrines were spread with much zeal through Syria, Egypt, and Persia.

One of the chief promoters of the Nestorian cause was Barsumas, created Bishop of Nisibis, A. D. 435. Such was his zeal and success, that the Nestorians, who still remain in Chaldea, Persia, Assyria, and the adjacent countries, consider him alone as their parent and founder. By him Pherozes, the Persian monarch, was persuaded to expel those Christians who adopted the opinions of the Greeks, and to admit the Nestorians in their place, putting them in possession of the principal seat of ecclesiastical authority in Persia, the see of Seleucia, which the patriarch of the Nestorians has always filled, even down to our time. Barsumas also erected a school at Nisibis, from which proceeded those Nestorian doctors who in the fifth and sixth centuries spread abroad their tenets through Egypt, Syria, Arabia, India, Tartary, and China.

He differed considerably from Nestorius, holding that there are two persons in Jesus Christ, as well as that the Virgin was not his mother as God, but only as man.

The abettors of this doctrine refuse the title Nestorians, alleging that it had been handed down from the earliest times of the Christian Church.

In the tenth century, the Nestorians in Chaldea, whence they are sometimes called Chaldeans, extended their spiritual conquests beyond Mount Imaus, and introduced the

Christian religion into Tartary, properly so called, and especially into that country called *Karit*, and bordering on the northern part of China. The prince of that country, whom the Nestorians converted to the Christian faith, assumed, according to the vulgar tradition, the name of *John*, after his baptism, to which he added the surname of *Presbyter*, from a principle of modesty; whence it is said his successors were each of them called *Prester John*, until the time of Gengis Khan. But Mosheim observes, that the famous Prester John did not begin to reign in that part of Asia before the conclusion of the eleventh century. The Nestorians formed so considerable a body of Christians, that the missionaries of Rome were industrious in their endeavors to reduce them under the papal yoke. Innocent IV. in 1246, and Nicolas IV. in 1278, used their utmost efforts for this purpose, but without success. Till the time of Pope Julius III., the Nestorians acknowledged but one patriarch, who resided first at Bagdad, and afterwards at Mousul; but a division arising among them, in 1551 the patriarchate became divided, at least for a time, and a new patriarch was consecrated by that Pope, whose successors fixed their residence in the city of Ormus, in the mountainous part of Persia, where they still continue, distinguished by the name of *Simeon;* and so far down as the last century, these patriarchs persevered in their communion with the Church of Rome, but seem at present to have withdrawn themselves from it. The great Nestorian pontiffs, who form the opposite party, and look with a hostile eye on this little patriarch, have, since the year 1559, been distinguished by the general denomination of *Elias*, and reside constantly in the city of Mousul. Their spiritual dominion is very extensive, takes in a great part of Asia, and comprehends also within its circuit the Arabian Nestorians, and also the Christians

40

of St. Thomas, who dwell along the coast of Malabar. It is observed, to the lasting honor of the Nestorians, that of all the Christian societies established in the east, they have been the most careful and successful in avoiding a multitude of superstitious opinions and practices that have infected the Greek and Latin Churches. About the middle of the seventeenth century, the Romish missionaries gained over to their communion a small number of Nestorians, whom they formed into a congregation or church; the patriarchs or bishops of which reside in the city of Amida, or Diarbeker, and all assume the denomination of *Joseph*. Nevertheless, the Nestorians in general persevere to our own times in their refusal to enter into the communion of the Romish Church, notwithstanding the earnest entreaties and alluring offers that have been made by the Pope's legate to conquer their inflexible constancy.

Nestorius, from whom the sect of Nestorian Christians derive their name, was born in Germanica, a city of Syria. He received his education at Antioch, where he was likewise baptized; and soon after his baptism, he withdrew himself to a monastery in the suburbs of that city. Upon his being admitted to the order of priesthood, he quickly acquired so great a reputation by the eloquence of his preaching, and the regularity of his life, that by the Emperor Theodosius he was deemed a fit person to fill the second see in the Christian Church, and was accordingly consecrated Bishop of Constantinople, in the year 429.

In one of his first sermons after his promotion, he publicly declared his intention to *make war upon heretics;* and with that intolerant spirit which has so often disgraced the preachers of the mild religion of Jesus, he called upon the emperor to *free the earth from heretics*, promising to give him heaven as a reward for his zeal. To this spiritual motive he added one that, though carnal, he possibly judged of equal force: "Join with me," said he, "in war against them, and I will assist you against the Persians." Although the wiser and better part of his audience were amazed to see a man, before he had tasted (as Socrates expresses himself) the water of his city, declare that he would persecute all who were not of his opinion; yet the majority of the people approved of this discourse, and encouraged him to execute his purpose. Accordingly, five days after his consecration, he attempted to demolish the church in which the Arians secretly held their assemblies; and he succeeded so far in his design, that these people, growing desperate, set it on fire themselves, and consumed with it some of the neighboring houses. This fire excited great commotions in the city, and Nestorius was ever after-wards called an *incendiary*.

From the Arians he turned his persecution against the Novatians, but was stopped in his career by the interposition of the emperor. He then let loose his fury upon those Christians of Asia, Lydia, and Caria, who celebrated the feast of Easter upon the 14th day of the moon; and for this unimportant deviation from the Catholic practice, many of those people were murdered by his agents, both at Miletum and at Sardis. One cannot be sorry that such a relentless persecutor should himself be afterwards condemned as a heretic, for holding an opinion which no man who speaks or thinks with philosophic accuracy will now venture to controvert. This obnoxious tenet, which produced a schism in the Church, and was condemned by a general council, was nothing more than that "the Virgin Mary cannot with propriety be called the mother of God." The people being accustomed to hear this expression, were much inflamed against their bishop, imagining that he had revived the error of Paulus Samosetenus and Photinus, who taught that Jesus Christ was a mere man. The monks declared openly against him, and, with some of the most considerable men in Constantinople, separated themselves from his communion. Several bishops wrote to him earnest persuasives to acknowledge that Mary was the mother of God; and when he would not comply, they procured his condemnation in the Council of Ephesus, which deprived him of his see. He then retired to his ancient monastery at Antioch, whence he was taken four years afterwards, by the emperor's orders, and banished in 435 to Tarsus. That city being taken and destroyed by the barbarians, he was removed to Panopolis, a city of Thebais; where he was not suffered to remain long, but was compelled to go from place to place, till, being in one of his journeys mortally bruised by a fall, death relieved him from the fury of his persecutors.

If we examine such of his writings as remain, we shall find that he was very unjustly condemned. It appears that he rejected the errors of Ebion, Paulus Samosetenus, and Photinus; that he maintained in express terms, that the divine Word was united to the human nature in Jesus Christ in the most strict and intimate sense possible; that these two natures, in this state of union, make but one Christ and one person; that the properties of the Divine and human natures may both be attributed to this person; and that Jesus Christ may be said to have been born of a virgin, to have suffered and died; but he never would admit that God could be said to have been born, to have suffered, or to have died. When we consider that every person partakes of the substance of his mother, and that it is this which constitutes the parental and filial relation between them, it is indeed surprising that the expression "Mother of God" should ever have been admitted into the Christian Church, or that any man who understands the meaning of the words should condemn Nestorius for not having used them.

PAGANS.

PAGANS are the worshippers of many gods, the heathen who were so called by the Christians, because, when Constantine and his successors forbade the worship of the heathen deities in the cities, its adherents retired to the villages (*pagi*, hence *pagani*, countrymen), where they could practise their ceremonies in secresy and safety. In the middle ages, this name was given to all who were not Jews or Christians, theirs being considered the only true religion and divine revelations; but, in more modern times, Mohammedans, who worship the one supreme God of the Jews and Christians, are not called *pagans*. The idea of heathenism is of early origin. Moses used every precaution to prevent an intercourse between the Hebrews and heathen nations, prescribed the renunciation of idolatry as a requisite to citizenship in the Hebrew state, and forbade any league with the Ammonites, Moabites, &c. When the kings relaxed in the observance of these regulations, the prophets raised their voice against the defection. The distinction between pagans and non-pagans, so far as claims to a revelation are concerned, is very slight, since there are many heathenish people who have traditions of revelations made to them. We also find in some religions of paganism (for example, with Zoroaster, Plato, and Socrates) pure and elevated notions, and precepts of morality, which would not disgrace even Christianity. Paganism has likewise her moral heroes, as well as Judaism and Christianity. And although St. Augustine declared that the virtues of the heathens were but splendid vices, yet this assertion is by no means borne out by facts.

40 *

The true point of distinction is therefore to be placed in the recognition or denial of one universal, perfect Being, that is, in the reception of monotheism or polytheism. The apostle Paul speaks (Rom. i. 23) of a law of God written on the hearts of the gentiles or pagans, and declares that pagans who live by this divine law in their consciences, are a law unto themselves; and that, to every man who does good, God will render "glory, honor, and peace, to the Jew first, but also to the gentile, for there is no respect of persons with God." (Rom. ii. 10, 15.) Clement of Alexandria, and many of the fathers, were of opinion that, as God had given prophets to the Jews, so he had raised up great men among the heathen, and thus rendered both capable of arriving at the enjoyment of divine happiness. These views, however, met with strong opposition. Augustine, although he acknowledged that the virtues of a Brutus, Decius, and Regulus, were subjects of admiration, and proper models of imitation, yet maintained the principle that all the noble and good actions of the pagans were done in the service of the devil, and from vain glory. His views obtained such an ascendency, that it came to be a generally received opinion that the hope of God's grace and eternal happiness depended on a belief in the doctrines of the church. Jerome adopted an intermediate principle, attributing to the heathens a willingness to receive the doctrines of the true church, should they become known to them. If this *fides implicita*, as it is called, be anything real, it can only be a desire and endeavor to know the truth and to act accordingly. Others have maintained the action of divine grace on the souls of heathens, independent of all instruction and knowledge on their part The influence which the writings of Augustine exercised at the time of the Reformation, and on the Reformers, led to the reception of the dogma of the damnation of the pagans, which acquired a new development from the doctrine of predestination. Marmontel's *Bélisaire* was condemned by the Sorbonne, because it professed a belief in the salvation of the pagans.

PAGANS OF CHINA.

THE primitive theology of China is supposed, by a number of learned men, to agree in its essential parts with the doctrine of the chosen people, before Moses, by the command of God himself, had consigned the explanation of it to the sacred records. The King, or canonical books of the Chinese, everywhere inculcate the belief of a Supreme Being, the author and preserver of all things; the principle of everything that exists, and the father of all living; he is eternal, immovable, and independent; his power knows no bounds; his sight equally comprehends the past, present, and the future; penetrating even into the inmost recesses of the heart. Heaven and earth are under his government; all events, all revolutions, are the consequences of his will; he is pure, holy, and impartial; wickedness offends his sight; but he beholds with an eye of complacency the virtuous actions of men. Severe, yet just, he punishes vice in a striking manner, even on the throne; and often precipitates from thence the guilty, to place upon it the man who walks after his own heart, whom he hath raised from obscurity. Good, merciful, and full of pity, he relents on the repentance of the wicked; public calamities, and the irregularities of the seasons, are only salutary warnings, which his fatherly goodness gives to men to induce them to reform and amend.

Some historians have also found in the Chinese religion

evident symptoms of the knowledge of the Trinity, as believed among Christians.

The present religion of China is Pagan; but it is said there are almost as many sects as persons among them. For as soon as a Chinese expects the least advantage from it, he is, without any consideration, to-day of one religion, to-morrow of another, or of all together. However, beside the worship of the Grand Lama, there are three principal sects.

I. The followers of Laokium, who lived five hundred years before Christ, and taught that God was corporeal. They pay divine honors to the philosopher Laokium; and give the same worship, not only to many emperors, who have been ranked with the gods, but also to certain spirits under the name of Xamte, who preside over every element. Their morality consists in calming the passions, and disengaging themselves from everything which tends to disquiet the soul; to live free from care, to forget the past, and not be apprehensive for the future. To remove the unavoidable fear of death, they pretend Laokium discovered an elixir, which confers immortality. They call this sect that of the Magicians, because the learned of it addict themselves to magic, and are believed to have the secret of making men immortal.

II. The most predominant sect is that of Foe, who flourished six hundred years before our Saviour, and who became a god at the age of thirty years. This religion was transplanted from India to China, sixty-five years after the birth of Christ. A large number of altars, temples, or pagodas, are reared to this deity, some of which are magnificent to the highest degree, and a number of bonzes, or priests, consecrated to his service. He is represented shining in light, with his hands hid under his robes, to show that he does all things invisible. The doctors of this sect teach a double law; the one *external*, the other *internal*. According to the external law, they say that all the good are recompensed, and the wicked punished, in places destined for each. They enjoin all works of mercy; and forbid cheating, impurity, wine, lying, and murder, and even the taking life from any creature whatever. For they believe that the souls of their ancestors transmigrate into irrational creatures, either into such as they liked best or resembled most in their behavior, for which reason they never kill any such animals; but while they live, feed them well, and when they die, bury them with splendor. They lay great stress upon acts of charity, and in building temples for Foe, monasteries for his priests, and providing for their maintenance, as the most effectual means to partake of their prayers, penances, and other meritorious actions towards the atonement of their sins, and obtaining a happy transmigration. These priests pretend to know into what bodies the dead are transmigrated; and seldom fail of representing their case to the surviving friends, as miserable or uncomfortable, that they may extort money from them to procure the deceased a passage into a better state. They also threaten the living with an unhappy transmigration, that they may procure money of them to obtain a happier one, or leave them to die in dread of the fatal change.

The interior doctrine of this sect, which is kept secret from the common people, teaches a pure, unmixed atheism, which admits neither rewards nor punishments after death; believes not in a providence, nor the immortality of the soul; acknowledges no other God but the *void*, or *nothing;* and which makes the supreme happiness of mankind to consist in a *total inaction, an entire insensibility, and a perfect quietude.*

III. A sect, which acknowledges for its master the philosopher Confucius, who lived five hundred years before our Saviour. This religion, which is professed by the literati, and persons of rank in China and Tonquin, consists in a deep inward veneration for the God, or King of heaven, and in the practice of every moral virtue. They have neither temples, nor priests, nor any settled form of external worship: every one adores the Supreme Being in the way he likes best.

Confucius did not dive into abstruse notions, but confined himself to speak with the deepest regard of the great Author of all beings, whom he represents as the most pure and perfect essence and fountain of all things; to inspire men with greater fear, veneration, gratitude, and love of him; to assert his divine providence over all his creatures; and to represent him as a being of such infinite knowledge, that even our most secret thoughts are not hidden from him; and of such boundless goodness and justice, that he can let no virtue go unrewarded, or vice unpunished.

The Chinese honor their dead ancestors; burn perfumes before their images; bow before their pictures; and invoke them as capable of bestowing upon them all temporal blessings.

PAGANS OF JAPAN.

The worship of the Japanese is Paganism, divided into several sects.

Among the various sects in this island, the three following are most conspicuous:

I. The Sinto, or ancient idol worship of the Japanese.

II. The Budso, or foreign idol worship, introduced into

Japan from the empire of China, and the kingdom of Siam; and,

III. The religion of their philosophers and moralists.

1. The religion of the Sintos. This denomination have some obscure and imperfect notions of the immortality of the soul, and a future state of bliss and misery; and yet worship only those gods who they believe are peculiarly concerned in the government of the world; for though they acknowledge a Supreme Being, whom they believe dwells in the highest heaven, and admit of some inferior gods, whom they place among the stars; yet they do not worship and adore them, nor have they any festivals sacred to them, thinking that beings so much elevated above mankind will concern themselves but little about human affairs. They, however, swear by their superior gods, but they worship and invoke those gods alone whom they believe to have the sovereign control over this world, its elements, productions, and animals; these, they suppose, will not only render them happy here, but by interceding for them at the hour of death, may procure them a happy condition in the next state of existence, in reward of their good conduct in the present state. Hence their dairis, or ecclesiastical emperors, being esteemed lineally descended from the eldest and most favored sons of these deities, are supposed the true and living images of their gods, and possessed of such an eminent degree of holiness, that none of the people dare presume to appear in their presence.

The Sintos believe that the soul, after quitting the body, is removed to the high subcelestial fields, seated just beneath the thirty-three heavens, the dwelling-places of their gods; that those who have led a good life find an immediate admission, while the souls of the wicked are denied entrance, and condemned to wander till they have expiated their crimes; but they do not believe in a hell, or a place of torment. One of the essential points of their religion is, that they ought to preserve an inward purity of heart, and to practise or abstain from whatever the dictates of reason, or the express command of the civil magistrate, direct or forbid.

The Sintos' religion enjoins abstaining from blood, from eating flesh, or being near a dead body; by which a person is, for a time, rendered unfit to go to the temples, to visit holy places, and to appear in the presence of the gods.

The other great points of their religion are, 1. A diligent observance of the solemn festivals in honor of their gods, which are very numerous. 2. Pilgrimages to the holy places at Isje; that is, to the temple of Tensio-Daisin, the greatest of all the gods of the Japanese. The last essential doctrine of their religion is, that they ought to chastise and mortify their bodies; but few of them pay much regard to this precept.

II. The Budso, or foreign pagan worship introduced into Japan, probably owes its origin to Budhe, whom the Bramins of India believe to be Vishnu, one of their deities, who, they say, made his ninth appearance in the world, under the form of a man of that name.

The most essential points of this religion are, that the souls of men and animals are immortal, and both of the same substance, differing only according to the bodies in which they are placed; and that after the souls of mankind have left their bodies, they shall be rewarded or punished according to their behavior in this life, by being introduced to a state of happiness or misery; that the degrees of both are proportioned to the different degrees of virtue and vice. They call their heaven a state of eternal pleasure. Their God Armida is the sovereign commander of this blissful region; and is considered as the patron and protector of human souls, especially of those who are removed to a state of felicity. These maintain that leading a virtuous life, and doing nothing contrary to the five commandments,* is the only way to become agreeable to Armida, and to render themselves worthy of eternal happiness.

On the other hand, all the vicious, whether priests or laymen, are, after death, sent to a place of misery to be tormented for a certain indefinite time, where every one is to be punished according to the nature and number of his crimes, the number of years he lived upon earth, his station there, and his opportunities for becoming good and virtuous. Yet they suppose the miseries of these unhappy souls may be greatly alleviated by the virtuous lives of their relations and friends; and still more by the prayers and offerings of the priests to their great god Armida, who can prevail on the almost inexorable judge to treat the imprisoned souls with somewhat less severity than their crimes deserve, and to send them speedily again into the world. For they believe that, when vicious souls have expiated their crimes, they are sent back to animate such vile animals as resembled them in their former state of existence. From the vilest of these transmigrating into others and nobler, they at last are suffered again to enter human bodies, and thus have it in their power, either by their virtue and piety to obtain an uninterrupted state of felicity, or, by a new course of vices, once more to expose themselves to all the miseries of confinement in a place of torment, succeeded by a new unhappy transmigration.

There are several sects of the Budso religion, all of which have their temples, their convents, and their priests.

---

* These five commandments are, 1. Not to kill anything that has life. 2. Not to steal. 3. Not to commit fornication. 4. To avoid lies, and all falsehood. 5. Not to drink strong liquors.

III. The religion of the philosophers and moralists is
very different from that of the two former, for they pay
no regard to any of the forms of worship practised in the
country. The supreme good, say they, consists in the
pleasure and delight that arises from the steady practice
of virtue. They maintain that men are obliged to be virtuous, because nature has endowed them with reason, that
by living according to its dictates, they might show their
superiority to the irrational inhabitants of the earth.
They do not admit of transmigration of souls, but believe
that there is a universal soul diffused through all nature,
which animates all things, and which reassumes departed
souls, as the sea does the rivers. This universal spirit
they confound with the Supreme Being. These philosophers not only admit of self-murder, but consider it as a
heroic and commendable action, when it is the only means
of avoiding a shameful death, or of escaping from the
hands of a victorious enemy.

They conform to the general customs of their country
in commemorating their deceased parents and relations, by
placing all sorts of provisions on a table provided for the
purpose; but they celebrate no other festivals, nor pay
any respect to the gods of the country.

There are innumerable temples and idols in this island,
among which the temples of those who profess the Budso
religion are the most remarkable, being distinguished for
their stately height, curious roofs, and numerous ornaments. One of the temples erected at Miaco is esteemed
the most sumptuous in the empire. This temple is said to
be as large as the church of St. Paul, London; and contains many idols, among which is one of gilt copper, of a
prodigious size, seated in a chair eighty feet broad, and
seventy feet in height. The festivals of the Japanese are
as numerous as their deities. The number of monasteries

is scarcely credible. The monks are either regulars or seculars. The regulars live in convents, some of which contain upwards of a thousand monks. The seculars are dispersed abroad, and live in private houses. The former are exceedingly abstemious, but the latter live in luxury and idleness

The Roman Catholic religion once made a considerable progress in this country, in consequence of a mission conducted by the Portuguese and Spanish Jesuits, in 1549, amongst whom the famous Saint Francis Xavier was employed, but soon relinquished the service. There were also some Franciscan friars of Spain engaged at last. At first the undertaking proceeded with the most rapid success, but ended in a most tragical manner, owing, it is said, to the misconduct of the Jesuits, and their conspiracy against the emperor. A persecution commenced of forty years' duration, which was terminated by a most terrible and bloody massacre, not to be paralleled in history. After this the Portuguese, as likewise the Christian religion, were totally expelled the country, and the most effectual means taken for preventing their return.

LAMAISTS.

THE name of the Grand Lama is given to the sovereign pontiff, or high-priest, of the Thibetian Tartars, who resides at Patoli, a vast palace on the mountain near the banks of Barampooter, about seven miles from Lahassa. The foot of this mountain is inhabited by twenty thousand lamas, or priests, who have their separate apartments around the mountain: and, according to their respective qualities, are placed nearer, or at a greater distance from, the sovereign pontiff. He is not only worshipped by the Thibetians, but also is the great object of adoration for the various tribes of heathen Tartars who roam through the vast tract of continent which stretches from the banks of the Wolga to Corea. on the sea of Japan. He is not only the sovereign pontiff, the vicegerent of the Deity on earth, but the more remote Tartars are said to absolutely regard him as the Deity himself, and call him *God, the everlasting Father of Heaven.* They believe him to be immortal, and endowed with all knowledge and virtue. Every year they come up from different parts to worship, and make rich offerings at his shrine. Even the emperor of China, who is a Mantchou Tartar, does not fail in acknowledgments to him in his religious capacity; and he actually entertains, at a great expense in the palace of Pekin, an inferior Lama, deputed as his nuncio from Thibet. The Grand Lama, it has been said, is never to be seen but in a secret place of his palace, amidst a great number of lamps, sitting cross-legged on a cushion, and decked in every part with gold and precious stones; where at a distance the people prostrate themselves before him, it not being lawful for any so much as to kiss his feet. He returns not the least sign of respect, nor ever speaks even to the greatest princes; but only lays his hand upon their heads, and they are fully persuaded they receive from thence a full forgiveness of all their sins.

The Sunniasses, or Indian pilgrims, often visit Thibet as a holy place; and the Lama always entertains a body of two or three hundred in his pay. Besides his religious influence and authority, the Grand Lama is possessed of unlimited power throughout his dominions, which are very extensive. The inferior Lamas, who form the most numerous, as well as the most powerful body in the state.

have the priesthood entirely in their hands; and besides, fill up many monastic orders, which are held in great veneration among them. The whole country, like Italy, abounds with priests; and they entirely subsist on the great number of rich presents which are sent them from the utmost extent of Tartary, from the empire of the Great Mogul, and from almost all parts of the Indies.

The opinion of those who are reputed the most orthodox among the Thibetians is, that when the Grand Lama seems to die, either of old age or infirmity, his soul, in fact, only quits a crazy habitation to look for another, younger or better; and it is discovered again in the body of some child by certain tokens, known only to the Lamas or priests, in which order he always appears.

Almost all the nations of the East, except the Mohammedans, believe the *metempsychosis* as the most important article of their faith; especially the inhabitants of Thibet and Ava, the Peguans, Siamese, the greatest part of the Chinese and Japanese, and the Monguls and Kalmucks, who changed the religion of Schamanism for the worship of the Grand Lama. According to the doctrine of this metempsychosis, the soul is always in action, and never at rest; for no sooner does she leave her old habitation than she enters a new one. The Dalay being a Divine person, can find no better lodging than the body of his successor; or the *Fo*, residing in the Dalay Lama, which passes to his successor; and this being a god to whom all things are known, the Dalay Lama is therefore acquainted with everything which happened during his residence in his former body.

This religion is said to have been of three thousand years' standing; and neither time, nor the influence of men, has had the power of shaking the authority of the

41 *

Grand Lama. This theocracy extends as fully to temporal as to spiritual concerns.

Though in the grand sovereignty of the Lamas, the temporal power has been occasionally separated from the spiritual by slight revolutions, they have always been united again after a time; so that in Thibet the whole constitution rests on the imperial pontificate in a manner elsewhere unknown. For, as the Thibetians suppose the Grand Lama is animated by the god Shaka, or Fo, who at the decease of one Lama transmigrates into the next, and consecrates him an image of the divinity, the descending chain of Lamas is continued down from him in fixed degrees of sanctity; so that a more firmly established sacerdotal government, in doctrine, customs, and institutions, than actually reigns over this country, cannot be conceived. The supreme manager of temporal affairs is no more than the viceroy of the sovereign priest, who, conformably to the dictates of his religion, dwells in divine tranquillity in a building that is both temple and palace. If some of his votaries, in modern times, have dispensed with the adoration of his person, still certain real modifications of the Shaka religion are the only faith they profess, the only religion they follow. The state of sanctity which that religion inculcates, consists in monastic confidence, absence of thought, and the perfect repose of nonentity.

BRAMINS.

BRAMA is the name of the first person in the Trinity, or Trimurti, of the Hindoos, consisting of *Brama*, the creator, *Vishnu*, the preserver or redeemer, and *Siva*, the destroyer. He is represented with four heads and as many arms, and the swan is consecrated to him. His name signifies *knowledge of the laws,* in allusion to his creative power. He is the god of the fates, master of life and death, and, by some, has been represented as the supreme eternal power; but he is himself created, and is merely the agent of the Eternal One. He is believed to die, according to some, annually, or, according to others, after a longer period, and to rise again. His character is no better than that of the Grecian Jupiter. He is considered as the author of the Vedas, and as the lawgiver and teacher of India. The worship of Brama is regarded as the oldest religious observance in that country.

The Bramins are the first of the four castes of the Hindoos. They proceeded from the mouth of Brama, which is the seat of wisdom. They form the sacred or sacerdotal cast, and its members have maintained a more absolute and extensive authority than the priests of any other nation. Their great prerogative is that of being the sole depositories and interpreters of the Vedas or sacred books. There are seven subdivisions of the Bramins, which derive their origin from seven penitents, personages of high antiquity and remarkable purity, who are said to have rebuked the gods themselves for their debaucheries. The great body of the Bramins pay equal veneration to the three parts of the mysterious trinity, but some attach themselves more particularly to one person of the triple godhead. Thus the Vishnuites are distinguished by an orange-colored dress, and the mark called *nama* on their foreheads. The devotees of Siva wear the *lingam,* and are distinguished from the former by their great abstemiousness. A Bramin should pass through four states. The first begins at about seven, when the duty of the young novice, or *Brachmacari,* consists in learning to read and write, studying the Vedas, and becoming familiar with

the privileges of his cast, and all points of corporeal purity
Thus he is taught his right to ask alms, to be exempted
from taxes, from capital, and even corporeal punishment.
Earthen vessels belonging to Bramins, when used by profane persons, or for certain purposes, must be broken.
Leather and skins of animals, and most animals themselves, are impure, and must not be touched by them.
Flesh and eggs they are not allowed to eat. The Bramin
is also taught to entertain a horror of the defilement of
the soul by sin; and rules for purification by ablution,
penances, and various ceremonies, are prescribed. The
second state begins at his marriage, when he is called
Grihastha. Marriage is necessary to his respectability
His daily duties become more numerous, and must be more
strictly performed. Regular ablutions, fasting, and many
minute observances, become requisite. The Bramins, however, engage in secular employments, political, commercial,
&c. The third state is that of the *Vana-Prasthas*, or
inhabitants of the desert, which is now, however, seldom
reached. They were honored by kings, and respected
even by the gods. Retiring to the forest, green herbs,
roots, and fruit were their food; reading the Vedas,
bathing morning, noon, and evening, and the practice of
the most rigorous penances, were prescribed. "Let the
Vana-Prastha," says Menou, in the Institutes, "slide back-
wards and forwards on the ground, or stand the whole day
on tip-toe, or continue rising and sitting down alternately;
in the hot season, let him sit exposed to five fires; in the
rain, let him stand uncovered; in the cold season, let him
wear wet garments; then, having stored up his holy fires
in his mind, let him live without external fire, without a
shelter, wholly silent, and feeding on roots and fruit.
When he shall have thus become void of fear and sorrow,
and shaken off his body, he rises to the divine essence."

The fourth state is that of a *Sunnyasi*, in which new and severer penances are to be performed. Suppressing the breath, standing on the head, and other such ceremonies are performed, till the devout patient rises to a participa'tion of the divine nature. The sanctity and inviolability of a Bramin are maintained in the eyes of his countrymen by the most severe penalties. The murder of one of the order, robbing him, &c., are inexpiable sins; the killing of his cow can only be expiated by a painful penance. To some travellers it appears that the number of Bramins respectable for knowledge and virtue is very small; that the great body of them are devoted to ambition, intrigue, and voluptuousness, and that their character is disgraced by avarice, meanness, and cruelty. Their charity extends only to those of their own caste. The objects of their worship, besides their innumerable gods, are almost every species of animals, and a variety of malignant demons. The transmigration of souls is one of their essential doctrines, and they believe in the existence of a hell. Some of the ceremonies of the Braminical worship are horrible; some are more licentious than the orgies of Bacchus. The sacrifices commonly consist of vegetables, but animals are sometimes sacrificed, and the burning of widows is a relic of the horrid practice of offering human victims.

Harrell computes the number of Bramins in all Asia at 80,000,000.

BUDDHISTS.

BUDDHA was the founder of the very ancient religion called after him. His worship, after the Bramins had put a stop to it in India, spread to Japan, Thibet, and China, where, as well as in Ceylon, it exists at the present day

Ritter, in his *Vorhallen Europäischer Völkergeschichten* (Introduction to the Histories of the European Nations), advances the opinion that the Buddhists also migrated to the North-West, to the shores of the Black Sea, to Colchis, to the modern Mingrelia, and thence to Thrace, where they laid the foundation of the civilization of the Pelasgi and Hellenes. Even in the doctrine of Asa, in the extreme north, traces of Buddhism have been thought to appear. According to Abel Remusat, Buddha, whose historical name was Tshakia-muni, was born under the reign of Tshao-Wang, of the dynasty of Tsheu, 1029 B. C., and died under the reign of Mou-Wang, 950 B. C. Before his death, he intrusted his disciple Mahakaya, a Bramin in the kingdom of Makata, which lay in the centre of India, with his mysteries. This Mahakaya, who lived under Hio-Wang, 950 B. C., is the first saint or patriarch of Buddhism, which was left by him to his successor, Ananta. The Japan Encyclopedia enumerates thirty-three patriarchs, including Mahakaya, in chronological succession, each of whom chose his successor, and transmitted to him the secret doctrine of Tshakia-muni, who was afterwards worshipped as a god, under the name of Buddha. Several of them died (or, to use the language of the Buddhists, emigrated) voluntarily in the flames.

Among them, Maming, the successor of Buddha (by the Chinese called *Phu-sa;* in Sanscrit, *Deva-Bodhisatua*), who gave names to the gods of the second class, was worshipped as his son, born from his mouth, because he perfected the doctrine of Buddha by his own philosophy, which is a metaphysical allegorical mysticism. His epoch must be fixed, according to the above-mentioned work, in 332, under the reign of Hian-wang, 618 years after the death of Tshakia-muni.

The twenty-eighth patriarch, Bodhidhorma, was the last

who lived in Hindostan. He afterwards fixed his residence in China, near the famous mountain Sung. He died A. D. 495. The secret of his doctrine was left by him to a Chinese, who was the twenty-ninth patriarch. After him, the above-mentioned book gives the names of four Chinese, who succeeded to the same dignity. The last of them died A. D. 713. Their history, like that of many other saints, is mixed with fables; their manner of living was the same as what the ancients report to us of the Gymnosophists and Samaneans. They devoted themselves to religious exercises and constant contemplation, and condemned themselves to the most severe abstinence; nay, several of them sealed their belief in the transmigration of souls with a voluntary death.

From that Indian patriarchate originated, A. D. 706, the sacerdotal dignity, which is common in China and among the Monguls, with the title *spiritual prince of the law*. These priests are, at the same time, a sort of confessors to the emperors. From this priesthood afterwards sprung the hereditary dignity of Grand Lama in Thibet; and, in process of time, the whole hierarchical system, when the monastical life of the Buddhists required regular superiors, or inferior lamas.

Besides many other monuments of the ancient worship of Buddha, there are two particularly remarkable — the ruins of the gigantic temple Boro-Budor, in Java, with works of sculpture; and the five large, subterranean halls, called *Pantsh-Pandu*, probably an old temple of the Buddhists, near the city of Bang, on the way from Guzurat to Malwa. Tradition ascribes these astonishing works of ancient Indian architecture and sculpture, which far surpass the skill of the modern Hindoos, to the Pandus, the heroes of Indian mythology.

Harrel computes the number of Buddhists in all Asia at 295,000,000.

PAGANS IN AFRICA.*

THE natives of Africa universally believe in a Supreme Being, and have some ideas of a future state. They address this being by a *fetishe* or *fetish*, which is a sort of charm or manner of conducting their worship. The term is often applied to whatever represents their divinities.

The negroes of Congo believe in a good and an evil principle, which are both supposed to reside in the sky. The former sends rain, the latter withholds it; but they do not seem to consider either of them as possessing any influence over human affairs. After death they all take their place in the sky, and enjoy a happy existence, without any regard being paid to their good or bad actions while here below.

Each town has a grand kissey, or presiding divinity. It is the figure of a man, the body stuck with feathers, rags, and bits of iron, and resembles nothing so much as one of our scarecrows. The chenoo of Gooloo had a kissey so redoubtable that if any person attempted to shoot at it, he would fall down dead, and the flint would drop out of the musket. This powerful divinity was the figure of a man, about two feet high, rudely carved in wood, and covered with rags.

Kolloh is the name of a great spirit, who is supposed to reside in the vicinity of Yangroo, in Western Africa. He makes his abode in the woods, and is rarely seen except on mournful occasions, such as the death of the king, or some

---

* Much valuable information respecting the religion of the tribes in the interior of South Africa, will be found in Dr. Livingston's Travels and Explorations in South Africa, published by J. W. Bradley, Philadelphia.

of their head men, or when a person has been buried without the usual ceremonies of dancing, drinking palm-wine,
&c., in remembrance of their departed friends.

The Kolloh is made of bamboo sticks in the form of an
oval basket, about three feet long, and so deep that it goes
on to the man's shoulders. It is covered with a piece of
net, and stuck all around with porcupine quills on the nose.
It has a frightful appearance, and has a great effect in
exciting the terror of the inhabitants.

A certain man pretends to have some very intimate intercourse with this Beelzebub, and therefore he is called
by the spirit to take the Kolloh on his head, and to go
about with it on certain occasions, to see that the various
ceremonies of the country are strictly observed, and if any
are absent, he seeks them out and drives them to the place
of assembly.

The Kolloh-man carries a stick in his hand, to show his
authority; and to give notice of his coming he rings a bell,
which is fixed inside of the Kolloh, or basket. These Kolloh-
men are a set of plunderers, who disturb the peace, and
greatly deceive the ignorant natives.

The fetishes of Whidah may be divided into three classes:
the *serpent*, *tall trees*, and the *sea*. The serpent is the
most celebrated, the others being subordinate to the power
of this deity. This snake has a large, round head, beautiful, piercing eyes, a short, pointed tongue, resembling a
dart: its pace is slow and solemn, except when it seizes on
its prey, then very rapid; its tail sharp and short, its skin
of an elegant smoothness, adorned with beautiful colors,
upon a light gray ground; it is amazingly familiar and
tame. Rich offerings are made to this deity; priests and
priestesses appointed for its service; it is invoked in extremely wet, dry, or barren seasons; and, in a word, on all
the great difficulties and occurrences of life.

42

The people of *Benin* believe in an invisible deity, who created heaven and earth, and governs them with absolute power; but they conceive it needless to worship him, because he is always doing good without their services. They also believe in a malignant deity, to whom they sacrifice men and animals, to satiate his thirst of blood, and prevent him from doing them mischief. But they have innumerable objects of worship, as elephants' teeth, claws, bones, dead men's heads, or any trifle that chance throws in their way, to which they make a daily offering of a few boiled yams, mixed with palm oil. On great occasions they sacrifice a cock, treating the divinity with the blood only, and reserving the flesh for themselves. Persons of high rank give an annual feast to their gods, at which multitudes of cattle are offered to the idols, and eaten by the people. Each offers his own sacrifices, without giving the priests any sort of trouble.

The religion of the Dahomans, like that of the neighboring kingdoms, consists of such a mass of superstition as can hardly be described. The objects of their devotion are the sun and moon, various animals and trees, and other substances. The Portuguese word *fetico*, or, as the English pronounce it, *fetish*, signifying witchcraft, has been adopted by most of the maritime natives of Africa, as well as by the Europeans who trade thither. Of their *amulets*, or *charms*, the principal is a scrap of parchment, containing a sentence of the Koran, which the natives purchase from the Moors who visit the country, and which they hang up in their apartments, and decorate with a variety of rude images. Among the objects of their idolatrous worship is a species of snake or serpent, called *Daboa;* they put it in a basket, and place it in the temple destined for it, where they secretly feed it with rats, but pretend that it lives upon air. The temple is served by priestesses, supported at the king's expense. Every year there is a festival in honor of this serpent, at which the grandees assist, and for which the king supplies the necessary articles. It lasts usually seven days, during which time the people abandon themselves to drinking, music, and dancing. Great faith is placed in the serpent. Those who labor under bodily pains, apply the animal to the part affected, and pregnant women offer prayers to it for a favorable delivery. The tiger is also held in veneration, and there is a temple dedicated to the devil, or bad demon. Notwithstanding these superstitions, the people have a confused idea of a Supreme Being, all-powerful and infinite, whom they endeavor to propitiate by their *fetish ;* but pay him no other worship, as they are convinced that he is too good to do them any evil.

The Ashantees are, perhaps, the most polished nation of negroes to be met with in Western Africa. They are, however, gross idolaters, and most lavish of human blood in sacrifices at their funerals and festivals. They say that, at the beginning of the world, God created three black men, and three white, with the same number of women, and placed before them a large box, or calabash, and a sealed paper. The black men had the privilege of choosing, and they took the box expecting it contained everything; but when they opened it, they found only gold, iron, and other metals, of which they did not know the use. The white men opened the paper, which told them everything. This happened in Africa, where God left the black men in the bush. The white men he conducted to the water side, where he taught them to build a ship, which carried them to another country. From hence they returned, after a long period, with various merchandise, to trade with the black men, who might have been superior people if they had chosen right. The kings and governors are believed to dwell with God after death, enjoying to eternity the luxuries and state they possessed on earth: the paradise of the poor affords only a cessation from labor. There are two orders of men attached to the inferior deities called fetishes. Every family has its domestic fetish, to which they offer yams, &c.; some of them are wooden figures; others are of fanciful forms, and different materials. When the Ashantees drink, they spill a little of the liquor on the ground, as an offering to the fetish; and when they rise from their chairs or stools, their attendants hastily lay the seat on its side, to prevent the devil, or evil spirits, from slipping into their master's place. This evil spirit is supposed to be white; doubtless from the same motives or feeling which induces Europeans to say that he is black: for, indeed, who would wish to resemble the devil, either in color or shape, however some of us may not object to a resemblance to him in character?

PAGANS OF MADAGASCAR.*

THE latest, and, no doubt, the most correct account of the superstitious rites and ceremonies of the people of Madagascar, is to be found in Ellis's History of Madagascar. From that work, the greater part of the information about to be given has been obtained.

It has long been thought that the people of Madagascar

---

* A particular account of the religion of the natives of Madagascar, and of the introduction of Christianity into that island, and the persecutions suffered by the native Christians up to the present time, is given in Ellis's "Three Visits to Madagascar," published by J. W. Bradley, Philadelphia.

were a people favorably prepared by circumstances to receive Christianity, for they have usually been represented as being free from popular idols and religious observances, to any extent that would render them averse to the influences of a better religion than their own. This impression, however, only arose from a want of that knowledge which has latterly been painfully obtained.

The same feelings and passions which move in the breasts of other people, are at work in the hearts of the Malagasy, and they. moved by the same hopes and fears, and joys and sorrows, that characterize humanity, have, in in their destitution of the light of revelation, sought a refuge to arm them against evil, and to inspire them with hope, in a belief of charms. They cannot regard creation around them without being convinced of an unseen and powerful agency, and being unable to account for effects visible to their eyes, and possessing no impression of a superintending Providence, they consider that charms alone could have effected what is above their apprehension.

But while the Malagasy believe in ody, (charms,) they have a conviction of the infallibility of the sikidy, or divination, by which the charm must be decided, and to this must also be added, an undefined belief in some superior, though unknown power, whose will the diviner's art is about to make known. The art of the diviner is considered as certain in its result, though the premises from which that result issues are avowedly laid in chances. The Mohammedan is not more wedded to the doctrine of fate than the Malagasy to their "vintana" — a stern and unbending destiny.

Though Madagascar has no visible objects of worship calculated to claim veneration, and charm the senses to any great degree, and recognizes no order of priests, yet it is not without its idols, its ceremonies, its sacrifices, and its divinations. It has, too, its altars, its vows, and its forbidden things, (forbidden because hateful to the supposed genius of the place,) as well as its mythology, oaths, and forms of benediction. No people surpass the Malagasy in credulity; ghosts, witches, apparitions, legendary wonders, and feats of ferocious giants and monsters, have their full influence over their minds. The people appeal to a superior but unknown power to protect them from sorcery, and to purge the land from the evils of witchcraft, the innocent blood is shed of numberless human victims, who are persecuted, poisoned, speared, strangled, or hurled over a fatal precipice. Being without divine truth, the Malagasy cling tenaciously to the superstitions of their forefathers.

Though they speak of God, pray to God, appeal to God, and bless in the name of God, yet is the notion they form of God so vague, uncertain, and, indeed, contradictory, that it can be hardly said with truth that they know anything of the creator, preserver, and redeemer of mankind. "Radama, king of Madagascar, was, a few years ago, offered the knighthood of the order of St. Patrick, which he declined, assigning as his reason that he could not take the oath which required him to say that he believed in God, meaning the God of the Europeans." There is no doubt that the real belief of the Malagasy concerning God, is far from being what the terms found in their language would seem to imply.

The terms for God in the native language are Andria manitra and Zanahary, or Andria-nanahary, but the notions entertained respecting them are of the most confused kind; whatever is great, or grand, or new, or extraordinary, is at once called Andriamanitra. Rice, money, thunder and lightning, with earthquakes, and other things, are called God. A book is god, a deceased king is god, velvet is son of god, and silk is god in the highest degree. "It is related of Radama, that in a heavy thunder-storm which occurred one evening, he amused himself in firing off some pieces of cannon. The British agent went to him, and inquired his reason for doing so. 'Oh!' said the king, 'we are answering one another — both of us are gods. God above is speaking by his thunder and lightning, and I am replying by my powder and cannon.' Mr. Hastie pointed out to him the presumption of his conduct, and the king ordered the firing to cease."

The Malagasy believe that when the body dies, the mind becomes "levona," — i. e. vanished, invisible, and that the life becomes "rivotra," — air, or wind, a mere breeze. Some of the inhabitants on parts of the coast believe in the existence of four superior divinities, or lords, who govern the four quarters of the earth — in the interior of the country this belief is regarded as a fable. The doctrine of a future state of retribution is not known to the Malagasy. No conceptions are entertained of the relation existing between the creator and the created, and no moral responsibility impressed on the mind. Chicanery, lying, and cheating, are considered but very light offences, compared with trampling on a grave, eating pork in places where it is forbidden, running after an owl, or wild cat, or preparing any kind of enchantment.

The Malagasy practise the ceremony of circumcision, purification, and offering sacrifice; but they have no traditions of the creation, the fall of man, the deluge, the favored people of God, or of the Messiah. The doctrine of a Mediator, the birth of a Redeemer, the salvation of man, the renewal of the heart, the resurrection, the general judgment, and the glory to be revealed, are unknown to them.

There are twelve or fifteen principal idols in the vicinity

ot Tananariva, which excite the religious dread of the people, and four of these are regarded as superior to the rest. They are supposed to exert more influence in protecting and benefiting the sovereign and the country than the others, and are therefore national idols. Different clans and districts have their own idols, which are little known beyond their immediate neighborhood. The idols of Imerina have no power among the Sakalavas, nor have the Sakalava gods any influence in Imerina.

Not only has every clan its own idol, but every house and family its ody, or charm; many wear crocodiles' teeth as receptacles of their ody, and in this they put their trust in all circumstances of sickness and peril, in life and in death.

It is not known whether the kings who raised the national idols to their present elevation, instituted any public worship, for none is now offered to them; yet still they are called God, and regarded as such. A native Malagasy thus describes the idol gods:—" The idols are called God, prayed to, praised, thanked, highly regarded, honored, and lifted up: they are said to be that which causes to live, and causes to die, and are supposed to see the future, the past, and the present, and to be able to cast down the thunderbolts, pour down the hail, to remove the disease, and inflict curses, and to assemble the snake tribe against all who calumniate them. It is said, also, that their calumniators are strangled by them. They are called ' means of life,' and are kept in boxes." The serpents of Madagascar are very numerous; they are regarded as the particular agents of the idols, and on this account are looked upon with much apprehension. The national idols of Madagascar are kept very secret: to endeavor to see them is a crime. No strangers are allowed to approach the houses where they are preserved, so that the materials of which they are made and the forms given to them cannot be described here. When one of them is carried in public, its appearance is that of a small image wrapped in red cloth. It is elevated on a pole, that it may be borne along with greater ease, and at the same time make an impression on the awe-struck multitude. Though it is carried along in this public manner, the people are forbidden to gaze upon it — an inconsistency that can hardly be accounted for. The sovereign gives the red velvet in which the idol is enveloped. A Malagasy idol was given on a certain occasion, and its appearance was of the most extraordinary kind.

The household gods of Madagascar are of many kinds; anything which strikes the fancy, or allures the eye, will do for a god. One man worshipped a piece of silver about the size of a walnut, shaped like a bullock; he called it his "bullock of money" An old chief had hung up in his dwelling an odd-looking bushy plant; this was his god.

The names of the principal idols already alluded to are as follows: —

1. Rakelimalaza.	6. Rafaronatra.	11. Razanaharitsimandry.
2. Ramahavaly.	7. Ratsimahavaly.	12. Ralehifotsy.
3. Ramanjakatsiroa.	8. Rabehaza.	13. Ralehimalemalema.
4. Rafantaka.	9. Ravalolona.	14. Ratsisimba.
5. Ramanjaibola.	10. Rafohitanana.	15. Ralandrema.

Of these fifteen, the two first are by far the most important.

At a distance of seven miles eastward of Tananariva, is situated the village of Ambohimanambola; this place is the residence of Rakelimalaza. The whole of the hill occupied by the village is looked upon as sacred. The signification of the name of the idol is "Renowned although diminutive."

There are certain animals and objects which may not be admitted within the sacred precincts, and they have the

name of Fady. Every idol has its own particular Fady
Gunpowder, pigs, onions, a shell-fish called sifotra, robes
that are striped or spotted, goats, horses, cats, owls, with
fire-arms, and anything of a black color, form, for the
most part, the Fady of Rakelimalaza. The benefits supposed to be conferred by this idol are, — rendering the
sovereign invisible and victorious, defending those who
cross rivers from crocodiles, protecting true worshippers
from sorcery, and extinguishing fires.

Ramahavaly ranks next in importance; the signification
of his name is, " Capable of replying :" his residence is at
Ambohitany, though a house is prepared at the capital for
his occasional residence. There is a steep hady or fosse
round the idol-house, and no stranger is allowed to draw
near to it, lest the power of the charms of the idol should
suffer injury. The Fady of articles forbidden to approach
Ramahavaly, are the flesh of animals killed at funerals,
and other things. This idol most strictly forbids the
killing of serpents.

Ramahavaly is considered as the physician of Imerina,
and is frequently taken from one place to another to arrest
the progress of disease. A ceremony, called Miafana,
takes place at the capital, almost every year, wherein a
guardian of the idol officiates as priest, and sprinkles the
people assembled as they pass by, in the presence of the
idol, with honeyed water. While the sprinkling goes on, the
priest cries out, " Take courage, you, your wives and children ! You have Ramahavaly ! take courage for yourselves and your property ! He is the preserver of life ; and
should diseases invade, he will suddenly arrest them, and
prevent them coming near to injure you."

The name of the idol kept at the capital is Raman-
jakatsiroa, — i. e., "There are not two sovereigns," or,

"The king is supreme." This idol is, however, considered to be inferior to both Rakelimalaza and Ramahavaly.

The idol called Ranakandriana, on a high mountain at Andringitra, is supposed to have imparted the knowledge of divination to the Malagasy; and he is said, also, to reply when any one addresses him. It is not an improbable supposition that this belief has been brought about by the echo of the place, every sound being reverberated very distinctly among the rocks. Some years ago, King Radama resolved to visit Ranakandriana, to ascertain whether it was really true that an answer was given by him to any question proposed. No sooner had the monarch entered the dark cavern of the idol, and saluted the invisible divinity, than he heard a low and solemn voice reply to him. He then presented a small donation of money, but immediately seized the hand that was gently put forth to receive it. This hand he held fast, crying out, "This is no god—this is a human being!" At his command the impostor was then dragged forth; and thus the spell was broken, and the disbelief of the king in the practised superstition confirmed.

There are many inferior idols, and among them Kelimanjaka-lanitra, "Little, but ruling the heavens;" Manara-mody, "The restorer to one's home;" Rakapila, "Half dishevelled;" Randrano-vola, "The silver water;" Randrano-mena, "The red water;" Ramandroany, "The governor of the past part of the day;" Rafortribe, and others. Ramanandroany is considered potent in punishing an unknown thief; and the owner of the lost property thus addresses him: "As to whoever stole our property, O Ramanandroany! kill him by day, destroy him by night, and strangle him! Let there be none among men like him: let him not be able to increase in riches—not even a farthing—but let him pick up his livelihood as a hen pecks rice

grains: let his eyes be blinded, and his knees be swollen,
O Ramanandroany!"

When any one wishes to obtain a favor from an idol, he
accompanies his request with a present and a vow. The
keeper of the idol receives the offering in the name of the
idol, and retains it for his own benefit. Whatever be the
object of desire, it is stated to the keeper, who repeats it
to the idol; and if the request be favorably received, a
wisp of straw is rapidly whirled round by the keeper; but
if the straw move not, it is a sign that the idol is not propitious. If the request be for a safe return from war, or
prosperity in any enterprise, or the birth of a child, the
vow made with the request must be fulfilled as soon as may
be after the benefit has been obtained. To fulfil the vow
is to bring the promised offering: this is called Manala-
voady, the signification of which is, "to fetch away, or
remove the vow."

Sacrifices and offerings are not compulsory. Each individual gives what he pleases, according to his riches or
poverty. In some places the idol has the head, the blood,
and the fat only, while the carcass is devoured by the sacrificers and their friends:—this is a very convenient arrangement for the sacrificers.

There are many occasions on which the idols are publicly exhibited, and their antipathies are then proclaimed;
the following is one of these proclamations:—"Practise
abstinence well; let each of you take good heed to avoid
what is prohibited by his idol, whose antipathies are the
pig;—let him take heed that it have no access to the villages of his abode. The snail, musket, and onions, let them
not be borne there; and the goat and the horse, suffer them
not to ascend his villages; and in the time of thunder (that
is, summer), the children shall not play at kicking each
other blue. Ye shall not throw dirt at each other; for these

things are his antipathies, so do not these things, but take good heed."

The processions of the idols are curious. In one of them the first man carries the symbol of the idol on the top of a pole twenty feet in height. Round the symbol, and round the top of the pole, is wrapped scarlet velvet, which hang down like the skirts of a child's doll. The next man bears a bullock's horn, filled with honey-water, while in his right hand he holds a bunch of twigs, to be used in sprinkling. Then come fifty fine young men, each one carrying in his left hand a bundle of grass containing a serpent; his right hand is left free, that he may seize the reptile with it when he pleases. These young men walk two abreast, and brandish their arms about continually. - When the procession arrives at any place considered to be affected with sorcery or evil of any kind, it is sprinkled to purify it, and preserve it from harm; and when any fence or building is approached that is repugnant to the idol, a small part of it is removed, as a sign that it must be taken down; and with this requirement the owner of it is obliged to comply.

It was once thought that no human victims were slain, but this impression is incorrect. Human sacrifices were offered in former times in the province of Vangardrano. An immolation took place every Friday, and chiefs and principal men were often slain as a more costly sacrifice to the blood-thirsty Moloch who presided. The victims were speared, and devoured by dogs and birds. These sacrifices were not, strictly speaking, offered directly to the idol. The victims were slain before an enormous pole, on the top of which ody, or charms, were suspended, and the incantation and sacrifices were, both together, expected to work wondrous effects.

There are two ceremonies connected with the religious rites of Ankova, called Frantra and Afana. The first is

43

anything chosen by the sikidy for the removal of diseases : it may be ashes, a sheep, cut money, or a pumpkin. The priest reckons upon it all the evils that may be hurtful to the person for whom it is made, and charges the Faditra to take them away forever. If the Faditra be ashes, the wind is allowed to blow it away; if money, it is cast into deep water; if a sheep, it is carried to a great distance on the shoulders of a man who runs along, complaining all the while of the evils the Faditra is carrying away; and if it be a pumpkin, it is carried to a distance. and dashed in pieces against the ground.

The Afana is performed at the grave of a person lately buried, and consists of slaughtering cattle and feasting, accompanied with firing of muskets or cannon. The skulls of the slaughtered cattle are fixed on poles, at the head of the tomb. This is done to take evil from the dead, that he may repose in peace. The last kind act which can be performed for the dead is the ceremony of the Afana.

The term Vazimba has three significations, but in its strictest sense it designates the aborigines of the interior of Madagascar. The graves of the Vazimba are numerous, and to violate them in the slightest degree is a very heavy crime. So terribly tenacious and revengeful are the ghosts of the Vazimba said to be, that an accidental stumble against one of their resting-places would bring down a terrible doom on the inadvertent offender.

There are two characters attributed to the Vazimba: When a Vazimba grants what is asked of him, he is called masina — holy, forgiving, and effective ; when he does not grant it, and occasions evil, he is called masiaka — fierce and implacable.

To convince the Malagasy of the folly of their fears respecting the Vazimba, the missionaries cut off a branch from a tree growing near the most popular Vazimba grave, and also carried away one of the stones. This absolutely terrified some young men who were present, and they doubted not that some terrible accident would avenge the impiety, or that the Vazimba would appear to resent the affront offered to the tomb. Day after day the missionaries inquired if the Vazimba had appeared, and the young men were convinced that their fears were groundless. When, however, the missionaries asked them whether their parents were convinced that no danger was to be apprehended, they replied — "No! our parents say that you white people have some strong charms which the Vazimba are not able to resist."

Reports were circulated, after the death of king Radama, that he was seen one night in his garden, dressed in one of the uniforms buried with him in his silver coffin, and riding on one of his best horses. Old Andrianamba, one of the principal ministers, was immediately sent by the queen, attended by many priests, to ask Radama why he came again to disturb them. The priests had with them the idols and sikidy, and they sacrificed a bullock on the occasion. The priests inquired of Radama whether they had not buried property enough in his tomb? and whether he did not turn his back upon them of his own accord, for they had not driven him away. It seems that this attention, in the opinion of the Malagasy, appeased the ghost of the old monarch, and it came again no more. It is not known what is the origin of the term *sikidy*. The word means, among the Malagasy, a certain kind of divination, to which they are devotedly attached. It is not astrology, nor is it necromancy. It has nothing to do with the flight of birds, the inspection of the entrails of slaughtered animals, nor the interpretation of dreams. It partakes neither of the nature of magic, legerdemain, nor ordinary incantation. It is the mode of working a particular process with peans, straw, rice, or sand. The rules for this are fixed and invariable, and the result is considered certain.

Missionary efforts have been successfully made in Madagascar; schools have been formed, and a Malagasy Bible has been printed: but since the death of King Radama, the queen has prohibited the profession of the Christian faith by the natives; indeed, the profession of Christianity and the observance of Christian ordinances are punishable with death. At the present time a strong persecution is carried on against the native Christians, and the missionaries have left the island. A young woman named Rassalama has been cruelly put to death. She was severely flogged for several days before her life was taken. Rafaralahy, a young man, has also been put to death for professing the Christian faith. He died with great firmness and constancy. The reported death of Rafaravavy, who was accused to the government of possessing the Holy Scriptures, and reading them, is not correct. There is now but little prospect of the superstitious rites and ceremonies of Madagascar being soon exchanged for the Christian faith.

PAGANS OF POLYNESIA.

POLYNESIA is a name given by geographers to the great body of islands scattered over the Pacific ocean, between Australasia and the Philippines, and the American continent. It extends from lat. 35° N. to 50° S.; and from lon. 170° to 230° E.; an extent of 5000 miles from north to south, and 900 from west to east. It includes, therefore, the Sandwich Islands, the Marquesas, Navigators,

Society, Mulgrave, Friendly, Ladrone, and Pelew Isles, the Carolines, Pitcairn's Island, &c.

A general similarity in respect to the objects of religious worship, as well as the forms of idolatrous and superstitious practices, obtains throughout the whole of Polynesia; although some differences may be found between groups of islands, and even between islands belonging to the same group.

The supreme deity of Polynesia, who is generally regarded as the creator of the world, and the parent of gods and men, has different names in different groups. By the Tahitians, he is called *Taaroa;* by the Hawaiians, *Tanaroa;* and by the inhabitants of the western isles, *Tangaroa.* According to one of the legends of the Tahitian mythology, Taaroa was born of Night, or proceeded from Chaos, as did his consort Ofeufeumaiterai. Oro, the great national idol of Raitea, Tahiti, Eimeo, and some other islands, was the son of the foregoing. Oro took a goddess to wife, who became the mother of two sons. These four male and two female deities constituted their divinities of the highest rank. This was the catalogue furnished the missionaries by the priests of Tahiti. Other gods of high and uncreated order, however, are mentioned, as Raa, Tane, &c. Besides the above, they had numerous other inferior deities.

The image of Taaroa cannot well be described. It may be stated, however, in respect to one, which was taken from the temple at Rurutu, that it bore some resemblance to the human figure. It was about four feet high, and twelve or fifteen inches broad, and was carved out of a solid piece of close, white, durable wood. On his face and body a great number of images were formed, denoting the number of gods which had proceeded from him; the image was hollow, and within was found a number of small idols

43 *

In the Sandwich Islands there is a resemblance among all their idols. The head has generally a horrid appearance, the mouth being large, and usually extended wide. exhibiting a row of large teeth, resembling the cogs in the wheel of an engine, and adapted to excite terror rather than inspire confidence. Some of these idols are of stone ' others are composed of wicker work covered with red feathers.

The Polynesian temples are of three classes — national, local, and domestic. In the first are deposited their principal idols, and in and around them are held their great festivals; the second belong to the several districts; the third are appropriated to the worship of their household gods. In the South Sea islands the name of their temples was Marae; these were buildings of a rude construction, and resembled oratories more than temples.

The worship of the Polynesians consists of prayers, offerings, and sacrifices. In their prayers, they address their gods either in a kneeling posture, cross-legged, or crouching. Like the Pharisees in the days of our Saviour, they extend their supplications to a great length, and use many vain repetitions, thereby hoping to recommend themselves to the special notice of the deity. Their offerings consist of fowls, fishes, beasts of the field, fruits of the earth, and manufactures of various kinds. When animals are offered, they are generally whole; but fruits are commonly dressed. Portions of the offerings are considered sacred, and may not be eaten; the remainder is monopolized by the priests, and other sacred persons, who are privileged to eat of the sacrifices. Human victims were formerly offered in great numbers, especially in seasons of war, at great national festivals, during the illness of their rulers, and on the erection of their temples.

When an individual had been selected for sacrifice, the family to which he belonged was said to be *tabu*, i. e. devoted; and, hence, if another victim was wanted, it was likely to be taken from such a family. When the person was about to be sacrificed, he was generally murdered at a moment when he was little expecting the stroke. As soon as dead, his body was placed in a long basket, and carried to the temple. Here it was offered, not by burning it, but by placing it before the idol. After a variety of ceremonies by the priests, among which one was to pluck out an eye of the victim, which, being placed on a plantain leaf, was handed to the king, who passed it to his mouth, as if he would eat it; the body was wrapped in a basket of cocoa-nut leaves, and frequently deposited on the branches of a neighboring tree. Here having remained a considerable time, during which it became dry and shrivelled, it was taken down, and the bones were buried beneath the wide pavement of the Marae.

The religious system of the Samoans differs essentially from that which obtained at the Tahitian, Society, and other islands. They have neither maraes, nor temples, nor altars, nor offerings; and, consequently, none of the barbarous and sanguinary rites observed at the other groups. On this account the Samoans were considered an impious race. When the people of Rarotongo upbraided a person who had neglected the worship of the gods, they called him " a godless Samoan."

The objects worshipped by them were of three kinds — their deified ancestors, their idols, and their etus. Many of their ancestors were deified for conferring supposed benefits upon mankind. It was believed that the world was once in darkness; but that one of their progenitors, by an absurd process, created the sun, moon, and stars. For this he was worshipped, until the light of Christianity

dawned upon them. The chief of Aitutaki gave a short
account of the relics of idolatry. The following selection
may give the reader a general idea of the whole: —

An idol named Te-rongo, one of the great deities, called
a kai-tangata, or man-eater. The priests of this idol were
supposed to be inspired by the shark.

Tangaroa, the great national god of Aitutaki, and of
almost all the adjacent islands. He holds the net with
which he catches the spirits of men as they fly from their
bodies, and a spear with which he kills them.

A rod, with snares at the end, made of the fibres of
the cocoa-nut husk, with which the priest caught the spirit
of the god. It was used in cases of pregnancy, when the
female was ambitious that her child should be a son, and
become a famous warrior. It was also employed in war
time to catch the god by the leg, to secure his influence
on the side of the party performing the ceremony.

Ruanuu, a chief from Raiatea, who, ages ago, sailed in
a canoe from that island, and settled at Aitutaki. From
him a genealogy is traced. He died at Aitutaki, and was
deified, as Te atua taitai tere, or the conductor of fleets.
The Raiateans have several interesting traditions connected
with Ruanuu. To this idol was appended an old tattered
silk handkerchief, and the foot of a wine-glass; both of
which were obtained from Captain Cook's vessel, and
dedicated to Ruanuu, the "god or guide of fleets," for
conducting that celebrated navigator to their shores.

Taau, with his fan, &c., the god of thunder. When the
thunder pealed, the natives said that this god was flying,
and producing this sound by the flapping of his wings.

PAGANS OF LAPLAND

FROM the time that so large a portion of Lapland fell under the dominion of Sweden, repeated attempts were made to convert the natives to the Christian faith; and the same object was diligently prosecuted by the Danish government. The Laplanders, however, continued to retain a strong attachment to their ancient mythology; and even so late as the middle of the eighteenth century, a great part of the nation secretly worshipped idols while publicly professing the Christian religion.

To these idols were presented various offerings and sacrifices. Upon any change of habitation, libations were made of whey or milk, to conciliate the guardian divinity of the place; and of brandy to the Lares or household gods, who were supposed to reside under the fire-place. To conciliate the favor of the deities to their children, sacrifices of sheep or deer were offered, before the child was born: a dog was buried alive at the moment of the birth; and some other animal killed when the infant was at the breast. Offerings and sacrifices were usually made for the removal of epidemic disorders, for success in hunting, &c. In these cases, sometimes the whole of the victim was presented, sometimes only a part, sometimes merely the bones, while the blood was sprinkled upon staves, which were left on the spot, or mingled with the waters of an adjacent river or lake. The liver of a bear, the horns and other parts of a deer, taken in the chase, were very frequently consecrated to the deity of the place.

The Laplanders, according to Picart, worship their gods under the form of a tree, or block of wood, the top of which they form into a rude resemblance of a man's head. In the head they were wont to drive a large nail, to which was fastened a flint stone, that he might make himself a fire when ever he found one needful. Sometimes their god was raised upon a kind of table, which served in capacity of an altar. Their domestic deity, or household god, they represented under the form of a large stone, carved in a rude manner, and bearing some resemblance to a human face. The sacrifices which were offered to these idols were presented by a privileged class of men, named Noaaids, who divided the victims with great expertness, and wore at the time of sacrificing a peculiar habit.

The Laplanders still retain much of their ancient super stitious spirit, even in the Christian rites which they have adopted. They particularly regard the sacrament as a powerful charm to preserve them from the attempts of evil spirits. It is not long since they used to take a cloth with them to church, into which they were accustomed to spit out the sacramental bread, which they wrapped up with great care, and afterwards divided into as great a number as possible of small crumbs. One of these crumbs was given to every one of their cattle, in the full persuasion that the herd would thus be secure from all injury. Their very deficient acquaintance with Christianity may, in some measure, be ascribed to the very inefficient manner in which they are instructed. It has generally been the practice of the Missionaries and pastors to address the natives by means of an interpreter, and the attempts of the Danish government to remedy this defect have hitherto proved unsuccessful.

PAGANS OF NORTH AMERICA.

THE aborigines of New England no⁺ only believed in a plurality of gods who made and govern the several nations of the world, but they made deities of everything they ima gined to be great, powerful, beneficial, or hurtful to man- kind ; yet they conceived an almighty Being, who dwells in the southwest regions of the heavens, to be superior to all the rest. This almighty Being they called Kichtan, who at first, according to their tradition, made a man and a woman out of a stone ; but, upon some dislike, destroyed them again, and then made another couple out of a tree, from whom descended all the nations of the earth : but how they came to be scattered and dispersed into countries so remote from one another, they cannot tell. They believed their supreme God to be a good being, and paid a sort of acknowledgment to him for plenty, victory, and other bene- fits. But there is another power, which they call Hoba- mocko (*i. e*, the devil), of whom they stood in greater awe, and worshipped—merely from a principle of fear. The im- mortality of the soul was in some sort universally believed among them. When good men die, they said their spirits go to Kichtan, where they meet their friends, and enjoy all manner of pleasures. When wicked men die, they go to Kichtan also; but are commanded to walk away, and to wander about in restless discontent and darkness for ever.

The original inhabitants of Canada, like other heathen, had an idea of a supreme Being, whom they considered as the creator and governor of the world. It is said that most of the nations which speak the Algonquin language, give this being the appellation of the Great Hare, but some call

him Michabou, and others Atahocan. They believe that
he was born upon the waters, together with his whole court,
who were composed of four-footed animals, like himself;
that he formed the earth of a grain of sand taken from the
bottom of the ocean; and that he created men of the bodies
of dead animals. Some mention a god of the waters, who
opposed the designs of the Great Hare, who is called the
great Tiger. They have a third called Matcomek, whom
they invoke in the winter season.

According to the Iroquois, in the third generation there
came a deluge, in which not a soul was saved; so that, in
order to repeople the earth, it was necessary to change
beasts into men. Besides the first Being, or Great Spirit,
they hold an infinite number of genii, or inferior spirits,
both good and evil, who have each their peculiar form of
worship. They ascribe to these beings a kind of immensity and omnipresence, and constantly invoke them as the
guardians of mankind; and they only address themselves
to the evil genii, to beg of them to do them no hurt. They
believe in the immortality of the soul, and say that the
region of their everlasting abode lies so far westward, that
the souls are several months in arriving at it, and have vast
difficulties to surmount. The happiness that they hope to
enjoy is not believed to be the recompense of virtue only,
but to have been a good hunter, brave in war, &c., are the
chief merits which entitle them to their paradise: this they
and other American natives describe as a delightful country,
blessed with perpetual spring, whose forests abound with
game, whose rivers swarm with fish, where famine is never
felt, but uninterrupted plenty shall be enjoyed without labor
or fatigue.

The Indians of Virginia gave the names of *Okee*, *Quioccos*, or *Kiwasa*, to the idol which they worshipped.
These names might possibly be so many epithets, which

they varied according to the several functions they, as cribed to this deity, or the different notions they might form to themselves of it in their religious exercises and common discourses. Moreover, they were of opinion that this idol is not one sole being, but that there were many more of the same nature, besides the tutelary gods. They gave the general name of Quioccos to all these genii, or beings, so that the name of Kiwasa might be particularly applied to the idol in question.

These savages consecrated chapels and oratories to this deity, in which the idol was often represented under a variety of shapes. They even kept some of these in the most retired part of their houses, to whom they communicated their affairs, and consulted them upon occasion. In this case they made use of them in the quality of tutelary gods, from whom they supposed they received blessings on their families.

The sacerdotal vestment of their priests was like a woman's petticoat plaited, which they put about their necks, and tied over their right shoulder; but they always kept one arm out to use it as the occasion required. This cloak was made round at the bottom, and descended no lower than the middle of the thigh; it was made of soft, well-dressed skins, with the hair outwards.

These priests shaved their heads close, the crown excepted, where they left only a little tuft, that reached from the top of the forehead to the nape of the neck, and even on the top of the forehead. They here left a border of hair, which, whether it was owing to nature, or the stiffness contracted by the fat and colors with which they daubed themselves, bristled up, and came forward like the corner of a square cap.

The Virginians had a great veneration for their priests; and the latter endeavored to procure it by daubing themselves all over in a very frightful manner; dressing themselves in a very odd habit, and tricking up their hair after a very whimsical manner. Everything they said was considered as an oracle, and made a strong impression on the minds of the people; they often withdrew from society, and lived in woods or in huts, far removed from any habitation. They were difficult of access; and did not give themselves any trouble about provisions, because care was always taken to set food for them near their habitations They were always addressed in cases of great necessity. They also acted in the quality of physicians, because of the great knowledge they were supposed to have of nature. In fine, peace or war was determined by their voice, nor was anything of importance undertaken without first consulting them.

They had not any stated times nor fixed days on which they celebrated their festivals, but they regulated them only by the different seasons of the year. As, for instance, they celebrated one day on the arrival of their wild birds, another upon the return of the hunting season, and for the maturity of their fruits; but the greatest festival of all was at harvest time. They then spent several days in diverting themselves, and enjoyed most of their amusements, such as martial dances and heroic songs.

After their return from war, or escaping some danger, they lighted fires and made merry about them, each having his gourd-bottle or his little bell in his hand. Men, women, and children often danced in a confused manner about these fires. Their devotions in general consisted only of acclamations of joy, mixed with dances and songs; except in seasons of sorrow and affliction, when they were changed into howlings. The priests presided at this solemnity, dressed in their sacerdotal ornaments, part of which were the gourd-bottle, the petticoat above mentioned, and the serpents' or weasels' skins, the tails of which were dexterously tied upon their heads like a tiara or triple-crown. These priests began the song, and always opened the religious exercise, to which they often added incantations, part of the mysteries of which were comprehended in the songs above mentioned. The noise, the gestures, the wry faces, in a word, everything, contributed to render these incantations terrible.

PAGANS OF MEXICO

THE deities of the ancient Mexicans are said to have exceeded two thousand, who had their respective temples, ceremonies, and sacrifices. There was hardly a street without its tutelary divinity, nor was there scarcely a disease which had not its peculiar altar, to which the Mexicans flocked in order to be healed. Their principal deity was *Vitzliputzli*, whom they considered the sovereign lord of all things, and creator of heaven and earth. The greatest god after Vitzliputzli was the *Sun*. Another of their divinities was *Tlaloch*, whom some writers confound with *Tescalipuca*. But these were considered brothers, of equal strength, and so similar in disposition, that the sovereign power of war was divided between them. *Tescalipuca* was, however, more appropriately the god of penance, whom the Mexicans invoked in seasons of adversity. The *Mercury* and *Plutus* of the Mexicans, the former of whom was sometimes called *Quitzalcoalt*, was represented under a human shape, except that it had the head of a bird, with a painted paper mitre upon its head, and a scythe in its hand. The body of it was covered with jewels of extraordinary value. Besides the foregoing, the Mexicans worshipped various other deities, among whom we shall mention only *Tozi*, a beautiful woman, for whom, at her death, Vitzliputzli procured divine honors. Nearly all their divinities were clothed with terror, and delighted in vengeance. The figures of serpents, of tigers, and of other destructive animals, decorated their temples. Fasts, mortifications, and penances, all rigid, and many of them excruciating to an extreme degree, were the means which they employed to appease the wrath of the gods. But of all offerings, human sacrifices were deemed the most acceptable. At the dedication of the great temple at Mexico, it is reported there were 60,000 or 70,000 human sacrifices. The usual amount of them was about 20,000

When the bloody sacrifices of the Mexicans took place, the victims about to be slain were assembled at a charnal-house on a terrace. A priest, holding in his hand an idol made of wheat-maize and honey, drew near to these unhappy wretches, and presenting it to each of them, cried out at the same time, "There is your god!"

This done, they withdrew, going off on the other side of the terrace, when the victims were immediately brought upon it, being the place appointed for the sacrifice. Six ministers of the idol here slaughtered these victims; and having torn out their hearts, they threw the bodies down the staircase, from the top to the bottom of the terrace.

They never sacrificed less than forty of these victims at a time; and those nations who either bordered on, or were tributary to, the Mexicans, imitated them in this bloody worship.

Another religious ceremony, which indeed does not seem so barbarous as the former, was the duel of the victim, if we may give this name to the liberty he was allowed of defending himself against the priest who was to sacrifice him. The captive, whose feet were tied to a stone, parried the instrument with which the priest struck at him, and even attacked him in his turn. If he had the good fortune to conquer the priest, he was released, and considered as a brave man; but if the priest came off conqueror, he first killed him, then stripped off his skin, and had his limbs dressed and served up at one of those meals called by them their religious meals.

The high priest was called Tapizlin in the Mexican language. It is pretended that his dignity was equal to that of the pope. He wore on his head a crown of beautiful feathers of various colors, with golden pendants, enriched with emeralds, at his ears, and a small blue tube, similar to that of the god of penance, ran through his lip. He was clothed in a scarlet robe, or rather mantle. The vestments of their priests were frequently changed according to the different seasons or festivals.

The priesthood of Vitzliputzli was hereditary, and that of the other gods elective. Children were often destined from their most tender years to the service of idols, and officiated as clerks, and singing boys, when but mere striplings. The priests used to incense four times every day the god, whose ministers they were; but at midnight, the principal ministers of the temple rose to perform the nocturnal office, viz., to sound a trumpet and horn for a considerable time, and to play on certain instruments, accompanied with voices, which together celebrated the praises of the idol. After this, the priest, whose turn it was, took the thurible, saluted the idol, and incensed it, himself being clothed in a black mantle. In fine, after the incensing was over, they all went together into a chapel, where they practised all those rigorous penances which have been already described.

The Mexicans, at the end of every month, which among them consisted of twenty days, used to observe a solemn

day of devotion, mixed with rejoicings. They then sacrificed some captives, and ran up and down the streets
clothed in the skins of those miserable victims that had
been just flayed. They danced, they sang, they collected
alms for the priests, the giving of which among them, as
in other places, was looked upon as an effect of real piety.
The great festival of Vitzliputzli was celebrated in the
month of May, two days before which, the nuns used t
make a figure of maize and honey, representing that god.
Then having dressed it in as magnificent a manner as
possible, they seated it on an azure throne, which was
supported by a kind of shaft. The nuns, who on that
festival used to call themselves the sisters of Vitzliputzli,
carried it in procession on their shoulders, to the area
before the temple, where the young monks before cited
received the idol, and, after having paid homage to it,
carried it also on their shoulders to the steps of the
sanctuary.

The festival of Tescalipuca was celebrated the nineteenth
of the same month, when the priests granted the people a
remission of their sins. At the same time they sacrifice a
captive, which we may almost consider as an imperfect
image of the death which our blessed Saviour suffered for
the redemption of mankind.

The Mexicans used to celebrate a jubilee every four
years, which was nothing more than the feast of penance,
such as we have already described, except that it was more
solemn, there being at that time a more general and
plenary remission of sins. We are assured that the Mexicans sacrificed many human victims at this season. And
the youth used to make a kind of challenge, who should
first, and in one breath, get to the top of the temple. This
enterprise was a very difficult one, since it gained applause
to all those who had the glory of coming first to the goal,

not to mention that they were distinguished from the rest of their countrymen, and, moreover, had the privilege of carrying off the sacred viands, of which they made the same use as Catholics do of relics.

Forty days before the feast of Quitzalcoalt, the merchants purchased a slave of a very fine shape, who, during that time, represented the deity to whom he was to be sacrificed as a victim on the day of the festival; but they first washed him in the lake of the gods, which was the name they gave to the water which fitted him for the fatal apotheosis which ended with his death.

Marriage was solemnized by the authority of the priests, and a public instrument was drawn up, in which were mentioned the particulars of the wife's fortune, which the husband was obliged to return in case of separation. After their having agreed upon the articles, the couple went to the temple, where one of the sacrificing priests examined their resolutions by certain precise questions appointed for that purpose. He afterwards took up the husband's mantle and the woman's veil, and with one of his hands tied them together at one corner, to signify the inward tie of the wills. They then returned to their house, bound in this manner, accompanied by the sacrificing priest. Then they went and visited the hearth or fire, which they looked upon as the mediator of all disputes between man and wife. They used to go seven times round it, successively, the sacrificing priest walking before; after which ceremony they both sat down, in order to be equally warmed by the heat of the fire, which gave the perfection to marriage.

Burials and all funeral rites were regulated by their priests. They generally buried their dead in their gardens or houses, and commonly chose the courtyard for that purpose; they sometimes buried them in those places where they sacrificed to the idols. In fine, they frequently burned them, after which they buried their ashes in the temples, together with their movables, their utensils, and all they thought might be useful to them in the next world. They used to sing at funerals, and even made feasts on those occasions, which custom, how ridiculous soever it may be, some Christian nations have not been able to persuade themselves to lay aside. Above all, they buried their great lords in a very magnificent manner, and used to carry their bodies with great pomp and a numerous train into the temples. The priests walked first with their pans of copal, singing funeral hymns with a melancholy tone, accompanied with the hoarse and mournful sound of flutes. They lifted the body several times on high, while they were sacrificing those who were appointed to serve the illustrious dead. The domestics were put to death to keep their masters company. It was a testimony of great affection, but very common among the lawful wives, to solemnize, by their deaths, the funerals of their husbands. They buried a great quantity of gold and silver with the deceased for the expense of his journey, which they imagined was long and troublesome. The common people imitated the grandees in proportion to their substance. The friends of the deceased came and made presents to him, and talked to him as if he were still living; the same ceremonies were practised whether they burned or buried the dead. We must not omit to state that they carried with them the achievements and trophies of the deceased, in case he were a man of quality, and that the priest who read the funeral service was dressed so as to set forth the glory of the idol whom the nobleman represented. The funeral lasted ten days.

The city of Mexico is said to have contained nearly 2000 small temples, and 360 which were adorned with steeples. The whole empire of Mexico contained about 40,000 temples, endowed with very considerable revenues For the service in the grand temple of Mexico itself, above 5000 priests were appointed; and the number in the whole empire is said to have amounted to nearly a million. The whole priesthood, excepting that of the conquered nations, was governed by two high priests, who were also the oracles of the kings. Besides the service in the temple, their clergy were to instruct the youth, to compose the calendars, and to paint the mythological pictures. The Mexicans had also priestesses, but they were not allowed to offer up sacrifices. They likewise had monastic orders, especially one, into which no person was admitted under sixty years of age.

PAGANS OF PERU.

THE Peruvians, previously to being governed by their Incas, worshipped a great number of gods, or rather genii. There was no nation, family, city, street, or even house, but had its peculiar gods; and for this particular reason, that they thought none but the god to whom they immediately devoted themselves was able to assist them in time of need. They worshipped herbs, plants, flowers, trees, mountains, caves, beasts, adders; in fine, everything that appeared wonderful in their eyes was thought worthy of adoration.

These ancient idolaters of Peru offered not only the fruits of the earth and animals to these gods, but also their captives, like the rest of the Americans. It was their custom to sacrifice their own children, whenever there was a scarcity of victims.

Some other idolaters offered their own blood to their deities, which they drew from their arms and thighs, according as the sacrifice was more or less solemn; and they even used, on extraordinary occasions, to bleed themselves at the tips of their nostrils, or between the eyebrows.

Such was the state of idolatry all over Peru, when the Inca *Mancocapac*, the lawgiver of that vast empire, taught the savages the worship of the *Sun*. From this time, sacrifices of various kinds of animals were offered in honor of the sun, and also cocoa, corn, rich clothes, and a liquor made of water and maize. They always presented the last offering to the sun in the following manner: When they were very thirsty, the first satisfied their hunger, and afterwards dipped the tip of their finger in the vessel into which the liquor was poured; this being done, they lifted up their eyes to heaven in a very submissive manner; shook that finger on which the drop hung, and offered it to the sun as an acknowledgment for his goodness in providing drink for them. At the same time they gave two or three kisses to the air. This oblation being made, they all drank as they thought proper.

Every time they entered their temples, the chief man in the company laid his hand on one of his eyebrows, and whether he tore off any of the hairs or not, he blew it into the air before the idol, as a mark of its being an oblation. They paid the same adoration to trees, and to all those things which a divine virtue had made sacred and religious.

ROMAN CATHOLICS.

ALTHOUGH, in ordinary language, the name *Roman Catholic Church* is often used to designate the ruling authority or power in the Catholic religion, as if distinct from the members of that communion, yet the definition which Catholics give of the Church is such as to comprehend the entire body of its members as well as its rulers, the flock as much as the shepherds. Thus we hear of Catholics being under the dominion of their Church, or obliged to obey it, as though it were something distinct from themselves, or as if they were not a part of their Church. This preliminary remark is made to explain a certain vagueness of expression, which often leads to misapprehension, and serves as the basis of incorrect ideas regarding the peculiar doctrines of that Church—a vagueness similar to what is frequent in writing and speaking on jurisprudence; as, for example, where the government of a country is considered as a power distinct and almost at variance with the nation which it rules, and not an integral part thereof.

The Catholic Church, therefore, is defined to be the community of the faithful united to their lawful pastors, in communion with the see of Rome or with the Pope, the successor of St. Peter, and vicar of Christ on earth.

Simply developing the terms of this definition, we will give a brief sketch of the constitution or fundamental system of this Church, under the heads of its government, its laws, and its vital or constitutive principle.

I. The government of the Catholic Church may be considered monarchical, inasmuch as the Pope is held in it to be the ruler over the entire Church, and the most distant bishop of the Catholic Church holds his appointment from him, and receives from him his authority. No bishop can be considered lawfully consecrated without his approbation. The dignity or office of Pope is inherent in the occupant of the see of Rome, because the supremacy over the Church is believed to be held in virtue of a commission given to St. Peter, not as his own personal prerogative, but as a part of the constitution of the Church, for its advantage, and therefore intended to descend to his successors — as the episcopal power did from the apostles to those who succeeded them in their respective sees.

The election of the Pope, therefore, devolves upon the clergy of Rome, as being their bishop; and it is confided to the college of cardinals, who, bearing the titles of the eldest churches in that city, represent its clergy, and form their chapter or electoral body. The meeting or chapter formed for this purpose alone is called a *conclave*. The cardinals are in their turn appointed by the Pope, and compose the executive council of the Church. They preside over the various departments of ecclesiastical government, and are divided into boards or congregations, as they are called, for the transaction of business from all parts of the world; but every decision is subject to the Pope's revision, and has no value except from his approbation.

On some occasions they are all summoned together to meet the Pope on affairs of higher importance, as for the nomination of bishops, or the admission of new members into their body; and then the assembly is called a *consistory*. The full number of cardinals is seventy-two, but· there are always some hats left vacant.

The Catholic Church being essentially episcopal, is governed by bishops, who are of two sorts, bishops in ordinary, and vicars apostolic. By the first are meant titular bishops, or such as bear the name of the see over which they rule; as the Archbishop of Paris, or of Dublin; the Bishop of Cambray or New Orleans. The manner of appointing such bishops varies considerably. Where they are unshackled by the government, the clergy of the diocese meet in chapter, according to old forms, and having selected three names, forward them to the Holy See, where one is chosen for promotion. This is the case in Ireland, Belgium, and perhaps in the free states of America. In most countries, however, the election of bishops is regulated by *concordat;* that is, a special agreement between the Pope and the civil government. The presentation is generally vested in the crown; but the appointment must necessarily emanate from the Pope.

The powers of bishops, and the manner of exercising their authority, are regulated by the canon law; their jurisdiction on every point is clear and definite, and leaves no room for arbitrary enactments or oppressive measures. Yet it is of such a character as, generally considered, can perfectly control the inferior orders of clergy, and secure them to the discharge of their duty. In most Catholic countries there is a certain degree of civil jurisdiction allowed to the bishops, with judicial powers, in matters of a mixed character; as in cases appertaining to marriages, where a distinction between civil and ecclesiastical marriage has not been drawn by the legislature. Some offences connected with religion, as blasphemy or domestic immorality, are likewise brought under their cognizance.

Where the succession of the Catholic hierarchy has been interrupted, as in England, or never been established, as in Australasia or some parts of India, the bishops who superintend the Catholic Church, and represent the papal authority, are known by the name of *vicars apostolic.* A vicar apostolic is not necessarily a bishop—an instance of

which we have now at Calcutta, where the vicar apostolic
is a simple priest.   Generally, however, he receives episcopal consecration; and as, from local circumstances, it is
not thought expedient that he should bear the title of the
see which he administers, he is appointed with the title of
an ancient bishopric now in the hands of infidels, and thus
is called a bishop *in partibus infidelium*, though the last
word is often omitted in ordinary language.   A vicar apostolic, being generally situated where the provisions of the
canon law cannot be fully observed, is guided by particular
instructions, by precedents and consuetude, to all which
the uniformity of discipline through the Catholic Church
gives stability and security.   Thus the vicars apostolic,
who rule over the four episcopal districts of England, have
their code in the admirable constitution of Pope Benedict
XIV., beginning with the words *Apostolicum ministerium*.
The powers of a vicar apostolic are necessarily more extended than those of ordinary bishops, and are ampler in
proportion to the difficulty of keeping up a close communication with Rome.   Thus, many cases of dispensation in
marriage which a continental bishop must send to the
Holy See, may be provided for by an English or American
vicar apostolic; and other similar matters, for which these
must consult it, could at once be granted by the ecclesiastical superiors of the Mauritius or of China.   The nomination of vicars apostolic is solely with the Pope.

The inferior clergy, considered in reference to the government of the Church, consists mainly of the parochial
clergy, or those who supply their place.   In all countries
possessing a hierarchy, the country is divided into parishes,
each provided with a *parochus* or *curate*,* corresponding

---

* To avoid mistakes, we may observe that the parish priest in Ireland corresponds to the curé in France the curato (or in the coun-

to the rector or vicar of the English Established Church. The appointment to a parish is vested in the bishop, who has no power to remove again at will, or for any cause except a canonical offence juridically proved. The right of presentation by lay patrons is, however, in particular instances, fully respected. In Italy the parish priests are generally chosen by competition; as, upon a vacancy, a day is appointed on which the testimonials of the different candidates are compared, and they themselves personally examined before the bishop in theology, the exposition of Scripture, and extemporaneous preaching; and whoever is pronounced, by ballot, superior to the rest, is chosen.

Under an apostolic vicariate, the clergy corresponding to the parochial clergy generally bear the title of *apostolic missionaries*, and have *missions* or local districts, with variable limits, placed under their care; but are dependent upon the will of their ecclesiastical superiors.

Besides the parochial clergy, there is a considerable body of ecclesiastics, who do not enter directly into the governing part of the Church, although they help to discharge some of its most important functions. A great number of *secular* clergy are devoted to the conduct of education, either in universities or seminaries; many occupy themselves exclusively with the pulpit, others with instructing the poor, or attending charitable institutions. A certain number also fill prebends, or attend to the daily service of cathedrals, etc.; for in the Catholic Church, pluralities, where the cure of souls exists, are strictly prohibited, and consequently a distinct body of clergy from those engaged in parochial duties, or holding rectories, etc., is necessary for those duties. Besides this auxiliary

---

try. arciprete) of Italy, and the cura of Spain. The curate in Ireland, as in the church of England, is equivalent to the vicaire of France and the sotto-curato of Italy.

force, the *regular* clergy, or monastic orders, take upon them many of these functions. The clergy of the Catholic Church in the west are bound by a vow of celibacy, not formally made, but implied in their ordination as *sub-deacons*. This obligation of celibacy is only reckoned among the disciplinary enactments of the Church. The clergy of that portion of the Greek and Armenian church which is united in communion with the see of Rome, may be married; that is, may receive orders if married, but are not allowed to marry after having taken orders. A similar discipline, if thought expedient by the Church, might be introduced into the west.

The only point concerning the government of the Catholic Church which remains to be mentioned is the manner in which it is exercised. The most solemn tribunal is a *general council*, that is, an assembly of all the bishops of the Church, who may attend either in person or by deputy, under the presidency of the Pope or his legates. When once a decree has passed such an assembly, and received the approbation of the Holy See, there is no further appeal. Distinction must be, however, made between *doctrinal* and *disciplinary* decrees; for example, when in the council of Trent it was decreed to be the doctrine of the Church, that marriage is indissoluble, this decree is considered binding in the belief and on the conduct, nor can its acceptance be refused by any one without his being considered rebellious to the Church. But when it is ordered that marriages must be celebrated only in presence of the parish priest, this is a matter of discipline, not supposed to rest on the revelation of God, but dictated by prudence; and consequently a degree of toleration is allowed regarding the adoption of the resolution in particular dioceses. It is only with regard to such decrees, and more specifically the one we have mentioned, that the council of Trent is said to have been received, or not, in different countries.

When a general council cannot be summoned, or when it is not deemed necessary, the general government of the Church is conducted by the Pope, whose decisions in matters of discipline are considered paramount, though particular sees and countries claim certain special privileges and exemptions. In matters of faith it is admitted that if he issue a decree, as it is called, *ex cathedrâ*, or as head of the Church, and all the bishops accept it, such definition or decree is binding and final.*

The discipline or reformation of smaller divisions is performed by provincial or diocesan synods. The first consist of the bishops of a province under their metropolitan ; the latter of the parochial and other clergy under the superin tendence of the bishop. The forms to be observed in such assemblies, the subjects which may be discussed, and the extent of jurisdiction which may be assumed, are laid down at full in a beautiful work of the learned Benedict XIV., entitled "De Synodo Diocesana." The acts and decrees of many such partial synods have been published, and are held in high esteem among Catholics ; indeed, they may be recommended as beautiful specimens of deliberative wisdom. Such are the decrees of the various synods held at Milan under the virtuous and amiable St. Charles Borromeo.

II. The *laws* of the Catholic Church may be divided into two classes, those which bind the interior, and those which

---

* The great difference between the Transalpine and Cisalpine divines, as they are termed, is whether such a decree has its force prior to, or independent of, the accession of the body of bishops to it, or receives its sanction and binding power from their acceptance. Practically there is little or no difference between the two opinions; yet this slight variety forms a principal groundwork of what are called the liberties of the Gallican church.

45 *

regulate outward conduct. This distinction, which corresponds to that above made, between doctrinal and disciplinary decrees, may appear unusual, as the term *laws* seems hardly applicable to forms of thought or belief. Still, viewing, as we have done, the Catholic Church under the form of an organized religious society, and considering that it professes to be divinely authorized to exact interior assent to all that it teaches, under the penalty of being separated from its communion, we think we can well classify under the word *law* those principles and doctrines which it commands and expects all its members to profess.

Catholics often complain that doctrines are laid to their charge which they do not hold, and in their various publications protest against their belief being assumed upon any but authoritative documents; and as such works are perfectly accessible, the complaint must appear reasonable as well as just. There are several works in which an accurate account is given of what Catholics are expected to believe, and which carefully distinguish between those points on which latitude of opinion is allowed, and such as have been fully and decisively decreed by the supreme authority of the Church. Such are Veron's "Regula Fidei," or Rule of Faith, a work lately translated into English, and Holden's "Analysis Fidei." But there are documents of more authority than these; for example, the "Declaration" set forth by the vicars apostolic or bishops in England, in 1823, often republished; and still more the "Catechismus ad Parochos," or "Catechism of the Council of Trent," translated into English not many years ago, and published in Dublin. A perusal of such works as these will satisfy those who are desirous of full and accurate information regarding Catholic tenets, of their real nature, and show that the popular expositions of their substance and character are generally incorrect.

Th? formulary of faith, which persons becoming members of the Catholic Church are expected to recite, and which is sworn to upon taking any degree, or being appointed to a chair in a university, is the creed of Pius IV., of which the following is the substance:

The preamble runs as follows: "I, N. N., with a firm faith believe and profess all and every one of those things which are contained in that creed, which the holy Roman Church maketh use of." Then follows the Nicene creed.

"I most steadfastly admit and embrace apostolical and ecclesiastical traditions, and all other observances and constitutions of the same Church.

"I also admit the Holy Scriptures, according to that sense which our holy mother the Church has held and does hold, to which it belongs to judge of the true sense and interpretation of the Scriptures; neither will I ever take and interpret them otherwise than according to the unanimous consent of the fathers.

"I also profess that there are truly and properly seven sacraments of the new law, instituted by Jesus Christ our Lord, and necessary for the salvation of mankind, though not all for every one, to wit: baptism, confirmation, the eucharist, penance,* extreme unction, holy orders,† and matrimony; and that they confer grace; and that of these, baptism, confirmation, and orders cannot be reiterated with-

---

* Under penance is included confession; as the Catholic sacrament of penance consists of three parts: contrition or sorrow, confession, and satisfaction.

† The clerical orders of the Catholic Church are divided into two classes, *sacred* and *minor* orders. The first consists of subdeacons, deacons, and priests, who are bound to celibacy and the daily recitation of the *Breviary*, or collection of psalms and prayers, occupying a considerable time. The minor orders are four in number, and are preceded by the *tonsure*, an ecclesiastical ceremony in which the hair is shorn, initiatory to the ecclesiastical state.

out sacrilege. I also receive and admit the received and approved ceremonies of the Catholic Church, used in the solemn administration of the aforesaid sacraments.

"I embrace and receive all and every one of the things which have been defined and declared in the holy Council of Trent, concerning original sin and justification.

"I profess likewise that in the mass there is offered to God a true, proper, and propitiatory sacrifice for the living and the dead; and that in the most holy sacrament of the eucharist there is truly, really, and substantially, the body and blood, together with the soul and divinity, of our Lord Jesus Christ; and that there is made a change of the whole substance of the bread into the body, and of the whole substance of the wine into the blood, which change the Catholic Church calls *transubstantiation*. I also confess that under either kind alone Christ is received whole and entire, and a true sacrament.

"I firmly hold that there is a *purgatory*, and that the souls therein detained are helped by the suffrages of the faithful.

"Likewise, that the saints reigning with Christ are to be honored and invocated, and that they offer up prayers to God for us; and that their relics are to be had in veneration.

"I most firmly assert that the images of Christ, of the mother of God, and also of other saints, ought to be had and retained, and that due honor and veneration are to be given them.

"I also affirm that the power of indulgences was left by Christ in the Church, and that the use of them is most wholesome to Christian people.

"I acknowledge the holy Catholic Apostolic Roman Church for the mother and mistress of all churches; and I promise true obedience to the Bishop of Rome, successor to St. Peter, prince of the apostles, and vicar of Jesus Christ."

Then follow clauses condemnatory of all contrary doctrines, and expressive of adhesion to all the definitions of the Council of Trent.

It is obvious that this form of confession was framed in accordance to the decrees of that council, and consequently has chiefly in view the opinions of those who followed the Reformation. It would be foreign to our purpose to enter into any explanations of the doctrines here laid down, much less into any statement of the grounds on which Catholics hold them, as we purposely refrain from all polemical discussion.

Such is the doctrinal code of the Catholic Church; of its moral doctrines we need not say anything, because no authorized document could be well referred to that embodies them all. There are many decrees of Popes condemnatory of immoral opinions or propositions, but no positive decrees. Suffice it to say, that the moral law, as taught in the Catholic Church, is mainly the same as other denominations of Christians profess to follow.

Of the disciplinary or governing code we have already spoken, when we observed that it consisted of the Canon Law, which, unlike the doctrinal and moral code, may vary with time, place, and accidental circumstances.

III. Our last head was the essential or constitutive principle of the Catholic Church. By this we mean that principle which gives it individuality, distinguishes it from other religions, pervades all its institutions, and gives the answer to every query regarding the peculiar constitution outward and inward of this Church.

Now, the fundamental position, the constitutive principle of the Catholic Church, is the doctrine and belief that God has promised, and consequently bestows upon it, a constant and perpetual protection, to the extent of guaranteeing it from destruction, from error, or fatal corruption. This principle once admitted, everything else follows. 1. The infallibility of the Church in its decisions on matters concerning faith. 2. The obligation of submitting to all these decisions, independently of men's own private judgments or opinions. 3. The authority of tradition, or the unalterable character of all the doctrines committed to the Church; and hence the persuasion that those of its dogmas which to others appear strange and unscriptural, have been in reality handed down, uncorrupted, since the time of the apostles, who received them from Christ's teaching. 4. The necessity of religious unity, by perfect uniformity of belief; and thence, as a corollary, the sinfulness of wilful separation or schism, and culpable errors or heresy. 5. Government by authority, since they who are aided and supported by such a promise must necessarily be considered appointed to direct others, and are held as the representatives and vicegerents of Christ in the Church. 6. The papal supremacy, whether considered as a necessary provision for the preservation of this essential unity, or as the principal depository of the divine promises. 7. In fine, the authority of councils, the right to enact canons and ceremonies, the duty of repressing all attempts to broach new opinions; in a word, all that system of rule and authoritative teaching which must strike every one as the leading feature in the constitution of the Catholic Church.

The differences, therefore, between this and other religions, however complicated and numerous they may at first sight appear, are thus in truth narrowed to one question; for particular doctrines must share the fate of the dogmas above cited, as forming the constitutive principle of the Catholic religion. This religion claims for itself a complete consistency from its first principle to its last consequence, and to its least institution, and finds fault with others, as though they preserved forms, dignities, and doctrines which must have sprung from a principle by them rejected, but which are useless and mistaken, the moment they are disjoined from it. Be this as it may, the constitution of the Catholic Church should seem to possess what is essential to every moral organized body—a principle of vitality which accounts for all its actions, and determines at once the direction and the intensity of all its functions.

To conclude our account of the Catholic Church, we will give a slight view of the extent of its dominions, by enumerating the countries which profess its doctrines, or which contain considerable communities under its obedience. In Europe, Italy, Spain, Portugal, France, Belgium, the Austrian empire, including Hungary, Bavaria, Poland, and the Rhenish provinces of Prussia, which formerly belonged to the ecclesiastical electorates, profess the Catholic religion as that of the state, or, according to the expression of the French *charte*, that of the majority of the people. In America, all the countries which once formed part of the Spanish dominions, both in the southern and northern portion of the continent, and which are now independent states, profess exclusively the same religion. The empire of Brazil is also Catholic. Lower Canada, and all those islands in the West Indies which belong to Spain or France, including the Republic of Hayti, profess the Catholic faith; and there are also considerable Catholic communities in the United States of North America. Many Indian tribes, in the Canadas, in the United States, and in South America, have embraced the same faith. In Asia there is hardly any nation professing Christianity which does not contain large communities of Catholic Christians. Thus, in Syria the entire nation or tribe of the Maronites, dispersed over Mount Libanus, are subjects of the Roman see, governed by a patriarch and bishops appointed by it. There are also other Syriac Christians under other bishops, united to the same see, who are dispersed all over Palestine and Syria. At Constantinople there is a Catholic Armenian patriarch, who governs the *united* Armenians, as they are called, large communities of whom also exist in Armenia proper. The Abbé Dubois, in his examination before a committee of the English House of Commons, in 1832, stated the number of Catholics in the Indian peninsula at 600,000, including Ceylon; and this number is perhaps rather underrated than otherwise. They are governed by four bishops, and four vicars apostolic with episcopal consecration. A new one has been added for Ceylon. We have not the means of ascertaining the number of Catholics in China; but in the province of Su-Chuen alone they were returned, September 22, 1824, at 47,487 (*Annales de la Propag. de la Foi*, No. XI., p. 257); and an official report published at Rome, in the same year, gives those in the provinces of Fo-kien and Kiansi at 40,000. There are seven other provinces containing a considerable number of Catholics, of which we have no return. In the united empire of Tonkin and Cochin-China, the Catholics of one district were estimated at 200,000 (*Ibid.*, No. X., p. 194); and, till the late persecution, there was a college with 200 students, and convents containing 700 religious. Another district gave a return, in 1826, of 2955 infants baptized, which would give an estimate of 88,000 adult Christians. A third gave a return of 170,000. M. Dubois estimated the number of native Catholics in the Philippine Islands at 2,000,000. In Africa, the islands of Mauritius and Bourbon are Catholic, and all the Portuguese settlements on the coasts, as well as the Azores, Madeira, the Cape Verde, and the Canary Islands.

The history of the Roman Catholics in this country begins with the discovery of Columbus, the Roman Catholic subject of a Roman Catholic government. Their first important movement in gaining a footing within the present boundaries of the United States was made by Lord Baltimore. He obtained from Charles I. the charter of Maryland, and appointed his brother Leonard Calvert to be governor of the new colony. The first body of emigrants consisted of about two hundred gentlemen of rank and fortune. They reached the shores of the Potomac in 1632.

The early missions of this denomination extended to all the principal tribes of the aborigines, and explored the countries of the great lakes and the Mississippi. That portion of the Roman Catholics which have descended from the early settlers of the country are comparatively liberal in their views, and many of them except to the exclusive spirit of the ancient hierarchy, and allow their Protestant brethren to be good Christians, so far as they adorn the Christian faith by a devout and charitable spirit. In the early settlement of Louisiana nearly all the people were Roman Catholics. The laws were originally made to favor that form of religion. They have been gradually changed or relaxed in their administration. So late, however, as 1834 or 1835, the Presbyterian church in New Orleans was not allowed to ring its bell for a week-day evening service, on the ground of an old law which restricted that right to the Roman Catholic churches. Yet, it ought to be said in perfect fairness that the Roman Catholics were not the persons to request the enforcement of the odious law. Its execution was threatened only by Protestants, and the Protestant council of the second municipality refused to grant the permission which the law gave them power to

46

grant as a special favor. Probably no portion of our population are more perfectly tolerant in their principles and feelings than the Roman Catholics of Louisiana.

From the period of the early settlement of Maryland and the banks of the Mississippi, there was but a slight increase of the people of this persuasion till within the last twenty years.

Lately the tide of foreign immigration has greatly swollen, and the increase of Roman Catholics is rapid. They now constitute more than one-twentieth of our population. Considering, however, the excess of Protestant increase from births and immigration, and the great mortality of the poor foreigners, it is doubted whether the ratio of increase of Roman Catholics is as great as that of the Protestants.

It ought also to be acknowledged with thankfulness to God, that in all their published declarations the Roman Catholic priesthood express their distinct disapprobation of all violence and unfairness in enforcing the claims of their religion. One of their gifted writers says, " If it [proselytism] imply the use of any means that are unfair, unhandsome, dishonorable, or uncharitable; of violence, bribery, false arguments, or any other means whatsoever than such as are dictated by the strictest truth and animated by pure benevolence, then, indeed, is proselytism as odious as it is unchristian; then, be it far from every Catholic and from every Christian. Be it hated and detested by every lover of honesty, of truth, and of charity."

The Roman Catholics have numerous institutions of learning, nunneries, orphan asylums, and various foundations of charity. Their colleges have accomplished professors, but they have never been able to place themselves on an equality with such institutions as Princeton and Yale colleges and Harvard University. Their female schools are more effective, because distinguished for the cultivation of those branches of learning and art which adorn he feminine character.

They have now (1860) in the United States, thirty-two Theological Seminaries, seven Preparatory Seminaries, thirty colleges, twenty-seven periodical publications, two thousand one hundred and eight clergymen, one thousand nine hundred and seventy-eight churches, and the Catholic population is estimated at twenty-five hundred thousand. In the British Provinces, six hundred and nineteen churches, three hundred and sixty-nine clergymen, and one million and seventeen thousand Catholic population.

The growth of this denomination appears of late years to have been very rapid; and this circumstance is probably owing to the large immigration from Europe.

SPIRITUALISTS.

SPIRITUALISM is a form of religion which existed from antiquity, but as a sect, Spiritualists are the youngest of the existing denominations. The first representatives of it resided in Rochester, New York, who, about the year 1848, began to attract the attention of the public, by declaring that they held communications with departed spirits by means of rapping on tables, knocking on the walls, and other mysterious and unaccountable noises.

So remarkable a phenomenon at once excited general attention, and several parties were formed in reference to the subject, some asserting the genuineness of the matter, others contending that the whole was an imposture, and that no communication had taken place, or possibly could take place, between the living and the dead. Notwithstanding the opposition which was arrayed against Spiritualism, facts continued to accumulate, and experiments were made which seemed to stagger the belief of the most incredulous, and made it very difficult for those who condemned Spiritualism as an imposition, to account for them.

The great principle of Spiritualism is, that the spirits of the departed, who are no longer "in the form," can and do hold intelligent and sensible intercourse with those still living; and that they accomplish this result in various ways, by raps on tables, by messages, by moving material objects about, by prophecies, by writing and speaking unknown tongues, by spiritual shocks and touches of the person, by spiritual melodies, and by the visible appearance of spirits to the living.

Within the last sixteen years thousands of persons have been thus used as mediums of communication with the spirits of the departed. Some are made to see and describe spirits, others are controlled to write out communications, often giving test facts unknown to the medium, and sometimes written in Phonography, Greek, Latin, or some language not understood by any one present. In the presence of some mediums, tables, chairs, and other articles are moved, and sometimes raised and carried about the room, by invisible means. Bells are rung, drums beaten, horns blown, guitars, dulcimers, banjoes, tambourines violins, accordeons, and pianos, are played upon by invisible operators. Impressional and inspirational mediums have had *positive demonstrations* of spirit influence; and hundreds of thousands have had tests which have fully convinced them of the possibility of communicating with departed friends and relatives.

The majority of Spiritualists contend, that these manifestations are not confined to the present or recent times, but that they have existed in all ages, though their real nature was unknown and unsuspected. Of this kind, they contend, were the revelations of God to Moses on Mount Sinai, in the Shekinah, those made to Isaiah, and the other Hebrew Prophets, the appearance of angels at the sepulchre of Christ, and various other events in the Scriptures.

The instruments by means of which communications are alleged to take place between spirits and the living, are called *media*. These media are of various kinds. *Writing* media, who write while in a state of trance, and whose hands are entirely under the control of the spirits. *Speaking* media, who, while in a state of trance, speak under the influence of spirits. *Seeing* media, whose development is so high and perfect, that they can see spirits with their physical sight. *Discerning* media, who, by placing a sealed letter on top of their heads, or on the palms of their hands, can read the contents. *Normal* media, who speak in a natural state, but are under the influence of a temporary inspiration. Some media are public, others are private; and media of both kinds possess different degrees of excellence and power.

Spiritualists also contend that spirits are themselves possessed of different degrees of capability to communicate with those "in the form," or who are still alive and in the body. Before a spirit can read, or communicate through the alphabet, it must possess the necessary acquaintance with letters. A spirit which left the body without being able to read, and without any acquaintance with science, cannot make communications which involve scientific knowledge. It is also alleged that the medium through which spirits communicate is a certain fluid in the atmosphere, which is more subtle than ether; hence the state of the weather has an important bearing on their communications. In damp, rainy, and dreary weather, when the atmosphere is heavy, they are restricted in their operations, because of the deficiency of this mysterious fluid.

By the use of these means, Spiritualists have arrived at the adoption of the following doctrinal opinions, which they regard as their system of belief: — They believe in the existence of a Supreme Being, and of the Father, Son, and Holy Ghost. But they do not regard these three as coequal, separate, and divine personages, according to the orthodox views of the Christian Trinity. They believe that all the spirits who now exist in the "Spirit world," once existed in connection with a physical body, or, as their jargon terms it, "in the form." That the Spirit world is composed of a great number of spheres, each one of which is divided and subdivided into a number of minor spheres, whose variety is equal to the variety of individualities which exist among men on earth. That the first sphere into which the spirit passes when it leaves "the form" is, in many respects, the counterpart of their condition here, and advanced but a single degree beyond their character and condition here. That the spirits of higher spheres can read the thoughts of all those spirits which belong to lower spheres. That the spirit of man is immortal; and that the nature of the sphere into which a man enters in the other world depends upon his character when he dies. If his character and feelings are base, he will enter into a base sphere. That for every injury inflicted on others, the spirit snall be punished by the suffering of mental tortures proportioned to the degree of his crime.

Spiritualists also hold that the natural tendency of spirits in the future world is one of constant progression from lower to higher spheres, and that every man's moral status at death is the starting point from which he enters the future state. As to infants, they think that, on entering the world of spirits, they are taken in charge by developed matrons, who educate them, and gradually introduce them into higher circles, and continue their care until they become adults. This is done, unless in the meantime the mother of the child arrives in the spirit world; in which case, if she be fit to enter the same sphere, the child will be entrusted to her custody, if not, it will be retained in the care of those who are more fit for the responsibility.

APPENDIX.

In this Appendix it is designed to give additional and later information on the various sects, correcting some errors, and bringing up all to the present time, 1871.

SPIRITUALISTS. Some recent developments of the origin and tendencies of the system professed by this new sect, have given it a startling importance. Wm. B. Potter, M.D., of Trenton, New Jersey, in a pamphlet dated June 7, 1866, entitled "*Facts, Fancies, and Follies of Spiritualism Explained*," has given a testimony which claims to be of the highest authority, from which we shall freely quote. The matter belongs to the public, if only in the way of warning. Dr. Potter, himself a leading medium, says :

"*Fifteen years' critical study* of Spiritual Literature, an extensive acquaintance with the leading Spiritualists, and a patient, systematic, and thorough investigation of the manifestations, for many years, enable us to speak from *actual knowledge*, definitely and positively of *Spiritualism As It Is*

"Spirit communications, full of the wildest fancies, and the most absurd and contradictory teachings, have been so common that it is no wonder that men of science and sound sense, who have not had the most ample test of spirit manifestations, look upon the whole thing as the vagaries of a diseased brain, the hallucinations of a moon-struck imagination, or the tricks of the vilest imposters.

"Among the innumerable follies, of which Spiritualists have been guilty, the greatest is following the advice of free-lovers, libertines and low spirits, in refusing to disfellowship the persistently vicious, when it is a notorious fact that many medi-

548

ums are practicing the most detestable trickery, deceit, fraud and falsehood. That leading teachers, noted mediums, and popular speakers, have deserted companions, obtained divorces, gone off with affinities, or practiced *promiscuous intercourse* to get spiritual elements, or to impart vital magnetism for the cure of diseases. Hundreds of families have been broken up, and many affectionate wives deserted by affinity-seeking husbands; many once devoted wives have been seduced and left their husbands and tender, helpless children, to follow some higher attraction; many well disposed but simple-minded girls have been deluded by affinity notions, and led off by affinity hunters, to be deserted in a few months, with blasted reputations, or led to deeds still more dark and criminal to hide their shame. Yet, in the face of all this, at the National Convention of Spiritualists, at Chicago, called to consider the question of a National Organization, the only plan approved by its committee *especially provided* that *No charge should ever be entertained against any member*, and that *any person, without any regard to moral character might become a member.*

"The fact of so much immorality and licentiousness among Spiritualists, is mainly due to three things : 1st. The teachings of *seducing spirits*, who have constantly and persistently, in every possible way, from the gentlest and most covert, to the boldest and most reckless, assailed the binding force of marriage bonds. Nearly every case of affinity, folly or free-love crime, from first to last, has been approved, if not planned, by spirits. 2d. The magnetism of low, selfish, sensual, deceitful spirits, tends to develop the same traits in mediums subject to their influence. The downward course of many mediums is owing to this cause. 3d. Sensual, deceitful, spirits, naturally seek mediums of like character, whom they aid and incite to practice the most debasing and detestable trickery, deceit and sensuality. The private history of many mediums, if made public, would *astound* and *disgust* the better class of Spiritualists."

EPISCOPALIANS. The right of convocation has been recently restored to the Church of England. The case of Dr. Colenso, missionary Bishop of Natal, South Africa, accused of infidelity, approaches its solution in a way that honors the Church of England as an ecclesiastical body, yet at the same time threatens its relation to the English Government. At the request of the diocese of Natal, the Archbishop of Canterbury, acting with the voice of his convocation, has appointed another Bishop, who will take the title of Bishop of Maritzburg. All the Bishops of South Africa will concur in his consecration. On the other hand Mr. Cardwell, Colonial Secretary, writes in a recent despatch that the Government will sustain Bishop Colenso, who holds letters patent from the crown.

The formal sentence of excommunication which the Bishop of Capetown has pronounced against Dr. Colenso, has been officially communicated to all the Anglican Bishops throughout the world, including the Bishops of the Protestant Episcopal Church of the United States. It has everywhere met with a cordial approval.

The reunion of the Southern dioceses of the Protestant Episcopal Church of the United States, with the General Convention, which had been interrupted for five years by the late Rebellion, is now complete; every diocesan convention of the South having passed resolutions to that effect, and the Bishops having officially announced the result to the presiding Bishop. In most of the conventions the resolutions were passed by a unanimous vote, and kind feelings expressed toward the Northern members of the Church : only in Virginia a strong, though ineffectual, opposition was made.

The wish for a large increase of the Episcopal Sees, by a division of the present dioceses in this country, is rapidly increasing. This is said to be a favorite scheme of the High Church party.

The first annual report of the Eastern Church Association contains some interesting statements on the progress of the movement, for effecting a union between the Anglican ard the Eastern Church. We learn from it also, that negotiations are pending for a reunion between the Greek and the Armenian Churches. The association has two hundred and eighty members, and among its patrons are English, Scotch, Colonial, American, and also two Servian Bishops. It contemplates a reunion of the English Church not only with the Greek, but also with the Russian, Swedish, Moravian and all other Episcopal Churches.

DUTCH REFORMED CHURCH. The General Synod which met in New York city in June, 1866, gives interesting reports of its work among the Freedmen of the South and its mission to Japan. A committee was appointed to consider the expediency and propriety of dropping the word Dutch in the name of the Church, and to report at the next Synod.

GERMAN REFORMED CHURCH. The unity of this Church is now fully restored, after the five years of separation, caused by the great Rebellion of the South. The classis of Virginia and the classis of North Carolina, the only ones of this connection belonging to the South, have returned to its jurisdiction. The increasing number of German emigrants into the Southern States is likely to add largely to the Southern membership of this denomination.

LUTHERANS. The General Synod of the Evangelical Lutheran Church, May 16, 1866, had no delegates present from the late Confederate States, and there seems as yet no prospect of reunion. The conflict between the High Church and Low Church party, which has for many years been widening, assumed this year a much more serious aspect. At the last General Synod, in 1864, the delegates of the synod of Pennsylvania withdrew from the General Synod, being dissatisfied with the indefinite declarations of the latter body as regards the obligatory character of the Augsburg Confession.

On calling the roll of delegates for this year's Synod, the president refused to call the names of the Pennsylvania synod taking that synod out of governing relation to the General Synod. This decision was sustained by the Low Church party, who were found to have a large majority, and who also carried a vote of censure against the Pennsylvania synod ; the delegates of which thereupon withdrew from the General Synod. A committee was appointed to correspond with the seceded Southern synod, with a view to reunion, and another committee was appointed to report at the next meeting a revision of the constitution of the General Synod, by which it shall be made not simply an advisory body, but the highest legislative and executive body of the Lutheran Church in the United States, whose acts and decisions shall be authoritative and final in all matters specifically intrusted to it by the constitution. Amendments specifying the ratio of representation and the doctrinal basis of admission to the General Synod, having been approved by a two-thirds vote of every synod, were adopted.

The General Synod of the South at their meeting June 14, 1866, concluded to adopt the name of the "Evangelical Lutheran Synod of the United States." This body, which consists of all the Southern synods except Texas, is decidedly under the influence of High Church tendencies, and gave a new proof of this by resolving to put itself squarely on a confessional basis. All ministers will henceforth be required to adhere strictly to the Augsburg Confession. The body also expressed its readiness to join the new General Synod of the North when it shall be formed as above ; but the synod of Texas, was not represented, and still declares its sympathy with the General Synod of the United States.

The secession of the Lutheran synod of Pennsylvania from the General Synod is now complete. This is the oldest and most numerous of all the synods of the United States. The cause of its secession is stated above. At its last annual meeting, June, 1866, it was resolved to dissolve its former

Connection, and to invite all Lutheran synods which accept the unaltered Confession of Augsburg as their doctrinal standard, to hold soon a general convention for the purpose of organizing a new (High Church) General Synod. Delegates to such a convention have already been chosen by the synods of Pennsylvania and Wisconsin.

METHODISTS. The latest representations of the various branches of this numerous and progressive body of Christians indicate general prosperity. Several organic changes have been adopted in the polity of the Methodist Episcopal Church, South. A proposition to change the name to "The Episcopal Methodist Church" obtained extensive favor, but finally failed to receive the constitutional sanction of a two-thirds vote, and, to the regret of many, the measure was not carried. This body made provision for the admission of lay members into both its general and annual conferences before the plan was sanctioned by the Northern section of the denomination. Some modification of the rule concerning class meeting has obtained, and a system of "District Conferences" inaugurated which brings the bishops into more immediate contact with the ministry and laity, and exerts a wholesome influence on the Sunday-schools, educational and financial interests of the church. The pastoral term has been extended, and certain restrictions in the discipline on minor points of deportment, dress, etc., removed. The bounds of this church have extended to Baltimore, Md., and also into some of the Western States, and California.

The Methodist Episcopal Church, since the close of the war, has very greatly enlarged the area of its operations in the South. Ten or more conferences have been organized, embracing an aggregate membership of over one hundred and fifty thousand. The distinctions long existing between white and colored persons are abolished, and both races stand on an equality in ecclesiastical privilege, in the conferences and various official positions of the church.

Theological institutions for the education of colored ministers have been established at Charlestown, New Orleans, and other places, and a liberal expenditure of missionary money has been made for church extension and ministerial support.

The African Methodist Episcopal Church has received very large accessions in the South since the emancipation of the slaves, and a new organization, embracing largely the colored membership of the Methodist Episcopal Church, South, has been formed, by which they now maintain an independent character, and have bishops elected from their own body.

The subject of a unification of all the sects of Methodism has received considerable attention of late. Conventions have been held, overtures made, and a friendly spirit obtains, giving promise that at no distant period a concentration of the strength and energy of the denomination will be effected, and most of the minor bodies in the United States and Canada will merge into one. The same spirit prevails in Great Britain, and a union of the great Wesleyan body with those called New Connection, Primitive, etc., will most likely be consummated.

In July, 1870, it was ascertained that the numerical strength of Methodism, including all branches and countries where it has been planted, amounted to between three and four million members, with a clerical force, embracing lay and travelling preachers, of over sixty thousand. The influence of Methodism is reacting on Germany and many other nations of the old world, through its converts in the United States, who return as missionaries to the fatherland. This is also the case with China and Japan. It is the policy of this church to enter every open door, and fulfill to the letter the saying of the celebrated Wesley—"The world is my parish."

KIRK OF SCOTLAND. Under this head the reader will find a brief account of the formation of the several bodies of Presbyterians, who have dissented from her communion.

The principal of these bodies, at the present time, are the " Free Church" and the " United Presbyterians," formed by a coalescence of dissenters of an earlier date

The General Assemblies of these two great bodies in both the Free Church and the United Presbyterian, this year (1866), devoted prominent attention to the question of union. Very important measures were taken to this end, which promise a happy result. The finances of the Free Church are in a flourishing condition, the total sum raised being £383,572, an increase of £25,374 over the last year. In the United Presbyterian Synod also, the contributions per member amounted to over 30 shillings. In seven years the missionary contributions had risen from £40,000 to £51,000. The num ber of congregations in the Synod, 592; of members, 172,752; of ministers 620; of elders 4466.

The General Assembly of the established Church (or Kirk) had an animated discussion on innovations, such as the use of organs and the use of a book of prayer, and decided against them by an overwhelming vote, 207 to 94.

UNITED PRESBYTERIANS. See the foregoing article.

FREE CHURCH. See the article, on KIRK OF SCOT-LAND.

AMERICAN PRESBYTERIANS. OLD SCHOOL. The Old School Assembly was divided at the beginning of the late war. In consequence of the passage of resolutions affirming loyalty and condemning slavery, the Southern delegates withdrew, and organized a new General Assembly, for the Southern States. Since the conclusion of the war, efforts have been made for reunion, but hitherto without success.

At the last General Assembly at St. Louis, May, 1866, new sources of difficulty arose. The Assembly was divided into three parties with regard to the deliverances by the last five Assemblies on the subjects of slavery and loyalty. The final

adoption of the motion of Dr. Gurley to censure the sentiments of the "Declaration and Testimony" of the Louisville
Presbytery as "slanderous and rebellious, and to summon
all the signers before the bar of the next Assembly, and in the
meanwhile to prohibit them from sitting in any church court
higher than sessions, has produced a great commotion in the
Presbyteries of the border States. A number of ministers
and churches in Maryland, Kentucky, and Missouri, have
taken ground openly against the Assembly. The seceders
have not yet declared in favor of a union with the Southern
Presbyterian Church, but it is understood that they will do
so as soon as the question of property is decided. Meanwhile
the General Assembly stands firm, and is acting with decision
in dissolving all defiant Presbyteries and constituting new
ones of loyal members. Their missionaries continue their
labor among the Freedmen, of whom, before the war and the
act of emancipation there were 11,000 belonging to the
Presbyterian Church

The New School General Assembly, which also met this
year in St. Louis, adopted unanimously a series of resolutions
and raised a committee of fifteen to meet a like committee of
the Old School Assembly on the subject of an organic union
between these important bodies of Christians, which for nearly
thirty years have been divided. Both have greatly prospered
the last year. The former now numbers 35 synods; 176
Presbyteries ; 2294 ministers ; 2608 Churches; and 239,306
Church members. The New School reports 109 Presbyteries ·
1739 ministers ; 1538 churches ; and 150,401 communicants.

The General Assembly of the "United Presbyterians," as
well as the annual meeting of the two branches of Reformed
Presbyterians, ("Synod" and "General Synod") appointed a
committee for making a plan of their organic union.

The General Assembly of the Cumberland Presbyterians
met last May (1866), and appointed a committee of twenty
members one from each synod, on the deliverances of the last
assembly. A majority of this committee pronounced the ac-

tion of 1864 and 1865 on the subject of slavery and the rebellion unconstitutional. The minority proposed in substance to let the whole matter stand where it is. The Assembly compromised by adopting a substitute, disclaiming any indorsement of the action taken on slavery and rebellion, and declared that "no opinion" on these subjects is expressed.

FREE-WILL BAPTISTS. This body has now 147 associations; 1252 churches; 1076 ordained ministers; baptized in 1865, 2034: total membership 54,076. They support a mission in India, and are making rapid improvement in education.

PROGRESSIVE FRIENDS. A portion of the Hicksite Quakers residing in the neighborhood of Philadelphia, about the year 1855, organized under this name, to indicate the progressive character of their inquiries and convictions on the subject of religion. They hold an annual meeting at Longwood, where large congregations assemble for addresses, consultations, etc., as well as public worship, and publish an annual report of their proceedings. They profess unlimited freedom of inquiry.

CHRISTIANS. It is an error to suppose that all this denomination are Unitarians. Many of them, especially in New England, are orthodox and evangelical in their creed. They accept the doctrines of the Trinity and the Atonement, and only object to the use of the word "person" in reference to that sublime mystery. These are the views expressed in their denominational organ.

WINEBRENNARIANS. This denomination is an anti-slavery Church, and numbers at present in ten annual "elderships" about 20,000 members. The "general eldership" of the present year (1866) was important. They accepted the offer of a denominational school in Centralia, Kansas, and

47*

will organize it as a denominational college. They will establish another in the Middle States. They also resolved to establish a Sunday School paper and a German paper, in addition to the Church Advocate, their present organ.

UNITARIANS. This body has also an organ in New York city, called the Christian Inquirer. From a late number we copy the following views of their denominational place in the Christian world. "We belong to and are part of a great religious movement which is sweeping down through the centuries, a central and foremost stream of influence it may be, but still only one of many streams springing from the same general cause and flowing to the same general destination; and whether we are to empty our accumulations into some other stream, or to absorb the others into our broader and deeper channel, we know not, nor ought we to care. We are what we are by the grace of God, who has raised us up for his own good purpose, and will do for us what he will; and the great thing for us to do, is to put ourselves entirely into his hands, and let him use us for his own holy ends."

The Unitarians of England, like those of our own country, are divided into a conservative (Evangelical) and radical party, the latter being opposed to the adoption of any creed, and, in particular, to defining in any way the Unitarian doctrine concerning the person of Jesus Christ.

UNIVERSALISTS. This denomination have recently established Tufts' College, at Somerville, Massachusetts.

CONGREGATIONALISTS. Within the last few years this intelligent body of Christians has put forth denominational efforts of extraordinary vigor. They have organized a general Union, and raised vast sums for the Freedmen, for schools and colleges, and for a Church Edifice Fund. Their progress in the Western States is very rapid. Congregationalism, which, in 1860, had not a single congregation in Missouri, has now a General Conference, with three distinct associations, embracing about thirty churches and more than thirty ministers The Congregationalists in Missouri, like those of the other Northern States, are unanimous in their devotion to the principles of freedom, progress, and impartial rights. See BAPTISTS.

MORMONS. There is a singular analogy between the origin and principles of this sect and those of the fanatic Anabaptists of Munster in 1535. Both claim prophetic powers, miracles, revelations, supplementary to and over riding the written word of God. Both practice polygamy.

ARMENIANS. It is a noticeable fact that, after so many centuries of alienation, there is now manifested a spirit of re-union between this body of Eastern Christians and the Greek Church. Negotiations to this end are now in progress.

GNOSTICS. This name (which properly signifies *Scientifics*) was an attempt of the philosophers of the East to blend the science of their time ("science," falsely so called) with Christianity. The same thing is repeated at this time in Germany and France, and with like corrupting effects.

RATIONALISTS. This is the name, not so much of an organized sect, as of a class of men diffused through many sects, whose distinguishing character is that they exalt their own reason above the divine reason, as revealed in the Scriptures, whether professing Christianity or not. In those who profess Christianity, this spirit is most dangerous as well as disingenuous.

The twaddle of bigotry and sectarianism, it has been justly said, is bad enough; but this modern cant of freedom of thought, which has degenerated into an utter disregard of all positive truth, and sacrifices the obvious import of Scripture, contemptuously called its letter, for a fanciful something termed its spirit, is infinitely worse

An eclectic reverence for the word of God is a virtual rejection of it as the word of God. If the New Testament be a revelation from heaven for the guidance of man, it must be accepted in its integrity. Our first business is to see to it that we have the inspired word *as God gave it*. In this investigation we should thankfully accept all the evidence furnished by manuscripts, by patristic quotations, by history, and by the various processes of a sound and reverential criticism. Our next duty is to ascertain the *import* of the testimony, as borne by the sacred book. Here, again, we should gladly avail ourselves of every aid which an enlightened and pains-taking investigation can afford. But when we have reached the goal of such inquiries, what then? Shall we proceed to eliminate from the book which we have just consented to receive as a divine revelation, all the authority and decisiveness which should stamp such a heavenly communication? Surely a God-inspired book should be treated as such; and unless its decisions be accepted as final, on *all* matters on which it has spoken, it is only treated as we should deal with any other book. If reason is to determine what portions are to be received and what rejected, the supposed revelation adds nothing to us whatever, for reason we already had. If a revelation is not to guide reason, of what use is it? If reason is to guide revelation, man is to be put above God. But verily this is a *reductio ad absurdum*. The fundamental idea of a revelation is that of a final, infallible, and authorita tive communication from our Maker, which is to aid the imperfections of reason, to correct her errors, and to enlarge the sphere of her knowledge—a communication, in fact, from whose decisions there is no appeal. If we pay only an eclectic reverence to God's word, we treat that blessed book as we should do the writings of Plato, or Cicero, or Shakespeare; and the Bible is of no more use to us than any other tolerably good volume of human origin. See DEISTS, LATITUDINARIANS, and ERASTIANS.

WICKLIFFITES. The influence of Wickliffe in preparing he Reformation of the sixteenth century seems to demand a more full development of his history and opinions than that given in the body of this book. Happily, new light has been recently shed upon the subject by the critical researches of Dr. Vaughan, of Dr. Boehring, and of Mr. Shirley; the first, a Congregationalist, the second, a learned German scholar, and the last, a clergyman of the Church of England, the editor of his newly-published works.

Dr John Wickliffe was born near Richmond, in Yorkshire, in 1324, and educated at Baliol College, Oxford, where he long resided, and acquired the reputation of extraordinary talents, piety, and scholarship. In 1361, he was chosen Master of Baliol College, and the same year, was presented with the rectory of Fylingham, in Lincolnshire. In 1363, he received his doctor's degree, and the appointment of Professor of Theology in the University. From this date, his public activity as a Reformer begins—nine years earlier than the common date of his appointment, as given by James, Le Bas, and even by Dr. Vaughn; but it has been fixed by Mr. Shirley.

From 1363 to the last days of 1384, the year of his death, in the reigns of Edward III. and Richard II., the reforming labors of Wickliffe were incessant: by his university lectures, his numerous publications, his personal preaching, his employment of a large body of pious and faithful men, under the name of "Simple Priests," to preach in all the villages of the kingdom, and, lastly, by the most important labor of his life, THE TRANSLATION OF THE WHOLE BIBLE INTO THE ENGLISH TONGUE. This last has been justly pronounced the greatest work in Anglo-Saxon history. True, the modern power of the press was then unknown, but he was for years surrounded by a band of active copyists and assistants... whom his writings and translations were widely diffused, notwith-standing all the efforts of his enemies. He never formally left the Church of Rome, but such was his unsparing exposure of her errors and corruptions, as his mind advanced in the knowledge and experience of the truth, that he was repeat-edly condemned as a heretic by the clergy and Pope, and would have been sacrificed as a martyr but for the protection of his powerful friends at court, and other providential inter-position. As it was, he was driven from the University early in 1382, and spent the last three years of his life in his rec-tory at Lutterworth, where his translations of the Bible and the best of his writings as a Reformer were produced. Such was the resistless influence of these, not only in England (where it is said that half the nation embraced his views), but on the Continent, in Germany and Bohemia, that the bigoted Council of Constance, in 1415, condemned not only his books, but ordered his very bones to be dug up and pub-licly burned to ashes, a sentence actually executed in 1428. But in vain did his enemies, the Romish clergy, thus insult the memory of the holy dead ; for, as old Fuller finely ob-serves, "The Swift conveyed his ashes into the Avon, the Avon into the Severn, the Severn into the narrow seas, they to the main ocean. And thus they are the emblem of his doctrine, which now is dispersed all the world over."

As Wickliffe's reformatory opinions were progressive, and never perhaps attained to an entire freedom from Romish errors, it may be asked on what grounds Mr. Crosby claims him as a Baptist. Our space forbids us to state them in full, but briefly they are three. First, Wickliffe adopted general principles which invariably tend to Baptist views, such as the sufficiency and supremacy of the Scriptures, the right of all men to read them, and that no doctrine or ceremony is to be received in the church which is not sanctioned by the word of God. "Wise men," he said, "leave that as impertinent which is not plainly expressed in Scripture." On this ground he rejected the authority of the Romish Church, Episcopacy, the efficacy of baptism to wash away sins, and the perdition of unbaptized infants—the very foundation on which infant baptism then rested. Secondly, he was charged by contemporary Catholic writers expressly with the denial of infant baptism. Among others, Thomas Waldensis, confessor to Henry V , who had access to his writings, and published a "*Fasciculi Zizaniorum*," or, Bundles of Tares, selected from them, says of Wickliffe : "He doth positively assert that children are not to be sacramentally baptized." Thirdly, it is certain that many of his followers, called *Lollards* in England, and *Picards* in Bohemia, were Baptists. The latter sect are thus described by a Roman Catholic, in a letter from Bohemia to the learned Erasmus, in 1519 : "They own no other authority than the Scriptures of the Old and New Testaments ; they believe or own little or nothing of the sacraments of the Church ; *such as come over to their sect must every one be baptized anew in mere water ;* they mutually salute one another by the name of brother and sister," &c. The writer of this letter admits that this sect had been in Bohemia for nearly a hundred years, that is, within thirty-six years after the death of Wickliffe, whose writings were so widely spread in Bohemia that, in, 1410, two hundred volumes of them were found and burnt in the University of Prague. The reader can now judge how far this first great English Reformer embraced the sentiments of the Baptists, and diffused them through Europe.

GREEK CHURCH. See ARMENIANS, in Appendix.

MAHOMETANISM. The computation of prophetic time in the last section of the article under this head, is evidently defective in its data, and false in its results. The date from which the 391 years are reckoned, is not mentioned, but it is evidently 1453, the year when the Turks conquered Constantinople ; but that was accomplished in their mid-career of conquest, rather than in its beginning. It is plain that their

movement from the Euphrates is the point of time contemplated in the prophecy in question, Rev. ix., 13–15. From the
year 1300 to 1691, their conquests were pushed, but closed
with the death of the Grand Vizier Kinjsrili Mustapha, in
1691, just 391 years. From that time the best historians
date the decay of the Turkish power, when it ceased to be a
terror to Europe. The date of its final fall does not seem to be
given in prophecy, though it is evidently near at hand. See
Article CHRISTIANITY, in this Appendix.

MANICHAEANS. It is a very serious error to confound
the Paulicians with the Manichaeans. It was the ignorance
or art of their enemies that led to this false imputation, which
has been perpetuated by so many better men in modern times.
But they themselves utterly denied the charge, as the learned
Photius, in the ninth century, candidly admits. See PAULI-
CIANS, in Appendix.

ANABAPTISTS: Those who require a new baptism
when, for any reason, the first is deemed invalid. Thus,
Paul is generally supposed to have required the twelve disciples at Ephesus to be baptized anew, because of their
ignorance of the real purport and design of John's teaching.
So, in the early Church, the Novatians and Donatists baptized all who joined them from the Catholic Church, on account of its alleged corruptions. And, in like manner, the
Catholics baptized anew those who had been baptized by the
Arians, Manichaeans, and other reputed heretics. So, at this
time, the Greek Church requires a new baptism of all who
unite with them, from either Romanists or Protestants, alleging, as one reason, that the Western Churches, by forsaking
immersion, have lost baptism. And the rule is rigorously
enforced on the intermarriage of royal families, as of a princess of Denmark or Prussia with a prince of Russia.

In Church history, however, the name of Anabaptists is
generally applied to a class of fanatical men who, at the be-

ginning of the Reformation in the sixteenth century, raised violent disturbances in the centre of Europe, and brought upon themselves a lasting odium. These men, who remarkably resembled the Mormons of our times, like them rejected the baptism of infants, and baptized all who adopted their views, which were really more political than religious. These religio-political fanatics were at the time confounded with the Baptists, from whom, however, they widely differed, except in the single point of baptism. Hence, also, much confusion has arisen in modern times, which needs to be cleared away.

Many modern historians have undertaken to do this, but the fullest and fairest account of the whole subject which we have seen, is found in the "History of the Netherlands Reformed Church," by Drs. Ypeig and Dermout, men of the highest standing in the Reformed Church of Holland. The work occupies four octavo volumes, and is written with great ability and candor. We shall quote a few extracts from it, sufficient, we think, to set this matter right.

"Since the peculiar history of the Anabaptists and Baptists has exerted so powerful an influence on the Reformation of the Church in this country, the nature of our historical work requires that we present in its true light the whole matter from its origin.

"The fanatical Anabaptists, of whom we are now to speak, were originally from Germany, where, under the bishopric of Spiers, they, by a rebellion had made known their displeasure at the oppressions of the so-called feudal system This was in the year 1491. Since that time they, by their revolts, had often caused anxiety, and given the Government no little trouble. This continued until the time of the Reformation, when these rebels sought in the new religion an augmented power, and made the most shameful misuse of it to the promotion of their harassing disturbances. These ought by no means to be considered the same as the Baptists. Let the reader keep this distinctly in mind in the statement which we now make respecting them. . . . .

48

"Although there were among the Romanists those who were better informed, yet even among these were some under the influence of prejudice, which does not spare even the learned. They would not see that which they might have seen. How evident it was that although the Baptists appeared to agree exactly with the Anabaptists in respect to the baptismal question, the former entirely disapproved of the course pursued by the latter. And yet the Romanists without dissent agree in ascribing these things to all the Baptists.

"We have nowhere seen clearer evidences of the injurious influence of prejudice. Nowhere have we met with a more obstinate unwillingness to be correctly informed, and a more evident disposition to silence those who better understood the truth of the matter. Prejudice, when once deeply imbibed, blinds the eye, perplexes the understanding, silences the instincts of the heart, and destroys the love of truth and rectitude."

"The Baptists are Protestant Christians, entirely different from the Anabaptists in character. They were descended from the ancient Waldenses, whose teachings were evangelical and tolerably pure, and who were scattered by severe persecutions in various lands, and long before the time of the Reformation of the Church, were existing in the Netherlands. In their flight, they came hither. In this country and in Flanders, in Holland and Zealand, they lived as quiet inhabitants, not intermeddling with the affairs of Church and State : in the villages tilling the land, and in the cities, working at some trade, or engaged in traffic, by which means each one was well supplied, and in no respect burdensome to society. Their manner of life was simple and exemplary. No great crime was known among them. Their religious teaching was simple and pure, and was exemplified in their daily conduct.— In the sight of the authorities they lived as peaceful citizens, obedient, and noted for their uprightness, honesty, conscientiousness, temperance and godliness. The earliest Romanist writers, who are willing to pay a proper respect to the truth, admit this to have been the fact.

" From this narrative it is not difficult to understand how greatly the Waldenses of the Netherlands, or so called Anabaptists, were pleased when Luther and his followers so zealously commenced the Reformation. They immediately made known this approbation. They glorified God, who in their time had raised up brethren with whom they could so well unite, at least in the main points. They also immediately put their hand to the work. Yet they adhered firmly to their own peculiar views, especially respecting the baptism of adults, although these were of less importance. These worthy Anabaptists, or as they may more properly be called Baptists, were to be found in great numbers in the Netherlands." ...... The case is thus summed up :

" The course which the work of the Reformation had taken required that we should give an extended account, both of the Anabaptists and of the Baptists. The former, as we have seen, exerted a very injurious influence upon the *outward* condition of the Protestant community. We think that the latter exerted an extensive *internal* influence upon all the Protestant Christians in the Netherlands." A conclusion so candid, from such men, must command respect.

There is a want of accuracy in the original article on this subject in the body of this work, which demands correction. In the first place, the definition is wrong, as it is restricted to a particular class of religionists, when it properly extends to all, who for any reason repeat baptism, in adult years. Immersion was in early times the practice of all parties. Besides, at the Reformation many rejected infant baptism, while they retained the use of sprinkling.

In the next place, there were two totally different classes of men at that period, as we see above, who were most injustly confounded under this common name, and the errors and crimes of the one wrongfully imputed to the other. Mosheim himself does not, but this article, though mostly taken from

Mosheim, is so carelessly written as to confound them. Once more, in the same way, the Peasants' War in 1525 is first charged upon them indiscriminately and solely; though it is afterward acknowledged that it was not a religious war at all, but a war for their civil rights and liberties, against the intolerable oppressions of the feudal system, and that the Anabaptists (so called) had no more to do with it than others— Lutherans and Roman Catholics.

LOLLARDS. See WICKLIFFITES, in Appendix.

PETROBRUSIANS. See WALDENSES, in Appendix.

PAULICIANS. It is an error in many writers to say, as is said in the article under this head, in the body of the work, that the Paulicians were a branch of the Manichaeans. Dr. Allix, Milner, and Jones, not to mention others, have cleared them of this calumny. They were Christians of an evangelical faith and spirit, who kept alive the flame of true piety in Europe in the middle ages. See WALDENSES and MANICHAEANS, in the Appendix.

MONOPHYSITES. The reader will find himself repaid for consulting on this point the articles ARMENIANS, NESTORIANS, JACOBITES, MARONILES, EUTYCHIANS, COPTS, MELCHITES, MONOTHELITES, and ABYSSINIAN CHURCH.

PAGANS. See CHRISTIANITY, in the Appendix, for some important general views of their condition and prospects.

BRAMINS: BUDDHISTS. See CHRISTIANITY, in this Appendix.
Since the great struggle of 1857, in India, to cast off the British dominion, and expel Christianity, a great change has come over the people. It is felt that the power of their gods, to whom they looked for success in that struggle, is gone, or

at least that it is now inferior, even on their ancient soil, to the God of the Christians. Hence Braminism is shorn of a great part of its former prestige, and there is growing up a disposition to hear Christian missionaries, and read Christian books with new respect and attention. Thousands are giving up their old belief and worship ; caste is broken with impunity ; and every thing betokens the speedy downfall of that mighty system of error.

PAGANS OF CHINA. The most astonishing changes have taken place in China within the last twenty years. Before 1845, no Christian was permitted to set foot upon the soil, beyond the Hong factories. Now, the whole empire is open to the gospel. Toleration is guaranteed by treaty with foreign nations, and Christian missions (Protestant) are in successful operation in the principal seaports, the interior cities, and in Pekin itself, under the eye of the Emperor. Chinese translations of the Scriptures are widely diffused, and many evangelical churches planted.

PAGANS OF JAPAN. After two centuries of interdict, Christianity has again gained a footing in Japan, and several Protestant missions have been established.

PAGANS OF AFRICA. On this great continent explorations are going on of a most important nature, and Christianity is pressing in on all sides.

PAGANS OF MADAGASCAR. Since that article was first written, there has been a most important change in the island in favor of Christianity. It is not only tolerated, but encouraged by the Court. The missionaries have returned, and been welcomed with the liveliest demonstration of joy. Churches have been established, the Scriptures circulated, and converts multiplied. Evangelical Christianity is now in the ascendant.

PAGANS OF POLYNESIA. Australia is filling up with a civilized and Christian population. New Zealand has received Christian missionaries. The gospel has signally triumphed, in overthrowing idolatry in the Society Islands, the Sandwich Islands, the Friendly, Fejee, and Marquesas Islands, and others, whose names have not yet become familiar to Christendom.

PAGANS OF AMERICA. The number of Indians of the various tribes within the territory of the United States, is now estimated at three hundred thousand. Most of these are yet Pagan. The number professing Christianity is not far from one hundred thousand. Beyond the United States, the number of the Pagan population is unknown.

ROMAN CATHOLICS. It is generally anticipated that a crisis must soon occur in the government of the Pope at Rome. By the convention of September 15, 1865, Louis Napoleon engaged to withdraw his troops from Rome, and in his recent manifesto, he declares that "this convention shall be faithfully executed," though " the emperor leaves there, as a guarantee of the security of the Holy Father, the protection of France." This language can only mean protection from personal violence, while the temporal power of the Pope is left to its fall. It was the interference of France that restored the Pope's temporal power, by subverting the Roman Republic of Mazzini in 1849, and for the last seventeen years French troops have kept guard at his palace gates ; though a Swiss body guard and a few Roman soldiers have helped to keep up some show of sovereign power. The withdrawal of the French regiments, now near at hand, will, therefore, inevitably be followed by some great change in his condition as one of the sovereigns of Europe. As Italy has now become a unit its king, Victor Emmanuel, will undoubtedly be welcomed to Rome as the grand old capital of the kingdom, and the Pope with his consistory of Cardinals, will be obliged to accept such arrangements for the future as they may be able to make with him. This would, of course, bring to an end that strange theocracy—the Papal sovereignty—at once the oldest and the feeblest government in Christendom.

The loss of the Pope's temporal power, is of little consequence to the Roman Catholic Church of itself; but only as it bears upon the future fortunes of that Church, of which the Pope is the visible head, the centre of the grand arch of its unity. This bearing will depend very much upon the situation of the Pope after his temporal power has fallen. There is here a very serious complication Victor Emmanuel, though a Catholic, is under the ban of the Pope, and is excommunicated from the church. To such a sovereign the Pope cannot surrender his temporal authority, or even intrust the guardianship of his person; nor can he enter into any relations of amity and concord with him He must either recall his interdict, or retire to a distance from Rome, whenever the king shall enter its gates. To do the former will be a great humiliation, and to do the latter will strip him of his prestige and change, perhaps destroy, what he delights to style "the centre of Christendom." Pius IX., has therefore to withdraw from Italy, and endure for himself the humiliation of the Pontificate, until the Catholic sovereigns of Europe shall be compelled by their pious subjects to reinstate him in independence at Rome. The vital question is, will they be likely to do this? It is not surprising that in such a crisis the greatest solicitude is expressed in every part of Catholic Europe. The Archbishop of Ireland, Dr. Cullen (now a cardinal) is in dismay, and thinks that within six months "his Holiness will be reduced to such a condition that he may not know where to turn his steps." The recent complete overthrow of Austria by Prussia, he says, has left no Catholic power able to support the Pope as a temporal sovereign.

To add to the consternation of Rome, the Italian Chamber of Deputies, June 9, 1866, by an almost unanimous vote, adopted the first article of the bill for the suppression of all the monastic institutions throughout Italy. Since then, we believe, the whole bill has been adopted, and gone into effect.

Protestants, however, should not be too sanguine about the effect of all these changes upon the Roman Church, and its hold upon the minds of men. The fortunes of the Pope are not the fortunes of the Church, however closely the two may be connected together. The name of the Pope may be stricken from the list of European sovereigns, and no shock be given to the Roman Catholic faith. Indeed, that faith might still control its votaries, if there were no Pope to be its visible representative. But the fall of the temporal papacy will be the beginning of a new era in the history of the Papal Church. The crisis is full of interest, and may well be watched with intense solicitude alike by the Protestant and Catholic world. It may give complexion to the future history of mankind.

The Roman Catholic Church in this country, consists (since July, 1850) of seven ecclesiastical provinces, at the head of each of which is an archbishop: namely, Baltimore, New York, Cincinnati, St. Louis, New Orleans, San Francisco, and Oregon, of which Baltimore ranks first. The number of priests exceeds two thousand five hundred; the number of the population connected with the Church is estimated at from four to five million.

National Councils in the Roman Catholic Church are convened by order of the Pope, and consist of all the Bishops of the country in which they are held. In the Old World, they are very rare, as in most countries, the meetings of the Bishops are made dependent upon the express permission of the Government. Only the Protestant government of England puts no obstacle in the way. In the United States, of course, it is the same. It is a curious fact that the Roman Church has this liberty only under the free political institutions which the Pope has never ceased to condemn.

At present but a small portion of the colored population of

this country is under the influence of the Roman Catholic Church; but it is understood that one·object of the present National Council of that Church, at Baltimore, is to devise measures for winning over that class so lately freed from bondage, and now recognized as American citizens.

WALDENSES. It seems to be a serious mistake into which some popular writers have fallen, who represent the Waldenses as originating in France about the year 1160, and deriving their name from the celebrated Peter Waldo. The evidence is now ample, that so far from being a new sect at that period, they had existed under various names as a distinct class of dissenters from the established churches of Greece and Rome in the earliest ages. It is an egregious error to suppose that when Christianity was taken into alliance with the State, by the Emperor Constantine, in the beginning of the fourth century, all the orthodox churches were so ignorant of the genius of their religion, as to consent to the corruption of a worldly establishment.

Crantz (in his History of the United Brethren) says, " These ancient Christians who, besides the several names of reproach given them, were at length denominated Waldenses, from one of their most eminent teachers, Peter Waldo, date their origin from the beginning of the fourth century; .when one Leo, at the great revolution in religion under Constantine the Great, opposed the innovations of Sylvester, Bishop of Rome."

The *Cathari*, or Puritan churches of the Novatians, also had at that very period (about A. D. 325) been flourishing as a distinct communion for more than seventy years, all over the empire; maintaining by the acknowledgment even of their enemies, the self-styled *Catholics*, the integrity of the true faith, together with the purity of discipline and the power of godliness, which had generally disappeared from the *Catholic* churches. These Puritans being exposed to severe and sanguinary persecutions for dissent, from age to age, were compelled to shelter themselves from the desolating storm in retirement ; and when at intervals they reappear on the pages of contemporary history, and their principles are propagated with new boldness and success, they are styled a new sect, and receive a new name from their enemies, though in reality they are the same people.

The same great principles of attachment to the word of God, and determined adherence to the simplicity of its doctrine, discipline, institutions, and worship, in opposition to the innovations of a secular spirit and policy on the one hand, and of false philosophy or of pretended apostolic tradition on the other, may be traced under the name of Novatians, Donatists, Luciferians, and Ærians, from the third to the seventh centuries. They reappear in the Paulicians, who have been falsely accused of Manichaeism, but who, from the middle of the seventh to the end of the ninth century, worthily sustained by their preaching, their lives, and their martyrdoms, their claim of being the genuine descendants of the primitive churches.

From Asia Minor they spread themselves over Europe, through Thrace, Macedonia, Epirus, Bulgaria, Sclavonia, Sicily, Lombardy, Liguria, and Milan ; whence, about the beginning of the eleventh century, they entered into France. The first discovery of a congregation of this kind in that country, was at Orleans, A. D. 1017. A Catholic council was immediately convened, and the Paulician missionaries, with their converts, among whom were many respectable citizens and several of the regular clergy, were all burnt alive. Other advocates of the doctrine were discovered in Languedoc, others in Picardy and Suabia. They were called in France Bougres or Bulgarians, Tisserands or Weavers, Bos Homos or Good Men.

They soon spread through Germany, where they were called by the old name of Cathari, or, by corruption, Gazari, *i. e.* Puritans. In Italy the same people were called Paterines, Josephists, Arnoldists, (and Fratricelli.) As early as the year 1100, it appears they began to be called Waldenses, sixty years before Peter Waldo. Their principles were powerfully advocated, and extended among the most intelligent classes in Languedoc and Provence, from 1110 to 1168, by the celebrated Peter de Bruys and Henry, his successor; from whom they received the name of Petrobrusians and Henricians From the places where they flourished they were called Toulousians, Albigenses, and afterward Poor Men of Lyons, and Leonists. They were condemned by a council at Toulouse in 1119, and again by the great Lateran council at Rome, in 1139. In 1160, some of them crossed from Gascony to England, where they were called Pophlicians and Publicans, corruptions of the original name, Paulicians About this time arose the celebrated Peter Waldo, of Lyons, whose labors, learning, zeal, and liberality, greatly extended their principles; in consequence of which many writers, both Catholic and Protestant, have most erroneously regarded him as the parent and founder of the proper Waldenses. Mr. Robinson, however, has shown that this name had a much earlier origin, that it signifies, " inhabitants of the valleys," and that it was applied to the persecuted people of whom we have spoken, simply for the reason that great multitudes of them made their residence in the valleys of the Alps and of the Pyrenees, where, age after age, they found an asylum from the tyranny of the Church of Rome. This view of the matter, also, is supported by the testimony of their own historians, Pierre Gillies, Perrin, Leger, Sir Samuel Morland, and Dr. Allix. The names imposed on them by their adversaries, they say, have been intended to vilify and ridicule them, or to represent them as new and different sects.

Their enemies confirm their great antiquity. Reinerius Saccho, the inquisitor, admits that the Waldenses flourished five hundred years before Peter Waldo. This carries us back to the year 660, the time of the appearance of the Paulicians, or rather of their great revival and increase under the labors of Constantine Sylvanus Indeed, there is not wanting evidence to show that churches of the Puritan faith existed at that time in the West, as well as in the East. In the year 553, nine bishops of Italy and Switzerland openly refused communion with the Pope of Rome, and the churches under their care persisted in their dissent. To say nothing of the labors of those noble reformers in the bosom of the Catholic Church, Paulinus of Aquileia, in the eighth century, Claude of Turin in the ninth, the council af Rheims in the tenth, and Berengarius, archdeacon of Angers, in the eleventh, which yet exerted a powerful influence in opening the eyes of men to the corruptions of Rome ; if we will believe the testimony of the suffering Waldenses themselves, their doctrine and discipline had been preserved in all its purity and efficacy from the days of the primitive martyrs, in Spain, France, Germany, Italy, and especially in the valleys of Piedmont.

The learned Dr. Allix, in his " History of the Churches of Piedmont," gives this account :—" That for three hundred years or more, the bishop of Rome attempted to subjugate the church of Milan under his jurisdiction, and at last, the interest of Rome grew too potent for the church of Milan, planted by one of the disciples, insomuch that the bishop and the people, rather than own its jurisdiction, retired to the valleys of Lucerne and Angrogne, and thence were called *Vallenses, Wallenses,* or *The People in the Valleys."*

M. Sismondi, in his late History of the Crusades against the Albigenses, says,." Those very persons who punished the sectaries with frightful torments, have alone taken it upon themselves to make us acquainted with their opinions, *allowing at the same time that they had been transmitted in Gaul from generation to generation, almost from the origin of Christianity* We cannot be astonished (he adds) if they have represented them to us with all those characters which might render them the most monstrous, mingled with all the fables which would serve to irritate the minds of the people against those who professed them. Nevertheless, amidst many puerile and calumnious tales, it is still easy to recognize the principles of the Reformation of the sixteenth century among the heretics who are designated by the name of Vaudois or Albigeois."

Dr Allix, speaking of the Paterines, some of whom, disciples of Gundulf, one of their teachers, went from Italy to the Netherlands, where they were thrown into prison, says, "Here, then, we have found a body of men in Italy before the year 1026, five hundred years before the Reformation, who believed contrary to the opinions of the Church of Rome, and who highly condemned her errors." Mr Jones adds, "Atto, bishop of Verceulli, had complained of such people *eighty years before, and so had others before him*, and there is the greatest reason to believe they had always existed in Italy. It is observable that those alluded to by Dr. Allix were brought to light by mere accident." About the year 1040, the Paterines had become very numerous at Milan, which was their principal residence; and in 1259, some of their churches in other Italian cities, we are informed by Reinerius the inquisitor, contained from five to fifteen hundred members. Their churches were organized into sixteen compartments or associations. They had no connection with the Catholic Church, which they regarded as Antichrist from the time of Pope Sylvester. Now, when we reflect that the Paterines, as well as the Paulicians, both in principles and practice, were the same people as the Waldenses, or *Leonists*, we shall not wonder at the following remarkable words of Reinerius concerning the *latter* :

"Of all the sects which have been, or now exist, none is more injurious to the Church, (*i.e.* of Rome,) for three reasons: 1. Because it is more ancient   Some aver their existence from the time of Sylvester; others from the very time of the apostles. 2. Because it is so universal. There is scarcely any country into which this sect has not crept.   And 3. Because all other heretics excite horror by the greatness of their blasphemies against God; but these have a great appearance of piety, as they live justly before men, believe rightly all things concerning God, and confess all the articles which are contained in the creed; only they hate and revile the Church of Rome, and in their accusations are easily believed by the people."

Such a concession, from such a source, speaks volumes. Here then is a succession of faithful men, whose apostolic origin, perpetuity, universal though often hidden diffusion, general orthodoxy, evangelical simplicity and sanctity of character, is admitted by the Church of Rome herself; a succession of faithful men, organized, too, into Christian churches, claiming to be the true successors of the apostles, protesting against all the corruptions of the patriarchate and the papacy, and for this reason subject to continual persecution from both, through the hands of the secular powers to which they are allied; a Church built not on St. Peter alone, but on the entire foundation of the apostles and prophets, Jesus Christ himself being the chief corner stone, and against which the gates of hell have not been able to prevail. May we not say then, in the language of Revelation, " Here is the patience and faith of the saints ? These are they that keep the commandments of God, and the faith of Jesus ?" Rev. xiv. 12.

It also appears that the recesses of the Alps and the Pyrenees were distinguished retreats of these persecuted Christians in the darkest ages of the Church. Or, as Mr. Robinson observes, in his Ecclesiastical Researches, " Greece was the parent, Spain and Navarre the nurses, France the step-mother, and Savoy (*i. e.* Piedmont) the jailor of this class of Christians called Waldenses."

Their principles.—From the united attestation of their enemies and their own confessions of faith, we learn that the ancient Waldenses were distinguished chiefly by the following points :—

1. *Their attachment to the Scriptures.*—They held that the Holy Scriptures are the only source of faith and religion, without regard to the authority of the fathers and tradition. Although they principally used the New Testament, yet, as

Usher proves, they regarded the Old also as canonical Scripture. "They translated the Old and New Testament," says Reinerius, "into the vulgar tongues, and spake and taught according to them." From their greater use of the New Testament, however, as Venema observes, their adversaries took occasion to charge them with despising the Old. "Hence, whatever a doctor of the Church teaches," says Reinerius, "which he does not prove from the New Testament, they consider it as entirely fabulous—contrary to the doctrine of the (Romish) Church. He adds, "I have heard and seen a certain unlearned rustic, who recited the book of Job, word by word, and many who perfectly knew the New Testament." This is high praise.

2. *Their Scriptural simplicity, and soundness* of belief.—Their adversaries frequently acknowledge this ; see the testimony of the inquisitor above. It is amply confirmed also by their own authentic monuments and confessions of faith, of which several are printed at length in Jones's History of the Church, and other standard works.

From a confession of their faith, in 1120, we extract the following particulars :—"(1) That the Scriptures teach that there is one God, almighty, all-wise, and all-good, who made all things by his goodness ; for he formed Adam in his own image and likeness : but that by the envy of the devil sin entered into the world, and that we are sinners in and by Adam. (2.) That Christ was promised to our fathers, who received the law : that so, knowing by the law their unrighteousness and insufficiency, they might desire the coming of Christ, to satisfy for their sins, and accomplish the law by himself. (3.) That Christ was born in the time appointed by God the Father ; that is to say, in the time when all iniquity abounded, that he might show us grace and mercy, as being faithful. (4.) That Christ is our life, truth, peace, and righteousness ; as also our pastor, advocate, and priest, who died for the salvation of all who believe, and is risen for our justification. (5.) That there is no mediator and advocate with God the Father, save Jesus Christ. (6.) That after this life there are only two places, the one for the saved and the other for the damned. (7.) That we ought to honor the secular powers by subjection, ready obedience, and paying of tribute."

3. *Their purity and excellence of life and manners.*—Though often accused of the most abominable crimes, the whole evidence goes to show that these accusations were vile calumnies, invented for party purposes by their malignant enemies, the papal priests. Indeed, an ancient inquisitor confesses that "these heretics are known by their manners and conversation, for they are orderly and modest in their behaviour and deportment. They avoid all appearance of pride in their dress; they neither indulge in finery, nor are they mean and ragged. They avoid commerce, that they may be free from deceit and falsehood. They get their livelihood by manual industry. They are not anxious about amassing riches, but content themselves with the necessaries of life. They are chaste, temperate, and sober. They abstain from anger. Even when they work, they either learn or teach, etc." Seisselius, archbishop of Turin, also admits, "Their heresy excepted, they generally live a purer life than other Christians."

4. *Their enlightened fervor, courage, and zeal.*—Reinerius assigns as one cause of their great increase, their great zeal. "All of them, men and women, night and day, never cease from teaching and learning. The first lesson," he adds, "which the Waldenses teach those whom they bring over to their party, is to instruct them what manner of persons the disciples of Christ ought to be; and this they do by the doctrine of the evangelists and apostles, saying that those only are the followers of the apostles who imitate their manner of life." Hence,

5. *Their steady opposition to all corruptions and antichristian usurpations.*—"The first error of the Waldenses," says an ancient inquisitor, "is, that they affirm that the Church of

Rome is not the church of Jesus Christ, but an assembly of ungodly men, and that she has ceased from being the true church from the time of Pope Sylvester, at which time the poison of temporal advantages was cast into the Church." They rejected images, crosses, relics, legends, traditions, auricular confession, indulgences, absolutions, clerical celibacy; orders, titles, tithes, vestments, monkery, masses, and prayers for the dead; purgatory, invocation of saints, and of the Virgin Mary; holy water, festivals, processions, pilgrimages, vigils, Lent; pretended miracles, exorcisms, consecrations, confirmations, extreme unction, canonization, and the like. They condemned the use of liturgies, especially in an unknown tongue. They condemned the mystical or allegorical interpretations of Scripture. They condemned, most of all, the wicked lives of both people and clergy in the worldly communion of Rome.

6 *Their enlightened views of liberty of conscience.*— "They affirm," says the inquisitor, "that no man ought to be forcibly compelled in matters of faith." On this point, as also on the next, they are far in advance of the reformers, Luther and Calvin

7. *Their just ideas of the nature and character of a church of Christ.*—"That is the Church of Christ which bears the pure doctrine of Christ, and observes the ordinances instituted by him, in whatever place it exists." "The sacraments of the Church of Christ are two, baptism and the Lord's Supper, and in the latter Christ has instituted the receiving in both kinds, both for priests and people." "We consider the sacraments as signs of holy things, or as the visible emblems of invisible blessings. We regard it as proper, and even necessary, that believers use these symbols when it can be done Notwithstanding which, we maintain that believers may be saved without these signs, when they have neither place nor opportunity of observing them" Hence Seisselius remarks, "They say that they also observe the evangelic and apostolic doctrine, on which account, by an intolerable

49 *

impudence, they usurp the name of the Catholic Church "
Reinerius also observes, " They declare themselves to be the
apostles' successors, to have apostolical authority, and the
keys of binding and loosing.   They say that a man is then
first baptized when he is received into their community : some
of them hold that baptism is of no advantage to infants, be·
cause they cannot actually believe."   On the whole, it is evi·
dent that they were, and that, too, on principle, dissenters, not
from the Church of Rome only, but from all national established
churches.   Their church officers, Reinerius says, were bishops,
elders, and deacons ; but the distinction between their bishops
and other elders seems to have been only that the former
were the official *pastors* of the churches.

That they understood and practiced immersion as baptism
is evident, but whether they generally practiced infant baptism has long been a matter of dispute.   The words of
Reinerius seem to imply that in his time (1250) they were
of different opinions on this point.   The modern Waldenses
in the valleys of `Piedmont do practise it ; but they have so
changed in many points, since their amalgamation with the
Calvinists at the Reformation, having also received their
pastors from them since 1663, that nothing decisive can be
hence inferred.   Dr. Murdock thinks that the followers of
Peter Waldo universally practised infant baptism ; but he
gives us no authority for this opinion.   The only one of their
ancient writings which sanctions it is the *Spiritual Calendar*,
but this, if genuine, is of doubtful date.   On the contrary, all
their other writings, from the Noble Lesson, in 1100, down
to their Confession of Faith, in 1655, Dr. Gill affirms to be in
favor of the baptism of believers only.   It appears certain that
the Cathari, the Paterines, the Berengarians, the Arnoldists,
Petrobrusians, and Henricians, *i.e.* the earlier Waldenses, as
far as history testifies, vehemently opposed infant baptism.
That there were, on the other hand, many among them in
after years who adopted the practice, is, in view of all the
facts, highly probable.   Mr. Jones, in the preface to the fifth

edition of his history, says that "the Waldenses were Anti-pedobaptists " Mr. Milner, after saying, "I cannot find any satisfactory proofs that the Waldenses were in judgment Anti-pedobaptists strictly," concludes thus : "I lay no great stress on the subject; for the Waldenses might have been a faithful, humble, and spiritual people, as I believe they were, it they had differed from the general body of Christians on this article. See ANABAPTISTS in this Appendix.

However this point may be decided, it is now generally acknowledged that the Waldenses were the witnesses for the truth in the dark ages, and that they gave the first impulse to a reform of the whole Christian Church, so called.

BAPTISTS. The Baptists in England, at this time, have a membership exceeding 200,000, with a population of about 1,000,000. In 1792, they began their famous India Mission —the pioneer of all Protestant Missions in the East. Of late years they have greatly prospered, and are now generally re garded as the most progressive body of Christians in England.

The Baptists of the United States established, in 1814, a Missionary Union for Foreign Missions ; a Home Mission Society in 1832 ; an American and Foreign Bible Society in 1838 ; a Bible Union for Revision in 1850, which, however, is not exclusively Baptist, being sustained by many of other denominations for the sake of a more exact version of the sacred text in the English tongue. It now employs the best scholars in the country in its work, without regard to denomination.

Besides the Home Mission Society, whose field is all North America, the Baptists have Conventions or General Associations in every State for Domestic Missions, and Education Societies for the aid of licentiates preparing for the ministry in colleges and theological seminaries, of whom there are over 1000. A Theological Institute for Freedmen was founded early in 1865, and has numerous branches The receipts and expenditure for these various purposes the last year was

about $500,000. If we add the sums expended in endow
ments of seminaries of all grades, it will exceed $1,500,000.
A liberal Baptist, of Poughkeepsie, New York, within five
years has given nearly $500,000 for founding a College for
female education, where 400 young ladies are now under the
tuition of accomplished Christian teachers. A single family,
near Philadelphia, has given $50,000 this year as a Fund for
the Freedmen, to be expended through the American Baptist
Publication Society, an institution whose total receipts for the,
last year were over $173,000. The annual outlay on new
church edifices exceeds $1,000,000. These facts and figures
show a remarkable development of energy and enlightened
liberality in this Christian denomination.

CHRISTIANITY : the religion of Jesus Christ, the Son
of God, as delineated in the sacred Scriptures. Its peculiar
and characteristic feature is, that it reveals the only way of
salvation for sinful men, through the incarnation and atoning
death of a divine Redeemer, in which " the righteousness of
God is manifest" in harmony with his mercy, " that he might
be just, and the justifier of him that believeth in Jesus."
(Rom. iii. 20, 21) To this, the Holy Spirit sets his seal.

All the variety of forms in which Christianity appears in
this book, may be reduced to two : namely, EVANGELICAL
CHRISTIANITY, which in the legitimate use of reason receives
the religion of Christ as it is—a revealed method of salvation
for sinners; and RATIONALISTIC CHRISTIANITY, which, by an
illegitimate use of reason, would exalt it as the ultimate
authority in regard to the matters revealed. (See RATION-
ALISTS, in this Appendix) RATIONALISTIC CHRISTIANITY
again, appears under four distinct forms. 1. *Philosophical*,
as in the Gnostics, Arians, etc ; 2. *Formal* or *Sacramental;*
3 *Hierarchical*, and 4. *Political*. Examples of the three last
divisions, which, indeed, are intimately allied, may be seen
in the Roman and Greek Churches, and in the principal Church
establishments of modern Europe. All three are strongly

pervaded also by the *Traditional* element; the Rationalistic remodelling Christianity to suit its own ideas of what religion ought to be, to fit it for the condition of the world, and the Traditional seeking to perpetuate the innovations thus introduced under the pretence of Conservatism.

But the object of this article is not to develop these points, but to present some general views of the present condition and prospects of Christianity, as the one true religion, designed to subdue and supersede all others, and become, like the sun in the firmanent, the fixed light and life of men. And we cannot, perhaps, do this better than by some extracts from a distinguished French philosopher, M. Jouffroy, in his Essay *On the Present State of Humanity.*

It must be remarked, that the writer here regards Buddhism as but a form of Braminism, from which it originally proceeded.

" We may regard the world as subject to the attraction of three different forms, or three systems of civilization : Christianity, Braminism, and Mohammedanism —A real religion is nothing but a complete solution of the great questions which interest humanity, that is to say, of the destiny of man, of his origin, of his future condition, of his relation to God and to his fellow-men. Now it is by virtue of the opinions which different nations profess on these questions, that they establish a mode of worship, a government and laws ; that they adopt certain manners, habits, and thoughts ; that they aspire to a certain order of things, which they regard as the ideal of the True, the Beautiful, the Right, and the Good, in this world. The true and radical difference between savage and civilized nations, consists in the fact that the former have only crude and vague ideas on the great questions which interest Humanity, so that these ideas could not be brought into a sufficiently precise form for the construction of a system.

" If in any part of the earth there were a great mass of savage nations in contact, as there was in the north and in the centre of Asia, during the fourth century, we might admit the possibility that a system suddenly appearing in the bosom of this mass, could gather around it the people who composed it, and create a fourth civilization, a fourth centre of attraction. But such a mass does not exist.

"We may then regard those three systems of civilization as the only systems which can exert an influence on the destinies of the world. To those systems, therefore, we must give our attention. What are their respective forces, the degrees of their vigor and attractive power?

"Now it is proved by facts that the Christian civilization is the only one of the three which is endowed at the present day with an expansive power. It is in truth the only one which makes any progress at the expense of the others, and which gains savage tribes to civilization.

"Braminism has few or no savages to civilize. Its dominion extends to the eastern borders of Asia, and on the west it approaches Mohammedanism and Christianity. It is therefore in contact with the other systems of civilization. And as it forms no foreign colonies, it remains unknown to savages of other countries. It will accordingly have no share in the mass of men who are yet to be civilized.

"Mohammedanism also forms no colonies; like Braminism, it keeps at home; the time when it subdued nations with the sword is past. Now, on the east toward Asia, on the north and on the west toward Europe, it is arrested by Braminism and Christian civilization. It comes in contact with savages only at the south, toward the centre of Africa. We know not whether it continues to extend in that direction, or whether the immense conquests which it formerly made are still increasing; but we may affirm with certainty, that if it does continue to make conquests among savage tribes, it is the mere result of contact, and not at all of design; for in the present day we do not discern in Mohammedanism the slightest trace of the spirit of proselytism which it once possessed, and which is now so ardently cherished by Christian nations.

"If we now turn our eyes to Christianity, we perceive that

with the exception of the barbarians of Africa—and even these it is on the point of disputing with Mohammedanism—it holds in its hand all the savages of the rest of the world. There is hardly an island of any magnitude where it has not taken a station on its coast, and visited with its ships ; and by degrees the population of every island of the ocean will fall under its system By holding the coast of New Holland (Australia) it surrounds with a thread which they cannot escape from, all the tribes of the fifth world—tribes the most barbarous which have yet been discovered. It will follow the same course there which it has followed in America.

"If we consider the conquests over one another which are made, or should be made by the three systems, we find new proof of the expansive power which is possessed exclusively by Christian civilization. Neither Braminism nor Mohammedanism penetrates, or attempts to penetrate, into Christian possessions. Christianity and its civilization everywhere advance with ardor, and with deliberate purpose, into the domains of Brama and of Mohammed. They openly meditate their conquest. The Bible and Missionary Societies are instituted for this express purpose. But there are two levers of still greater power in operation, to detach ancient Asia from its ancient doctrines. These levers are Russia and England. While Russia acts upon Asia on the north, from the Ural mountains to the extremity of Kamschatka, and opens a large third of this vast country to our civilization, England invades it in the south, and causes our power to penetrate into the very centre of Braminism.

"Now this superiority of power is a new circumstance, which appears to give Christianity brighter and brighter promise of the conquest of the world.

"The Christian system is making progress, and rapid progress, while the other two are decaying; the nations which compose it are every day becoming more united, and growing into a powerful aggregate which nothing on earth is able to resist It is impossible for the Christian system to be ab-

sorbed in either of the others ; on the contrary, it is beginning to absorb them both, or at least, to reduce the territory
which they occupy ; and there is every reason to believe
that these conquests will soon go on with increased rapidity.
We cannot then avoid the conclusion, that if the Christian
system of civilization be not destroyed by internal defect, it
is destined to gain possession of the earth. Its future condition involves the future condition of the world."

The argument of M. Jouffroy, a mere outline of which we
have given, seems perfectly satisfactory as to the general fact,
that Christianity *in some form* will gain dominion of the
world. But it may be asked, as a distinct question, In what
form will it prevail ? Will it be *Evangelical* or *Rationalistic* ?
We use these terms in the sense already defined in the beginning of this article. Now the same line of argument
pursued by M. Jouffroy, may be adopted to answer this latter
question, and we think with great success. The following
remarks of Isaac Taylor, in his *"Natural History of Enthusiasm,"* will show this :

" If we are to calculate the probable extension or extinction
of certain opinions, we must consult the evidence of facts on
a large scale, and especially must observe what manifestations of intrinsic power they have given us on certain peculiar
and critical occasions. This is the only course that can be
deemed satisfactory, or that is conformed to the procedures
of modern science.

" The early triumphs of the Gospel over the fascinating idol-
atries and the astute atheism of Greece and Rome, has been
often insisted upon (and conclusively) as evidence of its truth.
With that argument we have nothing now to do ; yet if the
subject were not such a very hackneyed one, it might well be
brought forward in all its details in proof of a very different
point—the innate power of the religion of the Bible to vanquish the hearts of men.

" But if there were room to imagine that the first spread of
Christianity was owing rather to an accidental conjuncture

of favoring circumstances than to its real power over the human mind, or if it might be thought that any such peculiar virtue was all spent and exhausted in the first expansive effort, then it is natural to look to the next occasion on which the opinions of mankind were put in fermentation, and to watch in what manner the system of the Bible then rode over the high billows of political, religious, and intellectual commotion. It was a fair trial for Christianity, and a trial essentially different from its first, when, in the fifteenth century, after having been corrupted in every part to a state of loathsome ulceration, it had to contend for existence, and to work its own renovation, at the moment of the most extraordinary expansion of the human intellect that has ever happened. . . .

"At such a time, which seemed to leave no chance for continued existence to aught that was not in its nature vigorous, might it not have confidently said, This must be the crisis of Christianity? if it be not inwardly sound, if it has not a true hold of human nature, if it be a thing of feebleness and dotage, fit only for cells and cowls and the precincts of spiritual despotism; if it be not adapted to the world of action, if it have not sympathy with the feelings of men—of freemen, nothing can save it: no power of princes, no devices of priests, will avail to rear it anew and replace it in the veneration of the people: at least not in any country where has been felt the freshening gale of intellectual life. The result of this crisis need not be narrated. . . .

"Whether the religion for which the Reformers suffered was from heaven, or of men,' is not our question; but whether it is not a religion of robust constitution, framed to endure and to spread, and to vanquish the hearts of men? With the history of the fifteenth and sixteenth centuries in view, it is asked if Christianity be a system that must always lean upon ignorance and craft and despotism, and which, when these rotten stays are removed, must fall and be seen no more?

" Yet another species of trial was in store to give proof of the indestructibility and victorious power of Christianity. It remained to be seen whether, when the agitations, political and moral, that were subsequent upon the great schism which had taken place in Europe, had subsided, and when the season of slumber and exhaustion came on, and when human reason, strengthened and refined by physical science and elegant literature, should awake fully to the consciousness of its powers; whether then the religion of the Bible could retain its hold of the nations, or at least those of them that enjoyed, without limit, the happy influences of political liberty and intellectual light. This was a sort of probation which Christianity had never before passed through. . . .

" It is difficult to imagine a single advantage that was lacking to the promoters of infidelity, or a single circumstance of peril or ill-omen that was not present to deepen the gloom of the friends of religion. The actual issue of that signal crisis is before our eyes in the freshness of a recent event. Christianity—we need not ask whether for the benefit or the injury of the world—has triumphed ; the mere fact is all that concerns our argument."

Once more : " The spread of the English stock and language and literature over the North American Continent, is a significant indication of the power of Christianity to retain its hold of the mind, and of its aptness to go hand in hand with civilization, even when unaided by those secular succors, to which its enemies in malice, and some of its friends in over-caution, are prone to attribute too much importance. The tendency of republicanism, and the connection of the colonies at the moment of their revolt (from the mother country) with France, and the prevalence of a peculiarly eager and uncorrected commercial temper, and the absence of every sort and semblance of restraint upon opinion, were concurrent circumstances belonging to the infancy of the American Union, of a kind which put to the severest test the intrinsic power of Christianity in retaining its hold of the human mind. Could infidel experimenters have wished for conditions more equita ble, under which to try the respective forces of the opposing systems? And what has been the issue? Christianity has gained rather than lost ground, and shows itself in a style of as much fervor and zeal as in England; and perhaps it has won the advantage in these respects. Wherever on that continent good order and intelligence are spreading, there also the religion of the Bible spreads."

It has, then, been proved that nothing inseparable from human nature, nothing invincible, stands in the way of the diffusion of our evangelical faith among either polished or barbarous nations, for already it has been victorious in both kinds. "Let it be affirmed that the religious infatuations of mankind are firm as adamant; still it is a fact that a hammer harder than adamant once shattered the rock to atoms. And now, when it is proposed to smite the same substance with the same instrument, are those to be deemed irrational who anticipate the same success?"

"There was a greater disproportion (as Mr. Douglas observes) between the resources of the first Christians and their success in changing the moral condition of the Roman empire, than there is at present between the means which Christians now possess and the universal conversion of the world. True benevolence will come in the train of genuine Christianity, and mankind, in promoting the welfare of each other, will find that happiness which has long escaped them. Then will be the harvest of the moral world; and the seed of noble thoughts and deeds that once seemed lost, shall suddenly shoot forth and ripen to maturity, and the success of wrong, even in this world, shall seem brief compared with the long ages that shall crown the efforts of wisdom and virtue."

RE-UNION OF THE PRESBYTERIAN CHURCH.

NOTWITHSTANDING the fearful shock which in 1837-8 rent this large and influential body of Christians in twain, and which was attended with violent controversies, trials for heresy and law suits, many hearts, in both sections of the Church, continued to be linked together in indissoluble bonds. Neither body attempted to alter, in the slightest manner, the doctrinal standards, or departed from the well known principles of the Presbyterian polity. There was a keen and wide-spread sense of the scandal to the Christian name and the cause of Protestantism and Presbyterianism, in this new breach of ecclesiastical unity. Multitudes on both sides never ceased to yearn for a healing of the breach, and the exscinded or New School portion, for a long time did not give up the hope of a satisfactory adjustment of difficulties and a restoration of the unity of the Church, and consequently delayed taking action, looking to the maintenance of a separate denominational existence.

The first steps, however, which they took, with this end in view, as the event turned out, were steps in an indirect, but sure road to reunion. They proved and they cultivated the genuine Presbyterianism of the body, and they gradually separated them from that co-operation with Congregationalists and with voluntary and outside societies, which was so distasteful to the Old School body and which was, in fact, the immediate cause of the division. Many leading New School men, whose sympathy with the Congregationalists was strong, resisted these movements for denominational and separate action, as ignoring the past record and destroying the comprehensive spirit of the body; but the majority perceiving no salvation for the denomination but in looking after its own Home Missionary, Educational and Publishing interests, continued to press them, until a degree of interior organization and success was reached, rivaling that of the Old School body itself.

In another course of action, the New School body was as surely, and yet as unexpectedly, preparing for the same remote result. The high ground it took on the subject of slavery, after estranging many of its conservative members North and South, at length, in 1857, culminated in a deliverance, mild, but firm and explicit, which drove off almost its entire Southern membership in a body. The Southern section of the Old School Church, on the contrary, powerful in numbers and in the extraordinary ability of some of its leading men, held back the Old School Assembly from any positive action and serious agitation of the subject thus maintaining its standing in the prevalent conservative sentiment of the country, and putting the New School Assembly at a disadvantage as a body of agitators, especially in the Middle States, where the great strength of the denomination lay.

All this seemed but to deepen and widen the division between the two bodies. But the unforeseen and mighty element of the Southern Rebellion was yet to come in play, as one of the forces bearing on the question. In 1861, the entire Southern constituency of the Old School Church was sundered violently from the main body, the General Assembly which met at Philadelphia that year having taken high loyal ground on the issues of the war. At the same time, the New School Assembly meeting in Syracuse, was establishing its Permanent Committee of Home Missions, and withdrawing finally from co-operation with the Congregationalists on that important field.

Thus the course of events brought the assemblies on a common platform, on two of the very subjects which had most widely divided them—Church-boards and slavery. And the various experiences of the ensuing four years' struggle, the common hopes, fears, trials, sacrifices and labors of that tremendous ordeal, continually strengthened every tie of sympathy between them.

The lively co-operation of the various Christian denominations in the vast sanitary, benevolent and Christian enterprizes for the benefit of the soldiers during the war, did more to break down denominational prejudices, and to cultivate a broad spirit of evangelical catholicity, than any other agency in the century. The Christian Commission, under the able and zealous leadership of George H Stuart, Esq., of Philadelphia, was especially serviceable in associating ministers and laymen of all denominations, in labors of Christian love, in the camp, on the march, in the hospital, and on the battle field. Amid these scenes of deep spiritual necessity and of imminent death, all human distinctions seemed trifling. Great and simple truths alone could reach and sustain the soul, in such times as these.

Doctrinal controversy had almost wholly ceased between the bodies. The popular interest in such discussions had subsided. The personal asperities of the conflict of a quarter of a century ago had worn away. Differences of opinion on unessential matters in the Calvinistic system were found to exist in both branches. New School men were called to Old School pulpits, and Old School men to New School pulpits, without any peculiar sense of incongruity among the parties concerned. Large-minded laymen, practical men of business, like Robert Carter, on the one side, and William E. Dodge, on the other, could see no reasons for prolonging the state of disunion between two churches of the same name, standard and spirit. Both bodies were rich in divines of standing and influence, recognized, like Gardiner Spring and Albert Barnes, throughout Christendom.

The first in the series of formal movements towards reunion was taken conjointly by the Old School Presbytery of Ogdensburg and the New School Presbytery of St. Lawrence, in a meeting held at Ogdensburg, N. Y., January 14th, 1862.

The joint meeting passed a unanimous resolution expressive of their desire to be united into one body, and under one General Assembly, and sent an overture in favor of reunion to the two assemblies which met in the following May.

The Old School Assembly, which met in Columbus, O., did not make a very encouraging response to the overture, but by a unanimous vote they resolved to commence the fraternal interchange of delegates or commissioners with the New School Assembly, provided that body met their proposals in the same amicable spirit. The New School Assembly, meeting at the same time, in Cincinnati, expressed themselves as cordially in sympathy with the spirit of the overtures on reunion, and declared that they had never shown a temper adverse to union, and that it would give them pleasure to unite with all occupying the same doctrinal and ecclesiastical position with themselves, and who agreed with them on the great moral questions of the day. Beyond this declaration of their views, however, they preferred not to advance at the present time. They had adjourned too early to receive notice of the proposal of the Old School Assembly for an interchange of delegates.

Meeting in Philadelphia the next year, the New School Assembly took up this proposal on the second day of the session, and by a standing and unanimous vote, accepted it, "with heartfelt pleasure and Christian salutations." Their action was telegraphed without delay to the other Assembly, meeting at the same time, in Peoria, who, by the same expeditious method, commissioned Rev. Septimus Tuslin, D. D., formerly Chaplain of the United States Senate, and Hon. George Sharswood, LL.D., of Philadelphia, to represent them on the floor of the New School Assembly. Rev. Robert W. Patterson, D. D., and Hon. Wm. H. Brown of Chicago, were appointed by the New School body to bear their salutations to the Assembly at Peoria.

Thus commenced a correspondence, in which, at once, the

scandal of the division was done away, and the mind of the Church, as represented in its highest judicatories, prepared for an organic union.

In 1866, both the General Assemblies met in St. Louis. This was the first meeting held in the same locality, and at the same time, by both bodies, since the question of re-union had been seriously agitated. The opportunity was taken to cultivate and strengthen the fraternal feelings which had sprung up between them. Joint religious services were held, and a joint communion was celebrated by vote of the two bodies. But, more important than all, each Assembly appointed a Committee of Fifteen, thirty in all, to consider and report a plan for the reunion of the two bodies. The Chairman of the Old School Committee was Rev. Jno. M Krebs, of New York, D. D., and that of the New School was Rev. Thomas Brainerd, D. D., of Philadelphia.

The appointment of this joint committee was the signal for a lively and wide-spread discussion of the whole subject of reunion, its bearings, its propriety, utility and season-ableness, and the exact nature of the terms on which it should be attempted. Ultra Old School men doubted whether the New School was thoroughly Calvinistic and Presbyterian, and feared lest the terms of reunion should be made so loose as to admit of, and sanction, serious doctrinal errors and unpresbyterian modes of action. Ultra New School men, on the contrary, were unwilling to risk the loss of the liberty of opinion which they enjoyed, on points which they considered unessential to the integrity of the Calvinistic system. And while there was a large and constantly increasing section of both churches, who stood between these extremes, who through lack of zeal for doctrinal niceties, or from a sentiment of charity that completely bore down all fears and prejudices, were unconcerned about guarantees for doctrinal soundness or for liberty of opinion, it was manifest, from the beginning, that great weight must be given to these opposite ideas, if a harmoni-

ous decision was reached, and a union formed, without lead
ing to further and painful divisions.

The death of Dr. Brainerd, during the summer of 1866,
and the long, and finally fatal, illness of Dr. Krebs, the
chairmen of each of the committees, deferred action until
the following year. The committee held their first meetings, separately and jointly, in February, 1867. Rev.
George F. Wiswell, D. D., of Philadelphia, was elected in
place of Dr. Brainerd, and Rev. William Adams, D D , of
New York, was made chairman of the New School Committee. Rev. C. C. Beatty, D. D., was made chairman of the
Old School Committee. The conferences opened with much
hesitation and embarrassment, which, however, under the
influence of prayer, and fraternal intercourse, rapidly wore
away, and the committee, after several meetings, agreed
upon a plan which they submitted to their respective
General Assemblies of 1867 : the one meeting in Rochester,
and the other in Cincinnati. The chief interest of the report centered in the First or doctrinal, article which was as
follows :

First.—The reunion shall be effected on the doctrinal and
ecclesiastical basis of our common standards. The Confession of Faith shall continue to be sincerely received and
adopted, as containing the system of doctrine taught in the
Holy Scriptures, and its fair historic sense, as it is accepted
by the two bodies, in opposition to Antinomianism and
Fatalism, on the one hand, and to Arminianism and Pelagianism on the other, shall be regarded as the sense in which
it is received and adopted; and the Government and
discipline of the Presbyterian Church in the United States,
shall continue to be approved as containing the principles
and rules of our polity."

The remaining articles related to details of organization.
It was provided, that the consent of three-fourths of the
Presbyteries belonging to each of the two Assemblies, must
be given to the plan within a year, in order to secure its adop-

tion. These proposals were unanimously adopted and transmitted to the Presbyteries by the New School Assembly; they were also adopted by a very decided majority by the Old School Assembly, who, however, also passed a resolution distinctly disclaiming any other purpose in their vote, than that of giving the Presbyteries the opportunity of deciding the question for themselves.

When the Presbyteries come to vote upon the plan in the ensuing fall, scarcely a tithe of those in the Old School body gave it their unqualified approval, and it was defeated in that branch of the Church by a very large majority. The New School Presbyteries by a large majority voted to approve the plan, but many of them objected to the vagueness of the doctrinal term, as an insufficient guarantee for doctrinal liberty.

Great discouragement was felt by the friends of the scheme, in both branches, at this result. And it seemed as if all specific efforts for reunion must be abandoned for the present. But the hopes that had received such a shock, were revived and carried to a higher point than ever, by the National Convention for a reunion of all the separated bodies of the Presbyterian Church, which was held in the city of Philadelphia, in November of the same year. This Convention, which was attended by leading men of the Old and New Schools, the United and the Reformed Presbyterian Churches, gave an opportunity for the discussion of the basis of reunion upon a still broader platform. The conclusions there reached, especially upon the doctrinal articles, showed that the two Schools were nearer together than the decisions of the Presbyteries just rendered, would indicate.

This Convention was not more remarkable for the widely varying shades of Presbyterian sentiment which it brought into cordial relations, as for the enthusiasm, earnestness and gratifying success which attended its deliberations. It would seem as if the strong undercurrent of reunion, which had been obstructed, and dammed up by the action of the Presbyteries, especially in the Old School Church, now broke vehemently over all restraints, and poured itself forth in a tide that could not be stemmed. Fuller guarantees for doctrinal soundness than even Old School men cared to have, were offered by New School men. By an amendment offered by Prof. Henry B. Smith, of Union Seminary, New York, subscription to the doctrinal basis of the Confession of Faith was described and defined as receiving the Confession in its historical, "that is Reformed, or Calvinistic sense;" it was also by the vote of the New School delegates, that the highly Calvinistic Shorter Catechism was included in the proposed doctrinal basis, adopted by the Convention. Guarantees for liberty beyond the limits of these terms were not demanded. Perhaps the great use of the Convention was to reveal the unexpected and uncontrollable strength of the hitherto latent feelings of sympathy and cordial Christian affection of Presbyterians for each other, in spite of their numerous and somewhat discreditable divisions. Where such feelings prevailed, technical objections and difficulties in the way of reunion, it was foreseen, must eventually give way.

The Reunion Committees of the two Assemblies now resumed their labors with a renewed hope of success. They modified their doctrinal article by inserting "the Smith amendment," as already described, and followed it up with a clause in the interest of liberty, proposed by the Rev. Dr. Gurley.

This celebrated addition, known as the Gurley amendment, read as follows:

"It is also understood that various methods of viewing, stating, explaining and illustrating the doctrines of the Confession which do not impair the integrity of the Reformed or Calvinistic system are to be freely allowed in the United Church, as they have hitherto been allowed in the separate Churches"

A new article, called the Tenth, was introduced, by which the right was conceded to the individual Presbytery to go back of the credentials of a member applying for admission, and satisfy itself by examination, of his soundness; at the same time leaving each Presbytery free to exercise the right or not as it saw fit.

With this amended Report, the Committees appeared in the General Assemblies of the Old School meeting in Albany, and the New School, in Harrisburg. Large majorities and leading men in both bodies, were found to be in favor of adopting the Report; but vigorous and able minorities in both contended, with such earnestness, for further modifications, that a harmonious adjustment seemed as remote as ever. In the New School Assembly, opposition was directed mainly to the Tenth article, and opportunity having been given before taking the vote, for the expression of dissent from any part of the basis, thirty-eight persons recorded their dissent from the Tenth article; four persons were excused from voting, and then the Report on reunion was adopted unanimously.

In the Assembly at Albany, opposition centered mainly on the explanatory clauses of the Second Article, [*i. e.* the Gurley amendment.] This opposition was so earnest and powerful, that the majority sent a deputation, consisting of Rev. Drs. C. C. Beatty and V. D. Reed, and Elders Robert Carter and Henry Day, from Albany to Harrisburg, to represent to the New School Assembly the delicacy and urgency of the situation, and to ask their consent to the omission of these clauses. Rules of order, however, made it impossible for the New School body, at that stage of the proceedings, to entertain a motion to reconsider, and the deputation was compelled to return, after a most cordial and respectful reception, without accomplishing their object.

Notwithstanding their failure, the Report, unamended, was adopted by the Assembly at Albany, the vote on the first and most warmly contested article being 186 to 79. After wards, however, by way of conciliating the minority, it was voted unanimously that the Assembly would prefer the basis with the explanatory clauses of the First article omitted; it was also resolved, that in adopting it they did not mean to give license to propagate doctrines, which have been condemned by either Assembly, nor to permit any Presbytery in the United States, to license or ordain to the work of the Ministry, any candidate who maintains any form of doctrine condemned by either Assembly.

This action, received by telegraph in the New School Assembly, just as they were adjourning, at eleven o'clock at night, made an unpleasant impression. The Union men in the Old School Assembly however, were in dead earnest. A protest against the action on reunion was presented by fifty-one members of their body, charging the New School with dangerous doctrinal tendencies. The Assembly's reply to the protest recognizes in the fullest and most unequivocal manner, the, soundness of the New School body, on all the fundamentals of the Calvinistic system.

The plan of the Joint Committees was once more submitted to the vote of the Presbyteries. One hundred of the one hundred and thirteen New School Presbyteries adopted the plan as it stood. Very few of the Old School Presbyteries approved of the plan without amendment, most of them reiterating the preference, expressed by the Albany Assembly, for the omission of the explanatory clauses from the doctrinal article, at the same time proposing to retain the Tenth Article, so much disliked by the decided men in the New School body.

When the Assemblies met in 1869, in New York City, the New School felt that, in adopting the Committee's plan with such a near approach to unanimity, they had done their part. It remained for the Old School body, whose Presbyteries had defeated that plan, to propose a new one. This responsibility the Old School Assembly promptly accepted, for it seemed a foregone conclusion, in spite of

51

all untoward appearances, that reunion must take place, and that all obstacles must be removed now.

· On the very first day of its session, that Assembly appointed an entirely new Committee of Conference, on the subject, which was responded to by the immediate appointment of a new Committee on the part of the other Assembly. In seven days, these Committees matured a new plan, which was submitted simultaneously in both Assemblies, and adopted with but eight dissenting votes in the Old School, and unanimously by the New School body.

The doctrinal article of this plan was as follows :

"The reunion shall be effected on the doctrinal and ecclesiastical basis of our common standards : The Scriptures of the Old and New Testaments, shall be acknowledged to be the inspired word of God, the only infallible rule of faith and practice ; the Confession of Faith shall continue to be sincerely received and adopted, as containing the system of doctrine taught in the Holy Scriptures ; and the government and discipline of the Presbyterian Church in the United States, shall be approved as containing the principles and rules of our policy."

No reference was made to the right of examination, which as recognized in the Tenth Article, in the plan of 1868, had caused such divergence of sentiment. The matter was left as the Form of Government leaves it—indeterminate. Certain Concurrent Declarations were also appended to the basis, not as parts of the plan nor of binding force, yet as just and equitable arrangements, to which both bodies were expected to assent. These declarations asserted the right of all ministers and churches to an equal standing in the United Church, with that which they held in the separate bodies. Imperfectly organized churches were counselled and expected to become thoroughly Presbyterian within five years, and no other such churches would hereafter be received. No rule or precedent which does not stand approved by both the bodies, should be of any authority in the re-united body, except as affecting property rights. The catalogues of the publications of both bodies should be revised, so as to exclude all invidious references to past controversies. The Theological Seminaries, it was suggested, might transfer their connections to the Synods adjacent, all Seminaries being counselled to come under Assembly or Synodical control. The second Sabbath in September, was also named as a day of prayer for divine guidance.

None of these "declarations" were overtured to the Presbyteries. It was resolved to send down for their action, the single doctrinal article as above recited, and each Presbytery was ordered to vote upon it, and forward the result of the vote to the stated clerk of its own Assembly, before the 1st day of November, following. The two Assemblies would adjourn to meet in the city of Pittsburg, on the second Wednesday of November, when and where, the stated clerks should report the vote, and if two-thirds of the Presbyteries in each branch had voted affirmatively, the union would be of binding force, and the two Assemblies should take action accordingly.

This report on reunion was adopted in the New School Assembly, by a unanimous rising vote, and in the Old School Assembly by 276 to 8 votes. The vote of the Presbyteries was a triumphant endorsement of the Assemblies' plan. Of the one hundred and forty-four Old School, one hundred and twenty-eight answered in the affirmative, and three in the negative; of the one hundred and thirteen New School every one sent up official answers in the affirmative There was a minority of one in each of three New School Presbyteries, in all other cases the vote was unanimous.

Nothing now remained but to give formal shape to the will of both bodies, thus emphatically expressed. The two Assemblies accordingly met in Pittsburg, on the tenth of November, and after making official record of the action of the Presbyteries and communicating the results in due form to each other, dissolved their separate sessions, and amid the most intense manifestations of joy and enthusiasm, united in a joint procession and a meeting in the Third Presbyterian Church, where several hours were spent in prayer, singing and addresses of congratulation. A resolution was adopted, that it is incumbent upon the Presbyterian Church, as thus united, to make a special offering to the treasury of the Lord of five millions of dollars, as a memorial of the reunion.

Thus closed a series of efforts, stretching over a period of three years and six months. The fears of the rigid men on the one side, and of the liberal on the other, exercised a constant influence upon the deliberations, delayed the progress of the movement, and shaped somewhat the final form of the basis. But while they could not prevent the result upon which the heart of the Church, in both branches, was set, it is wonderful how at last their opposition was almost entirely overcome, and that the acquiescence in the result was so nearly absolutely universal. The usual concomitant of an Ecclesiastical Union, the splitting off of fragments large or small, and the multiplying rather than the diminution of sects, was spared to the Christian world in this case. It is believed not an individual minister or Church—unless it be one or two partly congregational Churches—has left the body on account of reunion. The great size, the wealth, and the high standing in the Christian world of the body thus formed, exert a force of gravity which counteracts the centrifugal and separatist tendencies that might otherwise appear. Smaller Presbyterian bodies are likely rather to be drawn from their individual orbits and gathered like aerolites on the larger body.

The influence of this happy settlement of protracted and grievous denominational estrangements, upon the divided parts of the Protestant Church at large, must prove healthful. On all hands, this greatest of Ecclesiastical reunions since the dividing era of the Reformation, is viewed as the harbinger of a broader charity, and a wider and more comprehensive union among Christians.

The First General Assembly of the reunited Church was held in the First Presbyterian Church, Philadelphia, of which the late Rev. Albert Barnes, was pastor. This body, numbering 605 commissioners and delegates, is the largest Presbyterian Assembly, ever held in any part of the Christian world and represented the largest Presbyterian Church in existence. Accredited representatives from the Presbyterian Churches in England, Scotland, Ireland and Canada, besides the Lutheran, Congregational and other bodies in America, were in attendance. A full daily phonographic report of its proceedings was published. The necessary work of redistricting the Synods, and of consolidating the Boards and Committees was conducted with unusual harmony and dispatch, for so great a body. No jar or friction was perceptible, and the denominational lines so sharply drawn, a third of a century ago, disappeared under the magic breath of the spirit of Christian love.

The statistics of the United Church as reported at this Assembly are as follows; Synods, 51; Presbyteries, 259; Candidates and Licentiates, 879; Ministers, 4,238; Churches, 4,526; added to the Churches by profession, 32,003; whole number of members, 446,561; Baptisms, 26,598; Members of Sabbath Schools, 448,857; Contributions to Congregational purposes, $6,416,165; to Missions and other benevolent causes, $2,024,000.

51 *

THE FREE METHODIST CHURCH.

The Free Methodist Church had its origin, as the founders of the same believed, in necessity, and not in choice. It did not grow out of a secession, nor out of an unsuccessful attempt to bring about a reform in the government of the Methodist Episcopal Church, in which it had its origin. Those concerned in its formation never expected a separation from that Church until they were, as they believed unjustly, excluded from its pale. They sought redress at the proper tribunal. It was not granted. Even a candid hearing was denied them. Thus thrown out, and the possibility of a restoration being cut off, and believing that God still called them to labor for the salvation of souls, they had no alternative but to form a new organization. In doctrine, discipline, and spirit they were Methodists, and hence they could not offer themselves to any other denomination. The issue on which they were thrust out was, as they understood it, between dead formalism and the *life* and *power of godliness*, and so they could not feel at home with those branches of the Methodist family into whose formation other questions mainly entered.

A convention of ministers and laymen met at Pekin Niagara county, New York, on the 23d day of August, 1860 and adopted a Form of Discipline and Church Government.

The superintendency of the Church, instead of being in vested in a board of bishops, is held by a minister or minis ters elected to such office by each recurring General Confer ence, which is held once in four years. The supervision of the interests of the several districts of each Annual Confer ence is committed to a minister elected to the office by his Annual Conference, who is named chairman of the district, and may, in connection with the same, be a preacher in charge of a circuit, or may travel at large on his district, if so directed by his Annual Conference. The same preacher may be chairman of more than one district. The system is that of an itinerant ministry, the appointments being made annually, by a stationing committee composed of the chairmen of the several districts, and an equal number of the lay delegates of each Annual Conference, which lay members of the committee are elected by ballot.

The ministerial and lay elements enter equally into the formation of the General and Annual Conferences.

The Quarterly Conferences of the Church have jurisdiction over an entire district, and are composed of the itinerant and local preachers, exhorters, stewards, and class leaders of each circuit in the district, and the chairman of the district is president of the same.

The temporal and spiritual interests of each circuit are under the advisement of an official board elected from its membership, at the meeting of which the preacher in charge is expected to preside.

That the peculiar features of this body of Christians may be better understood, the following questions are subjoined, which are proposed to those who wish to unite in Church fellowship with them.

The candidate, having met in class six months on probation, and having been baptized, must give satisfactory answers to them before being admitted into full connection.

1. Have you the witness of THE SPIRIT that you are a child of God?

2. Have you that perfect love which casteth out fear? If not, will you diligently seek until you obtain it?

3. Is it your purpose to devote yourself the remainder of your life wholly to the service of God, doing good to your fellow-men and working out your own salvation with fear and trembling?

4. Will you for ever lay aside all superfluous ornaments, and adorn yourself in modest apparel, with shamefacedness and sobriety, not with broidered hair, or gold, or pearls, or costly array, but, which becometh those professing godliness, with good works?

5. Will you abstain from connection with all secret socie-

ties, keeping yourself free to follow the will of the Lord in all things?

6. Do you subscribe to our Articles of Religion, our General Rules, and our Discipline, and are you willing to be governed by the same?

7. Have you Christian fellowship and love for the members of this society, and will you assist them, as God shall give you ability, in carrying on the work of the Lord?

The person giving affirmative answers to the above questions shall, with the consent of three-fourths of all the members present at a society meeting, be admitted to all the privileges of a member. Any person in good standing in any evangelical church may be received into full connection, upon his meeting the other requirements of this section, without having been on probation in our Church.

The houses of worship of this denomination are built without any adornment of spire or stained-glass windows, and the seats are neither sold nor rented. The singing is done by the congregation, without the aid of a choir or instrumental music. All the modern devices for raising money so common in this age, such as festivals, fairs, oyster-suppers, pic-nics, lotteries, excursions, etc., are totally ignored by this "peculiar people," as they believe in giving directly to benevolent objects, and from the sole motive of obedience to the requirements of God, as revealed in his Holy Word.

The statistics of this Church are as follows, viz. : Five Conferences, which were organized in the order in which they are named, viz.: Genesee, Illinois, Susquehanna, Michigan and Kansas and Missouri Conference. Travelling preachers, 128, local preachers, 126, members, including probationers, 6756. Value of Church property, $234,700. A weekly paper, called the "Free Methodist," is published in New York City, by Joseph Mackey, and a monthly magazine called the "Earnest Christian," by Rev. B. T. Roberts, at Rochester, New York A school called the "Chili Seminary," is also in successful operation, located in North Chili, Monroe county, New York.

THE SOUTHERN PRESBYTERIAN CHURCH.

THIS body—represented by "*The General Assembly of the Presbyterian Church in the United States*," and consisting of some 1500 churches, 1000 ministers and 100,000 communicants—separated from the Old School body and organized a distinct Assembly at Augusta, Georgia, December, 1861.

The occasion which compelled this separation was a political deliverance of the General Assembly at Philadelphia, on the 28th May, 1861, declaring that, "in the spirit of Christian patriotism," the Assembly "do hereby declare and acknowledge our obligation to promote and perpetuate, so far as in us lies, the integrity of these United States, and to strengthen, uphold and encourage the Federal Government in the exercise of all its functions under our noble constitution, and to this constitution in all its provisions, requirements and principles we profess our unabated loyalty."

That such a deliverance by a Church court involves a dangerous usurpation of power, and is inconsistent with the fundamental idea of Presbyterianism, was then the deliberate judgment, not only of the Southern Presbyterians, who were thereby obliged to renounce either their allegiance to their *de facto* civil government or their allegiance to their Church, but the judgment also of the most enlightened and thoughtful men in the Northern Church.

Dr. Charles Hodge, of Princeton, with fifty-seven others, including the Moderator of the Assembly, entered their most earnest protest against the right of the General Assembly to make any such political deliverance in the following, among other emphatic terms:

" We protest, because we deny the right of the General Assembly to decide the political question to what government the allegiance of Presbyterians, as citizens, is due, and its right to make that decision a condition of membership in our Church."

" That the paper adopted by the Assembly does decide the political question just stated is, in our judgment, undeniable. . . . That the action of the General Assembly in the premises does not only decide the political question referred to, but makes that de-

2 o

cision a term of membership in our Church, is no less clear. . .
It puts into the mouth of all represented in this body a declaration of loyalty and allegiance to the Federal Government. But
such a declaration made by our members in what are called the
seceded States is treasonable. Presbyterians under the jurisdiction
of those States cannot make this declaration. They are therefore
forced to choose between allegiance to the State and allegiance to
the Church."

"The General Assembly, in thus deciding a political question,
and in making that decision practically a condition of membership
in the Church, has, in our judgment, *violated the constitution of the
Church and usurped the prerogatives of the divine Master.*"

With these views of Dr. Hodge in his protest the ecclesiastics
of the Southern Church fully concurred. In a solemn "*Address
to all the churches of Jesus Christ throughout the earth,*" issued by the
Southern General Assembly at its organization as explanatory of
the causes of their separation, December, 1861, it is declared:

"The only conceivable condition, therefore, upon which the
Church of the North and the South could remain together as one
body, with any prospect of success, is the rigorous exclusion of
the questions and passions of the forum from its halls of debate.
This is what always ought to be done. The provinces of Church
and State are perfectly distinct, and the one has no right to usurp
the jurisdiction of the other. The State is a natural institute,
founded in the constitution of man as moral and social, and designed to realize the idea of justice. It is the society of rights.
The Church is a supernatural institution, founded in the facts of
redemption, and is designed to realize the idea of grace. It is the
society of the redeemed. The State aims at social order, the
Church at spiritual holiness. The State looks to the visible and
outward, the Church is concerned for the invisible and inward.
The badge of the State's authority is the sword, by which it becomes a terror to evil-doers and a praise to them that do well.
The badge of the Church's authority is the keys, by which it
opens and shuts the Kingdom of Heaven, according as men are
believing or impenitent. The power of the Church is exclusively
spiritual, that of the State includes the exercise of force. The
Constitution of the Church is a Divine revelation, the Constitution
of the State must be determined by human reason and the course
of providential events. The Church has no right to construct or

modify a government for the State, and the State has no right to frame a creed or polity for the Church.

Had these principles been steadily maintained by the Assembly at Philadelphia, it is possible that the ecclesiastical separation of the North and South might have been deferred for years to come Our Presbyteries, many of them, clung with tenderness to the recollections of the past. Sacred memories gathered around that venerable Church which had breasted many a storm and trained our fathers for glory."

It will be perceived, therefore, that the thoughtful men, both of the Northern and the Southern sections of the Church, practically concurred in the judgment that the deliverance of 1861 compelled the separation. Nor was the issue of slavery or anti-slavery really involved in the primary cause of the separation, as has been so persistently asserted. For in the same "Address" the Southern Assembly declares, in December, 1861, before the question of slavery had become an issue of the war:

"In the first place, we would have it distinctly understood that, in our ecclesiastical capacity, we are neither the friends nor the foes of slavery—that is to say, we have no commission either to propagate or abolish it. The policy of its existence or non-existence is a question which exclusively belongs to the State. We have no right, as a Church, to enjoin it as a duty or to condemn it as sin. Our business is with the duties that spring from the relation—the duties of the masters on the one hand, and of their slaves on the other. These duties we are to proclaim and enforce with spiritual sanctions."

Such, then, were the grounds of this separation amid the opening strifes of the unhappy civil war. Obviously, this schism in the Presbyterian Church, like that of the Episcopal Church, might, by a kind and judicious policy, have been healed at the close of the war. But so far from this, the General Assembly at Pittsburg, in 1865, as though determined to give permanency to the separation, erected in the following ordinance an impassable barrier between the two bodies:

"It is hereby ordered that all our Presbyteries examine every minister applying for admission from any Presbytery or other ecclesiastical body in the Southern States on the following points:

"1. Whether he has in any way, directly or indirectly, of his own free will and consent, or without external constraint, been concerned at any time in aiding or countenancing the rebellion and the war which has been waged against the United States; and if it be found by his own confession, or from sufficient testimony, that he has been so concerned, that he be required to confess and forsake his sin in this regard before he shall be received.

"2. Whether he holds that the system of negro slavery in the South is a Divine institution, and that it is 'the peculiar mission of the Southern Church to conserve the institution of slavery as there maintained,' and if it be found that he holds either of these doctrines, that he be not received without renouncing and forsaking these errors.

"3. Church sessions are also ordered to examine all applicants for church-membership by persons from the Southern States, or who have been living in the South since the rebellion, concerning their conduct and principles on the points above specified; and if it be found that of their own free will they have taken up arms against the United States, or that they hold slavery to be an ordinance of God, as thus stated, such persons shall not be admitted to the communion of the Church till they give evidence of repentance for their sin, and renounce their error."

It has been claimed, however, and asserted not only by the commissioners sent to Louisville in 1870, but even officially declared, by implication, in a minute of the Northern Assembly of 1870, that these remarkable ordinances of 1865, together with all that resulted from them in the expulsion of the synods of Kentucky and Missouri in 1866–7, was in effect repealed by the "concurrent declaration of the two Assemblies that met in New York (prior to re-union), that no rule or precedent which does not stand approved by both bodies shall be of any authority in the reunited body." But aside from the incongruity of any such indirect and merely incidental repeal of an act, or series of acts, impugning the Christian standing of a vast body of people, this claim of repeal for lack of concurrence by both Assemblies very remarkably overlooks the fact that while the Old School Assembly at Pittsburg, in 1865, was enacting the extraordinary ordinance for examination just cited, the New School Assembly at Brooklyn the very same week also enacted the following:

"In the event that any of the ministers referred to in the overture (*i. e.*, Southern ministers) shall apply for admission into these Presbyteries, the assembly advises the *Presbyteries not to admit them, or in any way recognize them as ambassadors of the Cross of Christ, until they have given satisfactory evidence that they have sincerely repented of this sin* " (of aiding or countenancing the rebellion).

Thus it appears that, in fact, the "concurrent declaration" does not meet the case of the excluding ordinances of 1865 at all, since these ordinances "*do stand approved by both of the bodies.*" And, therefore, as the Southern churches were compelled originally to separate, so they are still compelled, under the ordinances of 1865–6–7, to make the separation permanent.

It would tend only to mislead the Christian public, however, to stop here and leave the impression that the differences which separate the Southern from the Northern Presbyterians are chiefly these questions of ecclesiastical punctilio. For, though holding the same symbols of faith and Church order, and even the same constitutional rules, the issues between them will be found, on examination, to involve principles fundamental in the Presbyterian faith and order. Nor can any pressure of popular sentiment in favor of union ever harmonize such differences. The true conception of Christian brotherly affection is not the withdrawal of all protest against error and witness for the truth, but of peaceful separation when differences are fundamental. The true model of Christian brotherhood is Abraham, the Father of the visible Church. "Let there be no strife, I pray thee. Separate thyself from me: go to the right or left, and I will take the opposite direction."

So far from being mere inconsiderable differences arising from temporary ill-humor or the idiosyncrasies of a few prominent men, as the popular judgment has it, and as men of feeble convictions and latitudinarian views of the Church regard it, the differences between the Southern and the Northern bodies of Presbyterians as now constituted are as wide as the differences between either and the other evangelical churches.

In the first place, it is well known that prior to 1861, and even as far back as the disruption of 1837, the Southern portion of the Old School Presbyterian Church (with a few exceptions on either side) was even far more earnest, more uncompromising and more united in antagonism to the "Broad Church" errors of the New School body in regard to the doctrine and order than the Northern portion. Indeed, but for the Southern portion of the Church, the testimony of 1837 could never have been maintained. Accordingly, it will be observed, in reviewing the proceedings of the ten years subsequent to 1860, that the movement first to exclude, and then to keep out, the Southern Churches, proceeded *pari passu* with the movement for bringing back the New School body. The intimation of any such purpose of reunion was indeed denounced as an uncharitable suspicion in 1861-2, but it will be difficult to find any other solution of the extraordinary ordinances of 1865, and the no less extraordinary expulsion of the synods of Kentucky and Missouri for resisting these ordinances, than that the motive for and the purpose of these ordinances was, by keeping out the South, to break down the power of resistance in the Church against the reunion with the New School and the withdrawal of the testimony of 1837.

It is of no force, as against this view of the case, that the Southern Assembly had in 1864 received the United Synod (New School of the Southern States), for that union was made really upon the basis of a solemn declaration in regard to the issues involved in the conflicts of 1837—viz.: "Concerning *The fall of man and original sin—The imputation of sin and of Righteousness—The Divine permission of sin—The Atonement—Regeneration—Justification and the Visible Church as Christ's agent for propagating the gospel.*" Which declaration, framed at a conference of both parties exhibiting an entire agreement of views, was reported to the Assembly with the following preface stating its purpose:

"Inasmuch as some have been supposed to hold the system of doctrines and Church order in different senses, the General Assembly and the United Synod do further adopt the following *Declaration,* touching former grounds of debate, in order to manifest our hearty agreement, to remove suspicions and offences, to restore full confidence between brethren, and to honor God's saving truth."

And though this "*Declaration*" was not formally made the basis of a union, because it was held that the General Assembly has no right to adopt any other doctrinal basis than the standards, yet it was an abundant guarantee to the Assembly (having been approved by the Presbyteries on both sides) that such union involved no withdrawal of the testimony of 1837.

Whatever, therefore, were the differences which separated the Old School and New School bodies for thirty years, the same differences now separate the Southern from the reunited Northern body.

In the second place, anterior to 1861, as well as since, the Southern Presbyterian churches have held in a much fuller sense than the Northern the *jure divino* view of Presbyterianism. This is the view universally taught in their schools and held generally by their pastors and Church courts. With exceptions on both sides, the issue between the Southern ecclesiastics and the Northern has been the same as that which created the rupture between the Westminster Assembly and the Parliament which called it to advise in the reconstruction of the English Church. While the Westminster Assembly, after thorough examination of the Scriptures, concluded that the Presbyterial Government of the Church and its ordinances were by direct authority of Christ the King, the Parliament stubbornly refused to accept Presbytery on any other ground than that "it is *lawful and agreeable* to the word *of God* that the Church be governed by congregational, classical and synodical assemblies." This discrepancy of views seems to have in some degree crept into the standards of the Presbyterian Church as accepted in the United States. While the Confession of Faith (chap. 30) and the Larger Catechism (Ques. 45) declares fully with the Westminster Assembly, "The Lord Jesus as King and Head of his Church hath therein *appointed a government*," etc., and—

"Christ executeth the office of a King in calling out of the world a people to himself, and *giving them officers*, laws and censures whereby *he visibly governs them*."

Yet on the other hand the *"Form of Government"* (chap. 8) seems to speak rather the non-committal language of the Parliament: "We hold it *to be expedient* and *agreeable to Scripture and the practice of the primitive Christians* that the Church be governed by congregational, Presbyterial and synodical assemblies."

Now, the Southern churches may be said to stand by the *jure divino* theory of the Confession of Faith and the Catechism, while the Northern churches accept the looser expediency view of Chap. 8th of the "Form of Government." The wide practical divergence of the two views is apparent in all the more notable utterances of the Northern and Southern Assemblies after the separation.

Thus, the Southern Assembly declares in reference to the natural functions and practical relations of the Church: "In regard to conflicts between existing governments, or as to movements in society, peaceful or otherwise, to effect political changes, the Church as such has no more control over them than it has over the polls of the country. If it has authority to uphold on the one side, it has equal power to condemn on the other; if to suppress a political movement, then also to instigate it. In truth, it has neither, and to assert the contrary is to corrupt the Church in its principles, for ever embroil it with the strifes of the world and plunge it headlong into ruin." (*See Minutes*, 1865, *page* 371.)

"The Assembly would declare anew the doctrine of our time-honored Confession, that Christ alone is King and Head of his Church, and that all ordinances of worship binding on us are ordained by him alone; that there are two commonwealths, equally appointed by God, the civil, whose object is to protect the persons and property and promote the well-being of men as they are members of civil society; and the religious, the commonwealth of Israel, whose object it is to train men, as they are sinners, for glory and immortality. Although these exist together in this world, each is independent of the other in its own sphere." (*See Minutes*, 1866, *pp.* 13, 14.)

"This argument, of visibly realizing the spiritual unity of the Lord's people, is enforced by the peculiar circumstances of the times in which we live, and by the nature of the controversies which now agitate the Church. The old conflict for the spirituality and independence of the Church is, to the amazement of many, renewed in our day and upon our own continent. The battle fought generations ago, by the Melvilles, Gillespies and Hendersons of Scotland, is reopened with singular violence, and the old banner is again floating over us with its historic inscription, "For Christ's covenant and crown." Upon no one subject is the mind of this Assembly more clearly ascertained, upon no one doctrine is there a more solid or perfect agreement amongst those whom this Assembly represents, than the non-secular and non-political character of the Church of Jesus Christ." (*See Minutes*, 1866, *pp.* 30, 31.)

An elaborate declaration of the doctrines and principles of the Southern Churches, prepared by the synod of Kentucky and accepted by the Assembly of 1867, may be found in the appendix to the minutes of that year, and in Vol. 10th of Wilson's Historical Almanac, pp. 297–316. A careful study of this paper must satisfy any one acquainted with the views of the Northern Presbyterians that the difference between the two bodies is radical as to some of the most practical questions of Christian duty. There is room for but a single extract:

"The doctrine of the kingly office of Christ is no abstract theory of theology, but of the very first practical importance in the gospel system, since to his office as a king, his prophetic and priestly offices stand related as means to an end. He is a teaching prophet and an atoning priest that He may be a reigning king. And His kingly office stands related to the government and discipline of the Church as His prophetic and priestly offices to the ordinances of the word and sacraments. While, indeed, the acceptance of the doctrine of His kingly office is not essential to the faith that is unto salvation in the sense in which the acceptance of the doctrine of His priestly office as exhibiting our justifying righteousness is essential, yet the obligation to present truly the doctrine of Christ's kingly office in the government and discipline of the Church to the faith of His people is of like force with the obligation to present truly the doctrine of His prophetic and priestly offices in the word and sacraments.

Therefore, the avoidance of all admixture of human maxims, policies and expediencies in the administration of the government and discipline of the Church is a duty of the same obligation as to avoid the admixture of human philosophies and theories with the dispensation of the word, or of human fancies with the dispensation of the sacraments.

It is therefore not only incompetent to the Church courts, but positively a perversion of the truth, that they shall assume to consider and determine any other questions than those which relate to the government, order and discipline of Christ's visible kingdom; or to determine these on grounds aside from the word of God; or to speak in Christ's name and by his authority, otherwise than to the faith and conscience of His people, concerning things to be obeyed as enjoined by the law of Christ.

Therefore, the Church has manifestly no commission either to discharge any functions of the State, or to direct, advise or assist the State; nor has the Church any light in regard to the affairs of the State which the State has not already; nor, since her authority is spiritual and resting on moral suasion only, has it any adaptation to the purposes of a government of force. Neither can the

State have any commission from God to discharge the functions of the Church, nor the ability to do so; since—aside from the fact that its compulsory power is inapplicable to things of religion—even though the State may have the advantage of the inspired word of God current among its citizens to give additional clearness and force to the teachings of nature and reason, yet the State has not the special illumination of the Holy Spirit, which alone can interpret the word for the purposes of the Church. Nor is anything plainer from experience than that the unconverted statesman, accepting the word of God intellectually merely, however he may thereby be made wiser as to natural things, is not made more competent to legislate for the Church than though he were merely a refined and enlightened Pagan. Nor has anything more certainly tended to enfeeble the spiritual life of the Church than the mistake of courting the favor and seeking the alliance of rulers and statesmen, who merely accept intellectually, and therefore treat respectfully the word of Christ and His ordinances, as though thereby the kingdom of Christ can be strengthened."

It may serve to complete this side of the proposed contrast to cite the following extract from the official response of the Assembly of 1870 at Louisville to the proposition for a renewal of correspondence and ultimately organic reunion:

1. "Both the wings of the now united Assembly, during their separate existence before the fusion, did fatally complicate themselves with the State in political utterances deliberately pronounced year after year, and which, in our judgment, were a sad betrayal of the cause and kingdom of our common Lord and Head. We believe it to be solemnly incumbent upon the Northern Presbyterian Church, not with reference to us, but before the Christian world, before our Divine Master and King, to purge itself of this error, and by public proclamation of the truth to place the crown once more upon the head of Jesus Christ as the alone King in Zion. In default of which the Southern Presbyterian Church, which has already suffered much in maintaining the independence and spirituality of the Redeemer's kingdom upon earth, feels constrained to bear public testimony against this defection of our late associates from the truth. Nor can we, by official correspondence even, consent to blunt the edge of this our testimony concerning the very nature and mission of the Church as a purely spiritual body among men.

2. The union now consummated between the Old and New School Assemblies, North, was accomplished by methods which, in our judgment, involve a total surrender of all the great testimonies of the Church for the fundamental doctrines of grace at a time when the victory of truth over error hung long in the balance. The united Assembly stands, of necessity, upon an allowed latitude of interpretation of the standards, and must come at length to embrace nearly all shades of doctrinal belief." Turning now to the contemporaneous deliverances of the Northern Assemblies, the irreconcilable difference of views between the two becomes at once manifest.

The action of the Old School Assembly in 1861 has been already cited. Here is the action of 1862, assuming to instruct the civil government:

"It is the clear and solemn duty of the national government to preserve, at whatever cost, the national Union and Constitution, to maintain the laws in their supremacy, to crush force by force," etc., etc. (*Minutes Old School Assembly*, 1862, p. 625.)

In the same year the General Assembly (New School) gave utterance to the following:

"*Resolved*, 4. That while we have been utterly shocked at the deep depravity of the men who have planned and matured this rebellion, and who are now clad in arms, manifested in words and deeds, there is another class found in the loyal States who have excited a still deeper loathing—some in Congress, some high in civil life and some in the ordinary walks of business—who never utter a manly thought or opinion in favor of the government but they follow it, by way of comment, with two or three smooth apologies for Southern insurrectionists, presenting the difference between an open and avowed enemy in the field and a secret and insidious foe in the bosom of his own family.

Resolved, 5. That, in our opinion, this whole insurrectionary movement can be traced to one primordial root, and to one only AFRICAN SLAVERY, and the love of it, and a determination to make it perpetual, and while we look upon this war as having one grand end in view—the restoration of the Union by crushing out the last living and manifested fibre of rebellion—we hold that everything—the institution of slavery, if need be—must be made to bend to this one great purpose, and while under the influence of humanity and Christian benevolence we may commiserate the condition of the ruined rebels once in fraternity with our-selves, but now—should the case occur—despoiled of all that makes the world dear to them, we must be at the same time con strained to feel that the retribution has been self-inflicted, and must add, *"Fiat justitia, ruat cœlum."* (*Minutes*, 1862.)

And in 1863 to the .following: "That the government of these United States, as provided for by the Constitution, is not only founded upon the 'great doctrine of human rights as vested by God in the individual man, but is also expressly declared to be the supreme civil authority in the land, for ever excluding the modern doctrine of secession as a civil or political right; that, since the existing rebellion finds no justification in the facts of the case or the Constitution of the United States, in any law human or divine, the Assembly can regard it only as treason against the nation and a most offensive sin in the sight of God, justly exposing its authors to the retributive vengeance of earth and heaven; that this rebellion, in its origin, history and measures, has been distinguished by those qualities which most sadly evince the depravity of our nature, especially in seeking to establish a new nationality on this continent based on the perpetual enslavement and oppression of a weak and long-injured race; that the national forces are, in the view of this Assembly, called out, not to wage war against another government, but to suppress insurrection, preserve the supremacy of law and order and save the country from anarchy and ruin."

So again, in 1864; the Old School Assembly felt free to make the following deliverance: "It is our judgment that the recent events of our history, and the present condition of our Church and country, furnish manifest tokens that *the time has at length come, in the provi-dence of God, when it is his will that every vestige of human slavery among us should be effaced, and that every Christian man should ad dress himself with industry and earnestness to his appropriate part in the performance of this great duty.* . . . Under the influence of the most incomprehensible infatuation of wickedness, those who were most interested in the perpetuation of slavery *have taken away every motive for its further toleration.* . . .

It is the President's declared policy not to consent to the reor-ganization of civil government within the seceded States upon any other basis than that of emancipation."

And the New School Assembly, in 1865, the following: "In An-drew Johnson, so unexpectedly called to the chair of our martyred

Chief, the Assembly recognize a man distinguished for a long course of earnest effort to elevate the masses, and for a steady, consistent patriotism that neither the power nor the favor of a treasonable oligarchy has been able successfully to assail or seduce. We desire to pledge to him, as our constitutional Chief Magistrate, our confidence and support in his efforts to vindicate the majesty of law; maintain the National Government in its just supremacy; destroy the spirit and counteract the workings of the evil system that created this war; inspire a just appreciation of the crime of treason and a true loyalty to the Government in the breasts of the masses of the white population of the South; and extend to the colored citizens of that section the practical enjoyment of those personal and political rights announced in the Declaration of Independence, but denied to them by a despotic aristocracy." (*Minutes*, 1865.)

And the following in 1866: "And, as promoting this end, which far transcends any mere political or party object, we rejoice that the active functions of the Freedman's Bureau are still continued, and especially that the Civil Rights Bill has become the law of the land. In respect to the concession of the right of suffrage to the colored race, this Assembly adheres to the resolution passed by our Assembly of 1865 (*Minutes*, p. 42): "That the colored man should in this country enjoy the right of suffrage in common with all other men is but a simple dictate of justice. The Assembly cannot perceive any good reason why he should be deprived of this right on the ground of his color or his race. Even if suffrage may not be universal, let it be at least impartial.

2. In case such impartial suffrage is not conceded, that we may still reap the legitimate fruits of our national victory over secession and slavery, and that treason and rebellion may not enure to the direct political advantage of the guilty, we judge it to be a simple act of justice that the constitutional basis of representation in Congress should be so far altered as to meet the exigencies growing out of the abolition of slavery, and we likewise hold it to be the solemn duty of our national Executive and Congress to adopt only such method of reconstruction as shall effectually protect all loyal persons in the States lately in revolt. (*Minutes*, 1866.)

3. As loyalty is the highest civic virtue and treason the highest civic crime, so it is necessary for the due vindication and satisfac-

tion of national justice that the chief fomenters and representatives of the rebellion should, by due course and process of law, be visited with condign punishment." (*Minutes*, 1866.).

From these citations in contrast, and more particularly from an official tract recently issued entitled "*The Distinctive Principles of the Presbyterian Church, commonly called the Southern Presbyterian Church*, the following may be enumerated as among the more distinctive principles of the Southern body, while accepting the same symbols of doctrine and order as the Northern Church:

1. More rigid adherence to the doctrinal symbols of Westminster, discarding all theories of "progress" and of "advanced thought" as inapplicable to doctrinal teachings derived directly from the infallible word.

2. More rigid adherence to the views of the Scottish Reformers concerning the nature and duty of the Church as a witness-bearer against all false teaching, and discarding all "Broad Church" schemes of comprehension as incompatible with the nature and purpose of the visible Church.

3. Asserting the Church of Christ, organized and visible, as an essential element of the gospel, and that the sinner born again is born into a visible family of God, with new relations not only to Christ, but also to Christ's organized body.

4. Asserting the Kingly office of Christ in his Church as a great practical truth which necessitates the *jure divino* character of all Church government and ordinances of worship.

5. Asserting a strict construction of the Constitution of the Church and a scriptural administration of the government and ordinances, as essential to purity of·doctrine as well as of Christian Liberty.

6. The absolute spirituality and independency of Christ's visible kingdom as against all tendencies to employ the Church and her agencies in the service of secular governments, or to accept secular aid in support of the Church, or to tolerate the interference of the secular power with the spiritual affairs of the Church.

Lightning Source UK Ltd.
Milton Keynes UK
UKOW07f2352251016
286164UK00007B/150/P

9 781171 605263